LISTENERS'
GUIDE
TO
CLASSICAL
MUSIC

KENNETH AND VALERIE MCLEISH

LISTENERS'
GUIDE
TO
CLASSICAL
MUSIC

AN INTRODUCTION
TO THE GREAT CLASSICAL COMPOSERS
AND THEIR WORKS

LONGMAN

LONGMAN GROUP LIMITED
Longman House
Burnt Mill, Harlow, Essex CM20 2JE, England
and Associated Companies throughout the World

First published 1986

Set in 11/13 pt Ehrhardt

Printed and bound in Great Britain by
Butler & Tanner Ltd, Frome and London

British Library Cataloguing in Publication Data

McLeish, Kenneth
  Listeners' guide to classical music.
  1. Music——Dictionaries
  I. Title   II. McLeish, Valerie
  780'.3'21   ML100
  ISBN 0-582-23569-3

For Martin McLeish

CONTENTS

INTRODUCTION

The main purpose of this book is to offer a guide to the huge repertoire of 'classical' music available to the concert-goer or home-listener. On every page, descriptions are given of suggested works, and cross-references (indicated by asterisks) lead to chains of listening in whatever direction the reader decides to go.

The bulk of the book consists of short articles on selected composers. Each article contains a brief description of the composer's life and musical style, a list of works and a set of detailed listening recommendations. (In these, the first works listed are recommended as the best or most characteristic to hear first, and the others, preceded by an arrow (→) offer follow-up listening in the same style. The symbol Ⓜ indicates a 'masterwork': that is, one which, in our opinion, makes a major contribution to the musical art.) Systematic use of the lists, and of the recommendations to works by other composers, should produce an ever wider and broader exploration of the repertoire.

The remaining entries take a more general view of works written for the main instrumental groups (e.g. woodwind), in specific centuries or forms (e.g. sonata), and in two particular geographical areas, the USA and the UK. All works mentioned in these entries are recommended listening, and descriptions are added only when appropriate. The book is concerned above all with music in the general concert or home-listening repertoire, and with compositions of substance. The bulk of this music was written between 1650 and 1950, and the book reflects that fact, venturing into 'early music' or 'contemporary music' (which, even for professional musicians, still tend to be specialist areas) only sufficiently far to indicate possible avenues of approach. For reasons of space, we have not dealt in detail with works of less than two or three minutes' duration (the sort generally performed or recorded in anthology-form): this has abbreviated our discussion of the song repertoire, both solo and part-song, of the repertoire of such specialist groups as madrigal choirs or brass ensembles, and (once again) of 'early music'.

Martin McLeish gave us much help and encouragement during the writing of the book, and Alison Mansbridge edited the manuscript. We are warmly grateful to them both.

Kenneth and Valerie McLeish

A

ADAM. See *One-work Composers.*

ALBÉNIZ, Isaac (1860–1909). *Spanish pianist and composer.*

Albéniz was born in an age of dazzling musical showmanship, when a performer with the right blend of personality and technique could earn fame to rival that of any eighteenth-century opera singer or twentieth-century pop star. From the start, both his piano playing and his temperament seem to have been equal to the task. He first played in public at the age of four; at seven (having failed to get into the Paris Conservatoire because he kicked a ball through a window) he ran away to America and supported himself for five years by giving piano displays in concert-halls, private drawing-rooms and circus tents. (A favourite showstopper was playing the piano with his back to the keyboard and his hands upside down – one better than the boy *Mozart's trick of playing with the keyboard concealed by a cloth.) As a young man, he was befriended by an eccentric millionaire who paid him to write an opera-cycle based on the legends of King Arthur and on a scale to rival *Wagner's *Ring*. (Albéniz gave this up halfway through, perhaps feeling that his talents were for display of a less grandiose kind.)

The showy side of Albéniz's character was balanced by hard work (he studied with *Liszt, for example, who gave his pupils encouragement but no quarter), and by a passionate love for the folk music of Andalusia – the same Moorish-influenced melodies and throbbing guitar chords that attracted *Falla. He wrote several hundred piano pieces in Spanish style, most of them influenced by folk music; they range from simple works for beginners to some of the most difficult music in the piano repertoire.

WORKS Apart from his vast output of piano pieces, Albéniz wrote five operas, three operettas, a handful of orchestral pieces (including a Spanish rhapsody, *Catalonia*, and a lacklustre Piano Concerto) and a dozen songs. None is outstanding; it is for the piano music that his name lives.

Seguidillas, Op. 47 No. 2 (1886) Albéniz grouped his descriptive pieces into sets with titles like *Travel Souvenirs* (Op. 71) or *Melodies of Spain* (Op. 232). The best known have picture-postcard titles like 'Tango', 'Granada', 'Malagueña' or 'Sevillanas'. Their detractors find them as brash as a Torremolinos night-club; for others, their folk-music roots, their cheerful harmonies and above all their tunefulness place them in the highest entertainment-music class.

→ 'Asturias' (Op. 74 No. 5); Falla 'Andaluza' (from *Four Spanish Pieces*); Grieg 'Wedding Day at Troldhaugen' (Op. 65 No. 6).

Ⓜ *Iberia* (1909) Twelve piano pieces in four books, each piece evoking a specific Spanish scene or mood (e.g. 'The Port'; 'Feast Day in Seville'; 'Málaga'). This music is deeply felt and poetic; it is difficult to play and the artistic aims – and achievement – are far higher than in Albéniz's lighter works. (It yields nothing to them, however, in tunefulness or grace.) Like much of his music, it is well known in arrangements (for orchestra; for guitar solo and duet); the original piano version remains the best.

→ *Characteristic Pieces*, Op. 92; Granados *Goyescas*; Debussy *Préludes*, Book 1.

ALBINONI. See *One-work Composers*.

AVANT-GARDE MUSIC

The phrase 'avant-garde', like the English word 'vanguard', originally meant the troops who went ahead of the main army, preparing the way and giving civilians a foretaste of what was to come. In the arts, the avant-garde work with the very latest styles. Their experiments lead the way for others – and are often about as welcome to ordinary listeners as the vanguard of an army was to the uneasy populace.

In music there has always been an avant-garde, and it has always been disliked. In the Middle Ages, church composers who experimented with the new-fangled idea of harmony (sounding more than one note at once) were considered to be polluting the pure worship of God, and some were excommunicated for doing so; in the sixteenth century, a Roman Catholic council complained that musical settings of the Mass were being strangled by the fashion of giving dozens of notes to every word, and insisted that each syllable be set to a single sound; Emperor Joseph II of Austria graciously informed *Mozart that his music had 'far too many notes'; a London critic said that *Beethoven's Symphony No. 8 was 'eccentric without being amusing and laborious without effect'; a Parisian wit called *Stravinsky's *The Rite of Spring* (*Le sacre du printemps*) 'The Massacre of Spring'; a New York critic gave his opinion that to have written *Pierrot lunaire* *Schoenberg must have been either 'crazy as a loon or a very clever trickster'; a *Bartók piano piece seemed to one hearer 'to represent the composer promenading the keyboard in his boots'; even gentle *Chopin was denounced in his day as 'a dealer in the most absurd and hyperbolical extravagances', whose entire works presented 'a motley surface of ranting hyperbole and excruciating cacophony'.

TWENTIETH CENTURY At the beginning of the twentieth century, the quest for 'new sounds for a new age' took avant-garde composers in two separate directions. Some used nineteenth-century harmonies and structures in ever wilder ways, until a musical language *Wagner or *Liszt would have recognized burst apart into what one critic (describing a piece by Richard *Strauss) called 'orgiastic noise'. The other direction led to sounds of a new kind altogether: the Italian 'futurist' Luigi Russolo composed for squeakers, tappers, whiners and other noise-machines; Alois Hába rebuilt traditional instruments to play quarter-tones, seventh-tones and even smaller intervals; Pierre Schaeffer spliced together tape-recordings of natural sound-effects and made what he called *musique concrète* ('concrete music'). In the USA in the 1940s, John Cage stuffed rubbers, pieces of cloth and woodchips in between the strings of a piano and composed a 'Concert' and other works for 'prepared piano' – once shocking, but now gentle-sounding and serene, untroubled music for meditation. In Poland, Penderecki asks his string-players to bow above the bridge as well as below – and his *St Luke Passion* and *Threnody for the Victims of Hiroshima* are masterworks.

Sometimes composers who once seemed avant-garde turn out by hindsight to have been creators of genius in their own right and the inspirers of countless followers. This was true of Beethoven and Wagner in the nineteenth century, and of such once-reviled figures as Bartók, Schoenberg, *Webern and Stravinsky in the twentieth. Other avant-garde composers did little in the end to advance musical art, but their experiments gave their own work individuality and vitality: good twentieth-century examples are *Ives, *Satie and György Ligeti. With other composers still, opinion remains divided. Was Edgard Varèse, for example, the lonely genius his admirers claim, or were his works (e.g. *Ionisation* for percussion, *Intégrales* for orchestra) no more than eardrum-lacerating junk? Will Milton Babbitt and Iannis Xenakis, who used computers to help them plot their note-sequences (e.g. in Babbitt's *Ensembles for Synthesizer* or Xenakis's *Antikhthon*), be remembered in future by humans or merely by computers? The present avant-garde favours 'endless' music, streams of incessantly-repeated chords or notes with only the minutest changes to divert the flow. Some of this music – e.g. Steve Reich's *Drumming*, Ligeti's *Melodien* or Brian Chapple's *Four Pianos* – is delightful, a series of ear-ravishing and entirely unalarming sounds. Will our great-grandchildren look back on it with the awe we reserve for our great-grandparents' bugbears Berlioz or Tchaikovsky?

Listening The least clangorous introduction to the early twentieth-century avant-garde is through the music of Satie (e.g. *Parade*) or of Ives (e.g. *The Unanswered Question*). Of middle-century music, Cage's *Sonatas and Interludes* and Foss's *Baroque Variations* are recommended, and later works might be Ligeti's Double Concerto, Feldman's *Projections* and Berio's *Sinfonia*. Anyone hungry for stronger meat might tackle the microtone music of Hába, the works of Varèse and such music-theatre pieces as Maxwell *Davies's *Eight Songs for a Mad King* or *Henze's *The Raft of the Medusa*. For further recommendations, see the articles on Boulez, Carter, Lutosławski, Messiaen, Schoenberg, Stockhausen, *Twentieth-century Music* and Webern.

B

BACH, Carl Philipp Emanuel (1714-88). *German composer.*

Bach was one of those rare people on whom the gods seem to smile from birth. His father was J. S. *Bach and his godfather was *Telemann; he had a cheerful disposition and a musical talent which, while hardly amounting to genius, was outstanding enough to guarantee a lifetime of congenial work. He spent twenty-eight years as a keyboard-player to the flute-playing King Frederick II of Prussia, who collected and played new pieces as avidly as a modern monarch might use the gramophone. (Bach complained about the boredom of having endlessly to accompany the King and to compose polite pieces for polite evening-audiences; but the length of time he stayed with Frederick tells another story.) In 1768 he succeeded Telemann as music-maker-in-chief to the town of Hamburg, and widened his scope to include church music and symphony concerts as well as keyboard-playing.

Bach was one of the most respected performers of his age; indeed, his instruction-book *Essay on the True Art of Playing Keyboard Instruments* is still influential. His writing for keyboard (often fortepiano rather than harpsichord) is in a transitional style, midway between the dance-suites of *Handel or J. S. Bach which preceded it and the sonatas of *Haydn or *Mozart which followed. Of all his music, only his church works (large, sonorous and uninspired) lack appeal; his solo music and his chamber and orchestral works are sunny with wit and craftsmanship, a musical counterpart to the comedies of manners and the poised, formal paintings of the age.

WORKS Twenty-two Passions; two oratorios; nineteen symphonies; fifty concertos; over two hundred chamber works and assorted pieces for keyboard; songs, anthems, etc.

Concerto in E flat for harpsichord, fortepiano and orchestra (1788) Generally speaking, the more instruments Bach wrote for, the more adventurous his music was. This Haydnish concerto makes play with the contrasting sounds of the solo instruments, and uses the orchestral wind instruments (especially oboes and bassoons) to sprightly effect.

5

→ Quartet in A minor for flute, violin, cello and piano; Telemann 'Paris' Quartet No. 3; Mozart Concerto for Flute and Harp.

J.C. BACH C. P. E. Bach's brother J. C. Bach (1735-82), known as 'the London Bach' because he settled there, wrote music less consistent than C. P. E.'s, but just as delightful at its best. In his heyday he was applauded for operas – a judgment which no longer stands. Mozart, rather more perceptively, admired his instrumental works, to the point of learning from and imitating their style. His Quintet in D for flute, oboe, violin, cello and harpsichord Op. 22 No. 1 is as sparkling as anything by C. P. E. Bach, and many of his early symphonies (e.g. the six in Op. 3) exhilaratingly, to modern ears, anticipate Haydn.

BACH, Johann Sebastian (1685-1750). *German composer.*

If anyone had asked him, Bach would probably have stressed two autobiographical facts above all others: his family background and his church. He belonged to one of the most prolific musical families in history. For four generations before him, the Bach men had been professional craftsmen-musicians as others were stonemasons or bakers; of Bach's own children, four (W. F. Bach, C. P. E. *Bach, J. C. Bach and J. C. F. Bach) followed him into the family business; in the seventeenth and eighteenth centuries as a whole, over fifty Bachs held positions of musical responsibility in the courts and towns of German-speaking Europe. Even more important than this family tradition (about which Bach himself once proudly began a pamphlet) was his membership of the austere Lutheran church, with its ungaudy rituals, its close connection with the German language and German folk music, and above all its authoritarian, puritanical approach to its adherents. Bach's – and Luther's – God was like a loving but stern father, and joy in his worship involved humble obedience as well as ecstasy.

When Bach was ten his father died, and his brother and uncle saw to his musical education, as a choirboy, in composition, and in playing violin, harpsichord and organ. From boyhood he was particularly drawn to the organ, and his first professional jobs were as organist (at Arnstadt, 1703-7; at Mühlhausen, 1707-8; at the court chapel of Saxe-Weimar, 1708-17). He won a reputation as one of Europe's finest players (one writer said that his feet 'flew over the pedals as if winged'), and another as a cantankerous young man determined to play the music his way regardless of the congregation. (When the authorities ordered him to stop surrounding the hymns with flourishes, he retaliated by stopping dead on the last chord, leaving the congregation high and dry; he introduced 'modern harmonies' and 'ear-tearing discords' into the music, to the bafflement of worshippers and the fury of his superiors.) During these years he wrote most of what are now his best-known organ works. Many (e.g. the chorale-preludes,

decorating familiar hymn-tunes) were for church use; others (e.g. the extrovert fantasias, toccatas and fugues) were like a modern cathedral organist's voluntaries, as much for the player's own satisfaction as for the congregation.

A complete change in Bach's life came in 1717, when he was appointed
court musician to the Prince of Anhalt-Cöthen. This aristocrat liked his
music instrumental and secular, and Bach served him for six years, pouring
out orchestral concertos and suites, partitas and sonatas for flute, violin,
viola da gamba and harpsichord, lightweight vocal pieces (e.g. *Coffee Cantata*, *Peasant Cantata*), and dozens of solo keyboard works, ranging from
the first twenty-four preludes and fugues of the *Well-tempered Keyboard*
to the flamboyant *Italian Concerto* and a couple of dozen large-scale suites
and partitas.

In 1723 Bach was appointed Kantor (musician-in-charge) of the
cathedral-school in Leipzig, a job he kept for the rest of his life (twenty-
seven years). His tasks were to supervise the choirboys' musical activities,
and to compose, rehearse and conduct music for the church of St Thomas
itself and for its three daughter-churches. As he had in previous church
appointments, Bach regularly grumbled about the inadequacy of the resources available (and equally regularly upset his employers by his uncompromising attitude to pupils, instrumentalists and congregations); but by
and large he was regarded by the city as an asset, and it was during his
Leipzig years that he composed his noblest church works, from a series of
cantatas (for each Sunday and holy day throughout the year) to the monumental B minor Mass and *St Matthew Passion*. Composing and conducting church music took up most of his time, and he seems to have used
keyboard-playing and instrumental writing as something of a relaxation.
The second twenty-four preludes and fugues of the *Well-tempered Keyboard*, *The Musical Offering*, and *The Art of Fugue*, his major keyboard
masterpieces, were all written in his fifties and sixties.

Bach's official appointments allowed him to work in the dignified obscurity he seems to have preferred to the operatic or virtuoso-soloist careers
of some contemporaries. Working for the Lutheran church also allowed
him to follow the conservative musical traditions of the previous century
rather than the more forward-looking styles of such contemporaries as
*Vivaldi (or of his own more worldly-successful sons C. P. E. Bach and
J. C. Bach). He was less an innovator than the bringer to culmination of
a glorious tradition, and the fact that he shunned musical fashion may
partly explain why his compositions were ignored, outside his own small
circle, throughout his life. After his death, a few of them lived on (*Mozart
and *Beethoven, for example, admired his keyboard works), but it was not
until the 1820s (when *Mendelssohn, for example, conducted the first
public performance of the *St Matthew Passion* since Bach's own day) that

Bach's works began to be sought out, published (often for the first time) and regularly played. And it has taken another century and a half for stolid nineteenth-century performing practices (e.g. the huge choirs, vast orchestras and lugubrious speeds which can still be heard in older gramophone recordings) to disappear from his music: the recent search for authenticity in performance has revealed a fleeter, slimmer composer than the Bach our grandparents knew.

(The BWV numbers attached to Bach's works refer to the Bach Werke-Verzeichnis, or 'Catalogue of Bach's Works' published by the scholar Schmieder in 1950.)

CHORAL WORKS Three Masses (including the B minor Mass); two Passions (*St Matthew* and *St John*); *Magnificat*; 295 church cantatas; seven motets, etc.

Jesu, Joy of Man's Desiring The heart of this popular piece, the last movement of Cantata 147, *Herz und Mund* ('Heart and Mouth'), is a plainly-sung chorale (i.e. Lutheran hymn, in long, slow notes in standard church style). In between the verses, and round the tune as it is sung, Bach entwines a glorious melody of his own, in faster notes, for oboe and first violins. The original piece is for choir and small orchestra, but it is also well-known in arrangements (for oboe and piano; for organ solo; for orchestra without choir; for piano solo, perhaps the best-loved version of all).
→ *Sheep May Safely Graze*; Mozart *Ave verum corpus*; Brahms *How Lovely Are Thy Dwellings Fair* (from his *German Requiem*).

Wachet auf ('Sleepers Wake') (Cantata 140; 1731) Most of Bach's cantatas (like this one) were designed as part of church services, and are variations and meditations on a Lutheran chorale appropriate to the particular day. Most are short (20-30 minutes); most contrast solo arias with choral sections, and include at least one straightforward singing of the chorale, whose words sum up the devotional theme of the whole cantata. Bach's music - as here - tends to be sunnier than these devout purposes might suggest, and offers exhilaration even to those who don't share his faith.
→ Ⓜ *Christmas Oratorio* (six linked cantatas on the Christmas story); *Wedding Cantata*; Mozart *Coronation Mass* K 317.

Ⓜ *St Matthew Passion* (1729) St Matthew's account of Christ's crucifixion and resurrection, set for soloists, choir and orchestra. The Bible words are treated as drama, somewhat in the manner of an oratorio (see *Choral Music*), with additional sections interspersed in cantata-style, reflecting on the meaning of the biblical events. Bach also uses chorales (some of them exceptionally well-known, e.g. *O Sacred Head Sore Wounded*) to involve the congregation even more. The work is solemn, majestic and devotional, best heard live, as records diminish its atmosphere.
→ *St John Passion*; Schütz *Christmas Story*; Brahms *A German Requiem*.

Ⓜ **Mass in B Minor** (1733) An enormous setting of the Latin Mass, treated in the manner of a Passion setting with solos, ensembles and choruses (but without reflective additional material). With the *St Matthew Passion*, Bach's supreme achievement in church music; some say the pinnacle of all his art.
→ Ⓜ *Magnificat* (brisker; lighter-weight); motet *Singet dem Herrn*; Beethoven *Missa solemnis*.

CHAMBER AND KEYBOARD WORKS

CHAMBER MUSIC *The Art of Fugue*; *The Musical Offering*; six partitas/sonatas for violin solo; twelve sonatas for violin and keyboard; six sonatas for flute and keyboard; four trio-sonatas; six suites for cello solo; three sonatas for cello and keyboard.
KEYBOARD SOLO Six *English Suites*; six *French Suites*; six *Partitas*; *Goldberg Variations*; *The Well-tempered Keyboard* (Forty-eight preludes and fugues); *Italian Concerto*; *Chromatic Fantasia and Fugue*; numerous inventions, toccatas, preludes, fantasias. All of these are for plucked-string keyboard instruments like the harpsichord, or for the clavichord.
ORGAN SOLO Six trio-sonatas; more than forty individual preludes/fantasias/toccatas and fugues; many other single pieces, including 150 short chorale preludes for use before or after church services, each decorating a well-known hymn-tune. (The best collection, *Orgelbüchlein*, or 'Little Organ Book', contains forty-six such pieces.)

Toccata and Fugue in D minor This is one of the best-known of all organ works, the piece played by James Mason as Captain Nemo in the film of *20,000 Leagues Under the Sea*, and arranged as a glossy orchestral 'pop' by Stokowski for Disney's film *Fantasia*. It offers the characteristic Bach blend of cerebral and physical pyrotechnics, as exhilarating to hear as it is challenging to play.
→Fantasia and Fugue in G minor; Ⓜ Passacaglia and Fugue in C Minor; Liszt *Prelude and Fugue on B-A-C-H*.

French Suite No. 5 for harpsichord. Bach's suites and partitas combine dance-rhythms (sarabands, minuets, jigs, etc.) with whistleable tunes and easy-going counterpoint; their urbane music is ideal for relaxation. Although they were written for the harpsichord, they are often nowadays played (to fine effect) on the piano: some listeners feel that the evenness of piano tone brings out detail in a way the harpsichord's generalized twanging can obscure. By and large, the six *French Suites* are shorter and more straightforward than the six *English Suites*; the six *Partitas* are display works, stirring technical brilliance into the musical mix.
→*Partita No. 1*; Ⓜ *Italian Concerto*; Handel Harpsichord Suite No. 10 in G.

Das wohltemperierte Klavier ('The Well-tempered Keyboard'; 'The Forty-eight') Forty-eight short preludes and fugues, two each in every key, for solo keyboard (the harpsichord is usual, but the piano is equally effective). The idea sounds dry (and the work was written as a result of Bach's dry interest in temperament, the identical spacing in the octave of all twelve semitones); in fact it offers the listener a kaleidoscope of keyboard playing-skills and styles, as varied and intriguing as (say) *Chopin's *Studies* or *Debussy's *Préludes*. The work is not meant to be heard complete at a sitting; the best-known individual items are Book I Nos. 1 and 2 in C, Nos. 3 and 4 in C minor, Nos. 5 and 6 in D, and Book II Nos. 15 and 16 in G.

→Fantasia in C minor; Ⓜ *Goldberg Variations*; Shostakovich *24 Preludes and Fugues* Op. 87.

Partita in E for violin solo. Bach's solo string-instrument works are akin to his French and English suites for keyboard: groups of dance-movements in lively style. There is no accompaniment: the solo line has its own implied harmonies, and the listening ear soon adapts.

→ Ⓜ Chaconne (from Partita No. 2, piano arrangement by Busoni also recommended); Cello Suite No. 3; Ysaÿe Sonata No. 1 for solo violin.

Ⓜ *The Musical Offering* (1747) King Frederick II of Prussia gave Bach a theme to improvise on, and was rewarded some months later with this huge work, a set of nine canons, ricercars and fugues manipulating the theme in every conceivable contrapuntal way. The work's heart is a twenty-minute, three-movement trio-sonata, in style like the *Brandenburg Concertos* (see below) and often heard on its own. The whole work is to Bach what the last string quartets are to *Beethoven, the fruit of a lifetime's creative experience.

→Trio-sonata No. 3; Ⓜ *The Art of Fugue*; Beethoven String Quartet No. 14.

ORCHESTRAL WORKS Six *Brandenburg Concertos*; four suites; five solo harpsichord concertos; two solo violin concertos; several concertos for more than one soloist, including one for two violins and one for violin and oboe. (Some of these miscellaneous concertos are adaptations from other composers, e.g. the four-harpsichord concerto is a version of Vivaldi's Op. 3 No. 10; others are rescorings of Bach's own works, e.g. the Concerto for violin and oboe also exists in C minor for two harpsichords.)

Brandenburg Concerto No. 2 (1721) Written for and named after the Margrave of Brandenburg, the six *Brandenburg Concertos* are for different solo groups and strings: in No. 2 the soloists are flute, oboe, trumpet and violin. Breezy outer movements (with prominent, high trumpet parts) surround a placid slow movement (highlighting oboe and violin).

→ Ⓜ *Brandenburg Concerto* No. 4 (two recorders, violin and strings); Concerto in D minor for oboe, violin and strings; Vivaldi *Il pastor fido* Op. 13 No. 1.

Concerto No. 5 in F minor for harpsichord and strings. This piece is typical of Bach's delightful solo concertos, generally lighter than his other orchestral works. It consists of the standard energetic first movement, lyrical slow movement and cheerful finale.

→ Ⓜ Harpsichord Concerto No. 1; Ⓜ *Brandenburg Concerto* No. 5; Handel Organ (or Harp) Concerto Op. 4 No. 6.

Suite No. 3 in D for orchestra The formal opening movement is followed by an Air (known separately as Air on the G String) and by four dance movements in a racy outdoor style. The orchestral sound (chiefly strings and oboes) is enlivened by three trumpets: especially in a resonant building, these offer spectacular and unusual close-harmony effects.

→ Suite No. 2 in B minor (for flute and strings: gentler and more reflective); Telemann *Don Quixote Suite*; Handel *Arrival of the Queen of Sheba* and *Fireworks Music*.

Ⓜ **Concerto in D minor/Double Concerto** for two violins and strings. Bach's most sublime concerto – some say his finest instrumental work. Brisk outer movements, sinewy and athletic in a particularly 'stringy' way, surround a central outpouring of ecstatic beauty, the two solo lines entwining and echoing as if the performers were singing rather than playing.

→ Violin Concerto in A minor; Sonata in E minor for violin and keyboard; Mozart *Sinfonia concertante* (for violin and viola) K 364.

BALAKIREV, Mily Alexeyevich (1837–1910). *Russian composer.*
For non-German-speaking musicians in the first half of the nineteenth century, the existence of the Germanic tradition was a mixed blessing. Not only had they to come to terms with challengingly great music by people like *Haydn, *Mozart and *Beethoven, but (except in opera, where Italy was supreme) all the best teachers, conservatoires and even instrument-manufacturers seemed to be in central Europe. Some countries (e.g. Britain and Scandinavia) gave in to the pressure, sent musicians to study in Leipzig or Vienna, and fawned on the Teutonic results. Others (notably France and the Slavonic countries) tried to develop styles of their own, suitable to local cultures, using local history or legend and often taking ideas from folk music.

Because of its enormous size, Russia was for generations musically schizophrenic. Many composers looked westwards to Europe, and produced symphonies, concertos and oratorios as heavy and Germanic as anyone else's; others turned east, and tried to create a musical tradition with its roots in Asian rather than European soil. The first composer to do this with distinction was Glinka (1804–57: see under *One-work Composers*), but the man almost single-handedly responsible for establishing a 'Russian' tradition was his pupil Balakirev. Balakirev spent most of his life as an administrator, heading music-schools, promoting concerts, encouraging talent and above all inspiring young composers to adopt the colourful forms and styles of Russian folk music. (His disciples included *Musorgsky, *Borodin and *Rimsky-Korsakov.) He had time to write only a handful of compositions of his own, but they are of high quality, in a melodious, uncomplicated and – to later, western ears – exotic style not unlike Borodin's.

WORKS Two symphonies; three overtures; two symphonic poems; Piano Concerto; numerous short piano pieces (nocturnes, waltzes, etc.) and a piano sonata; forty-three songs, etc.

Islamey (1869) This piano fantasy, using folk-tunes from oriental Russia, was advertised at the time as the hardest piano work ever composed. True or false, it remains a stunning showpiece, dressing up basically simple tunes and harmonies in finger-virtuosity which is an edge-of-seat spectacle in its own right. Orchestral arrangements exist, but lack the feeling of hair-raising technical risk which makes the piece so irresistible in its piano form.
→ *Overture on Three Russian Themes* (for orchestra); Liszt 'La campanella' (*Transcendental Study* No. 3) and 'Will o' the Wisps' (*Transcendental Study* No. 5); Debussy 'The Wind on the Plain' (*Préludes*, Book 2 No. 3).

Ⓜ **Symphony No. 1** (1898) Without losing the folk-music exuberance of *Islamey*, this is profounder and deeper music. It set the style for a particular kind of Slavonic symphony, far less monumental and earnest than (say) *Brahms's, but just as unified and just as intellectually coherent: the finest of all its descendants are the symphonies of *Tchaikovsky, and it is not eclipsed by them.
→ Symphonic poem *Tamara*; Borodin Symphony No. 2; Stravinsky Symphony in E flat (1904).

BALLET MUSIC

SEVENTEENTH CENTURY Although ballet is one of the oldest theatre arts – there were ballets in ancient Egypt, Greece and Rome – the first surviving ballet music comes from seventeenth-century France, from the court of the dance-loving Louis XIV. Jean-Baptiste Lully (1632–87) composed dozens of pieces for the king's pleasure: they range from individual minuets or sarabandes to full-length works blending dance, song and spoken dialogue. Lully's best-known surviving compositions are a series of comedy-ballets to words by Molière, and the best known of all is *Le bourgeois gentilhomme* ('The Would-be Gentleman'), available nowadays both in its original seventeenth-century dress and in a farcical and musically much frothier version by Hofmannstahl (words) and Richard *Strauss (music).

EIGHTEENTH AND NINETEENTH CENTURIES In the eighteenth and early nineteenth centuries, ballet had very little existence in its own right. A few full-length ballets were composed – e.g. *Mozart's lightweight *Les petits riens* ('Absolutely Nothing') and Beethoven's heavyweight *The Creatures of*

Prometheus – but the ballet music still remembered today was almost all composed for interludes in operas: the range is from short pieces like Gluck's 'Dance of the Blessed Spirits' (from his opera *Orfeo*) to longer suites like the enormously popular ballet music from Gounod's *Faust*.

Nineteenth-century Parisians were especially partial to ballet in operas. There was a tradition that any work performed at the Paris Opéra, whoever its composer and whatever its subject, should contain a ballet sequence. (Some composers, e.g. Meyerbeer, enthusiastically composed works with this in mind; others, e.g. *Rossini and *Verdi, equipped their operas with ballets especially for Paris productions.) Ballet also flourished at less august Paris theatres. At the Bouffes-Parisiens, for example, *Offenbach's operettas included cancans, polkas and barcarolles which were as popular with the public as the *Strauss family's waltzes, marches and polkas were in Vienna. Another composer of operettas, Adolphe Adam, wrote one of the first full-length ballets that has continued to hold the stage: *Giselle* (1841). Its silly plot (peasant girl loves anonymous count, dies of grief when she discovers his identity, then dances all night with him to save him from supernatural predators) offers plenty of scope for dancing, in a variety of colourful styles, without ever tumbling into meaningfulness; its music is a sequence of prettily-orchestrated tunes; it is danced operetta, and none the worse for it. Thirty years later, *Delibes's *Coppélia* (1870) and *Sylvia* (1876) triumphantly joined *Giselle* in the sweet-shop corner of the repertoire.

DRAMATIC BALLETS All ballets composed thus far, from Lully's to Delibes's, consisted of single 'numbers' loosely strung together to fit a story. The next dramatic advance took place in Russia. Russian companies, as well as favouring 'divertissements' (strings of speciality dances), also pioneered a kind of ballet in which full-scale dramatic narratives were told in dance. (The change was similar to the development, in mid-nineteenth-century *opera, from strings of show-arias to coherent 'music-drama'.) Dramatic ballets of this kind needed music of some symphonic substance, and Russian composers spectacularly provided it: the tradition includes Minkus's *Don Quixote*, Glazunov's *The Seasons* and *Raymonda*, and above all *Tchaikovsky's *The Sleeping Beauty*, *The Nutcracker* and *Swan Lake*. As well as this solid fare, Russian ballet companies served up plenty of *hors d'oeuvre*: typical are *Borodin's 'Polovtsian Dances' from the opera *Prince Igor* and *Chopin's *Les sylphides* (an orchestral arrangement of several well-loved piano pieces). In the early twentieth century Diaghilev took Russian ballet to France, and it is thanks to him that, for the rest of the century, ballet has remained a spectacle second only to opera in opulence and extravagance. Among the dozens of great ballets his company created are *Spectre of the Rose* (to *Weber's *Invitation to the Dance*), *Ravel's

Daphnis et Chloé, *Falla's *The Three-cornered Hat* and *Stravinsky's *The Firebird*, *Petrushka* and *The Rite of Spring*.

TWENTIETH CENTURY Twentieth-century composers have carried on both writing story-ballets (*Prokofiev's *Cinderella* and *Romeo and Juliet* are popular examples) and also arranging divertissement-ballets to their own or other people's music (Mackerras's *Pineapple Poll*, based on works by Sullivan, and Hossack's *The Prodigal Son*, based on pieces by Scott Joplin, are entertaining examples). In the 1930s a new form, 'symphonic ballet', began to dominate the repertoire: ballets arranged to pre-existing concert music, whether it was suitable (e.g. *Berlioz's *Fantastic Symphony*) or not (e.g. *Bach's Goldberg Variations or Beethoven's 'Choral' Symphony). The use of symphonic works in this way, and the high quality of some of the original ballet music of Tchaikovsky, Stravinsky and others, has finally dispelled the idea that ballet music is trivial and second-rate, the servant of the dance. Ballet commissions have led to some of the twentieth century's finest pieces of music (*Bartók's *The Miraculous Mandarin*; Stravinsky's *Apollo*; *Copland's *Appalachian Spring*), and the wheel has turned full circle: instead of ballet music being half-heard in the orchestra pit, serving chiefly to keep the dancers together, it has leapt from theatre to concert-hall, divorced itself from dance and been accepted on its own, purely musical, terms. Nothing, in cold blood, seems more absurd than listening to records or concert performances of music written to accompany something else – the same objection applies to film-scores – but who would puremindedly deprive themselves, on that account, of works like *The Firebird*, *Romeo and Juliet* or *The Nutcracker Suite*?

Listening Music for most of the ballets mentioned is regularly performed, either complete or in concert suites. Delibes's *Coppélia Suite* and Adam's *Giselle Suite* are excellent introductions, and Chopin's *Les sylphides* and Sullivan's *Pineapple Poll* agreeably continue their tradition. More substantial ballets (e.g. *Swan Lake* or *Cinderella*) are perhaps best sampled first in orchestral suites, then seen complete in the theatre; other ballet scores (e.g. *Petrushka*; *Appalachian Spring*; Debussy's *Jeux*; *Vaughan Williams's *Job*) work so well in the concert hall that some listeners even find the stage action a distraction. ('Symphonic ballets', except by those who like their classical music equipped with someone else's dramatic interpretations, are perhaps best appreciated by balletomanes, as are 'abstract ballets', where gymnastic movements, not stories, are all-important: Stravinsky's *Agon* and Starer's *Secular Games* are typical.) A whole series of well-loved concert 'lollipops' owes its existence to ballet, and is recommended for straightforward musical delight: the clog-dance from Hérold's *La fille mal gardée* (arranged by Lanchbery), the 'Adagio' from *Khachaturian's *Spartacus* (and the 'Sabre Dance' from his *Gayane*) and – somewhat more substantial – the ballet *Gaîté Parisienne* concocted from Offenbach by Manuel Rosenthal, Respighi's *La boutique fantasque* and

Britten's *Matinées/Soirées musicales* (all arrangements of pieces by Rossini) and the *Four Dance Episodes* from Copland's *Rodeo*. For details of works by the great ballet-music composers, see the articles on Bartók, Debussy, Falla, Milhaud, Prokofiev, Stravinsky and Tchaikovsky. For assorted titbits, see *One-work Composers*.

BARBER, Samuel (1910–81). *American composer.*

Barber belongs with Bliss (see *British and Irish Composers*) in Britain, *Khachaturian in the USSR or *Respighi in Italy. That is, he was one of the very best composers of the second rank, a 'modern' whose work is guaranteed to stimulate and satisfy, and who used twentieth-century techniques without wrenching the listener's ears. He trained as a singer as well as a composer, and a feeling of singability permeates his music. In the 1930s he made his reputation with the *Adagio for Strings*, and for the next forty years was regarded as one of the USA's leading composers. But his works are far less grand than this might suggest: they are tonal, fluent and romantic, high-quality examples of exactly the music people sometimes complain that 'nobody composes any more'.

WORKS Three operas (including *Antony and Cleopatra*); three symphonies and several shorter orchestral works; concertos for violin, cello and piano; chamber music including two string quartets; a sonata and other shorter works for piano (including the jolly *Four Excursions*, in jazz style); many songs, including *Dover Beach*, for baritone and string quartet.

Adagio for Strings (1936) Barber originally wrote this as the slow movement of a string quartet, and turned it into an orchestral piece at the suggestion of Toscanini; it has become one of the best-loved of all twentieth-century string works. A solemn, processional melody is passed from one string group to another, and the harmony rises to a heartfelt and touching climax.
→ Overture *The School for Scandal*; Delius *The Walk to the Paradise Garden*; Fauré Prelude from *Pelléas et Mélisande Suite*.

Violin Concerto (1939) An amiable three-movement work, harmonious and expertly-wrought, the kind of piece the conductor Beecham called 'lollipops' – they have to be sought out on records or in the concert-hall, but once discovered seldom disappoint.
→ Ballet suite *Medea*; Harty Violin Concerto; Britten Violin Concerto.

BARTÓK, Béla (1881–1945). *Hungarian composer.*

Bartók trained to be a concert pianist (he specialized in playing *Bach and *Liszt). He began serious composition in his early twenties, writing a

Liszt-inspired Rhapsody for piano and orchestra and a huge symphonic poem (*Kossuth*) which treats a Hungarian historical epic in the Romantic orchestral manner of Richard *Strauss. In short, at this stage he showed more talent than inspiration. Then, in the early 1900s, he went with *Kodály on a folksong-collecting expedition to the foothills of the Carpathian mountains, and found in the rhythms and melodic patterns of Magyar peasant music exactly the new ideas he needed. Collecting and editing folk music began to dominate his non-composing life; he noted down (or recorded on wax cylinders) tens of thousands of individual pieces, and in 1934 took a part-time job at the Hungarian Academy of Sciences specifically to put his collection in order and publish it.

Collecting folk music transformed the style of Bartók's own compositions. Previous enthusiasts for Central European folk-tunes (e.g. Liszt and *Brahms) had altered the tunes to fit art-music rhythm and harmony, and had had the words translated into German, often at the expense of the music. Bartók left everything exactly as he found it. The scales, to conservatoire-trained ears, were abrupt and bizarre; the rhythms followed the irregular patterns of local languages. In addition, when Bartók arranged folk music for concert use, he gave it piano accompaniments based on bagpipe-drones or percussive repeated notes instead of the usual chords and cadences. He used the same ideas in his original music (which was already full of counterpoint as intricate as Bach's and scored with the technicolour virtuosity he had learned from Strauss); by the early 1920s he had formed an instantly-recognizable personal style – a style almost universally reviled by critics, who claimed to find it ear-shatteringly barbarous and filled with as many nasty sounds as the human mind could possibly devise. (Percy Scholes – who later compiled *The Oxford Companion to Music* – wrote in 1925 that a Bartók piano recital had caused him more suffering than any occasion in his life apart from 'an incident or two connected with painless dentistry'; in 1928 the *Boston Christian Science Monitor* complained that Bartók had 'turned the grand orchestra into a mandolin' and 'gone after beauty with hammer and sticks'.)

Although in private life he was a shy, sensitive man, Bartók the composer seems totally to have ignored such hostility. For twenty years he went on refining his style, and in the process created a couple of dozen of this century's most towering masterworks. In many ways, he was like *Beethoven: he knew exactly what he wanted to do, he did it regardless of the world's opinion, and his refusal to compromise is, in part, what gives his music its power. Only once – in the USA, where he took refuge, aged fifty-eight, when the Nazis overran Eastern Europe – did Bartók compose in a deliberately 'gentler' style, to win some public acceptance. The results, the Concerto for Orchestra and the Piano Concerto No. 3, are today among his best-loved works, but they are by no means his best, and both are eclipsed by the Sonata for solo violin of the same period, as thorny a piece as any he ever wrote. Since his death his music has become part of the standard repertoire, and familiarity has shown that far from being the work of a 'demented blacksmith' or of 'someone old enough to know better', it ranks with the greatest artistic creations of the age.

WORKS Opera *Bluebeard's Castle*; ballets *The Miraculous Mandarin* and *The Wooden Prince*; three piano concertos and other shorter pieces for piano and orchestra; two violin concertos and two rhapsodies for violin and orchestra; Concerto for Orchestra; Music for Strings, Percussion and Celesta; Divertimento for Strings; Dance Suite and several other, shorter orchestral works; six string quartets; two sonatas for violin and piano; Sonata for two pianos and percussion and several other chamber works; Piano Sonata, *Mikrokosmos* (six books of graded teaching pieces), *Out of Doors Suite* and many collections of shorter pieces (e.g. Bagatelles) for piano solo; over seventy folksong-arrangements and original songs for voice or choir; *Cantata profana* for choir and orchestra.

Rumanian Folk Dances (1915) These six tiny pieces are based on collected tunes, and are Bartók's folk art at its freshest, an ideal first glimpse of his unique sound world. Originally for piano, the dances also exist in a sparkling arrangement for violin and piano (a favourite recital encore) and as an orchestral suite.
→*Allegro barbaro* for piano; *Village Scenes* (songs); Prokofiev 'Troika' (from *Lieutenant Kijé Suite*).

Concerto for Orchestra (1943) As its name implies, this five-movement suite gives every player in the orchestra the chance to star. Its tunes (Bartók's own) have all the zest of folksongs, its harmonies are lush and its orchestration rivals *Rimsky-Korsakov's *Sheherazade* or *Holst's *The Planets* for exuberance and drive. The first movement is athletic and sinewy; the slow movement is serious and deeply-felt, the exile reflecting on his beloved Hungary; the finale begins with bagpipe-imitations and ends with a brassy fugue.
→ Piano Concerto No. 3; Kodály *Dances of Galánta;* Janáček Sinfonietta.

Piano Concerto No. 3 (1945) The inspiration of this concerto, one of the best-loved of all twentieth-century works, is the piano's ability to move in an instant from spikiness to lyricism, and this switching-about is a feature of all three movements. The outer movements are fast and *Bachian; the central slow movement alternates chorale-like chords with note-flurries depicting nocturnal insects. (One of Bartók's hobbies was collecting moths.)
→ Piano Concerto No. 2 (brisker and clangier); Ravel Piano Concerto in G; Shostakovich Piano Concerto No. 1.

The Miraculous Mandarin (1919) Although composed for a ballet, this music is of symphonic size, and is usually heard as a concert work. Its opening depicts snarling New York traffic, and sets the scene for a story (at least in the ballet) of hoodlum violence and hopeless, yearning love. In its way, *The Miraculous Mandarin* is a musical equivalent of 1920s Cubist painting: once regarded as both shocking and naïve, it now seems cheerful, straightforward and absolutely clear in both what it sets out to do and how to do it.

→ Dance Suite; Ⓜ Violin Concerto No. 2; Stravinsky *The Song of the Nightingale*.

Ⓜ **Music for Strings, Percussion and Celesta** (1936) The seemingly bizarre combination of instruments leads to one of Bartók's finest works. The strings sometimes strum like folk-guitars, sometimes eerily foreshadow 1980s outer-space film music or synthesizer-sounds. Bartók's use of percussion here has never been outclassed, and the celesta, which in other hands can sound banal, adds a hard glint characteristic of the score. The opening movement is a complex fugue; the third movement is 'insect-music'; folk dances inspire movements two and four.

→ Divertimento for Strings; Martin *Petite symphonie concertante*; Martinů Concerto for two string orchestras, piano and timpani.

Ⓜ **String Quartet No. 6** (1939) Bartók's string quartets, regarded by many as the finest music for the medium since Beethoven's last quartets, make thorny but compelling listening. The Sixth is the most approachable, its four movements linked by a sad, folk-like melody and ranging in mood from march and burlesque (satirizing *Stravinsky) to a desolate lament. Of the other quartets, No. 1 is Debussyesque, No. 2 is in Bartók's fiercest folk-music style, Nos. 3 and 4 make gritty listening but are for many Bartók-lovers the finest of all his works, and No. 5 is relaxed and cheerful, in the mood of the Second Violin Concerto or the Divertimento for Strings.

→ Ⓜ String Quartet No. 3; Janáček String Quartet No. 2; Tippett String Quartet No. 2.

BEETHOVEN, Ludwig van (1770-1827). *German composer.*

Beethoven's father was a singer employed by the Elector of Cologne in Bonn. When alcoholism threatened his career, he saw the chance of enriching himself by exploiting his son as a child prodigy, a second *Mozart. To do this meant clipping several years from Beethoven's actual age, and neglecting his formal education in favour of endless music practice. As a money-making scheme, the attempt was a disaster – and it may also have soured Beethoven's character, encouraging the brusqueness and withdrawnness which marked his adult personality. In his twenties Beethoven was a barnstorming solo pianist and piano teacher, famous in aristocratic salons as much for displays of temperament (for example, refusing to play unless his audience stopped talking) as for his music. Deafness forced him to abandon his performing career in his early thirties, but by then he was sufficiently well-known as a composer to live from commissions, the profits of concerts and the sale of his works to publishers. He soon became the most revered composer in Europe, and was regarded (with his older contemporary, the poet Goethe) as the greatest living example of Romantic, wayward, artistic genius.

Although some of Beethoven's early works (those written before 1802, during his virtuoso years) do offer hints of the granite strength to come, his eighteenth-century music is generally as cheerful and uncomplex as (say) *Haydn's, though it is chunkier and less graceful than such comparisons might suggest. This is true not only of deliberately light works like the jolly Septet, but also of large-scale pieces like the First Symphony, the first two piano concertos, the first dozen or so piano sonatas (the 'Pathétique' Sonata, Op. 13, is typical), and the six string quartets Op. 18. In later years, even when his overall style had become darker and more intense, the same kind of 'classical' radiance can still break through – as in the 'Spring' Sonata, the Seventh Symphony or the Fourth Piano Concerto.

In 1802 Beethoven was told that his deafness was incurable and would increase until he could hear nothing at all. This produced a violent upheaval in his character (a combination of determination to 'seize fate by the throat' and the agony of depression from which it arose). The effects on his music were immediate. It lost none of its tunefulness or ease of flow, but shed most of the boisterousness of his virtuoso years. Reflectiveness, largeness of scale and 'innerness' became main elements; the feeling was no longer that of a brilliant adolescent hurling his talent about, but of a mature artist pondering and placing each effect. Many of Beethoven's most popular and tranquil works date from this time: the 'Emperor' Piano Concerto, the Violin Concerto, the Third to Seventh Symphonies, the 'Razumovsky' string quartets and several of his noblest piano sonatas (e.g. the 'Waldstein' and the 'Appassionata').

As his deafness increased – by 1819 he was stone deaf, unable to hear the orchestras he conducted, dependent for conversation on people writing down their remarks – his music became more like self-communion than public utterance, a mixture (sometimes startlingly abrupt) of intellectuality, experiment and serenity. (The last of his piano sonatas is typical: an angry first movement, furiously discordant, is followed by a set of peaceful variations, delicate necklaces of notes giving a feeling that Beethoven, in the poet Stefan Georg's phrase, felt 'the air of another planet'.) Among the works of his last fifteen years are two of the grandest utterances of the whole Romantic age (the 'Choral' Symphony and the *Missa solemnis*), and a series of chamber works which, though demanding and not easily accessible, are for many listeners the pinnacle of their musical experience. These include the last five piano sonatas and the last six string quartets.

ORCHESTRAL WORKS Nine symphonies; five piano concertos; Violin Concerto; Triple Concerto (for violin, cello, piano and orchestra); overtures; music for plays (e.g. Goethe's *Egmont*) and for a ballet (*The Creatures of Prometheus*), etc.

Overtures Overture *Egmont*, Op. 84 (1810). Just as many great writers' short stories compactly cover similar ground to their novels, so Beethoven's ten overtures are like pocket examples of his musical style, and of the emotions and ideas he expressed in longer works. Thus, *Egmont* (written, with other pieces, for Goethe's tragedy about the pull between political and private duty) is energetic music which progresses from an elegiac, fragmentary beginning to a heroic and affirmative end. Similar overtures (also good examples of Beethoven's style at its most heroic) are *Coriolan*, Op. 62 (for a play on the theme of Shakespeare's *Coriolanus*) and ⓜ *Leonora* No. 3 (1806), one of four written for Beethoven's opera *Fidelio*.
→ Overture *Prometheus*; Mozart overture *The Magic Flute*; Wagner overture *The Flying Dutchman*.

Symphonies ⓜ Symphony No. 5, Op. 67 (1807). The 'di-di-di-DAH' opening is one of the best-known ideas in music, and the rest of the first movement explores its rhythm in a miracle of taut construction. The second movement is a funeral march, the third a scherzo highlighting horns and double basses and leading to a ceremonial, joyous finale. This symphony's rhythmic energy, largeness of scope and powerful demonstration of how 'symphonic unity' (see *Symphony*) binds disparate movements into a meaningful whole, are features echoed in Beethoven's other most monumental symphonies, Nos. 3, 7, 8 and 9. The ⓜ Symphony No. 3 ('Eroica'), Op. 55 (1804), is, as its name suggests, in heroic style, with a muscular first movement (exploiting the contrast between a broad, upreaching theme and a brisker descending one), a funeral march and scherzo akin to those of the Symphony No. 5, and a variation-finale on a musical theme also used in the ballet *Prometheus* and the ⓜ 'Eroica' Variations and Fugue Op. 35 for piano. The ⓜ Symphony No. 7, Op. 92 (1812), though no less massive in scale, is in a more lighthearted and lyrical style; its compelling rhythms made *Wagner call it 'the apotheosis of the dance'. The Symphony No. 8, Op. 93 (1812), though shorter than any other Beethoven Symphony (*c.* 24 minutes), gives a similar impression of breadth and grandeur; the ⓜ Ninth ('Choral') Symphony, Op. 125 (1824), follows three orchestral movements (a hammering first movement and scherzo preceding a murmurous, ecstatic slow movement, the work's instrumental heart) with variations for chorus and orchestra setting Schiller's poem *Ode to Joy*, wishing unity and peace on all mankind. Of Beethoven's other symphonies, No. 1 (Op. 21, 1800), No. 2 (Op. 36, 1802) and ⓜ No. 4 (Op. 60, 1806) are relaxed, sunny and wittily scored; ⓜ No. 6 ('Pastoral'), Op. 68 (1808), is unlike any symphony composed before it: its five movements express (so Beethoven said) the emotions aroused by country scenes (and have subtitles like 'By the Brook' and 'Storm'), but the music avoids straightforward picture-painting (like that in, say, *Berlioz's *Fantastic Symphony*) in favour of (once more) 'symphonic unity', the work preserving the same mood and intellectual dignity throughout.

→ Good follow-ups to the more relaxed symphonies are Mozart's 'Jupiter' symphony, Schubert's Symphony No. 5, Bizet's Symphony and Mendelssohn's 'Scottish' and 'Italian' symphonies; after the 'Pastoral' might come Schubert's 'Unfinished' Symphony, Berlioz's *Fantastic Symphony* and Dvořák's Symphony No. 8; after the heavyweight symphonies might come Schubert's Symphony No. 9 and Brahms's Symphony No. 4.

Concertos ⓜ Piano Concerto No. 4, Op. 58 (1808). As with his symphonies, each of Beethoven's concertos is unique, making categories misleading. This one is gentle and serene, one of his most lyrical works (it reminded *Liszt of the legend of Orpheus singing to the Furies in the Underworld). Like Mozart's concertos (and unlike many later nineteenth-century ones), it treats the piano as a melodic rather than a percussive instrument. The ⓜ Violin Concerto, Op. 61 (1806), from the same stage in Beethoven's career, is in similarly relaxed style, with a rapt slow movement (violin-line soaring over gently-moving orchestral chords) and a spirited 'hunting' finale. Of the other concertos, the First Piano Concerto, Op. 15 (1798), and Second Piano Concerto, Op. 19 (1795), are cheerful, light counterparts to the First and Second Symphonies, and the Triple Concerto (Op. 56, 1804) for violin, cello, piano and orchestra, is the nearest of all Beethoven's concertos to the unsymphonic, fun-for-its-own-sake works of such contemporaries as Hummel and Spohr (whose concertos make excellent follow-up listening to it). His grandest concertos, the ⓜ Piano Concerto No. 3, Op. 37 (1801), and the ⓜ Piano Concerto No. 5 ('Emperor'), Op. 73 (1809), are a mixture of concerto showmanship and symphonic seriousness. Each follows a weighty first movement (the most complex musical argument) with a decorative slow movement and a cheerful finale; the *Chopin-like slow movement of No. 3 and the bouncing finale of No. 5 were especially admired and imitated by later concerto composers.

→ Good follow-ups to the Violin Concerto might be Mendelssohn's or Dvořák's violin concertos; the First and Second Concertos might lead to Mozart's Piano Concerto No. 23; the Fourth might lead to Mozart's Piano Concerto No. 27 and to Schumann's Piano Concerto; the Third to Chopin's Piano Concerto No. 2; and the Fifth to Liszt's Piano Concerto No. 1 and Brahms's piano concertos Nos. 1 and 2.

PIANO AND CHAMBER WORKS Thirty-two piano sonatas; seventeen string quartets; ten sonatas for violin and piano; five sonatas for cello and piano; six trios for violin, cello and piano; sets of variations (including *Diabelli Variations* for piano); other miscellaneous chamber works.

Lighter chamber works Septet Op. 20 (1800). This cheerful six-movement work, for clarinet, bassoon, horn and string quartet, is typical of a whole slice of Beethoven's output: it harks back to eighteenth-century music of patronage, to the serenades and divertimentos written (e.g. by Mozart) for aristocratic music-parties, or even to accompany food or cards. It is uncomplicated and unbuttoned, music intended solely for delight. Beethoven's many sets of variations, early trios (string trios Op. 9; piano trios Op. 1, Op. 20), quintets, sextets and octets for strings and/ or wind, all follow in the Septet's tripping footsteps, and one of the main pleasures for Beethoven-lovers is to see its geniality gradually transformed into something no less attractive but much weightier, in the early piano sonatas (Op. 2, Op. 10, Op. 13, Op. 14, Op. 22) and sonatas for piano and violin (No. 5, 'Spring' Sonata, Op. 24 No. 1, is typical).

→ Hummel 'Military' Septet; Schubert Octet; Dvořák Serenade for ten wind instruments.

Sonatas Piano Sonata No. 8 ('Pathétique'), Op. 13 (1798). Beethoven's thirty-two piano sonatas span his career, and are for his own favourite instrument: they give a clear indication both of his development as a composer and of his towering genius. The early ones, many composed for his own virtuoso recitals, are ebullient and often flashy; there are, however, plentiful original turns of mind and phrasing, hints (for us today, at least) of the greatness to come. No. 8 is typical: its subtitle means not 'pathetic sonata' but 'sonata full of feeling', and the work is an early example of Beethoven's (and Romantic composers' generally) concern for the dramatized, self-conscious presentation of private feeling in music. The first movement is turbulent and full of dramatic pauses; the second is serene; the third is a rondo whose decorous theme keeps breaking out in frenzied runs and emphatic discords. The same idea, of directly expressing feeling, is married to symphonic musical depth in the Ⓜ Piano Sonata No. 23 ('Appassionata'), Op. 57 (1805), which marks a peak in Beethoven's artistic development parallel to the Symphony No. 5: classical procedures are fully absorbed, transformed into a personal style, and the emotion is not dramatized and external (as in the Piano Sonata No. 8) but integrated, the driving-force inside the notes. (When this sonata ends 'as fast as possible', the instruction has less to do with virtuoso display than with the climax to the feeling of striving which underlies the whole piece.) The last half-dozen sonatas, from the same period as the Ninth Symphony and the last string quartets, are self-communing masterworks, each a unique reinvention of sonata form. The Ⓜ Piano Sonata No. 31, Op. 110 (1821), for example (one of the most accessible), begins with a slow movement, proceeds to a fast scherzo, a sobbing *aria dolente* ('griefstricken song') and fugue, and then unravels the aria and fugue in new keys (the fugue upside-down as well) and ends with a brief reference to the opening movement. The form is wholly unconventional and wholly satisfying (because of the overwhelming impression of inevitability, as if the piece had been written in a single afternoon instead of taking weeks of work).

→ After Piano Sonata No. 8, good follow-ups are the early sonatas: No. 14, Op. 27 No. 2 ('Moonlight') and No. 17, Op. 31 No. 2 are in the same exploration-of-emotion style, No. 4, Op. 7 and Nos. 5-7, Op. 10 are chunky display-pieces, Ⓜ No. 2, Op. 2 No. 2 is of a musical stature to rival the First Symphony. After the Piano Sonata No. 23, good follow-ups are Ⓜ No. 21, Op. 53 ('Waldstein') and the impassioned No. 26, Op. 81a ('Les adieux'); the Piano Sonata No. 31 might lead straight to the great, late group: No. 28, Op. 101 and No. 30, Op. 109 share its serenity and singing tone; Ⓜ No. 29, Op. 106 ('Hammerklavier') and Ⓜ No. 32, Op. 111 are monumental, equivalents of the Third and Ninth Symphonies respectively, among Beethoven's grandest works. Of other composers' works, good follow-ups to Beethoven's early sonatas are those by Haydn (e.g.

Sonata No. 52 in E flat); middle-period Beethoven might lead to *Schubert's sonatas (especially those in G and B flat), and the later sonatas lead directly to some of the most powerful works in the piano repertoire, Chopin's Sonata No. 3, Liszt's Piano Sonata in B minor and Brahms's *Variations and Fugue on a Theme of Handel*.

String quartets Ⓜ String Quartet No. 9 ('Razumovsky'), Op. 59 No. 3. One of three quartets written for the violin-playing Russian ambassador to Vienna, this work is contemporary with the Symphony No. 4 and the Violin Concerto, and like them is a blend of lyricism and closely-worked thematic development. The 'Razumovsky' quartets quite eclipse his earlier six quartets (Op. 18), and are typical of most of his mature chamber music – middleweight (akin, at their most serious, to the Piano Concerto No. 3), and relaxed rather than striving: good follow-ups are the Piano Trio No. 6 ('Archduke') Op. 97 (1810), the String Quartet No. 10 ('Harp') Op. 74 (1809), the Sonata No. 10 for violin and piano Op. 96 (1812), and the Sonata No. 3 for cello and piano Op. 69 (1809). Good follow-ups by other composers are Haydn String Quartet No. 81, Op. 77 No. 1, Mozart String Quartet K 428 and Schubert String Quartet No. 13 in A minor. Quite unlike these, or indeed any other chamber works at all, are Beethoven's last six quartets, regarded by some listeners as his greatest compositions in any medium. The Ⓜ String Quartet No. 15, Op. 132 (1825), is the most accessible: its slow movement (subtitled by Beethoven 'holy song of gratitude to the divinity, on recovering from an illness') is a hymn-like meditation of the utmost musical directness. The other late quartets offer music of comparable introversion (e.g. the opening fugue of the Ⓜ Quartet No. 14, Op. 131, 1826), and movements of extraordinary, athletic vigour, seeming almost too large-scale, too all-engulfing, to be performed by four players on fragile instruments: typical is the Ⓜ *Grosse Fuge* (Great Fugue), Op. 133 (1827). These quartets dwarf the rest of the repertoire: of other composers' chamber works, only Mozart's String Quintet No. 3 K 515 or Schubert's String Quintet offer experiences of anything like the same intensity.

VOCAL WORKS Opera *Fidelio*; two Masses; Choral Fantasia; Song-cycle *An die ferne Geliebte*; forty-nine folksong arrangements; three cantatas and other miscellaneous works.

Ⓜ *Fidelio* (1805, revised 1814) Beethoven's only opera – he was less a vocal than an instrumental composer – is passionate about revolutionary idealism and (a characteristic early Romantic theme) the redemptive power of true love. *Fidelio* is particularly thoughtful and thought-provoking, a 'symphonic opera', and needs to be both savoured on record and seen on stage to make its full effect; a short first approach is via the four *Leonora* overtures (based on the opera's musical themes: Ⓜ No. 3 is best heard first) and extracts such as the moving Prison Scene. The only other vocal work to match it (leaving aside the last movement of the 'Choral' Symphony) is the Ⓜ *Missa solemnis* (Solemn Mass), Op. 123 (1818), his second setting of the Catholic Mass, conceived less as a devotional work than as an affirmation of faith equally in God and in the creative and aspiring nature of humanity. (The music consistently goes beyond the specific religious meaning of the words, and is meant to speak of and to all humankind, believers or not.)

The size of the *Missa solemnis* daunts concert promoters, and it is rarely heard. But it remains a peak of the large-scale choral repertoire, a worthy companion to Bach's *St Matthew Passion* and B minor Mass (which are suggested follow-ups, along with Bruckner's E minor Mass and Mahler's Symphony No. 8).

SALON AND OTHER WORKS Among Beethoven's often-played, slighter pieces are *Für Elise* ('For Elise'), *Rage over a Lost Penny* and several other Bagatelles, for piano; *Wellington's Victory* (or, on the continent, 'Battle' Symphony) for grand orchestra; several sets of folksong arrangements for voice, violin, cello and piano; and assorted movements (often wildly disarranged) from longer works, e.g. the first movement of the 'Moonlight' Sonata as foxtrot, brass-band 'meditation' and popular song.

BELLINI, Vincenzo (1801–35). *Italian composer.*

At the beginning of the nineteenth century, when opera-composers in most countries were eagerly following the dramatic style pioneered by Gluck (see under *Opera*), the Italians took little interest in reform. They regarded Italy as opera's birthplace and its true home; they thought their opera-houses and opera-singers the finest in the world; they considered that the Italian style (where singing-display came first, and drama hardly mattered) was excellent as it was – and they had two outstanding composers (*Donizetti and *Rossini) to provide it.

It was Bellini who began the change. When his first opera was produced (in 1825, when he was still a student), show-arias were all-important; ten years (and ten Bellini operas) later, Italian opera had moved towards the dramatic style of the rest of Europe, and the foundation was laid for *Verdi and *Puccini, whose works are for many opera-lovers the pinnacle of the art. Bellini gave his singers plenty of scope for musical display – few composers have written more spectacularly agile arias – but he also made sure that each display-piece fitted its setting, so that each outburst of aria came at some climax of emotion or character-development. At first, singers found it hard to combine character-acting and florid singing, but the stars who managed the new technique took Bellini's operas into their repertoire, toured with them throughout Europe (and to Russia and America), and made his name before he was thirty. He died too young to fulfil the promise of the few works he wrote; even so, his operas are more than musical curiosities, and still both appeal to stars (in the twentieth century, Callas and Sutherland had particular success with them) and enthrall their audiences.

WORKS Apart from his eleven operas (the best-known are *La sonnambula*, *Norma* and *I Puritani*), Bellini also wrote an oboe concertino and a handful of solo songs and choral pieces for use in church.

'**Casta diva**' ('Chaste goddess') (from *Norma*, 1831) This hymn to the moon, sung by the opera's heroine (a Druid priestess tormented by unhappy love), shows Bellini's musical character-drawing at its best. A slow, beautiful melody symbolizes the heroine's longing for peace and purity, and it is decorated with every imaginable kind of trill and run, symbolizing her nervous tension which disrupts that peace. Thus, every ornament has dramatic point, and we sympathize with the character's predicament even as we gasp at the singer's skill.

→ 'Centa di fiori' (from *I Puritani*); Verdi 'Caro nome' (from *Rigoletto*); Puccini 'Vissi d'arte' (from *Tosca*).

La sonnambula ('The Sleepwalker') (1831) Complete opera. The gentle story of this work (about a country girl caught in a Count's bedroom at night, then cleared of guilt by being proved to be a sleepwalker) could have been farce, but Bellini makes it delicate, innocent and highly romantic (something like an opera-equivalent of one of the Brontë sisters' novels). Its superb central soprano role needs a star singer to do it justice (the music dies on lesser lips); the sleepwalking scene in Act II, the climax of the action, has an effect in the opera-house as electric as any piano-concerto cadenza in the concert-hall.

→ *Norma*; Donizetti *Lucia di Lammermoor*; Rossini *Le Comte Ory*.

BENJAMIN. See *One-work Composers*.

BERG, Alban (1885–1935). *Austrian composer*.

A small private income allowed Berg to take up composition as a career; when this money ran out after the First World War, he scraped a living from teaching and from royalties (especially performance-royalties from his opera *Wozzeck*). In his teens and twenties he was friendly with many of the avant-garde Viennese intellectuals of the time: the painters Kirchner and Kokoschka, the poet Altenberg, the architect Gropius, and above all the group of musicians centred on *Mahler's widow Alma and on the composer *Schoenberg.

Many of Berg's avant-garde colleagues created art chiefly for one another. They knew that the general public hated their works – there were rows and fights to prove it at every exhibition or concert they held – and they preferred to stay in a clique of friends, who understood and approved of what they were trying to do. Berg was an exception. Although he wrote some works for his friends (e.g. the Chamber Concerto, composed as a fiftieth-birthday present for Schoenberg) he consciously aimed others at the general public, choosing familiar forms (string quartet; grand opera), and asking for his music to be included in programmes alongside 'regular' works. (It was: his *Lyric Suite* was played with quartets by *Brahms or *Beethoven, and so won respect; *Wozzeck* became the one avant-garde opera included in every season.) His accessible musical style made (and makes) his works ideal ambassadors for 'modern' music. Although the avant-garde technique he used (e.g. the twelve-note system) gives his music a jagged surface sound, its direct expressiveness (nearer to *Verdi's music than to that of the twentieth century) makes it perfectly approachable, the sort of music whose difficulties disappear with frequent hearing.

WORKS Operas *Wozzeck, Lulu*; Three Pieces for Orchestra; Violin Concerto; Chamber Concerto for violin, piano and wind orchestra; String Quartet and *Lyric Suite* for strings; Piano Sonata and other smaller chamber works; *Wine*, Five Altenberg Songs, Four Songs, Op. 2, and over seventy other songs (mainly composed in his teens).

Ⓜ **Violin Concerto** (1935) Composed 'in memory of an angel' (Gropius's eighteen-year-old daughter Manon), this two-movement work is full of high-soaring, elegiac violin music (symbolizing the girl's beauty), contrasted with harsher orchestral outbursts (symbolizing the approach of death?). The second movement makes touching use of a folk-tune and ends with rapt variations on the chorale *Es ist genug* ('It is enough'), blending Bach's eighteenth-century harmonization (in his Cantata No. 82) with Berg's twentieth-century traceries.
→ Three Pieces for Orchestra; Bartók Violin Concerto No. 2; Shostakovich Violin Concerto No. 1.

Ⓜ *Wozzeck* (1920) Complete opera, based on Büchner's grim play about the degradation and destruction of a simple soldier. The events of the story (murder; betrayal; prostitution) are as sordid as those of (say) Leoncavallo's *Pagliacci* or *Puccini's *Tosca*, and *Wozzeck* is as sensational and gripping as they are; but Berg writes music so compelling that he elevates Wozzeck's sufferings into grander statements about the plight of humanity at large. His other opera, *Lulu*, has just as lurid a plot (its heroine is a prostitute betrayed by every man she meets and finally murdered by Jack the Ripper), but has less general relevance and consequently seems shocking where *Wozzeck* is moving, melodramatic where *Wozzeck* is true to life. (Good introductions to both works are the extracts Berg made for concert use: *Wozzeck Suite*, 1924, and *Lulu Symphony*, 1934. There were two versions of *Lulu*: the first should be ignored in favour of the three-act version first issued in 1979.)
→ Chamber Concerto; Bartók *Bluebeard's Castle*; Henze *Elegy for Young Lovers*.

Lyric Suite for string quartet (1926) This work, which Berg said was composed as 'an expression of lyrical love', echoes both the mood and chief musical lovetheme of *Wagner's opera *Tristan and Isolde*, and also makes characteristic use - Berg was a great one for codes and hidden meanings - of a musical cipher based on the initials of Berg and his beloved. There are six short movements, alternately spiky, spectral and passionate. *Three Movements from the Lyric Suite* is a sumptuous arrangement for orchestral strings.

→ String Quartet, Op. 3; Schoenberg String Quartet No. 3; Bartók String Quartet No. 4.

BERLIOZ, Hector (1803-69). *French composer.*

Berlioz's parents hoped that he would become a doctor like his father. But at the age of eighteen, disgusted by the dissection of corpses which was part of the training of medical students, Berlioz gave up medicine for music. He spent the next ten years studying, and was famous for refusing to abide by the strict rules of composition taught by his professors, and for standing up at concerts and shouting insults at conductors who tampered with the music being performed. His music also won a reputation: it was wild, unlike anything composed before, and seemed to some listeners like a chaotic nightmare, emotions and passions flung down on paper with neither order nor control. (The *Fantastic Symphony* dates from this time, and was a scandalous success.)

In his later life, Berlioz earned a living by conducting gargantuan concerts (some involving over 800 performers) of his own works, and by writing music criticism. He was fascinated by everything to do with the stage: his first wife was an Irish actress and his second an Italian opera-singer, and throughout his life he composed operas and incidental music for plays. His taste in literature was for tales of love and romantic adventure (he liked Virgil's *Aeneid*, especially the section about the doomed love-affair of Dido and Aeneas, Shakespeare's *Romeo and Juliet*, and Byron's poem *Child Harolde's Pilgrimage*, about a young man wandering through Europe trying to 'find himself'); his friends included such wild geniuses as Paganini and *Liszt (both said by their enemies to be inspired by the devil); he took opium, and believed in spirits of darkness and powers from other worlds.

Berlioz's highly-coloured personality is reflected in his music. He avoided neat, traditional forms (like sonatas) in favour of long, free-form works often based on literary originals. (*Harold in Italy* is typical: it is a 'symphony' for viola and orchestra, offering sound-pictures of four scenes from Byron's *Child Harolde's Pilgrimage* with the soloist's music taking the hero's part, reflecting on the scenes the orchestra depicts.) Berlioz wrote for the orchestra in a revolutionary way, unheard-of before his time: he was intrigued by the unexplored possibilities of instruments, exploited new inventions (like valves for *brass instruments), and even wrote a textbook on how to score music for orchestra. None the less, he thought that the human voice (especially the soprano) was the finest instrument of all, and that singing was the most natural form of human expression; the musical fruits of this enthusiasm are some of the richest of all his works.

WORKS Three operas (*Benvenuto Cellini*; *The Trojans*; *Beatrice and Benedict*); three 'Symphonies' (*Symphonie fantastique*; *Harold in Italy*; *Symphonie funèbre et triomphale*); six overtures (including *Roman Carnival*; *The Corsair*; *King Lear*); twenty-five choral works (including *Te Deum*; *Requiem*; *The Damnation of Faust*; *Romeo and Juliet*; *The Childhood of Christ*); songs and other works for solo voice (including *Nuits d'été* and *Lélio*, a 'monodrama' written as a sequel to the *Fantastic Symphony*). Berlioz also published his *Memoirs*, more like a comic novel than an autobiography, and a witty selection of his music criticism, *Evenings in the Orchestra*.

Hungarian March (Rakoczy March) (from *The Damnation of Faust*, 1846) Few pieces better show off Berlioz's orchestral wizardry: if he had lived a century later, he might have written a march like this for some enormous technicolour film. He based it on a popular revolutionary song, a Hungarian equivalent of the *Marseillaise*, and the piece affected audiences of the time rather as *Land of Hope and Glory* does British audiences at the Last Night of the Proms today.
→ Queen Mab Scherzo (from *Romeo and Juliet*) - orchestral portrait of the Fairy Queen and her attendants, quicksilver, gossamer music, glitteringly scored; Liszt Hungarian Rhapsody No. 15 (using the Rakoczy tune); Tchaikovsky *Marche Slave*.

Symphonie fantastique ('Fantastic Symphony'), Op. 14 (1831) Written to immortalize Berlioz's love-affair with his first wife, this work takes as its musical model *Beethoven's 'Pastoral' Symphony. Its movements show us 'five scenes from an artist's life' (some say hallucinations produced by drugs): 'Reveries, Passions'; 'The Ball' (a smiling waltz); 'Country Scene'; 'March to the Scaffold' (eerie and gloomy: the artist thinks he is the condemned victim, and the movement ends with the guillotine cutting short a last memory of his beloved); 'Dream of a Witches' Sabbath' (a supernatural jig, supposed to be taking place in a churchyard at midnight; the beloved is - oh horror! - one of the hags). The movement-titles give clues to the highly-coloured, melodramatic nature of the music, like no other 'symphony' before or since.
→ Overture *Roman Carnival*; Liszt *Les préludes*; Tchaikovsky *Romeo and Juliet*.

Overture *Carnaval romain* ('Roman Carnival'), Op. 9 (1844) This is a straightforward sound-picture of carnival festivities (including glimpses of lovers heedless of the crowds around them). It is as cheerful and bustling as one of Rubens's party-pictures, and though it works well enough on record, is particularly exhilarating to see performed, because of the spectacular demands it makes on the orchestral players.
→ Overture *The Corsair*; Dvořák overture *Carnival*; Beethoven overture *Egmont*; Weber overture *Euryanthe*.

Nuits d'été ('Summer Nights'), Op. 7 (1841) This set of six songs for voice and orchestra is one of even Berlioz's most Romantic works. He set out not only to fit music to the words, but also to produce the most ravishing possible vocal sounds. The music is mainly slow; the songs' subjects are loss and longing (e.g. 'Spectre of the Rose'; 'At the Cemetery'; 'The Unknown Island'); despite very different scoring, the mood is similar to *Chopin's piano nocturnes or the slow movement of *Beethoven's Violin Concerto.

→ Overture *King Lear*; Wagner *Wesendonck Songs*; Ravel *Sheherazade*.

(M) *Requiem* (*Grande messe des morts*), Op. 5 (1837) The biggest of all Berlioz's chorus-and-orchestra works, not so much a Mass for the Dead as a full-colour picture of the Day of Judgement, complete with Last Trump (trebling the usual number of orchestral brass), majestic angels, panic-stricken or humbly praying crowds and an overwhelming feeling that only belief in God can save humanity.

→ (M) *The Trojans* (enormous five-hour opera, Part 1 depicting the Fall of Troy, Part 2 – the better-known – Aeneas's love-affair with Queen Dido of Carthage); Verdi *Requiem*; Walton *Belshazzar's Feast*.

BERNSTEIN, Leonard (born 1918). *American conductor and composer.*

In the history of music, Bernstein's only real rivals for versatility are *Liszt and *Mendelssohn. He has had interlocking careers as concert pianist, professor, television lecturer, composer and conductor. He learned conducting from Koussevitsky, made his début deputizing for Bruno Walter, and has since conducted every major world orchestra. His eloquent platform manner – which runs the gamut from ecstatic hand-gestures to exuberant hip-wiggling when the beat hots up – has regularly made critics disparage him, claiming that there is an unbridgeable gulf between seriousness and show, between the intellectual and the frivolous. Bernstein's effervescent achievement proves them wrong: he is a one-man bridge.

Bernstein's compositions are a magpie's hoard. They are influenced by the composers he admires (*Mahler, *Stravinsky, *Britten, *Ives); they draw on twelve-note atonality, nineteenth-century Romantic harmony, jazz and swing; they range from film-scores (*On the Waterfront*) to religious choral works (*Chichester Psalms*) and from symphonies to Broadway musicals (*West Side Story*; *On the Town*). The diversity of his talent has hardly left him time for sustained creativity – in this, again, he is closer to Liszt or Mendelssohn than to *Bach or *Brahms – but taken all in all, his compositions, like his performances, have communicated more of the sheer delight of 'serious' music than those of almost any other twentieth-century composer.

WORKS Three symphonies; Mass; *Chichester Psalms*; *Songfest* (song-cycle with orchestra); opera *Trouble in Tahiti*; ballets *Facsimile*, *Fancy Free* and

Dybbuk; musicals *On the Town*, *Wonderful Town*, *Candide* and *West Side Story*; Serenade for violin and orchestra; chamber music including string quartet, violin sonata, clarinet sonata; songs, etc.

Overture *Candide* (1956) In the best traditions of mood-setting theatre over-tures, this is a breathless curtain-raiser, contrasting four minutes of orchestral high spirits with a hummable, lavishly-scored and utterly tongue-in-cheek 'big tune'.
→ Symphonic Dances from *West Side Story*; Glinka overture *Ruslan and Lyud-mila*; Kabalevsky overture *Colas Breugnon*; Walton *Johannesburg Festival Overture*.

Symphony No. 2 (*The Age of Anxiety*) (1949) This extended work (for piano and orchestra) is a musical reflection of W.H. Auden's bitter poem on our aspirin-dependent, anxiety-racked society. An emotional first movement (theme and fourteen variations) is followed by an anguished, discordant 'dirge' and a skittering jazz scherzo for solo piano and percussion; the work ends with a pensive epilogue. The symphony is a stylistic ragbag, but it combines approachability with seriousness in a way characteristic of Bernstein at his best.
→ Ballet *Fancy Free*; Piston Symphony No. 6; Copland *Dance Symphony*.

BIZET, Georges (1838–75). *French composer.*
Although Bizet regarded himself as a professional composer, his career reads like that of an amateur of genius. In his teens he wrote music of outstanding verve and charm; he won the Prix de Rome, the highest composition prize in France; he spent most of his twenties restlessly (and unsuccessfully) trying to make his name as a stage composer, working on a dozen projects from biblical grand opera to farce; he died in his thirties, just before his reputation became secure (with the incidental music for *L'Arlésienne* and the opera *Carmen*). His music, though seldom profound, is well-turned and tuneful – and the more unobtrusive its ambitions the more memorable it turns out to be.

works Six operas (including *The Pearl Fishers*, *The Fair Maid of Perth* and *Carmen*); incidental music for plays (including *l'Arlésienne*); Symphony; suite *Roma*; suite *Jeux d'enfants* ('Children's Games') and other short works for orchestra; numerous individual piano works (including the original four-hand version of *Jeux d'enfants*), songs and choral works.

In the Depths of the Temple (*Au fond du temple saint*) (from *The Pearl Fishers*, 1863) The story of *The Pearl Fishers* is an Arabian Nights fantasy, as inconse-quential as a pantomime. What the duettists here (tenor and baritone) are singing about matters little; what matters is Bizet's unfailing melody, as limpid and perfectly-proportioned as the play of a fountain.

→ Serenade (from *The Fair Maid of Perth*); Flower Song (from *Carmen*); Offenbach 'When I was King of the Boeotians' (from *Orpheus in the Underworld*).

Ⓜ **Carmen** (1875) Complete opera. Carmen's sensational story (about a
cigarette-smoking gipsy temptress, passion, betrayal and murder) is set by Bizet
rather in the manner of a twentieth-century musical, with show-stopping
'numbers' linked by spoken dialogue. Its exotic Spanish rhythms (Habañera; Se-
guidilla) and brash orchestral colour (e.g. in 'Entry of the Toreadors') have made
it one of the most popular pieces of music ever composed. It is best approached,
perhaps, through the extracts mentioned above, or through the rousing, glittering
Orchestral Suite.
→ Suites 1 and 2 from *L'Arlésiennne*; Mascagni *Cavalleria rusticana* (complete
opera); Smetana *The Bartered Bride* (complete opera).

Ⓜ **Symphony in C** (*c.* 1855) This sparkling, lightweight apprentice-work
equals, in joyous vivacity, anything by those other seventeen-year-old geniuses
*Mozart and *Mendelssohn. It follows the classical four-movement pattern, but
clothes its tunes in glowing nineteenth-century orchestral dress.
→ Suite *Jeux d'enfants*; Schubert Symphony No. 3; Mendelssohn 'Italian' Symphony.

BLOCH , Ernest (1880-1959). *Swiss/American composer.*
At first sight, Bloch might seem to have been a remarkably cosmopolitan,
not to say rootless, man. He was born in Switzerland, studied in Belgium
and Germany, had houses in Geneva, Paris and Rome, and eventually
settled in the USA, where he taught in Cleveland, San Francisco and
Berkeley before returning to Portland, Oregon. But beneath his surface
restlessness he had a secure, undeviating identity: Jewishness. He was
fascinated by the rituals and habits of mind of traditional Jewish religion,
and used Hebrew chants and melodies in his music as some Christian
composers used plainchant. In his heyday (the 1930s and 1940s) he was
likened to *Sibelius, and his work has similar ruggedness and individuality;
it is likely that when the current neglect of his music ends, he will be
reclaimed as one of the finest non-experimental composers of the century.

WORKS Opera *Macbeth*; *Sacred Service*; two symphonies; two *concerti grossi*;
several orchestral suites and symphonic poems (including *Helvetia* and
America); Violin Concerto; two piano concertos; *Schelomo*; five string quartets; two sonatas for violin and piano; two suites for violin solo; two piano
quintets; Piano Sonata; other chamber music including Suite for viola and
piano; many song cycles and instrumental pieces on Jewish themes, including *Baal Shem* and *From Jewish Life*.

Ⓜ *Schelomo* (1916) This rhapsody for cello and orchestra, depicting scenes from the life of King Solomon, is of concerto size and seriousness. It uses Jewish melody (some from the time of Solomon himself) in a highly romantic, exotic manner, likely to evoke a passionate personal response.
→ *Suite Hébraïque*; Janáček *Taras Bulba*; Strauss *Don Quixote*.

Concerto grosso No. 1 for strings and piano (1925) Bloch's non-Jewish music – to which this is an enjoyable introduction – is clean-sounding, brisk, and as twentieth-century as a Mondrian painting or a steel-and-plastic chair. This four-movement concerto borrows its form from *Vivaldi or *Telemann, but adds open textures and clangy twentieth-century harmony, so that it has a refreshing, athletic sound: press-ups for the mind.
→ Violin Concerto; Stravinsky Octet; Hindemith *The Four Temperaments*.

BOCCHERINI, Luigi (1743–1805). *Italian composer.*

Long residence in Madrid (where he was cellist and composer to the Spanish court) gave Boccherini's already Mediterranean musical style a delightful Spanish lilt. He worked for a short time for the cello-playing King Frederick William II of Prussia (for whom *Mozart and *Haydn also wrote); the Germans disparagingly called him 'Haydn's wife' – and the name fits, triumphantly, if sunny, Haydnish music (reams and reams of it) is what's required.

WORKS Twenty symphonies; a dozen concertos (including four for cello); Mass, two oratorios, several cantatas and over 400 shorter church works; two operas; innumerable chamber works, including 110 string quartets, sixty string trios, 140 string quintets, twelve piano quintets, eighteen quintets for guitar or wind instrument and strings, twenty-seven violin and piano sonatas, etc.

Minuet (from String Quintet Op. 13 No. 5) In the palmy days of the tea-time trio, this piece (often renamed 'In an eighteenth-century drawing-room') was one of the most requested of all classical works. Its air of innocent wickedness (based on a combination of strait-laced, plucked-string accompaniment and a syncopated tune) made it ideal theme-music for Alex Guinness's Ealing Comedy film *The Ladykillers* – and gives it enduring charm.
→ Introduction and Fandango for guitar and harpsichord; Haydn Serenade (from String Quartet Op. 3 No. 5); Mendelssohn 'Spring Song' (*Songs Without Words* Op. 62 No. 6).

String Quintet Op. 30 No. 6 Boccherini's string quintets are his most characteristic and exuberant works, often (as here) adding a second cello to the basic quartet and deliciously exploiting it. There are four short movements; the melodies are alert and witty; the cellos are given almost concerto-like showing-off.

→ Guitar Quintet No. 3; Mozart *Eine kleine Nachtmusik*; Rossini String Sonata No. 3.

Cello Concerto in B flat This splendid hybrid (Boccherini's carefree original dolled up by Grutzmacher in nineteenth-century style) is beloved by modern virtuosos. Enough Boccherini remains to ensure eighteenth-century grace and wit as well as virtuoso posturing.

→ Symphony Op. 12 No. 1; Haydn Cello Concerto in D; Mozart Bassoon Concerto.

BORODIN, Alexander (1833–87). *Russian scientist and composer.*

If he had concentrated on composition, Borodin might have been one of Russia's leading nineteenth-century artists, outranking even *Musorgsky or *Tchaikovsky. But he was a professional scientist (remembered in Russia today for chemical and medical research as much as for music), and he had time for composition only at weekends and on holiday. He left no more than a couple of dozen works, some in such a chaotic state that they had to be pulled into performability by such devoted friends as *Rimsky-Korsakov (who learned many of the most attractive features of his own style in the process).

Borodin's small output was not solely due to lack of time. He was a perfectionist, whose music was as intricately-worked as *Brahms's, teasing out every nuance of colour or expression. The combination of this craftsmanship with a jaunty, 'oriental' sound (learned from the Asiatic Russian folk music he admired) gives his work unique appeal, for lovers of 'serious' and 'light classical' music alike. (Several of his compositions were plundered for the 1950s hit musical *Kismet*, and even in this tawdry setting tunes like 'Stranger in Paradise' or 'This is my beloved' glow like gems.)

WORKS Opera *Prince Igor*; three symphonies; *In the Steppes of Central Asia* and Scherzo for orchestra; two string quartets; Piano Quartet; piano music (including Little Suite); music for choir and thirteen solo songs.

Ⓜ **Polovtsian Dances** (from *Prince Igor*, 1890) This colourful dance-sequence comes from Borodin's unfinished masterpiece, an opera based on a hot-blooded episode from twelfth-century Russian history, full of pacts-of-honour, contests of chivalry and epic fights. Famous in the concert-hall as an orchestral pop, these dances are even more striking in the theatre, the ancestors of every high-leaping, fast-whirling Eastern European dance-spectacular ever staged. The rhythms are irresistible; the tunes (as *Kismet* demonstrated) stick in the mind like burrs.

→ *In the Steppes of Central Asia*; Rimsky-Korsakov *Golden Cockerel Suite*; Ravel *Boléro*; Ippolitov-Ivanov *Caucasian Sketches*.

Ⓜ **Symphony No. 2** (1876) Of all concert 'lollipops' (see Barber: Violin Concerto), this is one of the most unfailingly delightful. It uses folk-like tunes (as in the Polovtsian Dances) and unexpected, catchy rhythms (particularly in the scherzo and finale) to champagne effect.

→ Symphony No. 1; String Quartet No. 2; Tchaikovsky Symphony No. 2.

BOULEZ, Pierre (born 1925). *French composer and conductor.*

Boulez began his career as one of the most daunting avant-garde composers of the century: few artists of any period have produced works so enthusiastically admired by their devotees and so incomprehensible to almost everyone else. The reason was 'total serialization': every note, every indication of loudness, speed or attack (ways of playing) was decided by means of graphs, charts and diagrams, so that at one point in the 1950s it seemed as though would-be listeners, never mind the composer, needed a degree in maths. (Computers and electronic instruments have since softened the complexities of this composing style; Boulez has in any case moved on to other things.) His works of this time include several masterpieces; some (e.g. *Le marteau sans maître*, 'The Masterless Hammer', a song-cycle for voice and chamber group) are immediately approachable, others (e.g. the Piano Sonata No. 2) require – and reward – considerable effort on the listener's part.

In the 1960s Boulez switched careers. He became a conductor of world rank, at first specializing in contemporary music (it is to him that we owe the present understanding of *Webern, both by orchestral players and by audiences), then broadening his repertoire until he conducted the celebrated, not to say notorious, centenary Bayreuth production of *Wagner's *Ring* in 1976. In the same year he returned to composition, heading a Paris research institute involved in the amalgamation of electronics and manually-created sound. During his years as a conductor, his compositions were few (and often incomplete, regularly revised and updated); since 1976 he has produced a dozen major scores, of a delicacy and attractiveness to make us wonder why we ever found his music hard.

WORKS Three piano sonatas; *Structures* for two pianos; Flute Sonatina and other short chamber works; many pieces for voices and instruments (chamber groups or orchestra) including *Le marteau sans maître*, *Pli selon pli*, *Le soleil des eaux* and *Cummings ist der Dichter*; orchestral music including *Livre pour cordes* (for string orchestra), *Éclats/Multiples*, *Domaines*, *Explosante-fixe* and *Répons*.

Ⓜ *Répons* (1981) If avant-garde music is ever to come out of the closet and be accepted as standard concert fare (as has happened to such once-daunting works as *Beethoven's 'Choral' Symphony and *Stravinsky's *Rite of Spring*), this is one piece that should lead the way. It is a masterpiece of organization and sound-manipulation, and more than that, it delights the ear. Six soloists and a small orchestra sit among and around an audience seated circularly; the music is fed through a computer, and the computer-operator alters and enhances the sounds, egging the performers on to 'respond' (hence the title) in a form of controlled improvisation similar (except in sound) to Indian classical music or jazz. *Répons* is predominantly quiet and hypnotic, but it periodically bursts out into virtuoso frenzy, when the computer-enhancement creates a glitter of notes beyond human breath or fingers. This kind of music requires, at first, a willingness to surrender to the experience; but it also has the quality to grow in the mind, to enhance our experience, which characterizes all great art.

→ *Pli selon pli* ('Improvisation on Mallarmé' for voice and orchestra); Ⓜ *Éclats/Multiples* for orchestra; Maxwell *Davies Symphony No. 1.

BRAHMS, Johannes (1833–97). *German composer.*

The son of a seamstress and a double-bass-player, Brahms grew up in a poor quarter of Hamburg's dockland. It is a tribute to his parents' strong-mindedness – and a sign that his musical gifts were apparent early – that despite their poverty they encouraged him to spend hours each day practising the piano and working at harmony and counterpoint, neither of them activities likely to boost the family income. As a young teenager Brahms played dance-music in the evenings in sailors' taverns, but at the same time he was rigorously practising *Bach and *Beethoven under the eye of one of the most formidable piano teachers of the time, who refused to let him sacrifice general education to musical facility. (The contrasts with Beethoven's early upbringing – and the similarities – are marked.) When he was eighteen, Brahms went on a concert tour with the Hungarian gypsy violinist Reményi; when he was nineteen he met the influential concert-violinist Joachim (who became a close friend), *Liszt and other members of the German musical establishment. His star was rising, and one year later – after *Schumann, impressed both by his piano-playing and by his sheaf of unpublished compositions, wrote an article welcoming him as the genius the musical world had long been awaiting – his career as a professional musician was assured. At first Brahms added to his income by conducting and performing; but after the enormous success of his *German Requiem* in 1869 he was able to devote all his time to composition.

By the 1870s, Brahms was one of the most respected composers in Europe. His devotees made him the centre of a clique, claiming that he stood for true musical values in an art corrupted by the outrageous experiments of men like *Wagner; they called him a second Beethoven. (Wagner's clique equally vociferously denounced everything he stood for.) Whether or not he regarded himself as Beethoven's heir, Brahms coped with his fame much as Beethoven had with his, by cultivating a prickly manner both in public and with his friends. He lived a quiet bachelor life in Vienna, composing, writing letters or visiting friends, attending concerts and (apart from summer walking-holidays in Italy and the Alps) avoiding travel wherever possible. He often conducted or played the piano in performances of his own music; this apart, his life was solitary and his character defensive and withdrawn.

Introversion also marked Brahms's composing style. Those admirers who talked of 'old-fashioned virtues' were right. Many of his contemporaries – especially Liszt, Wagner and *Tchaikovsky – were pushing music into new realms of form, harmony and expression, abandoning traditional methods in favour of a self-consciously dramatic and romantic style. Brahms, by contrast, based his music on the structures and methods of Bach, *Mozart and Beethoven, reinterpreted and developed in a personal way. In particular, he blended with the tight construction and intellectual density of conventional styles (*symphony, quartet, *sonata) a kind of yearning, arching melody which owed everything to romantic feeling and nothing to the past, and which opened out conventional forms and harmonies in an expressive way unknown before. Intellectual massiveness and romantic melancholy: these are the ingredients of his uniquely affecting style.

ORCHESTRAL WORKS Four symphonies; two serenades; two overtures; *Variations on a Theme of Haydn*; two piano concertos; Violin Concerto; Concerto for Violin, Cello and Orchestra; Hungarian Dances.

Shorter orchestral works Hungarian Dance No. 1. Originally for piano duet, Brahms's twenty-one Hungarian Dances have swept the world in arrangements of all kinds, including his own for orchestra (recommended above all others). This one, in full-blooded gipsy style, is perhaps the best-known of all. (It is the music to which Chaplin, in *The Great Dictator*, played a hilarious shaving-scene.) In the same way as he based the Hungarian Dances on folk-tunes, adapting them to his own (very unfolksy) purposes, Brahms used student-songs (e.g. *Gaudeamus igitur*) in his *Academic Festival Overture*, Op. 80 (1880), a riotous medley belying its pompous title (it was composed in gratitude for a university degree, and pokes sly fun at the dignitaries gathered for the first performance, expecting doctoral majesty). Equally easy on the ear, though deeper in content, are the Ⓜ *Variations on a Theme of Haydn/Variations on the 'St Anthony' Chorale*, Op. 56a (1873). Variation-form always inspired Brahms's best work, and few of his compositions are more mellifluous: the *Haydn Variations* are a jewel of the whole orchestral repertoire. (They also exist for two pianos, and the different scoring completely changes their character, and makes a fascinating comparison with the orchestral version.) Less well-known, but equally cheerful, are two Serenades (Op. 11, 1858; Op. 16, 1860), orchestral kin to such easy-going pieces as Beethoven's Septet; the Tragic Overture, Op. 81 (1881), is appropriately serious and sonorous, sharing the mood, for all its brevity, of the First and Fourth Symphonies.

→ After the Hungarian Dances, good follow-ups are Dvořák's Slavonic Dances and Janáček's Lachian Dances; the overtures and variations lead excellently to Dvořák's *Scherzo capriccioso* (cheerful) and Symphonic Variations (serious), to Beethoven's overture *Egmont* and to Parry's neglected Symphonic Variations; the Serenades might lead to such affable chamber works as Spohr's Nonet, Mendelssohn's *Octet* and Brahms's own String Sextet No. 1.

Symphonies and concertos Ⓜ Symphony No. 1, Op. 68 (1877). Hailed in its day as 'Beethoven's Tenth' (to Brahms's irritation), this is a large-scale work in his soberest and most vigorous style. Its first movement is hefty, its second and third are lyrical and its fourth is heroic; the construction-patterns (and the noble mood, though never the actual sound) recall Beethoven's Symphony No. 5. Of Brahms's other symphonies, only the Ⓜ Symphony No. 4, Op. 98 (1885), shares its general magnificence, though its outer movements are less monumental (the first is particularly graceful, with an almost Tchaikovskyan lilt) and its inner ones are more straightforward (a limpid slow movement and a headlong Scherzo). The Symphony No. 2, Op. 73 (1877), begins in a relaxed manner and progresses to a fast, brilliantly-orchestrated finale, with rushing strings and fiery brass. The mood of the Ⓜ Symphony No. 3, Op. 90 (1883), is lyrical throughout, its four movements integrated into a single impression of tranquillity after suffering as characteristic of Brahms as (say) Beethoven's 'Pastoral' Symphony or Violin Concerto is of him. The sunniest of Brahms's concertos is the Violin Concerto, Op. 77 (1879): heroic tunes keep trying to break in, and the violin has plenty of declamatory work to do, but the chief impression is of a stream of placid orchestral harmony and filigree musings from the soloist. The other concertos are among Brahms's largest and noblest works of any kind. The Piano Concerto No. 1, Op. 15 (1859), is a young man's work, bursting with ideas (not always ideally integrated, but full of personality), challenging both to play and to hear: its smoothly-flowing, Chopinesque slow movement and Bach-inspired finale are unlike anything else he wrote. The Piano Concerto No. 2, Op. 83 (1881), by contrast, is a serene, mature man's composition, absolutely certain of the moods it seeks to suggest (a typically Brahmsian combination of heroism, gentle flow and skittishness), and for all its enormous length (four movements, not three; 40 minutes) and stamina-problems for the soloist, an uncomplicated (and in the end un-concerto-like) work. Also more like a symphony with soloists than a concerto is the Ⓜ Double Concerto, Op. 102 (1887), for violin, cello and orchestra. The combination was unique, and Brahms solved its chief problem (not drowning the solo sound) by treating violin and cello rather as a separate chamber group within the orchestra, as if an eighteenth-century *concerto grosso* (see *Concerto*) had been welded into a large-scale Romantic symphony. With the Symphony No. 3, the Double Concerto is for many Brahms's supreme orchestral work; with the Symphony No. 1, it is one of the most challenging of all his works.

→ Beethoven's Symphony No. 7 and Schubert's Symphony No. 9 inhabit the same monumental but lyrical world as Brahms's Second and Third symphonies, and the First and Fourth symphonies might lead to Dvořák's Symphony No. 7 and Tchaikovsky's Symphony No. 5, respectively. The concertos are of their own kind, and lead less to other composers' music than to works in other genres by Brahms himself - the Piano Quintet and the Piano Sonatas Nos. 1 and 3, particularly. The nearest non-Brahms concertos of similar stature are Beethoven's Violin Concerto and 'Emperor' Piano Concerto; *Grieg's Piano Concerto and Tchaikovsky's Violin Concerto, though lighter and less symphonic, rival Brahms's for their energetic demands on both soloists and orchestra.

PIANO AND CHAMBER WORKS   Three piano sonatas; *Handel Variations* and *Paganini Variations* for piano solo; waltzes and other works for piano duet; several sets of short solo piano pieces: ballades, rhapsodies, intermezzos, etc; eleven chorale preludes and two preludes and fugues for organ; two string sextets; two string quintets; three string quartets; Clarinet Quintet; Piano Quintet; three piano quartets; three trios for violin, cello and piano; Trio for horn, violin and piano; three sonatas for violin and piano; two sonatas for cello and piano; two sonatas for clarinet (or viola) and piano.

Piano music Three Intermezzos, Op. 117 (1892). Brahms's six books of short piano pieces are chips from his workshop, concentrating on mood-expression (exquisite or robust) rather than on intellectual weight. These three pieces are all gentle: No. 1 (dreamy) and No. 2 (tender) are among his most-played works. Their poetic terseness is repeated in his other late collections, Op. 116 and Op. 119; the Rhapsodies Op. 79 are earlier and more swaggering, the Waltzes Op. 39 wistful and gentle, close in sound to Schumann's piano music, in a mood echoed in a lovely and little-known four-hand piano piece written in Schumann's memory, Ⓜ *Variations on a Theme by Robert Schumann*, Op. 23. His larger works are modelled on Beethoven's later sonatas and variation-sets. There are three sonatas, his earliest compositions (the works which impressed Liszt and Schumann); the Sonata No. 3, Op. 5, is the best. Of his many sets of variations, the finest are the *Variations on a Theme of Haydn*, Op. 56, for two pianos, the *Paganini Variations*, Op. 35 (two books of quicksilver virtuosity, some of the most extrovert music he ever wrote), and the Ⓜ *Variations and Fugue on a Theme of Handel*, Op. 24, his piano masterpiece, paying tribute to his own instrument, to his favourite musical form, and to the previous composer (apart from Beethoven) he revered above all others: it is a no-holds-barred, self-consciously 'big' display-piece similar in power to Beethoven's *Eroica Variations* or *Diabelli Variations*.
→ Good follow-ups to the short piano works are Schumann's Romances Op. 28; the sonatas might lead to Scriabin's Sonata No. 1, and the mood of the variations is matched in Chopin's Scherzos (especially No. 2) and Schumann's *Davidsbündlertänze*.

Chamber music Ⓜ Clarinet Quintet, Op. 115 (1891). Of Brahms's huge catalogue of chamber works, this is the best, a rapt product of his old age, written (as so much of his chamber music was) for a friend whose playing he particularly admired. Brahms tended to reserve his most serious thought for orchestral works, and his most lyrical feelings for songs; chamber music was for displaying composing-technique, and this part of his output has a feeling of craftsmanship, of a master relaxing with his own enormous skill, which in the Clarinet Quintet is married with mellow expressiveness to produce a serene, autumnal masterpiece. His other clarinet works, two sonatas and a trio (with cello and piano), are more muscular, and (perhaps to recapture the autumnal feel) he rescored the sonatas (Op. 120, Nos. 1 and 2) for viola and piano, considerably enhancing their gentleness. Of his three violin sonatas, ⓂNo. 1, Op. 78 is sunny and melodious, Nos. 2 and 3 are impassioned and turbulent. Their mood is matched in the eloquent cello sonatas (No. 1 is especially grand), and in the three piano quartets, of which No. 1, Op. 25 is the best, with a captivating gipsy finale worthy of *Dvořák. (*Schoenberg made a splendid arrangement of the whole work for symphony orchestra, claiming it as 'Brahms's fifth symphony'. It is more sensuous and frivolous than that suggests; both original and rescoring are recommended.) Brahms's Piano Quintet and his three piano trios are beefy and showy, almost piano concertos with solo-string accompaniment. His works for strings alone (quartets, quintets, sextets) are technically the most closely-argued of his chamber music, and some listeners find them emotionally arid; even so, the beautiful slow movement of the String Quartet No. 1 and the mellow String Quintet No. 2 come close in inspiration to the Clarinet Quintet itself. The Horn Trio is a bantamweight frolic which ends with a rollicking hunting-jig.

→ There are so many Brahms chamber works that the best follow-up to any of them is another of the same kind. Of other composers' music, the nearest equivalents are Schubert's 'Trout' Quintet and Dvořák's Piano Quintet in A (paralleling Brahms's lighter chamber style), Mendelssohn's Piano Trio No. 1 (paralleling Brahms's violin and cello sonatas) and, on a level of inspiration to match Brahms at his best, Schubert's Piano Trio No. 2 and String Quintet.

VOCAL WORKS *A German Requiem*; *Rinaldo*; *Song of Destiny*; *Song of the Fates*; *Song of Triumph*; *Alto Rhapsody*; song-cycles *Beautiful Magelone*, *Fifteen Romances from Magelone* and *Four Serious Songs*; twenty-two groups of short choral songs and twenty-eight German folksongs arranged for choir; over two hundred songs and seven books of German folksongs arranged for voice and piano.

Liebeslieder ('Lovesongs'), Op. 52 (1862) A century after his death, Brahms's instrumental music is among the most often-played in the repertoire, and ninetenths of his vocal music is practically unknown. He wrote prolifically for every kind of vocal combination, from tiny solo songs to choral cantatas with orchestra. Many of the forms he used were popular in their day but have since dropped out of fashion - and the loss is ours, for his vocal music is among his most delightful. *Lovesongs*, for example (and its sequel *New Lovesongs*, Op. 65), is for the nowadays uncommon drawing-room combination of four solo voices and piano duet: a sequence of waltz-time love-songs as lilting as any of the operetta-airs of Johann *Strauss. Brahms wrote many similar pieces for vocal consort or small choir: his part-songs, Op. 62, Op. 92 and Op. 112, for example, are delightful. His solo songs range from single 32-bar utterances (like the world-famous Lullaby, Op. 49 No. 4) to full-scale *Lieder* in the true *Schubert style (see *Vocal music*), where the piano part depicts mood and specifies emotion as clearly as the voice. Ⓜ *Vergebliches Ständchen* ('The Vain Serenade'), Op. 84 No. 4 (1881), is a sprightly example of his lighter songs, a popular recital encore whose witty words concern a soulful, serenading lover and a window-slamming girl. Ⓜ *Mainacht* ('Maynight'), Op. 43 No. 2 (1868), is a fine example of his more serious songs, the interplay between vocal melody and intertwining accompaniment particularly intense. Brahms grouped most of his songs in unrelated sets (e.g. *Nine Songs*, Op. 63, a splendid collection), and the nearest he came to an integrated cycle (see *Vocal music*) was in the brooding *Four Serious Songs*, Op. 121 (1896), settings of Bible words somewhat like the solo parts of the *German Requiem* (see below), and especially so when heard with orchestra rather than a piano. His finest voice-and-orchestra work is the Ⓜ Rhapsody for contralto, male choir and orchestra (*Alto Rhapsody*), Op. 53 (1869), written as a wedding-present for Schumann's daughter (with whom he was himself in love), and appropriately overlaying sensual vocal writing with feelings of wistfulness and loss. His choral works range from short and boisterous occasional pieces (e.g. the *Triumphlied*, 'Song of Triumph, Op. 55, written to celebrate the Prussian defeat of France) to drawn-out, poetic meditations on suffering and heroic resignation (e.g. *Schicksalslied*, 'Song of Destiny', Op. 54). His largest vocal work of all, *A German Requiem*, Op. 45 (1868), was inspired by the death of his mother, and sets not the usual Requiem words (Brahms was an atheist) but Bible texts of mourning and consolation. It is highly Victorian, somewhat morbid to some modern listeners; its lighter sections (e.g. the glimpse-into-paradise fourth movement, 'How Lovely are thy Dwellings Fair, O Lord of Hosts') and busy choral fugues (ending movements 3 and 6) stand out from a predominantly sombre score.

→ The best follow-up to Brahms's consort and solo vocal works is very similar music by Mendelssohn: *Six Songs*, Op. 48, or the part-songs of Op. 59, for ensemble, or the solo-songs Op. 47 (which include a typically Mendelssohnian *Spring Song*). Brahms's songs with orchestra might lead to those of Mahler (especially the *Kindertotenlieder*) and of Richard Strauss (*Four Last Songs*), and good follow-ups to his choral-and-orchestral music might be Mendelssohn's 'Hymn of Praise' (Symphony No. 2) or Nielsen's *Hymnus amoris*.

BRASS INSTRUMENTS

Brass instruments go back thousands of years: playable trumpets have been found in Tutankhamun's pyramid, and the Bible story of Joshua and the walls of Jericho shows how effective well-organized twelfth-century BC brass could be. But the brass instruments we know today are infinitely more recent, dating back only about two hundred years. Until then players had been restricted to the 'harmonic series' (about eight notes, and a brief scale, all made by the lips alone, as on a modern bugle); the eighteenth-century invention of valves and pistons allowed them to play five or six times as many notes, and to indulge in runs and trills as freely as players of any other instrument.

CONSORT MUSIC Early composers were wary of giving brass-players music too complex or too exposed. They wrote fanfares or other short pieces for outdoor occasions (such as processions or funerals), trusting to the wide open spaces to absorb any tonal imperfections. What these pieces sounded like at the time is anyone's guess; when modern players tackle them (either on modern instruments or using modern techniques on ancient instruments) they are exhilaratingly spectacular and tantalizingly brief. One of the most famous ancient brass works of all, Giovanni Gabrieli's *Sonata pian' e forte* ('Piece to be played soft and loud'), was written in the early seventeenth century for St Mark's, Venice, and involves two brass consorts answering each other across the resonant centre of the building; as its name suggests, its effect comes from contrasting tone-colours rather than from flurries of fast-moving notes. In recent years there has been a vogue for reviving pieces of this kind (short fantasias, fanfares, sonatas and ricercars, by such composers as *Josquin, Tylman Susato, Samuel Scheidt and Matthew Locke). There are record-collections in plenty, and despite the shortness of the pieces, the sound is satisfyingly clean and plump. (Unlike ensembles of some other instruments, e.g. viol consorts, brass groups have no weak-sounding members, so every part in the texture has equal weight.) The genre's popularity has encouraged twentieth-century composers to arrange all kinds of music for it (from *Byrd's virginals pieces to *Musorgsky's *Pictures at an Exhibition*) and to compose splendid new pieces of their own: Malcolm Arnold's engaging Brass Quintet and Gunther Schuller's Symphony for Brass and Percussion are examples of a thriving kind. Second only in interest are brass groups of two other sorts: brass bands and military bands. Once restricted to marches and to pithead-chapel hymns, their players (usually amateur) now tackle an immense variety of music with near-professional panache: at one end of the repertoire are such justly-popular classics as Sousa's marches or Hérold's *Zampa* overture; at the other are works of the extreme avant-garde, like Tōru Takemitsu's whispering *October Rain*. In some countries (notably the USA) 'symphonic bands' are popular. They consist of a blend of woodwind and brass instruments (an orchestra without strings), and many composers have provided works for them, including such giants as *Hindemith and *Copland, whose Symphony in B flat and *Fanfare for the Common Man* (respectively) show just what the medium can do. Unfortunately for brass-music of 'symphonic' stature, long works for brass can sound monotonous (one result, perhaps, of the perfect balance of the sound). The best brass pieces establish a single mood, explore it pithily, and stop.

SOLO AND CHAMBER MUSIC Because of the difficulty of playing early brass instruments, and their insecure pitch, solo music for them was extremely rare. The few exceptions (e.g. Giuseppe Torelli's trumpet concertos from the seventeenth century, and *Vivaldi's concertos for groups of trumpets and/or horns from the eighteenth) are nowadays revived more for curiosity than as treats, and *Bach's *Brandenburg Concerto* No. 2 (which features a high solo trumpet, treating it without mercy as a woodwind soloist like any other) wipes the floor with them. The first brass concertos of stature are *Mozart's four horn concertos: cheerful and tuneful, they exploit the horn's singing tone, and make concessions to its traditional nature only in open-air, 'hunting-style' finales. (For the same soloist, he wrote a Quintet for horn and strings, K 407: little-known but one of his finest chamber works.) *Haydn's horn concertos are less inspired than Mozart's, but his Trumpet Concerto is a masterpiece and its last movement (a lilting rondo) is justly one of his best-known works. In the nineteenth century, composers devoted more time to experimenting with brass tone in the orchestra than to solo concertos or sonatas. The chief exceptions are Hummel's Trumpet Concerto (very nearly as good as Haydn's) at the start of the century, and *Rimsky-Korsakov's jolly Trombone Concerto and Richard *Strauss's Horn Concerto No. 1 at the end of it. (Sixty years later, Strauss wrote a second Horn Concerto, in the mellow style of his Oboe Concerto and *Four Last Songs*.) Some composers wrote brass parts in their chamber works. The sound-blend between brass and piano is unsatisfactory, and even works otherwise as intriguing as *Beethoven's Horn Sonata tend to tire the ear. But softened by other instruments, brass sounds fine: Hummel's Military Septet and *Saint-Saëns's Grand Septet are dominated by solo-trumpet sound, and *Brahms's Horn Trio (for horn, violin and piano) shows how mellow, and how musical, brass can be. In the twentieth century, apart from Strauss's Horn Concerto No. 2, the best solo works are *Hindemith's Horn Concerto (poetic), Boris Blacher's Trumpet Concerto (jazzy) and *Vaughan Williams's Tuba Concerto (hearty). The brass – as *Stravinsky's jazz-inspired Octet shows – are now as much at home in chamber music as are any other instruments, and several heavyweight works (*Tippett's Sonata for four horns; Maxwell *Davies's Brass Quintet; Berio's *Sequenza* for trombone) simply ignore the players' problems and treat the instruments with as few concessions as if they were writing for string quartet – a sure sign that brass-playing, once music's Cinderella, has put on its finery and ridden to the ball.

Listening The best brass works to sample first are the short pieces collected on records with such titles as 'Renaissance Brass'; good follow-ups are the ensemble pieces mentioned in the text, Hummel's and Saint-Saëns's septets and Brahms's Horn Trio. For solo music, the best works to hear first are the Mozart and Haydn concertos, followed by Strauss's Horn Concerto No. 1, leaving twentieth-century works until later (when Hindemith's Horn Concerto might lead the fun).

BRITISH AND IRISH COMPOSERS

Britain's closeness to Europe, and love-hate relationship with it, have over the centuries produced a remarkable artistic schizophrenia. At times British artists have led the world, and their aggressive confidence (one result of being able to develop outside the mainstream) has taken their arts in directions unimagined and unequalled elsewhere; at other times they have shrunk into imitative mediocrity, peeping out at the parade of European art with a mixture of jealousy, complacency and hostility.

MUSIC IN TUDOR AND STUART TIMES In music, the first outburst of excellence was in the fifteenth to seventeenth centuries, during the reigns of the Tudor and early Stuart monarchs. Before the Tudors, there were individual composers of talent (e.g. John Dunstable, c. 1390-1453, whose church music rivals any from the continent), and in the late fifteenth and early sixteenth centuries a group of church composers developed a rich and intricate style that was peculiarly and renownedly 'English'. Then, because the early Tudor kings encouraged music (Henry VIII, for example, found time among all his other activities for playing, singing and composition), and because of the upheaval in church music brought about by the disestablishment of Roman Catholicism, the ground was prepared for the growth of one of the finest of all national artistic groups.

Sacred music The Tudors' ambivalent attitude to Rome made writing church music a lively occupation. Some composers (e.g. John Taverner, c. 1490-1545) worked in the Roman Catholic tradition, but at the time of the break with Rome (1534) abandoned music for less chancy professions (Taverner became a civil servant, assisting in the dissolution of the monasteries). Others (e.g. Thomas Tallis, c. 1505-85, and his pupil *Byrd) kept their personal religious options open, and wrote music of quality for whichever brand of Christianity was currently in favour. (Tallis, for example, produced both the intensely Catholic *Lamentations* and some still-sung hymns - e.g. the famous 'Tallis's Canon' - for the Anglican Psalter of 1567; Byrd wrote Anglican Services and Catholic Masses with apparently equal fervour and certainly with equal success.)

Secular music By and large, however, the greatest Tudor music was secular, composed for recreation rather than for devotion. A properly-educated lady or gentleman was expected to be knowledgeable both in instrument-playing and in singing, and composers provided instruction-books and hundreds of pieces for aristocratic enjoyment. The favoured solo vocal form was the lute-song (a short song in several verses, on the pangs or delights of love, for solo voice and lute: the finest examples are by John Dowland, 1563-1626). The vocal-ensemble equivalent was the madrigal (a song for three or more unaccompanied voices in harmony, often to pastoral or amorous words: the range is from the 'hey-nonny-nonny' trifles of Thomas Morley, c. 1557-1602, to the sombre, harmonically adventurous madrigals of John Wilbye, 1574-1638, and Thomas Weelkes, 1576-1623). Instrumental music either involved a solo instrument (e.g. Dowland's lute pieces, and the virginals music of such men as Byrd, Giles Farnaby, c. 1563-1640, and John Bull, c. 1562-1628, still part of the keyboard repertoire) or were for consort, groups of instruments similar to later chamber groups. (Dowland's *Lachrimae* or the viol-fantasies of Orlando Gibbons, 1583-1625, are typical, and fine.)

SEVENTEENTH-CENTURY MUSIC In the seventeenth century, British music lost creative impetus. While European composers busied themselves with such fruitful new forms as *opera and *sonata, British composers preferred the dead-end (if spectacular) masque or the increasingly old-fashioned viol-fantasy. (John Jenkins, 1592-1678, composed some especially fine fantasies.) While in Europe the growth of Lutheranism led to developments in church music of startling originality, British composers went on discreetly providing Anglican anthems, Services and voluntaries, the foundation of a tradition of second-rate competence which has cast its pall on British church music ever since. The only seventeenth-century British composer of international rank was *Purcell, and his greatness was due to his refusal rigidly to follow any model, whether continental opera or British solo song, but to synthesize them all in music of outstanding personality and dynamism.

EIGHTEENTH- AND NINETEENTH-CENTURY MUSIC The coming to Britain of European royalty (William of Orange; George I) encouraged an inflow of continental musicians which has never ceased. Some newcomers (e.g. *Mozart and *Haydn in the eighteenth century or *Weber and *Mendelssohn in the nineteenth) made their mark and left; others (e.g. *Handel, Clementi or the conductor Charles Hallé) stayed and took British nationality; all irrevocably turned public taste from native musical styles to continental ones. For two centuries, British composers produced agreeable and unremarkable pastiches of whatever European styles were fashionable. William Boyce (1711-79) and Thomas Arne (1710-78) wrote suites like Handel's and symphonies like J. C. Bach's; William Crotch (1775-1847) aped Haydn; Cipriani Potter (1792-1871) parroted *Beethoven; John

Stainer (1840-1901) mimicked Mendelssohn; George Macfarren (1813-87) and William Sterndale Bennett (1816-75) trudged after *Brahms. A host of minor masters did write music of originality, but it remained minor: Johann Pepusch's folksong score for John Gay's *Beggar's Opera*, the piano nocturnes and concertos of John Field (1782-1837) and the operettas of Gilbert and *Sullivan, while influential and delightful, succeed by modesty of ambition rather than by towering musical magnificence.

THE REBIRTH OF BRITISH MUSIC The second great period in British music – of a greatness to rival that of Tudor England – began at the end of the nineteenth century. The first signs of life were in composers who shook off the heavy cloak of Brahms: the choral and orchestral works of Hubert Parry (1848-1918) and the symphonies and concertos of Charles Villiers Stanford (1852-1924) add, respectively, mysticism and Irishness to a basically Germanic style, with agreeable if never earth-shaking results. In 1899 *Elgar's 'Enigma' Variations and *Delius's *Paris: Song of a Great City* announced the arrival of the first British musical geniuses for generations: their techniques were European (close in particular to Richard *Strauss), but their voices were one hundred per cent their own, with a distinctiveness of utterance that had been missing in native composers since Purcell.

Since Elgar's and Delius's time there have been two main strands to British music. One is mystical and nostalgic, looking back to Tudor compositional ideas and often drawing strength from folksong (collecting folksongs was a major activity in the years up to the First World War). Its leading figure was *Vaughan Williams, and its second rank included men as talented as the piano- and song-composer John Ireland (1879-1962), the symphonists Arnold Bax (1883-1953) and Edmund Rubbra (born 1901), and Gerald Finzi (1901-56), a song-composer almost in the league of *Wolf. The music of this group once seemed secure in the concert repertoire; recently it has receded in favour of works by the second, 'experimental' group. These are composers whose outlook is cosmopolitan, not insular, and who used international or avant-garde techniques to strengthen personal inspiration. As well as talented also-rans (Arthur Bliss, Alan Rawsthorne, Lennox Berkeley, Malcolm Arnold, Richard Rodney Bennett, Alexander Goehr) they include a handful of the finest world composers of the century: the work of *Britten, *Walton, Maxwell *Davies and *Tippett alone is a guarantee that, so far as music is concerned, Britain is now securely in a second Golden Age.

Listening The best introduction to British and Irish music is the work of composers discussed elsewhere in this book: Britten, Byrd, Delius, Elgar, Maxwell Davies, Purcell, Sullivan, Tippett, Vaughan Williams and Walton. Of work by others, there are few better introductions to Tudor music than Farnaby's short pieces for virginals (e.g. *His Humour, His Dreame*) and the madrigals of Morley (e.g. *Hard By a Crystal Fountain*) and Wilbye (e.g. *Sweet Honeysucking Bees*). Exploration might move from there to Dowland's lute-songs and consort-music (especially *Lachrimae*), and to the viol-fantasies and anthems of Gibbons. From the seventeenth and eighteenth centuries, Locke's consort-music and songs are well worth exploring, and Blow's anthems and Arne's symphonies agreeably echo Purcell and Handel, respectively. Characteristic nineteenth-century works are Field's piano compositions and the symphonies (especially the *Irish Symphony*) and church music (especially the *Te Deum* in B flat) of Stanford. Among the delights of twentieth-century British music – consistently under-rated – are Ireland's piano works (especially his Chopinesque Concerto), Rubbra's graceful Symphony No. 5, Finzi's mystical song-cycle *Dies natalis* and Berkeley's sparkling Serenade for Strings.

BRITTEN, Benjamin (1913–76). *English composer.*
Britten was a child prodigy. He wrote his first music at the age of four, and by the time he was twelve had composed a dozen large-scale works. (He later adapted themes and ideas from them into a delightful *Simple Symphony* for strings.) By the age of twenty-one he was self-supporting as a composer, chiefly from writing film-scores and incidental music for radio plays; the sensational success of his *Variations on a Theme of Frank Bridge* at the 1937 Salzburg Festival clinched his reputation. In his early twenties he was a member of a group of left-wing intellectuals centred on the poet W. H. Auden, but these left-wing views, based on a conviction (characteristic of the 1930s) that the 'ideal state', where everyone would be well-cared-for and happy, lay just around the corner, were brutally shattered by the Spanish Civil War and the rise of Nazism. Britten took flight, first to the USA, then to a fishing village on the Suffolk coast, where he finally settled. It is impossible to overestimate the effect on his character of this crushing of his youthful optimism: throughout his life he preferred isolation to public fame, and his work consistently shows an anguish at the dark side of human nature, a pessimism paralleled only in *Mahler and *Shostakovich. The other key to his work is his understanding and love of poetry: he shares *Schubert's ability to penetrate to the heart of a poem in a handful of ordinary-seeming notes.

In 1945 Britten's opera *Peter Grimes* was an international success, and thereafter composing operas was one of his two main preoccupations. (The other was the music festival he established in his home-village, Aldeburgh, in 1948.) He was inspired by the shape and sound of words, by the lonely fenland landscapes of East Anglia, and above all by suffering humanity (a recurring theme in his work is the tormented individual). Artists who visited the Aldeburgh Festival encouraged a third main strand: delight in virtuosity. His friends included some of the finest performers of the age (the tenor Peter Pears; the horn-player Denis Brain; the cellist Mstislav Rostropovich), and he wrote many works specifically tailored to their skills (there are definitive recordings of most of them, made by the dedicatees under Britten's direction: no other composer but *Stravinsky has left such a large first-hand recorded legacy); his own performing skills included playing the piano (e.g. accompanying Pears in *Schubert *Lieder*) as well as conducting.

WORKS Fifteen operas (including *Peter Grimes, Billy Budd, The Turn of the Screw* and *Death in Venice*); ballet *Prince of the Pagodas*; five song-cycles for voice and orchestra (including the *Serenade*); fifteen song-cycles for voice and piano (including *Winter Words* and *Canticles I-V*); choral works (including the *Spring Symphony* and *War Requiem*); the *Frank Bridge Variations* and *Simple Symphony* for strings; *Variations and Fugue on a Theme of Purcell, Sinfonia da Requiem, Four Sea Interludes* and other shorter works for orchestra; Piano Concerto; Violin Concerto; Symphony for cello and orchestra; chamber music including three string quartets and three suites for solo cello; many lesser works, some written for children.

Variations and Fugue on a Theme of Purcell/Young Person's Guide to the Orchestra (1946) This lively piece, originally composed for an educational film, shows off each orchestral instrument in turn in its own variation, then puts them all together in a rollicking final fugue. (A jolly-uncle spoken commentary, taken from the film, is sometimes superimposed on the music; the work is better heard without it, as a straightforward concert piece.)
→ *Simple Symphony*; Dukas *The Sorcerer's Apprentice*; Copland *Four Dance Episodes from Rodeo*.

Ceremony of Carols (1942) Fresh new settings of medieval carol words for boys' voices and harp. Hard-edged, clean sound: no trace of angelic flutings here.
→ *Missa brevis*; *Spring Symphony*; Stravinsky *Four Russian Peasant Songs*.

Four Sea Interludes (from the opera *Peter Grimes*, 1945) 'Dawn'; 'Sunday Morning'; 'Moonlight'; 'Storm'. The music is Britten at his most stripped-down: instantly and exactly, it conveys impressions of the loneliness, desolation and fury of the sea (which in the opera mirrors the emotions in Grimes's own soul).
→ *Serenade*; Debussy *La mer*; Sibelius *En saga*.

Ⓜ *Serenade for Tenor, Horn and Strings* (1943) Magnificent settings of seven poems on evening and darkness (including the 'Lykewake Dirge' and Keats's sonnet 'Sleep': Britten always knew exactly what words he needed, and took them from any source, however familiar or obscure). Atmospheric, haunting; perhaps Britten's masterpiece.
→ *Les illuminations*; Barber *Dover Beach*; Finzi *Dies natalis*.

(M) *War Requiem* (1962) A full-throated setting of the Latin Requiem Mass, for soprano, chorus and orchestra (as operatic and as powerful as *Verdi's), is interspersed with Wilfred Owen's bitter poems of protest at the First World War, searingly set for tenor, baritone and small orchestra. The work encapsulates all Britten's own feelings about war's futility and waste, and about the nature of consolation.

→ (M) *Holy Sonnets of John Donne*; *Sinfonia da Requiem*; Verdi *Requiem*.

(M) *Peter Grimes* (1945) (complete opera) Britten used this story of a dour, ostracized Suffolk fisherman who may or may not have killed the only person in the world he loved, to make an impassioned statement about loneliness and the freedom of the soul. The work's mood is caught in the *Four Sea Interludes* (see above), which are an excellent introduction to it.

→ *Billy Budd*; *Turn of the Screw*; Menotti *The Consul*.

A Midsummer Night's Dream (1960) (complete opera) Britten's most ravishing score: a comedy using Shakespeare's own words and miraculously preserving every element of the original play. The fairy music is atmospheric, the lovers' music intense and the mechanicals' music a glorious parody of Verdi at his most wooden.

→ *Albert Herring*; Verdi *Falstaff*; Henze *King Stag*.

BRUCKNER, Anton (1824–96). *Austrian composer.*

Bruckner's life was a remarkable mixture of distinction and humility. He was a fine church organist (for thirteen years at Linz Cathedral), and was famous throughout Europe for his improvising. For twenty-three years, from 1868 to 1891, he was a professor of composition at the Vienna Conservatoire. But despite this professional eminence, he had such a self-conscious manner, and was physically so uncouth, that his enemies dismissed him as a cretinous peasant floundering in areas he barely understood. In particular, the critic Eduard Hanslick (leader of the Viennese clique which supported *Brahms) mocked him mercilessly, calling his music 'greasy scraps from Wagner's table'. Well-meaning friends revised, re-orchestrated and generally hacked his works about – and it shows Bruckner's trusting nature (or his disastrous lack of self-confidence) that he let them do it. (Modern listeners, given a choice of recordings, will find 'original versions' closest to Bruckner's own intentions.)

Bruckner's simple faith led him to put his trust equally in God and in Richard *Wagner. For God, he wrote Masses and motets of unswerving fervour and devotion. For Wagner he wrote enormous symphonies, trying to equal in the concert-hall the overwhelming emotional force of Wagner's music-dramas. The resulting mixture is original, not to say unique: 'cathedrals of sound' which – like *Messiaen's equally bulky twentieth-century masterpieces – demand dedication from the listener, and reward it with an experience of rare magnificence.

WORKS Five Masses; *Requiem*; *Te Deum*; seven shorter religious choral works; nine symphonies (plus the early 'Symphony No. 0'); Overture in G minor; four Orchestral Pieces; String Quintet; a handful of other short keyboard and chamber works.

Te Deum (1881) Despite its symphonic scale, the mood of Bruckner's religious music is devotional and private rather than declamatory. The *Te Deum* is rugged, spare music, full of organ-effects and imitations of tolling bells. Its grandness belies its length (*c.* 20 minutes); in a short space, it sums up the distinctive qualities of Bruckner's style, and particularly his use of the simplest musical means (arpeggios, single chords, pauses) to achieve a mystical, almost transcendental religious effect.

→ Mass in F minor; Verdi *Four Sacred Pieces*; Rachmaninov *The Bells*.

Ⓜ **Symphony No. 9** (1894) The form of this symphony is a massive arch, two slow movements straddling an energetic Scherzo. Its long-breathed, many-times-repeated string melodies and sonorous brass chords (like Lutheran chorales sung by a choir of giants) are Bruckner fingerprints, common to all his works, but they are rarely more majestically used than here. More than any other of his symphonies, this one achieves what he set out to do: if Wagner's *Parsifal* (say) were recomposed as a concert work, it might very well sound like this.

→ Symphony No. 4 ('Romantic'); Symphony No. 7; Franck Symphony.

BRUCH See *One-work Composers*.

BYRD, William (1543–1623). *English composer*.

A man of considerable enterprise, Byrd contrived to hold prestigious Anglican appointments (at Lincoln Cathedral and as Elizabeth I's organist at the Chapel Royal) despite the fact that he was a practising Roman Catholic. He went into business with his colleague Tallis, and obtained from the queen an exclusive licence to publish music in England: one of the first-ever attempts at copyright. He was a prolific and gifted composer, of both church and secular music: he, rather than *Purcell, is the true 'father of British music', the first British composer of genius whose works are still performed.

WORKS Three Masses; 169 motets; two Anglican Services; twelve anthems; several other short choral works; madrigals; songs for solo voice and instruments; fantasias, In nomines and sets of variations for instrumental groups (usually viols); more than 120 pieces for solo keyboard (virginals or harpsichord).

The Bells for virginals Byrd's pioneering keyboard music (mostly written for Queen Elizabeth's favoured instrument) is challenging to play but light and tuneful to listen to. Some pieces (like this one) are descriptive, others (e.g. *The Carman's Whistle*) are sets of ever-more-elaborate variations on popular tunes. Most combine catchiness with a virtuoso clatter like that of *Scarlatti's harpsichord sonatas: well worth seeking out.
→ *Wolsey's Wild/The Woods So Wild* (also in guitar arrangements); Farnaby 'Loth to Depart' Variations; Gibbons *The Earl of Salisbury, His Pavan and Galliard*.

Mass for Five Voices (1605) Byrd's Latin church music – he wrote English church works too, in a more straightforward, functional idiom – enriches the severe, plainsong-based style of such men as *Palestrina with the sonorous new harmonies pioneered for St Mark's, Venice, by Giovanni Gabrieli and *Monteverdi. The result is sumptuous: church music of symphonic weight, emotional and devotional all at once, drawing from the unaccompanied choir music as varied and colourful as any composed at the time for instruments.
→ Mass for four voices; motet *Sacerdotes Domini*; Monteverdi Magnificat for six voices (1610).

C

CANTELOUBE. See *One-work Composers*.

CARTER, Elliott (born 1908). *American composer*.

Carter spent his non-composing life in a fascinating variety of ways. He taught at several conservatoires and universities (among them Columbia and Yale), lived in Paris, Berlin and Rome, and was for two years musical director of a touring ballet company. His music, similarly far-ranging, draws ingredients from *Schoenberg's academic formulas, from the lithe ballet-rhythms of *Stravinsky and from the jazzy glitter of *Ravel, and stirs them into a mixture distinctly Carter's and distinctly American (*Ives is another influence). Although it is far from easy at first hearing, its blend of personal, intellectual power and attractive outside references makes it flower in the listener's mind.

WORKS Two ballets; two symphonies, two concertos, Variations and other shorter orchestral works; three string quartets, Wind Quintet, Cello Sonata, Piano Sonata and other chamber works (including *Canonic Suite* for four saxophones); songs and cantatas for voice with piano or instrumental group (including *Six Poems by Elizabeth Bishop* and *A Mirror on Which to Dwell*).

Ⓜ **Sonata for flute, oboe, cello and harpsichord** (1974) This is an eighteenth-century trio-sonata (say, one of *Telemann's) seen entirely through twentieth-century eyes. That is, the breezy, Baroque blend of smooth wind lines and tinkly harpsichord is married to jazzy rhythms and pungent discords, and the music offers serious intellectual pleasure as well as ear-tickling entertainment.
→ Ⓜ Double Concerto for harpsichord, piano and two chamber orchestras; Symphony for Three Orchestras; Falla Harpsichord Concerto.

CHABRIER. See *One-work Composers*.

CHAMBER MUSIC

As its name suggests, chamber music is suitable for performance in a small room (compared, say, with *symphonies or *operas, whose large forces need large spaces). Chamber-music works involve anything from two to about a dozen players, and 'doubling' (more than one player playing the same part, as in an orchestra) is exceptional. Chamber music is one of the most intimate and domestic kinds of music; until the nineteenth century much of it was written for and performed by amateurs.

CONSORTS, SONATAS AND TRIO-SONATAS The earliest pieces of chamber music still in the repertoire are the instrumental consorts written in medieval and Renaissance times. They are short, scored usually for three to five players, and contrapuntal (see the Glossary: *Counterpoint*). The usual grouping is for instruments of the same family (e.g. recorders or viols of different sizes); a 'broken consort' mixes instruments of different kinds. In seventeenth-century Europe this civilized, highly-organized form gave way to another, far more extrovert: the *sonata. Solo sonatas were particularly popular in the seventeenth century; in the eighteenth they were over-shadowed first by the trio-sonata (see *Sonata*) and then by the string quartet (see below); they made a triumphant return in the nineteenth century, and have ridden high in the chamber-music repertoire ever since.

QUARTETS, QUINTETS, etc As the eighteenth century progressed, many composers began replacing the continuo (cello and harpsichord) in their chamber works. (One reason was that in the homes of the fashionable patrons who played or sponsored chamber music, harpsichords were giving way to pianos, and the tone of early pianos was too gentle to make a satisfying musical blend.) In place of the continuo, they added middle-voice instruments to the texture (viola in string music, horn or clarinet in wind), and as soon as players of these once-Cinderella instruments improved their technique enough to cope, the new consorts eclipsed all earlier ones. Favourite forms were the string quartet and quintet and the wind quintet (for details, see the last paragraph, below). At first the music was cheerful and simple, but in the second half of the century several great composers developed a chamber-music style that, for all the small playing-forces, was able to sustain musical argument as intricate as that of any symphony. *Haydn's string quartets and *Mozart's string quartets and quintets, for example, are among their finest works.

NINETEENTH-CENTURY CHAMBER MUSIC Once chamber music began to grow more complex, the inevitable happened: it progressed beyond most amateurs, and demanded players of professional ability. They in turn demanded paying audiences, and the end of it was that chamber music moved from the home into the concert-hall. Even so, there was more glory for a virtuoso in playing solos than in subordinating his or her personality to play one part in, say, quartets (even ones as demanding as *Beethoven's). The more career-minded players shied away from chamber music, and it fell out of fashion, to be kept up only by a few composers (notably *Brahms) who still wrote works for their own and their friends' domestic pleasure.

TWENTIETH-CENTURY CHAMBER MUSIC In the twentieth century the picture changed again. As orchestras grew ever larger and their music grew more demanding, many players turned to chamber music as a relaxed alternative. Some formed professional groups to play it, and nowadays it has an enthusiastic audience and a range of expert specialist players. It has become a fully public art-form, and the finest twentieth-century chamber works (e.g. *Bartók's string quartets) depend on the same feeling of occasion as do symphonies or operas, that is that players and audience are combining to create, and share, a unique experience. Paradoxically, however, chamber music has at the same time returned to the home: radio and records have revealed its delights, and allowed it to be enjoyed in its proper intimate setting, in a way unknown (except by the dedicated few) since Beethoven's time.

Listening Good introductions to seventeenth-century chamber music are the jolly consort pieces by Anthony Holborne (typical titles are *The Night Watch*, *Heartsease* and *Heigh Ho Holiday*), and *Purcell's Fantasies of three and four parts for viols, among the noblest of all pre-*Bach contrapuntal works. The vast sonata and trio-sonata repertoire, one of the largest and most enjoyable stretches of music of any kind, is outlined in the article *sonata in this book. Listening-recommendations for other kinds of chamber music are:

Piano trios (violin, cello, piano) Haydn Trio in G ('Gypsy Rondo'); Dvořák Trio No. 4., Op. 90 ('Dumky'); Beethoven Ⓜ Trio No. 7, Op. 97 ('Archduke').

String quartets (two violins, viola, cello) Mozart Ⓜ Quartet No. 17, K 458 ('Hunt'); Dvořák Quartet No. 12, Op. 96 ('American'); Wolf *Italian Serenade*.

String quintets (string quartet plus second viola or second cello) Boccherini Quintet, Op. 30 No. 6; Mozart Ⓜ Quintet No. 4, K 516; Brahms Ⓜ Quintet No. 2, Op. 111.

Wind quintets (flute, oboe, clarinet, horn, bassoon) Danzi Quintet, Op. 56 No. 3; Ibert *Trois pièces brèves*; Nielsen Ⓜ *Wind Quintet*.

Others Mozart Ⓜ Oboe Quartet, K 370 (oboe, violin, viola, cello); Beethoven Septet (clarinet, horn, bassoon, string quartet); Schubert 'Trout' Quintet (piano, violin, viola, cello, double bass); Mendelssohn Ⓜ Octet (two string quartets); Schubert Ⓜ Octet (clarinet, horn, bassoon, string quartet, double bass); Mozart Ⓜ Clarinet Quintet, K 581 (clarinet, string quartet).

For further recommendations, works by the greatest chamber-music composers, see the articles on J.S. Bach, Bartók, Beethoven, Brahms, Corelli, Dvořák, Fauré, Handel, Haydn, Mozart, Schubert, Telemann and Tippett. See also *Sonata*.

CHOPIN, Frédéric (1810-49). *Polish composer.*

When Poland submitted to the Russians in 1830, twenty-year-old Chopin was on a concert tour in western Europe. He decided to extend it to permanent exile, and settled in Paris, where he supported himself by giving piano lessons, appearing at occasional public concerts, and above all by giving piano recitals at the evening-parties of rich patrons. He became enormously popular, partly because of his dazzling piano-skill and partly because of his extraordinary good looks: he was handsome and consumptive, exactly suiting the Romantic notion of a frail genius marked for death. (His popularity survived even his love-affair with the notorious George Sand, with whom he ran away to Majorca in 1838, and later lived openly in Paris and at Nohant.) As his health deteriorated, he gave fewer recitals, concentrating on composition and on playing for his loyal friends. At the time of the 1848 revolution he was travelling in Britain; but he was mortally sick, and died shortly after his return to France.

For all its refinement and good manners, Chopin's music is as revolutionary as anything else composed in the nineteenth century. Its harmonies (helped by a quite new way of using the piano's sustaining pedal) constantly blur and melt into one another, and its decorative traceries cut across rhythmic regularity (often because they use all five fingers, and so expand the two-, three- or four-note divisions of the standard beat). He favoured short pieces whose forms were governed by fantasy rather than rules, and whose titles (ballade, nocturne, impromptu) suggest poetry or painting as much as music. Like *Mozart, he formed his style early in life, and rarely deviated from it. This means that virtually all his compositions, whether 'good' or 'not so good', start from the same generally high level, and have an instantly recognizable sophistication and elegance, which make criticism (such as the remarks quoted in the article on *Avant-garde music*) beside the point.

WORKS   Solo piano: three Sonatas; four Scherzos; four Ballades; twenty-seven Studies; nineteen Nocturnes; twenty-five Preludes; fourteen Waltzes; three Impromptus; ten Polonaises; fifty-five Mazurkas; a score of miscellaneous pieces including Berceuse, Fantasy in F minor, Fantasy-impromptu, and several sets of variations. Other: two Concertos and four shorter works for piano and orchestra; Trio for violin, cello and piano; Sonata and two shorter works for cello and piano; seventeen songs.

Nocturne, Op. 9 No. 2 This gentle 'night-piece' has been arranged for everything from brass-band to musical saw, but is still supreme in its original form: an ornamented right-hand tune floating above unhurried, uncluttered left-hand chords.
→Nocturnes Op. 32; Debussy *Clair de lune*; Ravel *Pavane pour une Infante défunte*.

Study, Op. 10 No. 12 ('Revolutionary') (1829-32). The nickname refers to fiery left-hand runs, set against an urgent melody in the right hand. Like all Chopin's studies, however, the piece is revolutionary in another way: its technical problems are audible to the listener only when triumphantly solved (that is, the piece is for listening to, not just for finger-loosening): we hear music that combines emotional directness with the exhilarating sense of a performer's virtuosity driving all before it.
→Study, Op. 10 No. 3; *Grande valse brillante*, Op. 18; Liszt 'Gnomenreigen' (from *Two Concert Studies*, 1863).

Ⓜ **Scherzo No. 2, Op. 31** Chopin's four Scherzos are large-scale works which add to the traditional hectic dash of scherzo-style a weightier, more closely-worked feeling, as if they were one-movement sonatas. Intellectuality, even so, is always balanced by tunefulness and showers of notes.
→ Ⓜ Scherzo No. 3; Ⓜ Ballade No. 3; Schumann Sonata No. 2.

Ⓜ **Sonata No. 2, Op. 35** (1839) The headlong urgency of the first two movements is abruptly halted by a solemn funeral march (often played separately, not least at solemn funerals), and is then taken up again in a turbulent, dark-toned finale. Many piano sonatas are serious and grand; this one is also a showpiece, a dazzler.
→ Sonata No. 3; Ravel *Gaspard de la nuit*; Scriabin Sonata No. 5.

Concerto No. 2, Op. 21 (1829) Chopin's concertos, though testing to play, are less duels between piano and orchestra than conversations, among his sunniest works. Large first movements are followed by nocturne-like slow movements and skittering finales (in this concerto, built on one of his most beguiling tunes).
→ Concerto No. 1; Scriabin Piano Concerto; Ireland Piano Concerto.

Arrangements by others *Les sylphides* (ballet). Orchestral version of seven pieces (Prelude No. 7, Nocturne No. 10, Waltz No. 11, Mazurka No. 44, Mazurka No. 23, Waltz No. 7, Waltz No. 1): charming as ballet music, but the arrangement saps the music's strength (which partly depends on its virtuoso element, the feeling of a performer's fantasy complementing the composer's). The ballet, in short, is gossamer, the piano originals gorse. *A Month in the Country* (ballet). Recommended: the score consists of three agreeable, less well-known works for piano and orchestra in their original (unadapted) form: *Fantasy on Polish Airs*, Op. 13, *Andante spianato and Grand polonaise brillante*, Op. 22, and *Variations on Mozart's 'Là ci darem la mano'*, Op. 2.

CHORAL MUSIC

Unlike *vocal music, which uses solo voices, choral music is performed by a choir, an orchestra of voices where several people sing the same line of notes at once. Its history is long and varied, ranging from competitive festivals in ancient Athens all the way through the choir of eunuchs with which Cleopatra delighted Julius Caesar and the choral hymns which preceded Aztec human sacrifice to the thousands-strong choirs which celebrate each anniversary of the Russian Revolution.

CHORAL MUSIC AND THE CHRISTIAN CHURCH From the beginnings of religion, choral music has played a key part in ritual. Often one soloist (the priest) would chant (i.e. half-speak, half-sing) the words of the service, and everyone else would chant in answer. In Christian churches this unadorned, unharmonized chanting is called plainsong, and has been used for seventeen centuries. In the late Middle Ages experiments began to enrich it by adding accompanying lines of different notes (in harmony or counterpoint), and by the fifteenth and sixteenth centuries they had turned church music into a breathtaking and sumptuous art-form. The Masses, motets and other choral works of *Josquin, *Palestrina, *Lassus and others are as far removed from the plainsong they are based on as cathedrals are removed from unadorned wood or stone.

No subsequent musical style has so well suited the Christian Church as unaccompanied choral singing. Since the Renaissance, Catholic composers' use of later styles (e.g. adding soloists and orchestras) has made their Masses and other religious works more suitable for the concert-hall than for church. (The seventeenth-century multi-choir works, for example, of Giovanni Gabrieli, *Monteverdi and others, turned St Mark's, Venice, into a kind of religious circus-ring: they dazzled the congregation with spectacle, made them constantly turn their heads to see where each new sound was coming from.) There are enjoyable Masses by *Mozart, *Haydn and *Schubert, but they intrude musical beauties on religious meaning, and so (it could be argued) fail in their devotional purpose. The trend was carried to its limits by later composers, in such attention-grabbing masterpieces as *Beethoven's *Missa solemnis*, *Bruckner's Masses and the Requiems of *Berlioz, *Verdi and *Britten.

A similar progression happened in Protestant music. In the seventeenth century, after the reforms of Luther, a thriving Protestant church music grew up, based on hymns and specifically intended to involve the hearts, minds and voices of the whole congregation. Then great composers (such as Heinrich Schütz and Dietrich Buxtehude) took hold of it, and extended its musical and emotional range to the point where, thanks to the complexity of the sound, the congregation had to listen instead of taking part. *Bach's cantatas, and his and other men's Passions, are musically supreme, but religious in no more than intent. In the oratorio (invented in the eighteenth century) composers such as *Handel went still further: an oratorio, to all intents and purposes, is an opera on a biblical theme, with large choruses, and was never meant to be performed in church. It has since become, with the Catholic Mass, the favourite large choral musical form, and many composers of genius have tackled it. But *Mendelssohn's *Elijah*, *Elgar's *The Dream of Gerontius*, Honegger's *Joan of Arc* and *Walton's overwhelming (and remarkably pagan) *Belshazzar's Feast* are religious works in nothing more than theme.

SECULAR CHORAL MUSIC Just as religious choral music celebrates (in theory at least) the relationship between human beings and God, so secular (i.e. non-religious) music celebrates more earthly matters (such as love, scenery, battle, or even food and drink). For many centuries, these subjects were considered more suitable for private, domestic performances than for public choirs, and the music was suitably small-scale: solo songs, madrigals, rounds and glees. (For details, see *Vocal music*.) When this kind of music outgrew the drawing-room, composers used the same large forms and styles for it as for their religious works, merely lightening the texture to suit light-hearted themes. There is little to distinguish Palestrina's or Monteverdi's secular from their sacred works: they use the same procedures in the same way and with the same surefootedness.

In seventeenth- and eighteenth-century Britain, *Purcell and his successors as Masters of the Royal Music developed a particularly sumptuous kind of secular choral music. This was the occasional or ceremonial Ode, a large work for soloists, choir and orchestra to mark a great occasion (such as a coronation) or a trivial one (such as a monarch's safe crossing of the English Channel). Purcell's *Birthday Odes* and Handel's *Chandos Anthems* are among the most sonorous of all choral works, and the tradition has both continued in Britain and spread to other countries (Berlioz's *Triumphal and Funeral Symphony* and *Brahms's jingoistic *Song of Triumph* are widely differing examples).

In the eighteenth century, when most composers still at least professed religious conviction, secular choral works were rare. (Bach's 'Coffee' and 'Peasant' cantatas, and Haydn's *The Seasons*, are fine examples of a scarce breed.) But in the nineteenth and twentieth centuries, when agnosticism or atheism have become more acceptable, non-religious choral music has flourished. The tradition began with Beethoven (whose 'Choral' Symphony includes a setting of Schiller's *Ode to Joy*), continued with Berlioz's giant choral-and-orchestral works based on Virgil and Shakespeare, and progressed to *Liszt's, *Schumann's, Brahms's and *Mahler's settings of Goethe. (Mahler's Symphony No. 8 is one of the most powerful non-religious choral works of any age.) One of the best-loved twentieth-century choral works, *Orff's *Carmina Burana*, goes as far from the church as seems possible: it is a pounding, sensuous setting of poems celebrating the joys of spring, gambling, drink and lust. Howard Hanson's *The Lament for Beowulf* sets Anglo-Saxon poetry as solemnly and magnificently as if it were *Genesis*; *Tippett's *A Child of Our Time* is an outcry against Nazi atrocity which borrows its form from that most devotional of all church works, Bach's *St Matthew Passion*. Other composers have worked equally confidently in church and secular styles: *Stravinsky's *Perséphone*, for example, is based on ancient Greek myth, and his *Les noces* pictures a Russian peasant wedding, but few devotional twentieth-century works can hold a candle to his *Symphony of Psalms* and *Requiem Canticles*.

Listening A fine, brief example of Palestrina's unaccompanied choral style – and of Renaissance church music at its best – is his *Stabat mater*. (It also makes a fascinating stylistic contrast with Pergolesi's *Stabat mater* of two centuries later, and with Poulenc's of two centuries after that.) At opposite eighteenth-century poles are Handel's coronation anthem *Zadok the Priest* and Mozart's effervescent *Missa brevis*, K. 192. Good introductions to nineteenth-century choral music are the *Shepherd's Farewell* from Berlioz's enormous cantata *The Childhood of Christ*, Rossini's *Petite messe solenelle* ('Little solemn Mass') and Fauré's ethereal *Requiem*. Twentieth-century religious music ranges from Stravinsky's austere Mass to Bernstein's bouncy *Chichester Psalms*, and few secular choral works rival Vaughan Williams's *Serenade to Music* (choral version) for placid beauty or Harris's Symphony No. 4 ('Folksong Symphony') for clean-cut verve. For major choral works by major composers, see the articles on J.S. Bach, Beethoven, Berlioz, Brahms, Britten, Bruckner, Elgar, Handel, Haydn, Josquin, Mahler, Mendelssohn, Monteverdi, Mozart, Orff, Palestrina, Penderecki, Purcell, Schubert, Stravinsky, Vaughan Williams and Walton; see also *Fifteenth-century music*, *Sixteenth-century music*, *Seventeenth-century music* and *Eighteenth-century music*.

CHURCH MUSIC

For general comments, see *Choral music*. For comments on some of the finest church-music composers, see the articles on J.S. Bach, Byrd, Josquin, Monteverdi, Palestrina, Purcell and Stravinsky.

CONCERTO

The word concerto means 'concert' or 'consort'. The concerto composer gives one or more instruments leading, solo parts; other instruments (usually those in the orchestra) provide support. The unfolding relationship between soloist(s) and supporting group is the essence of the musical experience. A good concerto also exploits and displays the qualities of the solo instrument.

CONCERTO GROSSO *Concerto grosso* ('grand concert', plural *concerti grossi*) was a popular form for approximately one hundred years (1650-1750). Often there were several solo instruments, and an orchestra of strings and harpsichord. Thus, the musical dialogue was between two contrasting groups, each complete in itself but with its own distinctive sound. In *Bach's *Brandenburg Concerto* No. 4, for example, a group consisting of two recorders and violin balances the string orchestra; in Handel's *Concerto grosso* Op. 3 No. 4 the solo group consists of oboe and two violins.

EIGHTEENTH-CENTURY SOLO CONCERTOS As well as *concerti grossi*, Baroque composers (especially Bach, *Handel and *Vivaldi) also wrote concertos for single soloists and orchestra. In these, the basic idea (of dialogue) was the same as in the *concerto grosso*, but because there was only one soloist to balance with the orchestra, his or her music tended to be more florid and assertive in style than theirs. Good examples are Vivaldi's *Four Seasons*, Haydn's Trumpet Concerto and Mozart's Clarinet Concerto.

NINETEENTH CENTURY In the age of great virtuoso players like Paganini and *Liszt, the imagination of both composers and public was caught by the idea of one person (the soloist) doing battle against huge odds (the orchestra). Thus the eighteenth-century idea of dialogue was converted to one of duel. Superstar soloists and their concertos range from Beethoven's Piano Concerto No. 3 of 1802 well into the twentieth century. Display-works with a fairly gentle, tuneful style include *Chopin's Piano Concerto No. 2 and *Mendelssohn's Violin Concerto; more grandiose, *Grieg's Piano Concerto, *Tchaikovsky's Piano Concerto No. 1 and Bruch's Violin Concerto No. 1 ride the crest of the gladiatorial wave.

TWENTIETH CENTURY In the twentieth century, though extrovert virtuoso concertos still abound (e.g. *Rachmaninov's Piano Concerto No. 3, *Sibelius's Violin Concerto), there has been a marked tendency towards a more conversational style, with the orchestral contribution balancing instead of being bludgeoned by the soloist's. Good examples are Rodrigo's *Concierto de Aranjuez* (for guitar and orchestra), Elgar's Cello Concerto and Ravel's G major Piano Concerto. There is also a trend back towards the *concerto grosso*, balancing groups of instruments against the fuller band. (Good examples are *Stravinsky's *Capriccio* for piano and orchestra and *Tippett's *Fantasia concertante on a Theme of Corelli*).

Most solo concertos have three movements; a few of the largest (e.g. *Brahms's Second Piano Concerto), and some *concerti grossi*, have four. In some nineteenth-century concertos (e.g. those of Liszt) the movements are played without a break, and the music makes a seamless whole. The usual three-movement pattern is of a bright, discursive first movement, a slow and lyrical second movement and a brilliant finale.

CONCERTOS FOR MORE THAN ONE SOLOIST As well as *concerti grossi* and solo concertos, there are a few distinguished concertos for two or more individual soloists and orchestra. Good examples are Bach's Concerto for two violins, Mozart's *Sinfonia concertante* (for violin, viola and orchestra), Beethoven's Triple Concerto (for violin, cello, piano and orchestra), and Brahms's Double Concerto (for violin, cello and orchestra). For some listeners, these are among the most cherished works in the whole concerto repertoire.

Listening For those new to concertos, recommended works are Handel's Organ Concerto No. 7, Mozart's Horn Concerto No. 3, Schumann's Piano Concerto and Rachmaninov's Piano Concerto No. 2. Good follow-ups are the other concertos mentioned in this article (particularly those by Mendelssohn, Rodrigo and Ravel); for other concertos by leading composers see the articles on J.S. Bach, Bartók, Beethoven, Brahms, Copland, Dvořák, Liszt, Martinů, Mozart, Rachmaninov, Schumann, Tchaikovsky, Vivaldi and Walton; see also *Brass Instruments*, *Keyboard Instruments*, *String Instruments* and *Woodwind Instruments*.

CONTEMPORARY MUSIC

For professional musicians, this phrase has a different meaning from either 'modern' or 'avant-garde' music. It refers to works written in the twentieth century, in experimental rather than traditional styles, and needing a certain amount of dedicated study and knowledge to be properly enjoyed. As with *Early Music, many works have, in the course of time, passed from the specialist to the wider world, and are now happily enjoyed by ordinary concert audiences. For listening recommendations to the best of these, see the articles on Berg, Boulez, Carter, Davies, Henze, Lutosławski, Messiaen, Schoenberg, Tippett and Webern. See also *Avant-garde Music* and *Twentieth-century Music*.

COPLAND, Aaron (born 1900). *American composer.*

Having decided at the age of eleven that he wanted to be a composer, Copland saved enough money over the next ten years to take him to Paris, where he studied with the leading composition-teacher of the day, Nadia Boulanger. He came back to the USA as a thorough-going 1920s modernist: his works were full of jazz rhythms, biting harmonies and shifting rhythms, in a style similar to that of *Milhaud or Honegger. His music won prizes – enough to secure Copland a living as well as a reputation – but most audiences hated it, and critics greeted it with such remarks as 'If there exists anywhere in the world a stranger concatenation of meaninglessly ugly sounds and distorted rhythms than Mr. Copland's Piano Concerto, Boston has been spared it' (*Boston Post*, 1927).

Copland went on for some years writing in this take-me-as-you-find-me style. But in the 1930s he decided that a composer's duty to his listeners includes not baffling them, and that there was no reason why high-quality music should not also be accessible and enjoyable. He radically simplified his style, and began producing works for 'popular' mediums (ballet, film, high-school orchestra) and in an idiom combining intellectual seriousness with aural appeal. The result, with its direct emotion, wide-spaced, clear harmony and unselfconscious use of folk-tunes, at once established a plain-speaking 'American' tradition and graced it with half a dozen masterpieces.

WORKS Four symphonies; Piano Concerto; Clarinet Concerto; *El salón México*, *Quiet City*, *Fanfare for the Common Man*, Orchestral Variations, *Connotations* and several other orchestral works; three ballets (*Billy the Kid*; *Rodeo*; *Appalachian Spring*); opera *The Tender Land*; Piano Quintet; Sonata for violin and piano; Piano Sonata; Nonet for Strings and other shorter chamber works; *Twelve Poems of Emily Dickinson*; *Old American Songs*; three choral works; *A Lincoln Portrait* for speaker and orchestra; scores for numerous films, including *Of Mice and Men*, *Our Town* and *The Red Pony*.

El salón México (1936) One of the first of Copland's 'popular' works, this lively orchestral impression of a Mexican dance-hall uses jazzy tunes (some folk-based), big-band scoring and catchy Latin-American rhythms.
→*Rodeo* (*Four Dance Episodes*); Chabrier *España*; Bernstein *Fancy Free*; Piston *The Incredible Flutist*.

Clarinet Concerto (1948) Written for the clarinet-playing band-leader Benny Goodman (who also regularly played *Mozart, and played him well), this concerto exploits both his velvety tone and the finger-snapping jazz style which earned him the nickname 'King of Swing'.
→ Ⓜ Symphony No. 3 (Copland's largest orchestral work, with a finale built on his earlier, world-famous *Fanfare for the Common Man*); *Billy the Kid*; Finzi Clarinet Concerto.
Ⓜ *Appalachian Spring* (1945) Originally a ballet, this music is most often heard nowadays in the concert-hall; many regard it as Copland's finest work. The

ballet story tells of the plain-dealing Shaker sect in the Appalachian Mountains (a religious offshoot of the Quakers), and the music incorporates several heart-easing Shaker tunes (e.g. 'The Gift to be Simple is the Gift to be Free'). Apart from a high-spirited barn-dance, *Appalachian Spring* is predominantly quiet, reflective and luminously beautiful.

→ Ⓜ *Old American Songs* for voice and piano/orchestra; Respighi *Brazilian Impressions*; Ives Symphony No. 3.

Piano Variations (1930) A splendid example of Copland's grittier, less compromising music. It is closely argued (somewhat in the manner of the fugue from *Brahms's *Handel Variations*); its style is urgent, rhetorical and discordant. It exists also in an orchestral arrangement (Orchestral Variations): this is easier on the ear, but a far less mind-stretching experience.

→Piano Sonata; *Short Symphony*; Bartók Piano Sonata.

CORELLI, Archangelo (1653-1713). *Italian composer and violinist.*

Corelli spent his life in musical service to the Italian nobility, most notably as household music-director to Cardinal Ottoboni in Rome. He was one of the leading violinists in Europe, the Paganini of his day, and died a rich man. His list of compositions was short (for the time): six opus numbers containing twelve works each. But few composers have had wider influence on their contemporaries. He developed two styles in particular, the *sonata and the *concerto grosso* (see *Concerto*), and they became the standard forms of instrumental music for the next half-century. (Only the *symphony, a century later, caught composers' imaginations to anything like the same extent.) Although some of the men Corelli influenced (e.g. *Vivaldi, *Bach, *Handel) wrote finer music, his works are today unjustly neglected compared to theirs. His music is expertly made, with tender slow movements (often showing off the expressive powers of the solo violin), neat counterpoint and lively jigs; they are crisp, to the point, and never a note too long.

WORKS Forty-eight trio sonatas; twelve sonatas for violin and continuo; twelve *concerti grossi*.

Sonata for violin and continuo Op. 5 No. 10 (1700) Corelli's sonatas (both those in Op. 5, for one soloist, and those in Opp. 1-4, for two) are of two kinds: 'church sonatas' (consisting of four contrapuntal movements, alternately slow and fast) and 'chamber sonatas' (consisting of an introductory movement followed by a suite of dance-movements). Op. 5 No. 10 is a typical chamber sonata, whose slow, decorated introduction leads to a jolly suite of *allemande, sarabande, gavotte* and *jig*.

→Sonata Op. 5 No. 11 (*La folia*: its unique form - for Corelli - is twenty-five increasingly lively variations on a popular tune); Handel Sonata Op. 1 No. 15; Bach Sonata No. 4 for violin and harpsichord.

Concerto grosso Op. 6 No. 2 (1714) This chirpy piece is scored for three soloists (two violins, one cello) and string orchestra. It has seven movements, each sub-divided into contrasting sections of fast and slow: the effect is like a mosaic of tiny musical experiences. As well as being one of Corelli's own most enjoyable concertos, this work also forms the basis for *Tippett's ecstatic twentieth-century *Fantasia concertante on a Theme of Corelli* (recommended).

→*Concerto grosso* Op. 6 No. 8 ('Christmas' Concerto); Geminiani *Concerto grosso* Op. 3 No. 3; Handel *Concerto grosso* Op. 6 No. 12.

COUPERIN, François (1668–1733). *French composer and harpsichordist.*

Couperin was the most distinguished member of a large family of musicians, with a tradition of professional work in France to rival that of the Bachs in Germany. He was a harpsichordist and organist, and spent most of his life in the service of the French court, where his duties were to provide church music for royal devotions and chamber music for royal delight. Apart from some polished church music, his chief compositions are instrumental: concertos, trio-sonatas, and a huge and delightfully quirky collection of pieces for solo harpsichord. (His book *The Art of Harpsichord-playing*, 1716, is a valuable guide both to his own music and to the extravagantly-embellished 'French' performing-style of the time, far more whimsical and flowery than the 'Italian' and 'German' styles favoured by such men as *Bach.)

WORKS 220 solo harpsichord pieces, grouped in twenty-seven *Ordres* (i.e. suites); forty-two solo organ pieces in two collections called *Masses*; assorted chamber and orchestral music including four 'Royal concertos', ten concertos subtitled 'The styles reunited', four trio-sonatas, and the large-scale *Apotheosis of Corelli* and *Apotheosis of Lully* for chamber ensemble; a couple of dozen church works including choral motets and the *Leçons de ténèbres*, passages from the Lamentations of Jeremiah for two voices and continuo.

Ordre No. 23 for harpsichord (published 1730, written many years before) Like all Couperin's *Ordres*, this is a sprightly collection of unrelated pieces in a style as fanciful as their titles: 'The Bold Girl'; 'The Knitters'; 'Harlequin'; 'The Gondolas of Delos'; 'Satyrs'. There is no Bach/*Scarlatti grandness here: these delicious sketches are ancestors of the picture-postcard piano pieces of *Albéniz or the *Préludes* of *Debussy.

→Ordre No. 2 (longer and more sonorous); Ordre No. 14 (plaintive; includes the famous 'The Nightingale in Love'); Rameau *Harpsichord Pieces* (fifty-six pictorial works, grouped in suites, with the same blend of virtuoso fingerwork and graceful charm).

Audite omnes et expavescite ('Hear, all of you, and tremble') This church motet, for solo voice, two violins and continuo, is less a devotional work than a vocal concerto, intended chiefly to delight. It is worth investigating the meaning of the words: Couperin's music (characteristically) exploits every possible pictorial opportunity. As word-setting, as music of sensual vocal delight, it rivals *Purcell's.
→ Ⓜ *Leçons de ténèbres*; *Concert royal* No. 2 (no voices: a splendidly Handelian sonata for chamber ensemble); Purcell *The Queen's Epicedium*.

D

DAVIES Peter Maxwell (born 1934). *English composer.*

Schoolteaching (for three years he was head of music at Cirencester Grammar School) and conducting (he was founder-director of a music-theatre group, the Pierrot Players) gave Davies a shrewd grasp of what makes music 'work' for both performers and audience. Unlike some avant-garde composers, therefore, he writes for ordinary music-lovers, not for a clique of specialists, and though his works are never easy on the ear, they are always purposeful, expertly-turned and memorable. (He resembles *Boulez in this, as well as in quality.) He applies *Webernian composition-methods to ideas and themes drawn from the Middle Ages: the texture of his music is an endlessly-intriguing blur of sound, as if old church motets and secular dances had been shredded and were being amazingly reconstituted before our ears. His most striking pieces are his music-theatre works (see *Eight Songs for a Mad King*, below); his best music, however, is abstract, on the largest scale, and often seems to be influenced by the bleak seascapes round his Orkney Islands home.

WORKS Four operas (including *Taverner*) and a dozen music-theatre pieces (including *Eight Songs for a Mad King*, *Miss Donnithorne's Maggot* and *Revelation and Fall*); three symphonies, two *Fantasias on an In nomine of John Taverner*, *Worlde's Bliss*, *A Mirror of Whitening Light* and other large orchestral works; *Leopardi Fragments*, *Mass on L'homme armé*, *Stone Litany*, *Hymn to St Magnus* and other solo vocal works; String Quartet, Piano Sonata, Brass Quintet, Trumpet Sonata, *Stedman Doubles*, *Antechrist* and many other chamber works, including chamber-orchestra recompositions of *Purcell, Gabrieli and other early composers in 1920s ragtime style; songs, choruses (including the carol-suite *O magnum mysterium*) and solo piano pieces (many for children).

Ⓜ *Eight Songs for a Mad King* (1969) In this unique and fascinating work, a solo singer takes the part of mad King George, going from one to another of a group of musicians in cages (symbolizing singing birds), trying by shouts, whines, moans and whispers to teach them the melodies in his mind. The piece assaults its audience as brashly as a Ken Russell film; it has to be seen (not heard on record) to be believed; its images as well as its sounds are unforgettable.

→ Ⓜ *Revelation and Fall* (for singer-speaker, acting the part of an entranced medium, and chamber group); Ⓜ *Stone Litany* (song-cycle, less exotic visually but musically just as sensational, for voice and orchestra); Ligeti *Le grand macabre* (theatre-piece depicting Death as a demented conjurer).

Ⓜ *First Fantasia on an In nomine of John Taverner* (1962) This 40-minute, single-movement work treats a huge orchestra as if it were a collection of chamber-music groups, and subjects a fifteenth-century theme to every conceivable kind of twentieth-century dislocation and reassembly. Its effect is a kind of intellectual hypnosis; like (say) *Bach's *Art of Fugue*, its purpose seems as much to make the listener think as to entertain.

→ Ⓜ Symphony No. 1 (similarly demanding, but with an expansive grandeur influenced by *Sibelius's Symphony No. 5, which was in Davies's mind as he planned the work); *Points and Dances from Taverner* (instrumental excerpts from Davies's best opera, a good introduction to his style); Stockhausen *Inori*.

DEBUSSY, Claude (1862–1918). *French composer.*

Debussy's career was of a sort to encourage late developers everywhere. Ambitious to become a concert pianist, he studied with a pupil of *Chopin, and entered the Paris Conservatoire at the precocious age of ten. Then his ambition faltered, and he turned from solo playing to accompaniment. At eighteen he became house pianist to Nadezhda von Meck, the wealthy Russian who also funded *Tchaikovsky; after six years of diligent application, he turned himself into a sufficiently formal, academic composer to win the Conservatoire's Prix de Rome (a three-year stay in Italy); it was not until six years later still, when he was thirty-two, that his own original composing style (flavoured not only by the French academic tradition, but also by Balinese gamelans, medieval plainchant and American ragtime) was finally revealed to the world, with the successful first performance of the *Prélude à l'après-midi d'un faune*.

Few composers have possessed a finer 'ear' than Debussy for musical sound. His works are meticulously noted down, with every nuance of rhythm, harmony or texture exactly calculated and precisely placed. But he used this Swiss-watchmaker technique to create music whose effect is, paradoxically, improvisatory and imprecise: pieces like 'Reflections in the Water', 'Clouds' or 'Play of the Waves', though solidly and logically constructed, sound as elusive as their titles suggest. Impressionist painters set out to place on canvas not objective images, but an exactly-controlled impression of the colours and light their own eyes saw; Debussy's goal in sound was similar. To create such shifting, original effects, he developed new scales, new ways of scoring for the orchestra (in blocks and washes of sound instead of precise melody or counterpoint), and above all, new ways of playing the piano. He was unlike any earlier composer, the father of musical modernism; what gives his work appeal is the relaxed, unassertive personality which makes every bar seem a fresh invention, a new discovery.

PIANO WORKS Twenty-four *Préludes*; twelve Studies; four Suites (including *Children's Corner*); two sets of *Images*; *L'île joyeuse* ('The Happy Isle'); two *Arabesques*; *Petite suite* ('Little Suite'), *Scottish March* and *Six épigraphes antiques* ('Six Ancient Epigraphs') for piano duet; suite *En blanc et noir* ('In Black and White') and other shorter works for two pianos.

Clair de lune ('Moonlight'; from *Suite Bergamasque*) (1895) A representation in sound of the limpid whiteness of moonlight, first still then rippled by passing clouds. The piece is often arranged for other forces, to its detriment: the piano original is evocative and clean.
→ *La fille aux cheveux de lin* ('The Girl with Flaxen Hair') (from *Préludes*, book 1); Satie *Gymnopédie* No. 1; Ravel *Pavane pour une Infante défunte* ('Pavane for a dead Infanta').

La cathédrale engloutie ('The Submerged Cathedral') (from *Préludes*, book 1) Each of Debussy's twenty-four *Préludes* (two books of twelve) paints a single poetic picture; even so, he liked them to be heard as pure music, without external 'meanings', and so printed their titles after the music, rather than before. This piece, about a cathedral bell tolling beneath the sea, together with *La fille aux cheveux de lin* (see above) and *Minstrels* (also from book 1), is the best-known; other immediate recommendations are: *Le vent dans la plaine* ('The Wind on the Plain') and *Des pas sur la neige* ('Steps in the Snow') from book 1; *Brouillards* ('Mists'), *Ondine* and *Feux d'artifice* ('Fireworks') from book 2.
→ *Reflets dans l'eau* ('Reflections in the Water') (from *Images*); the second *Arabesque*; Poulenc *Mouvements perpétuels*.

Ⓜ *Estampes* ('Engravings') (1903) This work is characteristic of Debussy's larger-scale piano (and orchestral) compositions: a suite of separate movements which, without losing individuality or charm, cohere into a grander, more 'symphonic' statement than a mere collection of miniatures. Its movements are *Pagodes* ('Pagodas'), *Soirée dans Granade* ('Evening in Granada') and *Jardins sous la pluie* ('Gardens in the Rain').
→ Suite *Pour le piano* ('For the Piano'); Ireland suite *Decorations*; Ravel suite *Miroirs* ('Mirrors').

ORCHESTRAL AND CHAMBER WORKS Three *Nocturnes*; three *Images*; *La mer*; three ballets (including *Jeux*); *Prélude à l'après-midi d'un faune*; *Printemps*; half a dozen lesser works, including *Fantaisie* for piano and orchestra; String Quartet; sonatas for violin and piano, cello and piano, and flute, viola and harp; *Syrinx* for solo flute; *Rapsodie* for clarinet and piano.

Prélude à l'après-midi d'un faune ('Prelude to the Afternoon of a Faun') (1894) An orchestral impression of Mallarmé's poem about adolescent daydreams on a summer afternoon: the faun is a mischievous forest creature, half boy, half goat. As a scandalously erotic ballet (by 1900s standards), it made Nijinsky famous. Debussy seldom bettered the languid, floating style of this sensuous piece.

→ Ⓜ *Nuages* ('Clouds') (from *Nocturnes*); d'Indy *The Sorceror's Apprentice*; Liadov *The Enchanted Lake*.

Ⓜ *La mer* ('The Sea') (1904) 'Three symphonic sketches' ('From Dawn to Midday on the Sea'; 'Play of the Waves'; 'Dialogue of the Wind and the Sea') – and for once all the titles are incidental: this is an urgent three-movement symphony in all but name.

→*Images* (1909 – no connection with the piano suite of the same name); Janáček *Taras Bulba*; Sibelius *Pohjola's Daughter*.

Jeux ('Games') (1912) Ballet score originally commissioned for Nijinsky. Its story deals with games (tennis, flirtation) played by a young man and two girls. Debussy's subtlest, most evanescent score, influential on later composers; for listeners, though hard to penetrate at first, eventually revealing enduring poetic power.

→Suite *En blanc et noir* ('In Black and White') for two pianos; Ravel *La valse*; Szymanowski Symphony No. 2.

String Quartet (1893) Not at his happiest in chamber music, Debussy nevertheless left this one masterpiece, personable rather than profound, nearer to Borodin than to Beethoven, and full of un-quartetlike sonorities which surprise and delight the ear.

→Sonata for flute, viola and harp; Wolf *Italian Serenade*; Bartók String Quartet No. 1.

VOCAL MUSIC Opera *Pelléas et Mélisande*; two cantatas; eight song-cycles for voice and piano (including two sets of *Fêtes galantes*; *Chansons de Bilitis*; and *Proses lyriques*); *Chansons de Charles d'Orléans* for choir; other, less significant works including the incidental music for *King Lear* and *The Martyrdom of St Sebastian*.

Ⓜ *Fêtes galantes* (set 1, 1903; set 2, 1904) The poet Verlaine claimed that in his poetry 'the music was in the words'; in these settings, which fit his limpid or fantastical verses as skin fits flesh, Debussy proved him wrong. Of all French songwriters only *Fauré ever matched the coolness and freshness of Debussy's style here.

→ *Three Ballades of François Villon*; Fauré Verlaine song-cycle *La bonne chanson*; Duparc *Au pays où se fait la guerre* (extended single song).

Ⓜ *Pelléas et Mélisande* (1902) Complete opera. Though quintessentially Debussy, *Pelléas* is unlike any other opera: a long, predominantly quiet and conversational setting of Maeterlinck's symbolist play about doomed lovers. Its atmosphere recalls Cocteau's film *Beauty and the Beast* (or even Resnais' *Last Year at Marienbad*) – an elusive, hypnotic and (perhaps) unsettling work.

→ Cantata *Le martyre de Saint Sébastien*; Fauré *Pénélope*; Bartók *Bluebeard's Castle*.

DELIBES, Léo (1836-91). *French composer.*

Much of Delibes' working life was spent in the thankless chores of teaching singers their notes and playing for rehearsals at the Paris Opéra and Théâtre Lyrique. His ambition was to succeed as a stage composer – and in the end he did, for although his name is hardly on everyone's lips, his music (e.g. for *Coppélia*) is universally known and loved.

works Five operas (including *Lakmé*); half a dozen operettas (with titles like *Two of the Old Guard* and *The Scots Girl of Chatou*); four ballets (including *Coppélia* and *Sylvia*); incidental music; several large-scale vocal works including a cantata and a Mass; fifteen songs.

'Bell song' (from opera *Lakmé*, 1883) One of those instantly-recognizable show-pieces beloved by star sopranos and their audiences everywhere: spun-sugar chains of trills, runs and twiddly bits. Candy-floss music? The very best.
→'Pizzicato' (from ballet *Sylvia*; no voice, but one of Delibes' – and light music's – enduring hits); Strauss 'Laughing Song' (from *Die Fledermaus*); Gounod 'Waltz Song' (from *Romeo and Juliet*).

Coppélia (1870) Gorgeously tuneful ballet (about a young man who falls in love with a beautiful, lifesize doll, and his girl-friend's trick when she finds out who her 'rival' is); the score is a string of separate 'numbers' (e.g. waltz, bolero, mazurka) which are often played as a concert suite.
→*Sylvia* (complete ballet, and concert suite); suite *Le Roi s'amuse*; Offenbach *Gaîté Parisienne*; Rossini/Respighi *La boutique fantasque*.

DELIUS, Frederick (1862-1934). *English composer.*

As a young man, Delius was shipped out of Bradford, Yorkshire (then a thriving industrial town of cobblestones and black, Satanic mills), to manage an orange-farm in Florida. In his mid-twenties he went to Europe, and spent several years in Germany and Scandinavia before settling in Grez-sur-Loing, in the flowery French countryside favoured by the Impressionist painters. For the last ten years of his life, though blind and paralysed, he continued composing, dictating his works to his amanuensis Eric Fenby (whose book *Delius As I Knew Him* interestingly describes how the feat was done). In the 1920s he was one of the most-played of all English composers; more recently (and especially since the death of his main champion, the conductor Beecham) his music has, sadly, fallen out of the repertoire.

Delius's music often sounds as if composed by someone completely different from the man who lived his life: a mittened eccentric unaware of any innovations in the art since *Wagner or César *Franck. It is dreamy, decadent, meltingly Romantic and orchestrated for ravishing effect. Occasionally (in his concertos, for example) he tried to add robustness: it pulled the works apart. His best work is unique: sunsets, reveries and Indian summers transfixed in sound.

WORKS Six operas; four concertos; twenty-one orchestral works (including *Brigg Fair*; *North-country Sketches*; *a Song before Sunrise*); twelve works for choir and orchestra (including *Sea Drift*; *A Mass of Life*; *Songs of Sunset*); String Quartet; three sonatas for violin and piano; Sonata for cello and piano; a couple of dozen songs and nine piano pieces, none of them substantial.

(M) *On Hearing the First Cuckoo in Spring* (1912) Though its basis is a Norwegian folksong, and its title clearly states what season Delius had in mind, this short orchestral rhapsody is the very picture of an Edwardian summer afternoon, tea on trim lawns beside heady-scented delphiniums. From its first, unmistakably Delian chord (a sensuously-orchestrated dissonance) its mood never falters: it is a poem in sound, a single inspiration.
→*Summer Night on the River*; *In a Summer Garden*; Butterworth *The Banks of Green Willow*.

Brigg Fair (1907) The form of this 'English Rhapsody' for orchestra is a set of variations (on a Lincolnshire folksong); but the separate sections coalesce and fuse in Delius's ripest, most heartfelt vein, as if trying to capture a single vision of long-past rural happiness. Delius's admirers make claims for his larger works; but his best music is like this piece, unpretentious and exact, like a Monet poppyfield-painting turned into notes.
→ *Song Before Sunrise*; Violin Concerto; Wagner *Siegfried Idyll*; Kodály *Summer Evening*.

DONIZETTI, Gaetano (1797–1848). *Italian composer.*
Donizetti began his musical career as an army bandsman, and it was not until he was twenty-five, when his fourth opera triumphed in Rome, that he was able to work full-time for the theatre. From then until his retirement (for reasons of ill-health) twenty-two years later, he produced operas as a journalist produces news reports: fast (two to five operas a year), effectively and to the point, with little concern for posterity (or even for the day after tomorrow). Many of his operas are empty and slick, strings of showy arias to please audiences greedy for novelty; a handful rise above this competence to excellence (usually because of believable dialogue and lively plots); a very few of those (*L'elisir d'amore*; *Don Pasquale*; *Lucia di Lammermoor*) are outstanding, and put their composer, briefly, in *Rossini's or *Bellini's class.

WORKS Sixty-two operas (including the comedies *L'elisir d'amore*, *La fille du régiment* and *Don Pasquale*, and the serious operas *Lucia di Lammermoor* and *Lucrezia Borgia*); twelve string quartets (charming but shallow); a handful of solo songs and short orchestral works (including a Concertino for cor anglais and orchestra); *Requiem* (composed in memory of Bellini).

'Una furtiva lagrima' ('A Furtive Tear') (from *L'elisir d'amore*, 1832) This is a sobbing tenor love-song, half ironical (he's piling on the grief to convince the girl he loves), half serious. The mixture of farce, cardboard heroics and full-throated melody is what Italian comic opera (especially this one) does best of all.
→ 'Spirto gentil' (from *La favorita*); Verdi 'Celeste Aida' (from *Aida*); Puccini 'O mio babbino caro' (from *Gianni Schicchi*; for soprano).

Ⓜ *Lucia di Lammermoor* (1835) Complete opera. A hot-blooded tale of passion and betrayal, based on Scott's novel *The Bride of Lammermoor*. Splendid skulduggery over forged letters and a false marriage contract (Donizetti was excellent at clothing swift-moving intrigue with tunes); in the superb Act 3 climax, the heroine (unsurprisingly) goes mad and sees visions of her dead true-love. Sublime nonsense, but treated seriously by Donizetti, to sublime effect.
→ *Lucrezia Borgia* (complete opera, this time with fake potions instead of letters); Bellini *La sonnambula*; Verdi *La forza del destino*.

DUKAS. See *One-work Composers*.

DVOŘÁK , Antonín (1841-1904). *Czech composer.*
Dvořák's life progressed as serenely as one of his own symphonies. Until he was thirty-two he worked as a violinist in the orchestra of the Prague National Theatre; he then took a less demanding job in order to spend more time composing. After that the fame of his music spread rapidly: he won a succession of prizes; he was taken up (on *Brahms's recommendation) by Brahms's publisher; leading performers (e.g. the violinist Joachim and the conductor Richter) asked him to write new works. He was showered with honours: a Cambridge doctorate, the directorships of the National Conservatoire of Music, New York, and of the Prague Conservatoire. By the end of his life, this village butcher's son had achieved worldwide fame, and had reached the pinnacle of his profession.

There is nothing extraordinary about this: Dvořák's life has been lived, with minor variations, in a thousand trades. What makes him special is that despite his upward progress towards social and professional eminence, he never lost the innocent freshness of his village childhood, and miraculously recaptured it, time after time, in music. Like *Schubert, he had a gift for spontaneous melody; though he seldom used actual folk-tunes, his music is so steeped in their turns of phrase that real Bohemian folk music, to ears used to Dvořák, tends to sound fake. His admiration for Brahms and *Wagner, and his experience as an orchestral player, helped to discipline his scores: though his works are packed with tunes, the tendency to sprawl is generally kept at bay with careful organization, a balance of bar with bar which (remarkably) seems to increase rather than spoil the freshness of his themes.

ORCHESTRAL WORKS Nine symphonies; five symphonic poems; five overtures (including *Carnival*); Symphonic Variations; *Scherzo capriccioso*; Violin Concerto; Piano Concerto; Cello Concerto; several shorter works including *Serenade for Strings* and *Serenade for Wind*.

Slavonic Dance Op. 46 No. 8 (1878) A fast, rhythmic dance in gypsy style, summoning images in notes alone of every folk-dance ensemble ever seen. Originally for piano duet, it works even better in this red-blooded orchestral version.
→ *Slavonic Dance* Op. 46 No. 1; Smetana *Polka* and *Furiant* (from *The Bartered Bride*); Rimsky-Korsakov *Dance of the Tumblers* (from *The Snow Maiden*).

Serenade for Strings, Op. 22 (1875) Officially a five-movement suite, this sounds more like a chain of endless melodies, delectably scored. As often with Dvořák, this music is insidious: once heard, it is hard to get out of one's head.
→ *Serenade for Wind*, Op. 44; Grieg *Holberg Suite*; Wirén *Serenade for Strings*.

Ⓜ **Symphony No. 9** ('From the New World'), Op. 95 (1893) This is one of the great orchestral warhorses, as beloved as *Beethoven's Symphony No. 5 or *Tchaikovsky's Piano Concerto No. 1 - and like them, every time it's played it comes up fresh as paint. Beguiling; exhilarating; essential.
→ Overture *Carnival*; Ⓜ Symphony No. 5; Tchaikovsky Symphony No. 4.

Cello Concerto, Op. 104 (1895) Concerto fireworks take second place throughout to ravishing melody, with the cello treated as an operatic solo voice singing to the orchestra. It is unlike any other concerto, but nevertheless - as concertos should? - it seems to express the very soul of the solo instrument.
→ Violin Concerto; Tchaikovsky *Rococo Variations*; Saint-Saëns Cello Concerto No. 1.

Ⓜ *Scherzo capriccioso*, Op. 66 (1883) Bouncy tunes, heroic fanfares and exuberant orchestration combine to make a piece that both satisfies and leaves you wanting more. (Fortunately, Dvořák's other works precisely satisfy such wants.)
→ Symphonic Variations; overture *My Home*; Smetana *Vltava* (from *Má vlast*).

Ⓜ **Symphony No. 6,** Op. 60 (1880) Unfairly neglected in favour of Symphonies 7-9, this is Dvořák's orchestral masterpiece, as carefully organized (and as satisfying to the mind) as any Brahms symphony, but crammed with tunes in a way Brahms could only envy. (He once said 'If only I could invent a main theme as glorious as Dvořák's passing thoughts . . .').

→ Ⓜ Symphony No. 7; Symphony No. 5; Schubert 'Unfinished' Symphony.

VOCAL MUSIC   Ten operas (including *The Big-headed Peasants*; *The Jacobin*; *The Devil and Kate*; *Rusalka*); *Stabat mater*, Mass, *Requiem*, *Te Deum* and other shorter works for choir and orchestra; *Amid Nature* for choir; seven song-groups for solo voice and piano (including *Cypresses*; *Gypsy Songs*; *Biblical Songs*).

'Songs my Mother Taught Me' (from *Gypsy Songs*, Op. 55) (1880) This beautiful, sentimental ballad is familiar both as a song and as an instrumental piece beloved of string players (Casals made a swooping cello recording in 1929). It's not the best of the *Gypsy Songs*, even so: the whole group repays exploration.

→ *Moravian Duets*, Op. 32; Brahms *Von ewiger Liebe* ('Everlasting Love'), Op. 43 No. 1; Mendelssohn *Auf Flugeln des Gesanges* ('On Wings of Song'), Op. 34 No. 2.

Ⓜ *Ten Biblical Songs*, Op. 99 (1894) Extracts from the Psalms, set by Dvořák at the climax of his career, and as varied in mood and style (within their devotional framework) as the Psalms themselves.

→ *Four Songs*, Op. 82; Schumann *Six Songs*, Op. 90; Sibelius *Six Songs*, Op. 36.

'Hymn to the Moon' (from opera *Rusalka*) (1900) This smoothly-flowing aria with orchestra is usually performed on its own, and is justly favoured by sopranos, as it gives an unrivalled chance to show off sustained purity of tone. The rest of the opera is forgettable; this aria is a glorious example of Dvořák's effortlessly lyrical vocal style.

→ *Four Duets*, Op. 38 (two voices and piano); Bizet 'In the Depths of the Temple' (*The Pearl Fishers*); Puccini 'One Fine Day' (*Madama Butterfly*); Grieg 'Solveig's Song' (from *Peer Gynt*).

Ⓜ *The Jacobin* (1889) Complete opera. Little-known, but as light-hearted a boy-meets-girl tale of rustic wooing as Smetana's *The Bartered Bride*. Cheerful dialogue, lilting songs, witty ensembles (e.g. the scene where the hero tries to train a band of willing but over-effervescent village musicians).

→ *The Devil and Kate* (complete opera); Smetana *The Bartered Bride*; Weinberger *Schwanda the Bagpiper* (complete opera).

Ⓜ *Stabat mater*, Op. 58 (1877) Our present-day preference for instrumental music over large-scale vocal works has led to unjustified neglect of Dvořák's choral music. This is a notably melodious setting of what in some hands has been a ponderous, over-solemn religious text.

→ Ⓜ *Te Deum*; Mass in D; Schubert Mass in A flat.

CHAMBER AND PIANO WORKS   Eight string quartets (plus several more, early and only recently discovered); two string quintets; String Sextet; four trios for violin, cello and piano; two quartets for violin, viola, cello and piano; Quintet for piano and string quartet; Sonata and other shorter works for violin and piano; roughly 100 short piano pieces, grouped into sets of *Mazurkas*, *Humoresques*, *Eclogues*, etc; sixteen *Slavonic Dances*, *Legends* and *From the Bohemian Forests*, for piano duet; miscellaneous shorter chamber works.

Slavonic Dance Op. 46 No. 4 (1886) Though delightful in orchestral arrangements (especially the set Op. 72), some of the *Slavonic Dances* are equally bubbly in their original piano-duet form. (The rhythmic zest of this one, for example, is smoothed out on the orchestra.) Both versions, in short, are worth exploring.
→ *Slavonic Dance* Op. 72 No. 6; *Legends* Op. 59 (piano-duet version); Handel *Arrival of the Queen of Sheba* (piano-duet version); Martinů *Three Czech Dances* for two pianos.

Ⓜ **Trio No. 4** for violin, cello and piano ('Dumky'), Op. 90 (1891) A *dumka* is a Czech folk-dance with alternating sections of slow and fast (often adapting the same basic material). Dvořák blends this idea with more serious-minded sonata-form, to charming effect. Like his Cello Concerto, the 'Dumky' Trio is less a solemn concert work than a passing-show of melody, grave and gay.
→ Trio No. 2, Op. 26; Schubert Trio No. 1 in B flat; Mendelssohn Trio, Op. 49.

Ⓜ **Quintet for piano and strings**, Op. 81 (1887) In this sunny four-movement work, bright piano tone is contrasted with sinuous or strenuous string lines, but the feeling is one of friendly dialogue rather than of rivalry. Chamber music can wear a forbidding frown, as if daring the listener to enjoy it; this work smiles.
→ Piano Quartet No. 2, Op. 87; String Quartet, Op. 96 ('American'); Borodin String Quartet No. 2.

E

EARLY MUSIC

Professional musicians use this term for music composed before the turn of the seventeenth century, performed nowadays in styles and on instruments as close as possible to the originals. The growth of 'authentic' performing methods has been particularly strong in the last twenty years or so, and they have begun to be applied, with startling and exhilarating results, to the music of later composers too, notably that of *Bach, *Handel, *Haydn and composers of the early nineteenth century. But while this aspect of 'early music' has caught the general public imagination, pre-seventeenth-century music still remains something of a specialist interest, and the work even of its greatest masters (Dufay, *Josquin des Prez, *Monteverdi) is taking longer to enter the musical mainstream than devotees might wish. For listening recommendations, see the articles on Byrd, Corelli, Josquin des Prez, Monteverdi and Palestrina, and especially the composers and works mentioned under *Fifteenth-century Music*, *Sixteenth-century Music*, *Seventeenth-century Music*, and the appropriate sections of *Brass Instruments*, *British and Irish Composers*, *Chamber Music*, *Choral Music*, *Keyboard Instruments*, *String Instruments* and *Vocal Music*.

EIGHTEENTH-CENTURY MUSIC

STYLE AND FORM Eighteenth-century composers were concerned, above most other things, with style and form: not so much what the music 'said' as the way it said it. At the start of the century there were three main styles, each associated with one of the great European nations and as distinctive as a language. French music was generally graceful; German music was generally serious; Italian music generally favoured virtuoso display. A composer could choose a style like a suit of clothes, and let its rules govern his inspiration: *Bach's *Italian Concerto* for harpsichord, for example, is a showpiece, while his *French Suites* are tuneful and gentle and his German-style Partitas combine runs and flourishes with solemn counterpoint.

Less national than these styles, but just as dominating for composers, were a number of strictly-organized musical forms, developed in the seventeenth century and now at a high point of perfection which led most composers to use them above all others. *Opera consisted of alternate recitatives and arias, each written according to specific rules. Religious music (whether German-style Passions, Italian-style Masses or English-style oratorios) also used recitatives and arias, but added large-scale choruses and orchestral interludes. Music for instruments chiefly used the forms of suite, *sonata and *concerto. Each of these major forms, and a score of smaller ones, was followed as closely as cooks follow a recipe, and there were many instruction-books to make sure that everyone used the right ingredients in the proper way.

CONVENTION AND INDIVIDUALITY The strict control of style and form homogenized music: listeners were cosseted against experiments much as readers of romantic novels or thrillers are today. At first, when national styles were dominant, each French-style harpsichord piece, Italian-style *concerto grosso* or German-style motet was much like another. Later, when national styles began to disappear (thanks to the ease with which musicians could travel abroad, and the eagerness of music-lovers in every country to hear and copy the latest foreign fashions), composers devised an international style which became popular everywhere. They called it *le style galant*, 'gallant' or 'elegant' style, and it was notable for its good manners, its undemanding fluency and – compared to even the slightest *Handel or *Mozart piece – for the resolute second-rateness of the music it inspired. J. C. Bach (see the article on C. P. E. Bach) was the *galant* composer whom everyone admired, and while the similarities between his musical language and, say, *Haydn's are obvious, the difference in quality is just as clear. J. C. Bach respected the rules, and they fenced him off from greatness; Haydn used the rules as a starting-point, and it was when he struck out from them that his music leapt in quality.

Striking out was all very well for Haydn: his employers understood that his genius lay in his individuality, and encouraged it. But most patrons and music-lovers took exactly the opposite view. They distrusted individuality, and thought that musical craftsmen, like craftsmen of any other kind, should respect the rules of their trade. Just as a square-wheeled cart, however much it expressed its maker's feelings, would hardly make people rush to buy, so composers who manipulated the standard forms and styles to suit themselves had problems with their customers. Bach regularly quarrelled with the authorities; Mozart found it impossible to stay in regular employment at all; whatever we may think today, the greatest composers of their time were considered to be men like *Vivaldi, *Telemann and J. C. Bach, whose musical carts, however delightful, were

fashioned always with exactly the regulation number and shape of
wheels.

PATRONS, CONCERTS AND PUBLISHERS It may seem extraordinary, given these
conditions, that any musical originality survived at all. It is one of the
miracles of eighteenth-century music that great composers not only per-
severed, but in the process totally changed the public's view of what 'good'
music really was, wrenching them away from good-mannered craftsmanship towards acceptance of the artist's right to self-expression in his work.
The nineteenth century was the great age of musical individuality, but its
roots lay in the work of a handful of eighteenth-century non-conformists,
among them some of the greatest geniuses in the history of the art.

The main reason for their success was the evident superbness of the
works they wrote. Faced with a Mozart opera, a Haydn string quartet or
one of *Beethoven's early piano sonatas, who can seriously quibble about
quality? But there was a second reason, almost equally important: a major
change in the way composers earned their living. Once, patrons had employed them, and naturally expected a say in what they produced. This
tended to breed conformity: if you failed to write the sort of music your
patron required, you could lose your job. But during the eighteenth century patronage of this kind gradually became old-fashioned: more and
more people began going to concerts, and for many composers concert-
giving became an important source of income. Concert listeners are patrons
for one occasion only, and in those days (unlike today) were hungry for
novelty, for the feeling that their ticket-money had bought something
unique: the growth of concerts was thus a powerful incentive towards
experiment. Publication, too, once a way of fawning on your patron (sending gorgeously-printed copies with extravagant dedications), became a
money-making venture: both Handel at the start of the century and
Beethoven at the end of it spent much of their non-composing time hag-
gling with publishers, and Mozart's widow supported her family for years
after his death by the careful control of his publication rights.

Listening Few kinds of 'light' music better suit the gramophone than the
entertainment-works of the eighteenth century. They were written with no more
substantial aims than to give pleasure, and succeed admirably. Since form and
style were so all-controlling, there is delightful continuity: all works for any given
medium, whoever they are by, offer similar pleasures. Three composers, leaders
of the second rank, are particularly worth exploring. Jean-Philippe Rameau (1683-
1764) wrote harpsichord-pieces in the same fanciful, ornate French style as *Couperin, and two dozen operas wittily sending up stories from ancient history or
myth: Les Indes galantes and Platée are among the most enjoyable. Johann Quantz
(1697-1773) was to the flute what Paganini later was to the violin; his concertos
and chamber works (sonatas and trio-sonatas) are plentiful (over 400), expertly

written and unfailingly enjoyable. Michael Haydn (1737–1806) is overshadowed by his brother Joseph and by Mozart (who worked – for a time – for the same employer, the Archbishop of Salzburg); he was one of the most fluent entertainment-music writers of the century, and his symphonies, concertos (especially the Concerto for harpsichord and viola) and church works deserve more hearings than they get. For more music of the same kind, albeit by composers of greater renown, see the articles on C. P. E. Bach, Boccherini, Gluck, Pergolesi, Telemann and Vivaldi. For the most substantial music of the century, see the articles on Bach, Couperin, Handel, Haydn, Mozart, One-work composers (Albinoni) and Scarlatti. See also *Concerto*, *Sonata*, and *Symphony*.

ELGAR , Edward (1857–1934). *English composer.*
The most substantial British composer since *Purcell, Elgar ended Britain's dismal nineteenth-century reputation as 'the land without music', and began the glorious renaissance of the last hundred years. Except that he worked in the arts, not in business, he was an excellent example of the Victorian 'self-made man': by his own efforts he made his way from nowhere (teaching piano and violin and playing in local orchestras) to eminence (international fame with the *'Enigma' Variations* in 1899, a knighthood in 1904 and membership of the Order of Merit, Britain's highest artistic honour, in 1911).

Elgar's music is put together with all a professional's cunning (he was, for example, as dazzling an orchestrator in his style as Richard *Strauss was in his); although at first it seems to swagger with Edwardian self-confidence, a persistent feeling of self-questioning, allied to most un-Edwardian professional skill, undercuts all its ponderousness. (A century or so before, *Haydn's irreverent genius had undercut stiff traditions in much the same way.)

WORKS Two symphonies, Violin Concerto, Cello Concerto, *'Enigma' Variations*, *Falstaff*, *Introduction and Allegro*, *Serenade for Strings*, many marches (including five *Pomp and Circumstance*), overtures (including *Cockaigne* and *In the South*) and suites (including two *Wand of Youth*) for orchestra; several pieces for small or 'light' orchestra, including *Chanson de matin* and *Sospiri*; four oratorios (including *The Dream of Gerontius*), three cantatas and other large works for chorus and orchestra; String Quartet, Piano Quintet, Sonata for violin and piano and a dozen shorter chamber or solo piano works; many (now seldom-performed) part-songs for choir, solo songs and works for speaker and orchestra.

Land of Hope and Glory (*Pomp and Circumstance* March No. 1) (1901) Even without its jingoistic words (of which Elgar disapproved) this is one of the best-loved patriotic pieces in existence, second only to 'Rule Britannia' as an anthem of blazing national pride. It is also magnificent music in its own right: its alternation of bustling excitement and plump big tune sets the style for a thousand imitations, and it beats them all.

→ *Pomp and Circumstance*, March No. 4; Verdi 'Grand March' (*Aida*); Chabrier *Joyeuse marche*; Walton March *Crown Imperial*.

Ⓜ *'Enigma' Variations*, Op. 36 (1899) The inspired idea behind this work (thirteen variations each taking the character of someone Elgar knew, followed by a finale depicting the composer himself) allows the typical Elgar blend of extrovert, public music and haunting private emotion. The variations range from the dashing to the delicate; 'Nimrod' (often played separately) is some of the most sonorous slow music ever written by an Englishman.

→ Overture *Cockaigne*; Tchaikovsky *Rococo Variations* (cello and orchestra); Borodin *Polovtsian Dances*; Strauss *Till Eulenspiegel*.

Ⓜ *Introduction and Allegro*, Op. 47 (1904-5) This is an opulent Edwardian *concerto grosso*: a solo string quartet set against full string orchestra. Much of the music was planned by Elgar on walks in the Malvern Hills, and is as clean-limbed and open-air as that suggests; the solo quartet contributes wistful tunes in quieter vein, and the whole piece ends with a tumbling fugue.

→ *Serenade for Strings* (smaller and lighter); Vaughan Williams *Fantasia on a Theme of Thomas Tallis*; Ireland *Concertino pastorale*.

Ⓜ **Cello Concerto**, Op. 85 (1919) This eloquent work is in Elgar's most affecting 'twilight of empire' style: its slow movement in particular tugs the heart. He wrote it at the end of his composing life, and it stands as a summary of all his art aspired to, and all it could achieve.

→ Violin Concerto (bigger and far more extrovert); Symphony No. 1; Barber Cello Concerto.

Symphony No. 2, Op. 63 (1911) Apart from its funeral-march slow movement (written in memory of Edward VII, and seeming, now, a lament for all the imperial certainties for which he stood), this symphony is ebullient and forceful, in marked contrast with the elegiac Symphony No. 1. Like the *Introduction and Allegro*, it shows Elgar's public manner in full mutton-chop-whiskered, self-assured display.

→ Ⓜ *Falstaff*; Brahms Symphony No. 2; Bliss *A Colour Symphony*.

The Dream of Gerontius, Op. 38 (1900) In Elgar's day, large-scale, dramatic choral works were the peak of a British composer's ambition (as operas were in Italy, symphonies in Germany). Elgar himself composed half a dozen; although sprawling by today's brisk standards, they contain many of his finest pages. Less an oratorio (c.f. *Messiah*, *Elijah*) than a meditation on the soul's immortality (the words are by Cardinal Newman), *The Dream of Gerontius* is predominantly reflective and slow-moving, with some exquisite moments (e.g. 'Angel's Farewell') for both soloists and choir.

→ *Sea Pictures* (heartier, breezier work for soloist and orchestra); oratorio *The Kingdom*; Vaughan Williams *Sancta civitas*.

F

FALLA, Manuel de (1876-1946). *Spanish composer.*

Although he studied at the Madrid Conservatoire (and made his composing début writing *zarzuelas*, Spanish comic operas), Falla really found his style when he moved to Paris in the 1910s and made friends with *Stravinsky, Picasso, Nijinsky and other associates of Diaghilev's Ballets Russes. He blended the sharp-edged modernism he learned from them (as clean-lined as cubist painting) with the long-drawn-out, wailing melodies and twanging guitar-harmonies of Andalusian folk music, and produced a style at once entirely personal and as castanet-clickingly 'Spanish' as the music of a flamenco dance-troupe. Above all, his music has the feeling of melancholy aloofness, of aristocratic disdain, which marks the work of many of the great Spanish artists, the portraits by Goya, say, or still-lifes by Zúrbaran.

WORKS Three operas (including *La vida breve*); two ballets (*Love the Magician*; *The Three-cornered Hat*); *Nights in the Gardens of Spain*, for piano and orchestra; Harpsichord Concerto; a dozen solo piano works (including *Four Spanish Pieces* and *Fantasia Baetica*); *Psyche*, for voice and four instruments; two sets of songs (*Three Songs*; *Seven Popular Spanish Songs*); *L'Atlantida* ('Atlantis'), unfinished cantata for chorus and orchestra; a handful of lesser vocal works.

'Ritual Fire Dance' (from ballet *El amor brujo*, 'Love the Magician') (1915) Originally for orchestra, this was arranged by Falla for piano and by others for every instrumental combination conceivable. It is a fast, foot-stamping dance, originally meant to accompany a garish magic ritual. One of the great pop classics, it is startling, exhilarating, and (especially as a recital encore) enormous fun.
→Whole ballet; 'Spanish Dance' (from *La vida breve*, 'Life is Short'), Prokofiev Toccata Op. 11.

Ⓜ *El sombrero de tres picos* ('The Three-cornered Hat') (1919) Complete ballet. A simple story of rustic trickery, in which a miller and his wife outwit a pompous and lecherous official. Falla's music, often in folk style, is vivid and colourful; the slow music (e.g. 'Miller's Dance', played separately, and in arrangements) is particularly languorous and seductive.

→*Nights in the Gardens of Spain* (an exotic sound-picture of evening scenes, for piano and orchestra); *Four Spanish Pieces* (piano solo); Milhaud *Le Carnaval d'Aix*.

Ⓜ *Seven Popular Spanish Songs* (1922) Epigrammatic song-settings, catching the atmosphere of Spain in short, simple melodies and uncluttered chords. Also arranged for violin, and as a solo piano suite.
→*El retablo de Maese Pedro* ('Master Peter's Puppet Show', a chamber opera based on a story from *Don Quixote*); *Three Songs* (French words); Ravel *Histoires naturelles*.

Ⓜ *Harpsichord Concerto* (1926) The harpsichord clatters and jangles in sprightly, neo-eighteenth-century style (like *Scarlatti made over by *Stravinsky); the five accompanying instruments (there is no orchestra) provide a primary-coloured accompaniment. The central movement is wonderfully solemn, a pigeon-toed processional. A short, superbly crafted work, Falla's instrumental masterpiece.
→*Fantasia Baetica* (piano solo); Ravel *Introduction and Allegro* (harp and six instruments); Martinů Harpsichord Concerto.

FAURÉ, Gabriel (1845-1924). *French composer.*
When he was nine, Fauré was one of the first pupils at the newly-formed Niedermeyer 'School of Religious and Classical Music' in Paris; he stayed for eleven years, became a skilled organist and choir-trainer, and also (in his senior years) assisted with the teaching, an experience which formed his life. After army service and some time as a provincial organist he settled in Paris, where he led a hectic life conducting choirs, playing the organ at several churches (including the Madeleine), teaching at the Niedermeyer School and at the Paris Conservatoire of Music. When he retired from teaching in 1905, he was immediately appointed Director of the Conservatoire, and - somewhat unexpectedly after such a conformist early life - became one of the most forward-looking figures in French musical life, brushing stuffier traditions aside and encouraging 'new music' and the work of such 'advanced' young composers as *Ravel, Koechlin and Florent Schmitt.

Until he was in his sixties, Fauré specialized in the smaller forms of composition: incidental music to plays, piano pieces and songs (at which he was a supreme master). The works of his last two decades are much larger in scope: the songs are grouped in cycles, there is a full-length opera (*Pénélope*) and there are seven big chamber works. He used to be regarded as a composer of easy-going, exquisite trifles (and the description certainly fits his best-known works, e.g. *Pavane* or *Dolly Suite*); now that his longer works are better-known, he is clearly a far more substantial composer, similar in stature to *Schumann or *Chopin.

WORKS Three stage works (including the opera *Pénélope*, based on Homer's *Odyssey*); seven orchestral suites, some based on incidental music for plays (including *Masques et Bergamasques* and *Pelléas et Melisande*); a number of other short orchestral works including *Pavane* and Ballade for piano and orchestra; *Requiem* and several shorter choral works; ninety-six songs (including song-cycles *La bonne chanson*, *Mirages* and *L'horizon chimérique*); thirty-four opus numbers of nocturnes, impromptus, barcarolles and other solo-piano pieces; *Dolly Suite* for piano duet; String Quartet; two piano quintets; two piano quartets; Trio for violin, cello and piano; two sonatas for violin and piano; two sonatas for cello and piano; other smaller chamber works including *Élégie* for cello and piano.

Pavane (1887) Fauré was attracted by the cool clarity of ancient Greek civilization, and wrote several works in limpid classical style. This is the best-known: a beautiful flute melody over plucked strings, like a grave dance on a painted vase.
→ *Élégie* (cello and piano); Satie *Gymnopédie* No. 1; Debussy *Syrinx* (solo flute).

Ⓜ *Masques et Bergamasques* (1919) A suite of four short movements in charming, bustling style. Like *Sibelius, Fauré produced a large quantity of delightful light music, a smiling counterpart to his larger concert works. Though unpretentious, this suite is one of his best compositions: the overture in particular is a near-perfect miniature, equalled only by the tiny overture in *Tchaikovsky's *Nutcracker Suite*.
→*Dolly Suite* (for piano duet or orchestra); Debussy *Petite suite* (piano duet or orchestra); Sibelius suite *King Christian II*.

Ⓜ *Requiem* (1888-9) One of the best-loved of all choral works, this quiet, reflective music avoids the declamatory gestures of most composers' *Requiems*. One movement, 'Pié Jésu', for solo treble (often sung separately), seems exactly the right music to be sung by angels in renaissance paintings of heavenly choirs. It could be sugary or sentimental; thanks to brevity and sincerity, it never is.
→*Cantique de Jean Racine*; Verdi 'Ave Maria' (from *Four Sacred Pieces*); Poulenc Mass in G.

Piano Pieces Op. 104 (1910) Fauré consciously modelled his piano music on *Chopin's, giving his pieces poetic titles (Impromptu, Caprice, etc.), and working them up into often substantial compositions without losing the rhapsodic, improvisatory feeling. This set contains pieces in his favourite styles, Nocturne and Barcarolle.
→*Three Nocturnes*, Op. 33; *Préludes*, Op. 103; Chopin Nocturne, Op. 72.

Ⓜ Piano Quintet No. 2, Op. 115 (1921) Piano quintets are fairly rare, as the combination of forces seems to require a too-sonorous, too 'symphonic' composition-style. This is one of the three or four masterpieces in the genre; opaque and elusive at first, on rehearings it reveals tough construction under the unruffled surface.

→Piano Trio, Op. 120; Schumann Piano Quintet; Elgar Piano Quintet.

Ⓜ *L'horizon chimérique* (1921) Fauré's individual songs (e.g. 'Après un rêve', Op. 7 No. 1; 'Clair de lune', Op. 46 No. 2; 'Le parfum impérissable', Op. 76 No. 1) may be better known, but his reputation as France's greatest song-writer, the equal of Schumann or *Wolf, rests on his half-dozen song-cycles, of which this is the last and greatest. Four poems of turbulence and yearning (the lover's quest compared to a traveller's) are linked in mood and style to form a coherent, weighty chamber work.

→Song-cycle Ⓜ *Mirages; L'invitation au voyage*; Poulenc song-cycle *Tel jour telle nuit*.

FIFTEENTH-CENTURY MUSIC

For music historians, few periods are more rewarding than the fifteenth century. Until then, although there had been a few individual musicians of genius (e.g. Guillaume de Machaut, whose church music is still occasionally heard), most music was anonymous, and the function it served (church worship or secular entertainment) was more important than any individual artistic contribution. By the end of the century, however, things had completely changed. Not only had the art of composition developed to the point where music tended to dominate the occasions at which it was performed, and not only had the seed been sown for the glories of sixteenth-century church music (one of the most sumptuous of all human artistic achievements), but several world-ranking composers – Dufay, Ockeghem, *Josquin des Prez – had produced work as individual and staggering for its time as *Haydn's or *Mozart's was for theirs.

One of the main reasons for this growth in excellence was the existence of hundreds of small European courts (over 300 in Germany alone), each seeking to outdo the others in magnificence. Fifteenth-century princes employed artists of all kinds, including musicians, and encouraged them to advance their arts in the most sumptuous and extravagant ways possible. Ducal chapels, in particular, and the monasteries allied to the courts or favoured by them, were places for extravagant public show, for forms of worship as flamboyant as a modern coronation. To serve this grandeur, court composers began using elaborate, winding counterpoint, and the kind of warm harmony people had previously considered more suitable for secular love-songs than for the worship of God. Choirs were formed (often with their own choirschools, offering a magnificent training to boys of musical ability), and the more skilled they became the more challenging was the music composers wrote for them.

In social life away from church, music provided either ceremony or entertainment. Ceremonial music consisted of fanfares, praise-songs, celebrations of birth, marriage and victory (e.g. the rollicking *Agincourt Song*, popular, in Britain at least, from 1415 right through to Shakespeare's time), and – a favourite form of the time – 'deplorations', or laments for some distinguished person's death. Entertainment music was intended either as a background to eating, hunting, embroidery or conversation (and was suitably self-effacing) or to be listened to and enjoyed for its own sake. Some of this secular music remained robustly simple, but composers at the more extravagant courts combined the rich new church styles with folk-dance rhythms, with everyday instruments (banned from church) and with distinctly frivolous, non-religious words (e.g. about hunting, sex and love), producing a secular style more 'artistic' and elegant than anything known before in music.

Listening For modern listeners, whether at concerts or on records, the easiest way to enter the fifteenth-century repertoire is through anthologies. In the last thirty years there has been enormous interest in 'early music', and many soloists and groups now specialize in performing pre-Renaissance court, ceremonial and religious works. (Since many of the pieces are short, they are grouped together in a way no fifteenth-century listener would have expected or understood, but the music is little the worse for that.) The fifteenth-century Burgundian court was particularly rich in composers, and anthologies of Burgundian music are recommended above all others.

The second way into the period is to listen to music by four of its leading composers. Guillaume Dufay (*c.* 1400-1474) was a Burgundian composer, renowned in his day for church music (e.g. the Mass *Se la face ay pale*), but also remembered nowadays for the syncopated rhythm, bright harmony and witty tunes of his songs and other secular works. Antoine Busnois (died 1492) was court composer to Charles the Bold of Burgundy, and specialized in cheerful part-songs, ancestors of the jolliest kind of madrigal (see *Vocal Music*) or of the patter-songs in comic operas. Johannes Ockeghem (*c.* 1410-1497), master of the French Chapel Royal, was considered the finest church composer of the age. His pupils (among them Josquin) carried his style throughout Europe; he is the true father of the sensuous counterpoint which dominated church music for the next two centuries, and his own works (e.g. the Mass *Ecce ancilla Domini*) are among its jewels. For music by the fourth and greatest composer, the *Beethoven of the fifteenth century, see the article on Josquin des Prez.

FRANCK, César (1822–90). *Belgian/French composer.*
Like *Fauré, Franck spent his non-composing life teaching, and playing the

organ. (His organ-playing was famous: the Archbishop of Paris once said to his priest, 'What a marvellous intercessor you have here, my son. He'll bring more souls to God than we ever can.') His teaching was chiefly done at the Paris Conservatoire. But unlike Fauré (who encouraged his pupils there to follow their own inspiration, however far it seemed to lead them from usual paths), Franck taught adherence to the rules. Because his favoured composers were *Bach and *Liszt, the rules he taught were those of Bachian counterpoint and lush Lisztian harmony. His own works show exactly the style he meant. At their worst they ramble, sounding like any competent organist's after-the-service improvisations; but whenever he built a piece on really good tunes (e.g. the works recommended below), he gave it wings.

works Three operas; Symphony and three symphonic poems for orchestra; *Symphonic Variations*; two Masses and six other religious choral works (including *Panis angelicus*); String Quartet; Piano Quintet; four trios for violin, cello and piano; Sonata for violin and piano; forty-seven pieces for organ (including *Three Chorales*) and fifty-nine for harmonium (or organ without pedals) for church use; half a dozen solo piano works (including *Prelude, Chorale and Fugue*).

Symphonic Variations for piano and orchestra (1885) Franck admired Liszt's idea of building works on ever-changing aspects of one or more main themes. Here a languishing, sighing idea is first treated with *Wagnerian solemnity, and is then gradually perked up until the work closes with a skipping dance-movement, the theme transformed into a paper-boy-whistleable tune.
→Symphonic poem *Les djinns* ('The Sprites') (piano and orchestra); Saint-Saëns *Wedding-cake Caprice*; d'Indy *Symphony on a French Mountain Song*.

Symphony (1888) Once overplayed, this long, Wagnerian work is now sadly neglected. It is somewhat 'samey' in sound, but its purposeful exploration of a single, memorable theme and its urgency of mood affect in much the same way as *Bruckner's (not dissimilar) Wagner-inspired orchestral works.
→Symphonic poem *Le chasseur maudit*; Liszt *Faust Symphony*; Saint-Saëns Symphony No. 3 ('Organ' Symphony).

Ⓜ **Sonata for violin and piano** (1886) Franck is thought to have been the model for the composer Vinteuil in Proust's novel *Remembrance of Time Past*, and this sonata may have suggested the one whose 'little phrase' (the opening, questioning few notes? the striding, canonic theme of the last movement?) is an instantly-recognizable signal of good taste to all Parisian high society. It is instantly recognizable to non-Proustians too, one of the best-known and happiest works in the chamber-music repertoire. (Versions exist for viola, cello and even flute, and prove that Franck's first choice of violin was right.)
→Ⓜ *Prelude, Chorale and Fugue* (forceful virtuoso work for solo piano); Grieg Violin Sonata No. 3; Saint-Saëns Violin Sonata No. 1.

G

GERSHWIN, George (1898-1937). *American composer.*

When he was six, Gershwin heard a mechanical piano playing Rubinstein's *Melody in F*, and decided to become a professional musician. His parents thought he was a budding concert-pianist (and indeed in adult life he often played the solo parts in his own Piano Concerto and *Rhapsody in Blue*), but when he left school he went to work for a music-publisher, accompanying 'song-pluggers' (salesmen who demonstrated new songs in music shops). His first composition was published when he was eighteen; his first hit ('Swanee', made famous by Al Jolson) was written when he was nineteen; his first Broadway musical (*La La Lucille*) was performed when he was twenty. From then until his death he poured out hit songs, Broadway shows and film musicals: he specialized in the kind of light-hearted, soft-shoe-shuffle-and-tap, boy-meets-girl dance-romances immortalized by Fred Astaire (for whom he wrote *Funny Face* in 1927 and *Shall We Dance?* in 1937). Apart from his songs' success with crooners and big-band singers, they were enormously popular with jazz musicians too, their unexpected rhythms and cunning harmony (influenced by, among others, *Debussy and Richard *Strauss) offering inspiration and challenge which outran the usual Tin-Pan-Alley products as tigers outrun pussy-cats.

In parallel with his popular music, Gershwin also wrote 'serious' works (the ones chiefly recommended here). He brought to them sharp jazz rhythms and the urgent melancholy style of Blues singing; above all he filled them with the instantly-hummable tunes which make them hits.

WORKS Operas *Porgy and Bess*, *Blue Monday/135th Street;* nineteen musicals (including *Lady Be Good*, *Funny Face* and *Girl Crazy*); six film musicals (including *Shall We Dance?* and *The Goldwyn Follies*); Concerto, *Rhapsody in Blue*, Variations on 'I got Rhythm' and *Second Rhapsody* for piano and orchestra; *Cuban Overture*; *An American in Paris*; three Preludes for solo piano; over 150 songs (including 'Swanee', 'Embraceable You', 'I got Rhythm', 'S'Wonderful' and 'Lady be Good').

Ⓜ*Porgy and Bess* (1935) Gershwin's masterpiece, at once an opera to match anything by, say, *Puccini and a musical show crammed with hits. Its songs (e.g.

87

'Summertime'; 'I got Plenty of Nuthin' '; 'Bess, You is my Woman now'; 'It ain't Necessarily So') are often sung separately; there are also the 'Symphonic Picture' *Porgy and Bess* and the suite *Catfish Row* for orchestra, excellent abridgements of the music though lacking the wit and pathos of the words. But the whole opera (a tragic love-story set among poor Southern blacks) turns its potentially maudlin or patronizing material into a moving work of art.

→Individual songs: 'S'wonderful'; Ⓜ 'I got Rhythm'; 'Shall we Dance?'; musical *Funny Face*; Kern *Showboat*; Puccini opera *La bohème*.

Rhapsody in Blue (1924) Jazz-style fast music; big blues tune; piano-and-orchestra style recalling *Rachmaninov's Concerto No. 2 - this is Gershwin's blend of light and serious music at its breeziest. (There is a fascinating recording by Gershwin himself, transcribed from a 1920s piano roll.)

→*An American in Paris* (orchestra alone); Piano Concerto; Rodgers *Slaughter on Tenth Avenue*.

GLINKA. See *One-work Composers*.

GLUCK, Christoph Willibald (1714-87). *German composer*

After university (where he studied philosophy as well as music) Gluck spent eighteen years travelling about Europe, providing operas and other stage-entertainments of all kinds, and giving recitals on the cello and the musical glasses. In 1754 he became composer-in-chief of the Imperial Theatre in Vienna. There, with four like-minded colleagues (one of them the poet and librettist Ranieri Calzabigi), he founded an operatic 'reform group'. The group's aim was to bring opera nearer to the style of old Greek tragedy (its starting-point: see the article on *Opera*); in particular, they wanted to cut down show-arias and to remove all voice-and-harpsichord recitative (see Glossary: *Recitative*) so that the effect would be continuously dramatic instead of a sequence of loosely-connected 'turns'.

Gluck composed six 'reform' operas, all on stories from Greek myth, and they made him one of the most admired composers in Europe. (He was particularly well-liked in Paris, where his last three operas had their *premières*.) His work paved the way for the grand operas of the nineteenth century (e.g. *Wagner's music-dramas and the operas of *Verdi and *Puccini); but instead of nineteenth-century blood-and-thunder they are cool and classical, very much in the manner of the Greek myths he chose to tell. To opera-lovers brought up on the later composers he influenced, this can sometimes make Gluck seem tame; but for those who love his style, his works are as refreshingly far away from tub-thumping as a glass of water is from a goblet of heady wine.

WORKS Thirty operas (the six 'reform' operas are *Orfeo, Alceste, Paris and Helen, Iphigenia in Tauris, Iphigenia at Aulis* and *Armide*); two ballets (*Don Juan, Semiramide*); six trio-sonatas; nine symphonies; *De profundis* for un-accompanied choir.

'Divinités du Styx' (from opera Ⓜ *Alceste*, 1767) *Alceste* was Gluck's second 'reform' opera, and is the most 'Greek' of them all in style. Its story (based on Euripides' play about a queen who sacrifices her life to save her husband's), for all its passion and intensity, is told in calmly-flowing melodies and serene harmonies which seem, paradoxically, to increase rather than to lessen its emotional power. (It is close in mood to the French classical tragedies of Racine and Corneille: no wonder Gluck was so popular in France.) The whole opera takes several hearings to make its full effect; this aria gives an ideal flavour of its – and Gluck's – gentle style.
→'O del mio dolce amor' (from opera *Paris and Helen*); Purcell 'When I am Laid in Earth' (from opera *Dido and Aeneas*); Mozart 'Ruhe sanft' (from opera *Zaide*).

Ⓜ *Orfeo* (1762) Complete opera. Gluck's best-known opera tells the story of Orpheus and Eurydice (a favourite of opera-composers: see, e.g., Monteverdi and Offenbach). It is in 'reform' style, except that it uses the earlier eighteenth-century idea of having a male soprano as the hero (nowadays, the part is sung by a woman): this casting gives it a remote, unearthly atmosphere ideally suited to the story. Its calm beauty comes over particularly well on records: this is one of the rare operas as effective in the imagination as in the theatre. Two extracts are popular in their own right: the lament Ⓜ 'Che farò senza Eurydice' ('What shall I do without Eurydice') and the 'Dance of the Blessed Spirits', a poised flute melody contrasted with rushing strings.
→*Armide*; Purcell *Dido and Aeneas*; Fauré *Pénélope*.

GOUNOD. See *One-work Composers*.

GRANADOS, Enrique (1867–1916). *Spanish pianist and composer*.
Although he had some success as a theatre composer (with light operas in folk style, Spanish equivalents of *The Bartered Bride*), Granados's musical life centred on the piano. He ran a piano-academy in Barcelona, and was an international concert soloist, touring as far afield as the USA and Hungary. (He died on his way home from one of these tours, when his liner was torpedoed during the First World War.) His lighter piano pieces are enormously popular, known to many people who have never heard of Granados himself: they are in a bright 'Spanish' style close to that of *Albéniz. But Granados was a far more refined composer than this implies,

with a sensitivity and delicacy reminiscent of *Chopin's. This side of him is best heard in his plaintive *tonadillas* (songs, usually to words about wistful love-affairs) and in his masterpiece, the piano suite *Goyescas*: without sacrificing Spanishness or tunefulness, they reach worlds of feeling far beyond his lighter works.

WORKS Six operas; five suites, *Three Spanish Dances* and two other orchestral works; Piano Trio; eight sets of solo piano pieces (including *Goyescas*; *Twelve Spanish Dances*); three song-sets (including *La maja dolorosa* and *Songs in the Ancient Style*) and a handful of individual songs.

'Andaluza' (*Spanish Dance* Op. 37 No. 5) Originally a piano solo, this piece is most popular in a thrumming guitar arrangement: the essence of Spain, and of the guitar, it seems, in a handful of chords.
→'La maja de Goya' (*Tonadillas* No. 1) (song, arr. guitar); Albéniz *Asturias* Op. 47 No. 5 (arr. guitar); Villa Lobos Guitar Prelude No. 1.

Ⓜ *Goyescas* (1911) This suite of seven piano pieces after Goya paintings is best heard complete, though No. 4, 'The Girl and the Nightingale', a gentle lament, is often played separately (sometimes as an orchestral interlude, taken from the opera *Goyescas* derived from these pieces).
→*Poetic Scenes*; Falla *Four Spanish Pieces*; Fauré *Barcarolles*, Op. 105.

GRIEG, Edvard (1843–1907). *Norwegian composer.*
When Grieg was a boy, his teachers forecast a brilliant future for him as a concert pianist. But he studied so hard that he ruined his health, and had to settle for a quieter life teaching and composing in Oslo and Copenhagen. In 1874, however, he was given a life-pension by the Norwegian government, and the financial security this brought enabled him to begin a gentler concert career than that of piano virtuoso: he went on tours with his wife (a soprano), giving recitals of songs and piano pieces. His pension also freed him from the need to write in the large-scale forms (*sonata, *symphony, *opera) expected of the day's leading composers, and to concentrate on the shorter kind of works at which he excelled. His finest pieces are Romantic miniatures (songs, piano pieces, dances) in a simple style derived from Norwegian folk music. He gathered many of them into groups (orchestral suites; *Lyric Pieces* for piano; sets of songs) and so satisfied the taste of the time without betraying his own intimate, poetic style.

WORKS Piano Concerto; Symphony (early; uncharacteristic); *Symphonic Dances*; overture *In Autumn*; nine orchestral suites (including two *Peer*

Gynt suites, *Sigurd Jorsalfa Suite* and *Holberg Suite*); seven works for chorus, or solo voice, and orchestra; three violin sonatas; Cello Sonata; String Quartet; Sonata and twenty-two opus numbers of individual pieces for piano (including ten books of *Lyric Pieces*); *Four Norwegian Dances* and three other works for piano duet; 143 solo songs in twenty-three sets (including song-cycle *The Mountain Maid*).

Peer Gynt Suite No. 1, Op. 46 (final version 1888) Out of his incidental music for Ibsen's huge poetic play, Grieg made two self-contained orchestral suites. This one has four movements ('Morning'; 'Aase's Death'; 'Anitra's Dance'; 'In the Hall of the Mountain King'), among the most enduring light music he composed.
→*Peer Gynt Suite* No. 2, Op. 55; suite *Sigurd Jorsalfa*, Op. 56; Bizet *L'Arlésienne Suite* No. 1.

Songs: 'Solvejg's Song', Op. 23 No. 1; 'I Love Thee', Op. 5 No. 3; *Haugtussa* ('The Mountain Maid') (song-cycle, Op. 67) Grieg's songs have the simplicity of folksongs – straightforward melodies accompanied by unfussy chords. Even the eight songs in *Haugtussa*, his most elaborate collection (telling of a young shepherd girl's life and love), are more like a group of folksongs than the grand song-groups of *Schumann or *Brahms. The precision is that of poetry; the inspiration seems instantaneous, exact, requiring no artifice. Two of his most heartfelt songs, 'Heart's Wound' and 'Last Spring' (from Op. 33), exist also in plaintive orchestral arrangements.
→'Autumn Song', Op. 18 No. 3; 'From Monte Pincio', Op. 39 No. 5; Wolf *Italian Songbook*.

Lyric Pieces There are altogether sixty-nine lyric pieces for piano, in ten books. Some (e.g. 'The Butterfly', Op. 43 No. 1; 'Notturno', Op. 54 No. 4) are miniature concert-pieces, like Mendelssohn's *Songs without Words*; others (e.g. 'Halling', Op. 47 No. 4; 'March of the Dwarfs', Op. 54 No. 3; 'Wedding-day at Troldhaugen', Op. 65 No. 6) are in Grieg's most pictorial, 'Norwegian' style. Several (including 'Wedding-day' and four pieces from Op. 54 regrouped as the *Lyric Suite*) also exist in lively orchestral arrangements.
→*Ballade* (*Variations on a Norwegian Folksong*), Op. 24; Schumann *Album for the Young*, Op. 68; Macdowell *Piano Pieces*, Op. 55.

Symphonic Dances, Op. 64 (1898) Originally for piano duet, these four pieces were later orchestrated. They are an exact Norwegian parallel, for gaiety and colour, to *Dvořák's *Slavonic Dances*.
→*Four Norwegian Dances*, Op. 35; *Holberg Suite*, Op. 40; Weinberger Polka and Fugue (from *Schwanda the Bagpiper*).

Ⓜ **Piano Concerto**, Op. 16 (1868) Grieg's largest and most popular work, this combines the wistfulness and tunefulness of his folksong style with all the heroic bravura required by the concerto form. One of the half-dozen best-loved works in the concert repertoire.
→ Piano Sonata; Schumann Piano Concerto; Mendelssohn Piano Concerto No. 1.

H

HANDEL, George Frideric (1685-1759). *German/English composer.*

By the time he was seventeen (and at university, studying law), Handel's gifts as a keyboard-player were evident, and it was not long before he settled for a musical career. At first he concentrated on playing – he became one of the most renowned virtuosos of the day, on both organ and harpsichord – but when he was twenty he had great success with an Italian opera, and decided to turn his talents to composing for the stage. For the next four years he worked in Italy, met leading musicians (e.g. the aging *Corelli, whose violin-playing he thought old-fashioned but whose compositions he admired) and wrote his first big church and theatre works. In 1710, attracted by the popularity of Italian opera in London, he went to England, where he stayed for the rest of his life. (He took British nationality in 1727.)

Handel was idolized by fashionable Londoners. Queen Anne (and later George I) favoured him with a royal pension, lords and ladies vied to have him play at high-society parties, and his Italian operas, written for the Queen's Theatre in the Haymarket (which he also managed), were the talk of the town. He became a kind of unofficial Master of the Royal Music, and his works for state occasions (e.g. the *Birthday Ode for Queen Anne*, the *Te Deum* and *Jubilate* to celebrate the Peace of Utrecht, the four coronation anthems for George II) were as glitteringly successful as *Purcell's had been a generation earlier. He wrote chamber music for aristocratic parties, and suites and other teaching-pieces for his keyboard-pupils. And once or twice each year, for twenty years, he wrote and produced a new opera for the Haymarket.

In the early 1730s, the fashion for Italian opera waned. It was a showy, artificial form, notable chiefly for the singers' vocal gymnastics and the expensive dazzle of sets and costumes. Gay's *The Beggar's Opera* (first performed in 1728) set a new fashion for English theatre-entertainment, much less gaudy, more interesting dramatically and far easier to follow. After its success, Handel wrote a few more Italian operas, but he also turned to a new musical form: the oratorio. For this, he had Bible stories dramatized (in English), then set them to music with the same verve as his operas, but in a more forthright musical style and incorporating the kind of majestic choruses which had given his odes and church works their dignity. As interludes during oratorio-performances he played organ solos or concertos, recalling the virtuosity of his youth. Thus the new recipe brilliantly used ingredients from all his past successes, and brought him a second twenty years of public acclaim. He went on performing well into his seventies, despite failing health (and, for his last seven years, blindness); when he died he was considered the greatest composer to have lived in Britain, and more than 3000 people attended his funeral in Westminster Abbey.

Handel was a devout Christian, and the Lutheran Protestant roots of his musical style were similar to *Bach's. (They can be heard particularly clearly in his church and ceremonial works.) His years as an opera-composer, however, lightened and softened his style. He was ready to move in an instant from intellectual seriousness to dramatic show, and the balance between them gives his music a surefooted clarity some of his contemporaries lacked. He composed an enormous amount of music, even for the time, and regularly adapted or recomposed works he liked. (The same music, for example, serves as the chorus 'Lift Up Your Heads' in *Messiah* and, speeded up, as one movement of the orchestral *Concerto a due cori* No. 2; the Recorder Sonata Op. 1 No. 11 reappears as the Organ Concerto No. 4.) For 150 years after his death, his church works and oratorios fascinated the British, who performed them in a heavy-footed, solemn way (with massed choirs and enormous orchestras) which had little to do with Handel's own lean style. It is only recently, as the rest of his music has become known (especially his operas and chamber works), and particularly since efforts have been made to play it in the way he wrote it instead of in plump Victorian arrangements, that he has been revealed as one of the most dexterous and witty composers of his century. (Although the music is quite different, stripping the varnish from it has had the same beneficial effect as it has on Bach's.)

VOCAL WORKS Forty-six operas (including *Agrippina*; *Ariodante*; *Berenice*; *Julius Caesar*; *Serse*); thirty oratorios and other large-scale dramatic works (including *Acis and Galatea*; *Alexander's Feast*; *Judas Maccabaeus*; *Messiah*; *Occasional Oratorio*; *Samson*; *Saul*); eleven Chandos anthems, four coronation anthems, two *Te Deums*, *Gloria*, *Birthday Ode*, *Funeral Ode* and other smaller choral works; over 150 chamber cantatas, duets and solo songs.

Oratorios and other choral works Ⓜ *Messiah* (1741). Few musical works have ever caught public affection so quickly, or held it for so long, as this dramatic presentation of the life and nature of Christ. The reason is partly its subject-matter, partly the sturdy certainty with which it is treated – Handel's own sure faith seems to blaze in every bar, a remarkable musical phenomenon – and perhaps most of all the magnificence of the music. *Messiah* uses operatic forms (recitatives, arias, choruses) but is meant for concert use, not stage: this allows Handel to give

the narrative dramatic shape without the distractions of stage movement or costume. The work's chief glory is its choruses ('For unto Us a Child is Born'; 'All We Like Sheep'; 'Hallelujah!'), which draw the listener into the experience in a uniquely affecting way; the arias ('He Shall Feed His Flock'; 'Why do the Nations so Furiously Rage Together?'; 'I Know that my Redeemer Liveth'; 'The Trumpet Shall Sound') personalize the work's message in a different way, allowing us as it were to reflect on individual Christian testimony. This shifting involvement is what makes *Messiah* such a personal experience – of other similar works, only Bach's *St Matthew Passion* depends on and controls the listener's response to anything like the same extent – and although Handel's other oratorios are fine works, none shares its incandescent power. Of the oratorios on biblical themes, the best-known (and best) are *Saul, Israel in Egypt, Samson,* Ⓜ *Judas Maccabaeus* and *Solomon*. They are full of splendid movements (e.g. Ⓜ 'Let the Bright Seraphim' from *Samson,* 'See the Conquering Hero Comes' from *Judas Maccabaeus* or the bustling string-orchestra 'Arrival of the Queen of Sheba' from *Solomon*), but never 'gel' as musical experiences as *Messiah* does. If unity as well as musical magnificence is a criterion, Handel's non-biblical oratorios are better, and the best of them are Ⓜ *Alexander's Feast* (1736), an ornate setting of Dryden's *Ode for Saint Cecilia's Day*, bubbling with the feeling of occasion, and his version of Milton's *L'Allegro, il Pensieroso* (and, in an added section, *Il moderato*) (1740), which treats somewhat ponderous philosophical poetry ('Hence, loathéd melancholy!') as if it were a vigorous opera-libretto. Of Handel's other choral works, the majority are solemn odes for church or state use: the coronation anthems (especially *My Heart is Inditing* and *Zadok the Priest*) are majestic, slow-moving and ideal for the solemnities they adorn, the eleven Chandos anthems, written for a private chapel, are graceful and intimate, nearer in spirit to Purcell than to Bach.
→ The works mentioned above lead best to one another, and offer plenty of Handelian splendour to feast the ear. Good follow-ups by other composers might be, to the oratorios, *Telemann *The Day of Judgement* and *Haydn *The Creation* and *The Seasons*, and to the big choral works, Purcell *Ode on Saint Cecilia's Day* and Bach *Magnificat*.

Operas and cantatas 'Ombra mai fù'/'Handel's Largo' (from opera *Serse*, 1738) For over 150 years, Handel's operas were quarried for short, single pieces, like this beautiful slow melody, the orchestral Minuet from *Berenice* or firework-display arias like 'V'adoro pupille' from *Julius Caesar*. In the last fifty years or so, complete operas have been revived, and some (e.g. *Agrippina,* 1709, *Julius Caesar,* 1724, and Ⓜ *Alcina,* 1735) have taken the stage admirably. But there are problems. Operatic fashions have so drastically changed (see *Opera*) that the style of Handel's librettos, and even some of his music, has been left uncomfortably high and dry. In particular, his audiences loved intrigue, plot and counter-plot conducted in long stretches of recitative (see Glossary, *Recitative*): this can take up over half the opera's performance-time, and (especially to audiences without Italian) can be a trial of patience. The arias come regularly every ten minutes or so, as if rewards for good behaviour, and although they are often superb, their effect can be diminished both by their musical surroundings and by their inordinate length. Add to this the fact that the leading male roles were often written for *castrati* (male sopranos) and are nowadays either transposed for tenors or sung by women dressed as men, and the obstacles to enjoying a Handel opera, at least in the theatre, are manifest. Those who surmount these obstacles maintain that the operas contain his finest work; other listeners may prefer to enter their world through short extracts like those mentioned above, or by less demanding doors such as the delightful pastoral interlude (in English) Ⓜ *Acis and Galatea* (1718), on a boy-meets-girl-meets-monster story from Greek mythology, or the short dramatic cantatas, like twenty-minute operas for solo voice, which he wrote for favoured singers. (Fine examples are *Ah, crudel!* ('Oh, cruel!'), a furiously griefstricken denunciation, and *Mi palpita il cor* ('My Heart Flutters'), an expression of tremulous passion as immediate and touching as Cherubino's aria 'Non so più' in *Mozart's opera *The Marriage of Figaro*.)

→ Pergolesi *La serva padrona* (cheeky, short and comic); Bach *Coffee Cantata* (bucolic and whimsical – the lady's addiction is to coffee, when it should be to love); Bononcini *Griselda* (an intrigue-opera to equal any of Handel's, by the 1720s rival whose feuds with him made one wit remark, 'Some say that next to Bononcinny/Mynheer Handel's but a ninny; /Others aver that he to Handel/Is scarcely fit to hold a candle').

INSTRUMENTAL WORKS *Water Music*, *Music for the Royal Fireworks* and twenty-five *concerti grossi* for orchestra; eighteen organ concertos (several also arranged for other solo instruments); several dozen sonatas and trio-sonatas for wind or string instruments and continuo; sixteen suites, six fugues and many shorter pieces for solo harpsichord.

Orchestral music and concertos Ⓜ *Water Music* (probably 1717). This group of twenty short pieces (airs, minuets, fugues, hornpipes and arias) was written for a royal barge-procession on the Thames, and is given an appropriately outdoor sound by the highlighting of oboes and horns in the orchestra and by the striding simplicity of its tunes and harmony. It is light music, with no ambition except to entertain, and its bright runs and breezy counterpoint show Handel at his most debonair. Later conductors pillaged it for concert suites – one of the best, full of the sound of horns and drums, is Harty's arrangement of five movements for modern orchestra – but all are eclipsed by Handel's clean-cut original, now usually performed complete but easily sampled movement by movement or in the three *concerti grossi* he himself assembled from the music. Similar bustle marks his organ concertos: though they were written for insertion in oratorio-performances, they use no solemnity at all, replacing it with decorous slow movements and fast movements combining orchestral fugues with displays of finger dexterity from the soloist. (No. 13, nicknamed 'The Cuckoo and the Nightingale', is the most often played; No. 6 is also popular as a harp concerto; Nos. 5, 6, 7 and 8 are musically the best.) More serious orchestral music comes in the *concerti grossi*. Though Handel is said to have composed these quickly even for him (rushing the pages to the publisher before the ink was dry), they are substantial and carefully-planned, more like Bach's *Brandenburg Concertos* than Handel's own more random suites. The scoring of the six Op. 3 *concerti grossi* (1734), for oboes, bassoons and strings, makes them closest in sound to the *Water Music*; the twelve *concerti grossi* of Ⓜ Op. 6 (1739), for strings alone, are large-scale and serious, music for reflection as well as entertainment.

→ A pendant to the *Water Music* is the six-movement, equally jolly *Music for the Royal Fireworks* (1749), and good pieces by others in a similar uncomplicated style are Purcell's *Abdelazer Suite* and Telemann's suite/overture *Hamburg Ebb and Flow*. Good follow-ups to the concertos are Vivaldi Concerto for viola d'amore, lute and strings (RV 540) and Bach Concerto for three harpsichords; the *concerti grossi* might lead to Handel's own *Tre concerti a due cori*, to Boyce's charming Symphonies and to Avison's weightier *Twelve concerti grossi* after sonatas by Scarlatti.

Chamber music Ⓜ Fifteen Sonatas Op. 1 (1724). Most of Handel's chamber music was written for pupils or for single performances at evening concerts, and is suitably disposable and middle-weight. The exception – as engaging to hear as to play – is the set of sonatas collected and published as Op. 1. (Six are for violin and continuo, four for recorder and continuo, three for flute and continuo and two for oboe and continuo.) Like the *concerti grossi* (see above), they have integrated movements, linked by mood and style, and repeated hearings enhance rather than extinguish their appeal. Good samples are Op. 1 No. 4 (recorder) and Op. 1 No. 10 (violin). Op. 1's only real rivals for quality among Handel's chamber works are his sixteen suites for solo harpsichord: though some of the movements were clearly teaching-pieces, the majority reflect Handel's own virtuoso talent, and are mindful of the listener's fun as well as the player's. (Good samples are the Bachian Suite No. 9 and the chirpy Suite No. 14; Suite No. 5 contains the 'Harmonious Blacksmith' variation set.)

→ Anyone pleased by the Op. 1 sonatas will find plenty to enjoy in Handel's dozens of other chamber works: the meatiest are perhaps the nine trio-sonatas of Op. 2. Good follow-up works by others are Quantz's trio-sonatas and the solo sonatas in Telemann's *Essercizii musici*. After the harpsichord suites, good works to hear next are Arne's eight sonatas and Bach's *French Suites* and *Italian Concerto*.

HAYDN, Joseph (1732–1809). *Austrian composer.*

When Haydn was eight, he won a scholarship to the choir-school of St Stephen's Cathedral in Vienna. He stayed nine years, and if he had been a star pupil he might have remained in church music all his life. But he found maths and classics boring, and his schoolmasters considered him a dunce, far inferior to his younger brother Michael. Accordingly, when he was seventeen and his voice broke, instead of keeping him on as choir tenor or bass in the usual way, they threw him out. He was penniless – he owned nothing but a cloak, a harmony text-book and three shirts – and he scraped enough to eat by playing in dance-orchestras, giving music-lessons and finally by taking a job as manservant to the aged composer Porpora, who paid him in handed-down clothes and harmony-lessons. Haydn survived this life for ten years, and while he survived he composed and learned his trade. His music gradually caught the attention of aristocratic patrons, until in 1760, in the greatest stroke of luck of his life, he was appointed to the court of Prince Esterházy, one of the richest men in Europe and a devoted music-lover.

Haydn served the Esterházy family for thirty years. Much of his time was spent at the family's superb palace at Esterháza, on the site of an old hunting-lodge beside a lake. It was modelled on Louis XIV's palace at Versailles, but was bigger and even more extravagant. There were over 200 rooms, and the vast body of staff (everyone from gamekeepers to footmen, opera-singers to laundry-maids) made it more like a small town than one family's private residence. Haydn, as music-director, was in charge of an orchestra, a chapel choir, a company of opera-singers and a brass band, perhaps 150 people altogether. He had to provide music, each week the Prince was in residence (i.e. thirty or forty weeks a year), for two two-hour orchestral concerts, two opera performances, a puppet-play, three Sunday services and as many chamber-music concerts as the Prince required. It is no wonder that Haydn produced so many works: the wonders are when he found time to write them down, and how he kept their quality so high.

By 1790, when a non-music-loving Esterházy succeeded to the princely throne, Haydn's music was famous all over Europe. (The princes had travelled widely, for example as ambassadors; word of Haydn's genius had travelled with them, and many European aristocrats had heard his music-making at first hand, on visits of their own to Esterháza.) In 1791, therefore, as soon as his employer gave him leave of absence, he was showered with invitations. He chose to go to Britain, and made two extensive, happy and profitable concert-tours, playing and conducting in London (where he fell in love with the wife of one of his hosts), accepting an honorary degree from Oxford University, going to the races in Ireland and visiting the Highland Games. Moves were made to persuade him to stay in Britain, but he loyally went back to his Esterházy employer in 1795, and stayed in his service till his retirement in 1803. Then he settled in Vienna, where he held a kind of musical court in his lodgings, welcoming kings, princes and visiting musicians of every class and kind. There is a painting of him at a concert given in his honour in the early 1800s: a frail old man in dandyish clothes and a powdered wig, sitting in an armchair and surrounded by admirers.

The last fifteen years of Haydn's life, although they must have been gratifying to him personally, are not the period of his true greatness. This was the thirty years he spent at Esterháza. He was cut off from avant-garde experiments elsewhere – he once said he was 'forced by isolation to become original'. (*Mozart achieved the same objective by exactly opposite means, refusing to bind himself to any single patron.) He had everything he needed: he could write a piece in the morning, hear it played in the afternoon, and extend his art by daily experience as well as by imagination. Above all, the Esterházy magnificence gave him the chance to write music of almost every kind, from dances to full-length operas, and the princes' own musical enthusiasm guaranteed praise for his efforts and constant encouragement to rise above routine, to make each new work surpass the last. His musicians affectionately called him 'Papa', and few composers have been so industrious, so easy-going and so well-beloved.

ORCHESTRAL WORKS Over 100 symphonies (the official tally is 104, but there are a dozen others, mainly early); twenty-four concertos including eight for organ, two for cello and one for trumpet; *Sinfonia concertante* for four soloists and orchestra.

Symphonies (M) Symphony No. 48 ('Maria Theresia') (*c.* 1769). One of the most effervescent of Haydn's Esterházy symphonies, this was performed at a state visit by the Austrian empress, and is suitably equipped with fanfares and joyous whoops for horns. Like most of his earlier symphonies, it has bubbly outer movements, a graceful slow movement and a minuet and trio as stiffly decorous as footmen on parade. (Some early symphonies also incorporate solo parts, showing off favoured members of the Esterházy orchestra: a typically Haydnish idea, combining musical interest with friendliness. Nos. 6-8, nicknamed 'Morning', 'Noon' and 'Evening', are fine examples.) At the time of the 'Maria Theresia' Symphony he came under the influence of a German literary movement called *Stürm und Drang* ('storm and stress'): it was a sort of prototype Romanticism, an attempt to break open eighteenth-century formality and express direct emotion. Haydn's symphonies using this idea (e.g. No. 49, 'La Passione'; No. 52) are among his most striking middleweight works, of a stature to equal such well-known pieces as the (M) Symphony No. 45, the 'Farewell', or the dignified Symphony No. 22, 'The Philosopher'. For his British visits in the 1790s he composed twelve new symphonies (Nos. 93-104) in his ripest, wittiest style. Throughout the nineteenth century they entirely eclipsed his other works, and some (e.g. No. 100, the 'Military'; No. 104, the 'London') equalled *Mozart's symphonies in popularity. They are fine works, but show occasional signs of haste (e.g. the last movement of No. 104), so that some of the lesser-known symphonies are even better. ((M) Symphony No. 99 and (M) Symphony No. 102 match Mozart's Symphony No. 39 and Symphony No. 41, respectively.) In the last few years the earliest symphonies of all have been dusted off, played on original instruments and found to be enchanting. They were written before Esterháza, for Haydn's previous patron Count Morzin, and are short, pretty works in a style of outstanding elegance. (Nos. 10 and 18 are typical.) → There are so many musical riches in Haydn's symphonies that they are their own best follow-ups. Among the finest not mentioned above are No. 44 ('Mourning'), in the *Stürm und Drang* style, the ebullient No. 63 ('La Roxolane'), (M) No. 95 and No. 92 ('Oxford'), the latter one of his happiest works. Of other composers' symphonies, Schubert's Symphonies 1-5 follow Haydn at his most elegant (the best is No. 5), and Mozart's middle symphonies (especially No. 33 and No. 36) rival Haydn's for tunefulness and dash.

Concertos With two exceptions, Haydn's concertos are much less good than his symphonies. He seems to have shied away from the display element needed for a concerto, preferring to integrate show into the texture of longer works. His most frequently-played concertos are for cello, but his best are the Trumpet Concerto (where the unusual nature of the solo instrument, equipped with newly-invented keys and so capable of previously-unknown dexterity, inspired one of Haydn's most extrovert works), and the Ⓜ *Sinfonia concertante* (1794), composed for London and exploiting not only the fine first oboist, bassoonist, violinist and cellist but all the members of Salomon's famous orchestra. This, with Symphonies 99 and 102, is one of his finest works of any kind.

→The best follow-up to the Trumpet Concerto is Hummel's Trumpet Concerto, closely modelled on it and with a last-movement tune as whistleable as Haydn's. Good follow-ups to the *Sinfonia concertante* are Mozart's *Sinfonia concertante* K 297*b* (for four wind instruments and orchestra) and Spohr's Concerto for String Quartet and Orchestra.

CHAMBER MUSIC AND PIANO WORKS Eighty-three string quartets; thirty-two trios for piano, violin and cello; 126 trios for baryton, viola and cello; dozens of partitas, serenades, divertimentos and other small-scale entertainment-works; fifty-two sonatas and the *Andante and Variations* for solo piano.

Smaller chamber works Baryton Trio No. 63 (date unknown). Most of Haydn's chamber music is like this delicious piece: written for instant use and immediate delight, with no thoughts of grandeur or posterity. (The baryton was an instrument part cello, part guitar, now obsolete; Haydn's patron played it, and these trios were written to show off his skills. Haydn played the viola part, and gave himself – and the third musician, a court cellist – discreet professional underpinning of the royal dexterity. The works are a triumph of tact as well as tunefulness.) In the same agreeable way, Haydn wrote many of his piano sonatas and piano trios as presents for talented players (often pretty young ladies: he knew the way to a musical maiden's heart), and made them effective and charming without too many technical demands. His divertimentos and serenades (e.g. the Divertimento in B flat for wind instruments, on the slow movement of which *Brahms based his *Variations on the St Anthony Chorale*) were party-music pure and simple. But although many of his chamber works are personable and little more, with nothing to distinguish them from pieces by a dozen contemporaries (e.g. Haydn's own brother Michael or the cellist-composer Boccherini), the last dozen or so piano trios (e.g. the justly-famous Trio in G, nicknamed the 'Gipsy Rondo') are meaty as well as melodious, closer to symphonies than to divertimentos, and the last half dozen piano sonatas are difficult, sonorous and fine. (Ⓜ Sonata No. 52, for example, is as darkly Romantic as any of Beethoven's early sonatas.)

→Good follow-ups to Haydn's lighter chamber works are Krommer's Nonet, Op.79 (for wind instruments), and Mozart's Divertimento K 138 (for strings);

there is rich listening of a similar kind in Boccherini's and Dittersdorf's chamber works. The early piano sonatas might lead to the piano sonatas of C.P.E. *Bach and to Clementi's six Sonatinas, Op. 36, and the late piano sonatas to Haydn's own Ⓜ *Andante and Variations* and to Beethoven's Piano Sonata No. 4, Op. 7. The piano trios are agreeably like Mozart's (e.g. No. 2, K 496), not to mention his superb Piano Quartet K 493.

String quartets Of all Haydn's chamber music, the best is for the medium he perfected, the string quartet. When he began writing them, quartets were little more than accompanied cadenzas for the first violin, empty and frivolous; he built up the other parts, notably viola and second violin, until quartets became solid musical dialogues. (The change begins with the six quartets of Op. 33 (the 'Russian Quartets'), admired and imitated by, among others, Mozart, who played them with Haydn and two friends, and was so impressed that he revised his own quartet-composing style.) Haydn's late quartets (the six of Ⓜ Op. 76 and the two of Ⓜ Op. 77) are among the glories of the repertoire. They have the intimacy of all his chamber works – he never forgot that chamber music should first and foremost be fun to play – but they are musically rich and intellectually compact, and, without once overstepping eighteenth-century civilized manners, they strikingly foreshadow the Romantic feeling of the nineteenth century.

→Since the string quartet is very much Haydn's invention, the best listening-recommendations are his own works. Op. 20 No. 4 is sprightly and lively (especially for the first violin); Op. 64 No. 5 (the 'Lark') and Op. 76 No. 3 (the 'Emperor') show his mature style at full stretch. There are few better follow-ups by others than the set of six quartets Mozart wrote after playing Haydn's Op. 33: Mozart's Quartets Nos. 14-19, the six 'Haydn' Quartets (the 'Hunt' Quartet, K 458, is the most Haydnish of all).

VOCAL WORKS Twenty operas (including *The World on the Moon* and *The Desert Island*); thirteen Masses (including the *Mass in Time of War*, the *Nelson Mass* and the *Wind-band Mass*); six oratorios (including *The Creation* and *The Seasons*); cantatas, songs and other works for solo voice (including twelve *English Canzonets* and 450 arrangements of British folksongs).

Ⓜ **Harmoniemesse** ('Wind-band Mass') (1802) Although he wrote plenty of vocal music, Haydn was rarely at his most confident with voices. His music is witty rather than dramatic, poised rather than fanciful, neat rather than passionate – and these qualities fight against the pull of words. His finest vocal works are the six large Masses he wrote after his 1790s tours. (His new Esterházy employer was more devoted to the church than to music, and these Masses were designed to be adornments of the Esterháza chapel as sumptuous as the symphonies or quartets were of the concert-room.) Haydn (who had given up writing symphonies) gave the usually sprawling Mass-form symphonic unity: this makes the Masses virtually unusable in church (where they need to be split up with prayers and chants), but ideal for the concert-hall. The *Wind-band Mass* (so-called because of prominent woodwind parts) is exuberant and radiant, full of Christian zest; the Ⓜ *Nelson*

Mass and the *Mass in Time of War* are more pensive, the *St Theresia Mass* and the *Holy Mass* more grandly ceremonial. All of them eclipse Haydn's oratorios (even *The Seasons*; even *The Creation*), which have splendid individual moments (e.g. the opening of *The Creation* and choruses such as 'The Heavens are Telling the Glory of God'), but lack a sense of unity or conviction. In the same way, Haydn's operas are charming but hopelessly undramatic, ideal concert- or record-works. (Their overtures, e.g. the sparkling *L'infideltà delusa* overture, and individual arias such as 'Dice benissimo' from the Molière-inspired farce *La scuola di gelosi*, are the best of them.) The *English Canzonets* (e.g. 'My Mother Bids me Bind my Hair') have, naturally enough, always been popular in Britain, but are pretty rather than inspired. In short, Haydn's vocal music was composed for tastes different from those of today, and his best vocal works – the Masses, the solo cantata Ⓜ *Ariadne on Naxos* (1789) – live not because they served the trends of the time but because they broke away from them.

→The nearest sound-equivalents to Haydn's Masses are those of Schubert (e.g. the Mass in A flat), and his solo vocal works are almost exactly paralleled by those of Beethoven (the dramatic scena *Ah, Perfido!*; the forty-nine settings of Scottish songs). The best follow-ups to his operas are those of *Rossini (e.g. *The Italian Girl in Algiers*), which add to Haydn's musical distinction a swaggering sense of what works well on stage.

HENZE, Hans Werner (born 1926). *German composer.*

When Henze was growing up in Germany, the Nazis were in power and modernism was banned. In 1945, therefore (when Henze was nineteen), the lifting of restrictions must have been like the bursting of a dam. He flung himself into discovering *Stravinsky, *Schoenberg, *Bartók, *Debussy, *Weill and Richard *Strauss, and his early compositions are a mish-mash of influences. It was not until 1952, with his opera *Boulevard Solitude*, that he found both his style and his feet: it is a tragedy (on the same story as *Puccini's *Manon Lescaut*, about a doomed love-affair), and its music contrasts emotional lyricism for the singers with unsentimental orchestral sounds in much the same way as Weill's or *Britten's. *Boulevard Solitude* made Henze's name, and ever since he has poured out operas, concertos, cantatas, chamber works and symphonies: he is one of the most prolific composers of the age.

In the 1950s and 1960s Henze spent much time in Italy, and the works of these years (e.g. *Muses of Sicily*: see below) are among his most relaxed and sensuous; after the 1968 student uprisings, by contrast, he became a fervent left-wing revolutionary, moved to Cuba and produced a string of politically strident theatre-pieces (e.g. *El Cimarrón*, about an oppressed slave who runs away), intended for working-class audiences but so hectic and discordant that they have rarely had popular success. His best music is not like this at all. It is warm, lush and fits voices as comfortably as well-tailored clothes: left-wing politics apart, he is another Britten, and his music has a similar energetic charm.

WORKS Thirteen operas (including *King Stag*, *Elegy for Young Lovers*, *The Bassarids* and *We Come to the River*); eleven ballets (including *Undine* and *Orpheus*); ten cantatas or song-cycles for voices and instruments (including *Novae de infinito laudes* and *The Raft of the Medusa*); six symphonies, ten concertos (including the Double Concerto and the Double Bass Concerto) and a dozen other, shorter works for orchestra; five string quartets, a wind quintet and many shorter chamber works (including *Royal Winter Music* and *Shakespeare Music* for solo guitar).

Ⓜ *Elegy for Young Lovers* (1961) (complete opera) This opera, set in the Swiss mountains in 1910, is about a 'blocked' writer who finds inspiration by engineering a love-affair between his stepson and his mistress. Its claustrophobic atmosphere recalls the novels of Thomas Mann, and its musical style is particularly close to Britten's (e.g. in *Peter Grimes*). Twentieth-century opera can be gritty, and this one is by no means all easy arias; but anyone who enjoys (say) Puccini's *Turandot* should find its music no harder on the ear, and just as sumptuous.
→ Opera Ⓜ *The Bassarids* (based on Euripides' *Bacchae*); Menotti opera *The Saint of Bleecker Street*; Britten opera *Death in Venice*.

Ⓜ *Muses of Sicily* (1966) A rapt setting for choir, wind instruments, two pianos and percussion of a pastoral poem by Virgil, full of images of summer meadows, gentle breezes and soothing songs—and seemingly an attempt on Henze's part to wring out of himself the most exquisite sounds possible with twentieth-century orchestration and harmony.
→ Symphony No. 4 (1955, based on his fairy-tale opera *King Stag* and full of similarly ravishing sounds); *Being Beauteous* (1963, setting Rimbaud's extravagant, sensuous poetry); Maw *Scenes and Arias* for solo voices and orchestra.

Double Concerto for oboe, harp and orchestra (1966) The unusual scoring (the work was commissioned by Heinz and Ursula Holliger) evoked from Henze both his usual lyrical outpourings and a rhythmic and harmonic sharpness not unlike Stravinsky's. It may seem at first like modern music without tears (a lot of Henze's non-political music does); but (again characteristically) it seems to grow in lasting quality with each new hearing.
→ *Compases para preguntas ensimismadas* (1970, a concerto for viola and small orchestra); Martinů Oboe Concerto; Ligeti Double Concerto for flute, oboe and orchestra.

HINDEMITH, Paul (1895-1963). *German composer and teacher.*

Even in a profession where early success is commonplace, Hindemith's achievements were extraordinary. At twenty he was a professional violinist, at twenty-five a front-rank viola soloist and string-quartet player, and by the time he was thirty he had produced a couple of dozen of the most notorious works of a lively decade and was considered a leader of the avant-garde. Then, in 1927, he took a teaching-post at the Berlin Academy of Music, and creative vitality gave way to pedagogic zeal. He determined to provide music for all who wanted it, and (rather as *Copland later did in the USA) simplified his style to make his works accessible.

Copland's simplification led to his finest work; Hindemith's did not. He turned out a dozen new pieces each year, of every kind and length from operas to recorder trios, and evolved a style for them which was efficient, effective and boringly, regularly very nearly very good. (He wrote sonatas, for example, for almost every available instrument, and except for their scoring there is little to tell them apart.) The contrast between this plastic predictability and his vigorous 1920s output is total (as if the two kinds of music were by different people); he would be remembered not as a composer but as a teacher of genius were it not that when his works *are* good they are among the most characterful and striking of the century.

WORKS Nine operas and three children's stage-works; four ballets (including *Nobilissima visione*, a work of *Vaughan Williams-like limpidity on the life of St Francis); six large choral works (including the moving requiem *When Lilacs Last in the Dooryard Bloom'd*, to words by Whitman) and two dozen sets of madrigals, motets, choruses and other works for choir; *Lieder* and solo songs (including the beautiful cycle *The Life of Mary*); seven *Kammermusiken* ('Chambermusics') for solo instruments and chamber groups; four symphonies (including *Mathis der Maler*), twelve concertos and over a dozen other large orchestral works (including *Four Temperaments* for piano and strings, *Symphonic Metamorphoses* and *Konzertmusik* for strings and brass); six string quartets, forty solo sonatas (for almost every instrument from flute to tuba, from cor anglais to solo violin), octet, septet, wind quintet and many other chamber works; *Schoolwork*, *Play-and-sing-music*, *Solos for group singing* and other educational works. Hindemith also wrote several university course-books including *The Craft of Musical Composition*.

Symphonic Metamorphoses on Themes of Carl Maria von Weber (1943) The title is the only boring thing about this work, which is a lively four-movement suite updating some *Weber piano pieces. The scoring is extrovert, the tunes (Hindemith's as well as Weber's) are gorgeous and the harmony is full of twentieth-century spice. Except for its slightly 'modern' sound, this is a work from the same delightful corner of the repertoire as *Borodin's *Polovtsian Dances* or *Dvořák's *Carnival Overture*.

→ *The Four Temperaments*; Shostakovich suite *The Gadfly*; Martinů suite *Revue de cuisine*.

Ⓜ *Der Schwanendreher* ('The Swan-turner') (1935) This is a meditative, gentle viola concerto based on old German folksongs (including the one which gives it its name). Writing for his own favourite instrument, and using beloved traditional songs, Hindemith produced a work of tender inspiration, wistful, eloquent and not a note too long.

→ Organ Sonata No. 3 (also based on folk-tunes); Ⓜ *Kammermusik* Op. 46 No. 1 (concerto for viola d'amore, in his more energetic 1920s style); Honegger *Concerto da camera* for flute, cor anglais and strings.

Ⓜ *Mathis der Maler* (symphony) (1934) The three movements of this symphony are based on sections of an opera about the sixteenth-century church painter Matthias Grünewald (and the symphony's movements reinterpret his paintings *Angels' Concert, Christ's Entombment* and *The Temptation of St Anthony*). There are brisk tunes and brassy harmonies, but the symphony's mood is mainly lyrical, sharing (for all its twentieth-century sound) the Lutheran simplicity and intensity of *Bach's choral works.

→ Ⓜ *Konzertmusik* for strings and brass (1930); Ⓜ *Das Marienleben* ('The Life of Mary': song-cycle, version with voice and orchestra recommended); Roussel Symphony No. 3.

HOLST, Gustav (1874-1934). *British composer.*

Until he was twenty-nine, Holst was an orchestral trombonist; then he switched to teaching, and worked at two London girls' schools (Dulwich; St Paul's), at Morley College (an adult evening institute) and at the Royal College of Music. At each of them, he wrote pieces for his pupils far beyond the usual range of student works (the best-known are *St Paul's Suite* and *Hymn of Jesus*: see below). He was fascinated by British folksong, by the occult and above all by religious mysticism. (He set the apocryphal *Acts of St John*, on the 'dance of Christ's divine grace', and he learned Sanskrit especially to study and set Indian religious texts.) He is world-famous for one work, *The Planets* (see below); unlike some of his other music (which is emotionally reticent) it is bustling with humanity, full of the warmth of life.

WORKS Four short operas (including *Savitri* and *At The Boar's Head*); two concertos, ten suites (including *The Planets*) and several shorter works for orchestra (among them the brooding tone-poem *Egdon Heath*); several hundred choruses, part-songs and other works for choir (many small-scale, for pupils' choirs, but including a *Choral Symphony*, a *Choral Fantasy* and the large-scale *Hymn of Jesus*); a dozen sets of solo songs (including *Hymns from the Rig Veda* and the masterly *Twelve Songs of Humbert Wolfe*); assorted small chamber works (including a *Terzetto* in three keys at once) and folksong-based piano pieces.

Ⓜ *The Planets*, Op. 32 (1916) One of the most popular orchestral works of the century, this suite takes seven planets (not Earth; not Pluto, which was undiscovered when Holst was writing), and paints sound-pictures of their astrological associations: Mars is warlike, Jupiter jolly, Neptune mystical and so on. The music is characterful and catchy, and the work is a showpiece as extrovert as anything by Chabrier (see *One-work Composers*) or *Rimsky-Korsakov.
→ Ballet music from *The Perfect Fool*; Ⓜ *Hymn of Jesus* (a wonderfully unsolemn religious cantata, full of pounding rhythms and 'magic' chords); Rimsky-Korsakov *Sheherazade*; Smetana *Vltava*.

Ⓜ *St Paul's Suite* for strings, Op. 29 No. 2 (1913) All school orchestras should attract music as good as this. Its four short movements (Jig; Perpetual Motion; Aria; Finale) tease the players without stretching them too far, and provide easy pleasure for the listener. Holst wove folk-tunes into the texture with exhilarating dexterity: in the last movement, for example, he blended the fast, hypnotically-repeated *Dargason* with *Greensleeves*, appearing majestically and unexpectedly from the tumult – a magical effect.
→ *Brook Green Suite* (written for similar forces and similarly gay); *Fugal Concerto* (whose title is the only forbidding thing about it: it is a *Bach-like concerto for two violins and orchestra); Vaughan Williams *Five Variants of 'Dives and Lazarus'*.

I

IVES, Charles (1874-1954). *American composer.*

Although he trained as a musician, Ives spent his working life in the insurance business (which made him a millionaire). He composed at weekends and on commuter-trains, and was totally unbothered about publication, performance or the opinion of the musical establishment. (Most of his works stayed undiscovered until after his death.) His lack of interest in the musical mainstream, coupled with unconventional boyhood training by a bandsman-father addicted to experiment (inventing new instruments, having pieces sung in several keys at once, writing into the hymns birdcalls, churchbell-sounds and the whistling of passing errand-boys) turned Ives into one of the great natural eccentrics of the arts. He did just as he pleased: if he felt like adding a dozen bars of flute music to a piano sonata, writing fugues on hymn-tunes which then broke out into *Columbia, Gem of the Ocean* or *Darktown Strutters' Ball*, or telling his instrumentalists to play *con fistiswatto*, that's exactly what he did.

Ives's works are like musical patchwork quilts. They move in a moment from genius to banality; they can be as pure-harmonied as hymns or shatteringly discordant; most of all, their anthology of snippets from musical-hall, organ-loft and parade-ground gives them an Americanness which (it must be admitted) some listeners find more appealing than others. After his music became known in the 1950s, he influenced a generation of composers; but his influence has begun to fade, and he now seems not so much the Grand Old Man as the Grandma Moses of American music.

WORKS 4 Symphonies, *Holidays Symphony, Three Places in New England, Central Park in the Dark, Tone Roads 1-3, The Unanswered Question, Orchestral Set 2* and other shorter orchestral works; two string quartets, three violin sonatas, *Concord* piano sonata, Piano Trio and a score of smaller chamber works; over 100 works for choir, ranging from the huge *Lincoln the Great Commoner* for chorus and orchestra to the homely *Three Harvest-home Chorales*; over 120 solo songs.

Ⓜ *The Unanswered Question* (1908) Three things happen at once in this short piece. A trumpet sends out calls and arpeggios, sometimes discordantly blaring, sometimes querulous; flutes whistle in an empty-headed way; among all the uproar the strings move in quiet chords, as serene as the procession of clouds across the sky. It is like no other orchestral piece (even by Ives), and it is irresistible. What does it mean? Is *that* the question of the title?

→ *The Housatonic at Stockbridge* (a beautiful river-picture, calm and flowing, from the suite *Three Places in New England*); Symphony No. 2 (half *Dvořákian, half a collection of barn-dances, harmonium-hymns and music-hall quotations: cf. String Quartet No. 1 – but beware String Quartet No. 2!); Copland *Quiet City*.

Ⓜ **Symphony No. 3** (*The Camp Meeting*) (1911) A gentle three-movement work largely based on hymn-tunes. Like no other composer, Ives could conjure up the homespun simplicity and dignity of nineteenth-century New Englanders, church-going, honest folks from clapboard houses and in sturdy shoes. The miracle is that the music avoids such applecheeked banality: without abandoning those plain-dealing qualities, it is inspired, finely put together and intellectually compelling.

→ *Central Park in the Dark in the Good Ol' Summertime* (another quietly-moving orchestral evocation); Ⓜ *Concord Sonata* for piano solo (sound-picture of such figures of the New England past as Hawthorne, Thoreau and the Alcotts: enormously hard to play – it took one virtuoso ten years to learn – but regarded by many as Ives's best work); Virgil Thomson Symphony No. 1.

JANÁČEK, Leoš (1854-1928). *Czech composer.*

Until he was sixty-two Janáček led a busy but unremarkable life running an organ-school in his native town and conducting local choirs and orchestras. His music was small-scale, chiefly folksong arrangements for choir and folk-dances and similar works for piano or orchestra. Then, in 1916, his opera *Jenůfa* was triumphantly performed in Prague, and he began a love-affair – by letter, but none the less passionate for that – with a girl forty years his junior. These two events changed his life. For the next twelve years he behaved like a student of genius, writing his beloved hundreds of love-letters and pouring out works inspired by her, in a heady, intoxicated style unlike anything he'd written before and unlike anyone else's music before or since.

The basis of Janáček's music is hot-blooded nineteenth-century harmony, but he overlays it with chirping, skittering runs of notes based on the uneven rhythms of the Czech language: it is as if someone were eagerly trying to blurt out the love welling up in his heart, but each time breaking off in mid-syllable and leaving the declaration half-spoken in the air. This is a magnificent style for opera, and Janáček's operas are his finest works. But he also turned it to good use in chamber music (especially the two string quartets inspired by his beloved: see below), and in the lively *Sinfonietta* composed for an athletics festival.

WORKS Nine operas (including *Jenůfa*, *Katya Kabanova*, *The Cunning Little Vixen*, *The Makropoulos Affair* and *From the House of the Dead*); *Sinfonietta*, rhapsody *Taras Bulba* and several shorter orchestral works; *Concertino* and *Capriccio* for solo piano and chamber group; two string quartets, Violin Sonata, Cello Sonata and other chamber works; Sonata *1:x:1905*, suite *By Overgrown Paths* and other piano works; *Slavonic* (*Glagolitic*) *Mass* and many other choruses and songs (including the song-cycle with women's choir and piano, *Diary of One Who Disappeared*).

Ⓜ *Sinfonietta* (1926) The work's athletics-festival origins are audible in robust fanfares for a huge brass choir (including twelve trumpets); the wind instruments squeal above them and the strings rush impetuously about, producing an exhilarating open-air effect. Under it all, as calm water underlies a white-horsey, porpoise-dancing sea, is an unhurried and tuneful Czech folksong suite.

→ *Taras Bulba* (fiery orchestral rhapsody about a Cossack folk-hero); Concertino for piano and chamber group; Kodály *Peacock Variations*.

Ⓜ *The Cunning Little Vixen* (complete opera) (1923) In some ways Janáček's operas are a special taste: their abrupt musical style and their glove-like setting of the Czech language mean that the listener has to put in more work than usual to unlock the experience. This one is perhaps the best to try first: it is a lyrical, folk-like story about a happy vixen, her innocent, tumbling cubs, the forester who falls in love with her and imprisons her, and the lumpish, ridiculous humans who inhabit the village beside the wood. A bilingual libretto is a more-than-usually useful key to enjoyment.

→ *Katya Kabanova* (complete opera: human, unfolksy but just as emotionally supercharged); Ⓜ *Glagolitic Mass* (enormous, but lively and folksy, Mass setting in the Old Church Slavonic language for choir and orchestra); Ravel *L'enfant et les sortilèges*.

Ⓜ **String Quartet No. 2** (*Intimate Letters*) (1928) Few composers, whether seventy-four years old or not, have ever conceived a string quartet like this. Each of its four movements is a musical love-letter, and Janáček wrote of the way in which the music expresses both his beloved's character (tender, lively, frolicsome) and his own desire for her.

→ String Quartet No. 1 (*Kreutzer Sonata*, based on Tolstoy's story of unhappy love; more anguished and hence more musically strident, but with balancing passages of equal radiance); *Mládi* ('Youth') (1924), a light-hearted, pastoral suite for six wind instruments; Delius String Quartet.

JOSQUIN DES PREZ (*c.* 1440–1521). *French composer.*

In Josquin's day it was common to regard artistic ability as a loan from God, to be repaid in the form of loyal service: Christ's parable of the stewards and the talents was powerful in people's minds. Josquin himself certainly took this view. Though contemporaries hailed him as a prince among composers, the 'moon of all music', he spent his life humbly in the service of the Church, first as a choir-singer (at Milan Cathedral and in the Papal Chapel in Rome, where he served the Borgia Pope Alexander VI), and then, in his sixties and seventies, as Provost (i.e. religious overseer) of a church and choirschool of Our Lady (for whom he had always had strong personal devotion). Put this way, his life may seem austere. But for all his sense of religious duty, he had a marked taste for worldly pleasures too. He was at ease with kings and courtiers, fond of hunting, good food and wine, and seems particularly to have enjoyed the folk music of the time (the kind of bagpipe-playing, high-kicking merriment so often painted by his contemporary Brueghel).

Josquin's secular interests affected his music. Although he wrote in the learned, approved style of the time (he was taught by Ockeghem, its greatest master), he warmed his counterpoint with 'worldly' harmony, sounds of a passionate, earthy kind not heard in church before. (When a Josquin motet tells of love for the Virgin Mary, for example, the music adds more than a hint of sensual yearning to the formal Latin words.) His technical skill (as dazzling for its day as *Bach's for his) was what earned his contemporaries' respect; his music's humanity and passion are what make it live today.

WORKS Josquin was so famous that many compositions were credited to him, both in his own day and after, which modern scholars think were never his at all. (The same thing happened with *Beethoven in the nineteenth century: putting his name on a piece guaranteed sales.) Surviving works regarded as genuine are eighteen Masses (including *Pange lingua* and *L'Homme armé*) and eighty motets (e.g. *Ave Maria*) for unaccompanied choir, and over a hundred short songs and dance-pieces for voices and/or instruments.

Ⓜ **Mass *Pange lingua* for four-part choir (date unknown)** The plainsong for the words *Pange lingua* ('Tell, my tongue, the glorious story') was a favourite basis for fifteenth-century composers' Masses, and it inspired one of Josquin's most sumptuous works. (One reason is the rich harmonic scope of the plainsong notes, so different from the bare contrapuntal suggestions of some other chants.) The work is in the usual five sections, and its *Agnus Dei* ('Lamb of God', the closing section, similar in its rounding-off effect to a symphony's finale) is especially sonorous. Like *Palestrina's Masses, this one needs a resonant building to do justice in live performance to its overlapping sound-effects; on records, paradoxically, a small choir, perhaps with accompanying instruments, works just as well. → Mass *L'Homme armé*; motet *Benedicta es coelorum regina* ('Blessed art thou, Queen of Heaven'); Taverner Mass *Western Wind*.

Ⓜ ***Basiez-moy*** ('Kiss me') (date unknown) This two-minute song (a flirtation between shepherd and shepherdess) is three things at once: a double canon, for those who relish technicalities (that is, the same words keep deliriously recurring, in different voices, like lovers' murmurings), wittily tuneful and unexpectedly passionate. (If any music can titillate, this does.) Josquin's 100 or so secular songs, all written for court enjoyment, are either earthy and charming in the same way, or are splendidly melodramatic laments (e.g. *Plain de deuil*, 'Full of Mourning'), where the harmonies are deliberately stretched and squeezed to make them as heart-rending as possible. The artifice in all these pieces, the wish to please, is one of their most delightful traits.

→ *Bergerette Savoyenne*; *Cueurs desoles* ('Broken Hearts', a lament on which Rubbra based a beautiful twentieth-century piece for recorder and harpsichord, *Meditazioni*, herewith recommended); Jannequin French *chansons* (e.g. *Ce mois de May*; *Resveillez-vous*).

K

KEYBOARD INSTRUMENTS

On most instruments, the players make the notes by unaided breath- or muscle-power. Keyboard instruments give them mechanical (or, nowadays, electronic) help, making possible a wider variety of sounds and far more notes. All musical instruments are examples of the human mind using technology to control natural sounds; keyboard instruments are applied technology at its most ingenious.

ORGAN FAMILY In a **pipe organ**, sets of differently-sized pipes are arranged in rows (like wind instruments stacked on end), and each is tuned to a different note. When the player presses a key, a valve lets compressed air into the corresponding pipe and so makes the sound. In **reed organs** (such as harmoniums and accordions), the air passes not through a pipe but across a shaped cane or reed (as on a clarinet or oboe); in **electronic organs**, pipes and reeds are non-existent, and pressing the key completes an electrical circuit and generates sound through a loudspeaker.

Early organs were primitive. In ancient Greece they used water to compress the air; medieval organs often needed one person to carry them, another to pump the bellows and a third to play the notes. It was not until the sixteenth century that the pipe organ was perfected, and it was another 150 years before it became a standard instrument in church. In the sixteenth and seventeenth centuries composers treated it as interchangeable with the harpsichord: if they wanted sustained, wind-instrument sounds they used the organ, if they wanted crisp, plucked-string sounds they used the harpsichord. The organ was a favourite instrument in chamber music (playing the *continuo* or accompaniment), and had a small solo repertoire of fantasias, toccatas and ricercares similar to those written for harpsichord or virginals. Three of the leading composers of this unassuming kind of music were Bull, Frescobaldi and Sweelinck; of the great composers of the age, only *Byrd left any organ pieces to rival theirs.

The organ's first heyday was the end of the seventeenth century and beginning of the eighteenth. Lutheran church organists, especially in Germany, began using the organ not only to accompany singing but to play interludes and solo pieces in its own right. These works began as simple meditations on chorale tunes, usually at the beginning or end of the service, and many were improvised (made up on the spot); but as the pieces grew more complex, and as more and more composers began writing them down, a magnificent repertoire was created of toccatas, fantasias, preludes, fugues, passacaglias and sonatas: its greatest contributors were Buxtehude and J. S. *Bach. Other composers, especially in England, used the organ not only for church music but for entertainment too. A favourite form was the *concerto, setting the wind-sound of the organ against a string orchestra and giving the soloist scales, trills and arpeggios of the most demanding kind. (*Handel's organ concertos show just how enjoyable such works could be.)

In the eighteenth and early nineteenth centuries, composers turned their attention to other kinds of music (especially orchestral and piano music), and organ works were rare. (Haydn's eight exuberant organ concertos, for example, make up less than one-thousandth of his total work.) At the same time, public concerts became more common, and large concert-halls were built for them, equipped with organs – and the larger the hall, the larger the organ. By the mid-nineteenth century the science of organ-building had reached a peak of grandeur and magnificence: the organs of this time are among the largest and most powerful ever made. (Some were even steam-powered; the use of electric power was a late nineteenth-century development.) This was the organ's second heyday. One player on one instrument could rival a whole orchestra in both volume and variety of sound, and musicians began treating the organ seriously again, rediscovering the works of Bach and others and composing organ works of their own as grand as the largest piano sonatas or symphonies. In the last 150 years, several fine composers (e.g. Reubke, Rheinberger, Vierne and Widor) have specialized in organ music, and others, better known for music of other kinds, have composed organ works as magnificent as anything else they wrote. (*Franck, *Liszt and *Messiaen are among leading organ-composers; *Mendelssohn, *Elgar and *Hindemith wrote fine sonatas; *Saint-Saëns's 'Organ' Symphony and *Poulenc's Organ Concerto have been concert favourites since the day they were first performed.)

HARPSICHORD FAMILY In this group of instruments (the **harpsichord** and its smaller relatives the **spinet** and the **virginals**) the keys work quill or leather 'jacks' which pluck the strings. (In another related instrument, the **clavichord**, the strings are not plucked but gently struck by 'tangents' to produce a miniature version of harpsichord sound.) The sound is quiet, like a harp's, and dies quickly away; for this reason the strings are laid in a resonating wooden case which adds echoes and amplifies the sound. The harpsichord, which has a larger case than the other instruments of its family, is the loudest; the spinet, virginals and clavichord are more effective in small rooms than in concert-halls.

Queen Elizabeth I of England was a keen amateur virginals-player, and English aristocrats favoured it above most other instruments. The variations, fantasias and character-pieces (with names like 'Humour', The 'Earl of X's Pavane' or 'The Bells') of the composers of the 'English virginals school' (e.g. *Byrd, Bull, Morley, Farnaby) are among the earliest and most delightful keyboard music still performed. In other countries, composers preferred the harpsichord: Sweelinck in the Netherlands and Frescobaldi in Italy were its finest masters. Like the organ, the harpsichord reached its heyday at the turn of the seventeenth century. It was not only a major chamber-music instrument (see *Sonata*), but had a sizeable repertoire of its own, ranging from the character-pieces of such French composers as *Rameau and *Couperin and the virtuoso one-movement sonatas of *Scarlatti to suites, toccatas and fugues of the most substantial kind (e.g. those of J. S. Bach), and to large-scale concertos for one, two, three and even four harpsichords and string orchestra. (Apart from J. S. Bach's, the most often played today are *Vivaldi's and C. P. E. *Bach's.)

For the first half of the eighteenth century, harpsichord and piano existed side by side. But the piano continued to grow in size and reliability; the harpsichord (perfected centuries before) did not. By the time of Mozart and Beethoven, the piano was the standard instrument for keyboard concertos, sonatas and chamber works. Neglect of the harpsichord family continued throughout the nineteenth century: if people played harpsichord music at all, they played it on the piano. It was not until the early twentieth century that interest revived: old harpsichords were renovated, new ones were built and the first modern generation of professional harpsichordists appeared. At first the aim was to rediscover old music and to re-create its original sound in an archaeological sort of way; but soon people began to treat the harpsichord not as a curiosity but as a unique and beautiful sound-source like any other, not the piano's ancestor but an alternative. Composers began specifying it in works, and nowadays it is firmly re-established both for the playing of pre-nineteenth-century music and in a sizeable repertory of modern works. (*Falla, *Martinů, *Poulenc, Martin, *Milhaud and *Carter have written splendid concertos for harpsichord, with or without other soloists; *Henze, Ligeti and Berio have written notable harpsichord-solo works.)

PIANO Pressing a piano key works a system of levers and springs which cause a felt-covered wooden hammer to hit the strings. In modern pianos there are generally three strings for each of the upper notes and one or two for each of the lower; 'dampers' (worked by a pedal) let the player stop the strings vibrating, or, by releasing them, prolong the sound for as long as he or she requires. The power to sustain sound and the fact that hard pressure on the keys makes a louder noise than soft pressure (hence the name *pianoforte*, 'soft-loud') are the crucial differences between piano and harpsichord (where the sound is short-lived and of much the same loudness).

The piano was invented *c*.1709, and by the end of the century had almost completely replaced the harpsichord. Apart from mechanical superiority, the main reason was a series of late-eighteenth-century piano masterworks: no harpsichord music had ever been written as grand as Mozart's piano concertos, say, or *Beethoven's first half-dozen piano sonatas – and where geniuses led, other composers eagerly followed. In the first thirty years of the nineteenth century, manufacturers continued vigorously improving the actual instruments (stretching the strings on iron frames, for example, instead of wooden ones, and so tripling or quadrupling the sound); composers like Clementi, Field and Czerny extended the technique and style of keyboard-playing in ways unimagined before their time.

Soon, pianos were everywhere. Upright pianos were popular household instruments; chamber music with piano was a favourite concert form; every new concert-hall was equipped with a grand piano powerful enough to play concertos with the largest orchestras and strong enough to survive even the most demonic recital soloists. Once, the violin had been the virtuoso's instrument, favoured by musical showmen throughout the world; now the piano rivalled its supremacy. Reams of virtuoso music were composed; most of it is now forgotten, but it paved the way for some of the greatest of all nineteenth-century composers, who adapted virtuoso playing-styles to suit musical as well as showy purposes. *Chopin's scherzos, studies and ballades and the piano suites of *Schumann, for example, are as poetic as they are hard to play; *Liszt's piano works, as well as being fabulously spectacular, are nineteenth-century Romanticism at its most heart-felt; the sonatas of *Beethoven and *Schubert and the piano works of *Brahms contain some of their composers' finest thoughts.

The piano's enormous popularity has continued ever since. Nothing is a more sure-fire concert item than a piano concerto (Grieg's, say, or Tchaikovsky's Concerto No. 1, or Rachmaninov's Second); virtuoso pianists are, with conductors, among the most admired and pampered of all twentieth-century classical-music stars. Few other instruments have a finer repertoire of twentieth-century music: from the suites of *Granados, *Debussy and *Ravel to the concertos of *Bartók, from Rachmaninov's neo-Romantic Preludes to such avant-garde works as *Boulez's Sonata No. 1, *Messiaen's *Catalogue d'oiseaux* and *Stockhausen's *Piano Piece II*, the modern pianist's library is crammed with masterworks.

Listening The best early keyboard works to sample first are the virginals pieces of Byrd and Farnaby and the organ works of Sweelinck; good follow-ups are Gibbons's fantasias and Frescobaldi's toccatas and ricercares. **Organ music**. From the eighteenth century, Handel's Organ Concerto No. 13 ('The Cuckoo and the Nightingale') and Mozart's Fantasia for mechanical organ, K 608, are recommended first, followed by Buxtehude's preludes and fugues and then by the organ works of J. S. Bach (beginning with the Trio-sonata No. 6 and the Toccata and Fugue in D minor). From the nineteenth century, Mendelssohn's Sonata No. 2 (straightforward) and Franck's *Pièce héroïque* (extrovert) might lead to more specialist, darker-toned works like Liszt's *Fantasia on 'Ad nos ad salutarem undam'* and Widor's solo-organ Symphony No. 5 (whose last movement, Toccata, is a favourite classical-organ 'pop'). Saint-Saëns's Symphony No. 3, for organ and orchestra, is a sprightly nineteenth-century counterpart to Handel's concertos. From the twentieth century, Poulenc's Organ Concerto amiably follows in Saint-Saëns's footsteps, Hindemith's Sonata No. 2 is a good introduction to the solo repertoire, Ligeti's *Volumina* is a fascinating and murmurous avant-garde work, and Messiaen's organ works (e.g. *Les corps glorieux*) are the specialist repertoire at its most approachable and spectacular. **Harpsichord music**. The best introductions to the eighteenth-century repertoire are Scarlatti's sonatas and Bach's Concerto No. 1 for harpsichord and strings; good follow-ups are Couperin's Ordre No. 24 and Bach's *Italian Concerto* and Partita No. 1. From the twentieth century, good first works are Falla's and Martinů's harpsichord concertos and Martin's *Petite symphonie concertante*. **Piano music**. So much piano music is available, and its enjoyment depends so much on individual listeners' tastes, that recommending specific works would fill this book. For composers whose piano music is a main part of their output, see Albéniz, Chopin, Debussy, Granados, Liszt, Rachmaninov, Ravel, Schumann and Scriabin; for other major composers' piano works see Bartók, Beethoven, Brahms, Fauré, Grieg, Haydn, Mendelssohn, Mozart, Prokofiev, Ravel, Satie and Schubert. For further keyboard-music recommendations, see *British and Irish Composers, Concerto, Eighteenth-century Music, Nineteenth-century Music, One-work Composers* (Litolff, Sinding), *Seventeenth-century Music, Sixteenth-century Music, Sonata* and *Twentieth-century Music*.

KHACHATURIAN, Aram (1903–78). *Russian composer.*

An Armenian, Khachaturian was so fascinated by the folk music of his native area that he decided to become a composer. He was nineteen before he began to study music, and his apprenticeship lasted seven years. But he began winning prizes almost immediately after that, and quickly climbed the artistic hierarchy of the Communist Party, surviving disagreements with Stalin and being notably helpful both to younger composers and to such temporarily-disgraced older ones as *Prokofiev and *Shostakovich. His music had an international vogue in the 1930s and 1940s, and some of it (e.g. the Adagio from *Spartacus*) still does. At its worst (e.g. *Poem about Stalin*) it is bombastic and piffling; at its best (e.g. Symphony No. 1, Piano

Concerto: see below) it blends Armenian exuberance with traditional forms in a technicolor way reminiscent of *Rimsky-Korsakov or *Borodin at their bounciest.

WORKS Two ballets (*Gayane, Spartacus*); three symphonies and several suites (including *Masquerade*) for orchestra; concertos and concerto-rhapsodies for piano, violin and cello; Violin Sonata, Trio for violin, clarinet and piano, Piano Sonata and various shorter pieces of chamber music; music for films (e.g. *The Battle of Stalingrad*) and plays (e.g. *Macbeth*).

Gayane Suite No. 1 (1943) Whatever else he was good at, choosing ballet stories was not Khachaturian's strong point. *Spartacus* is about the gladiator's revolt in ancient Rome, a sort of *Ben Hur* with leaps and twirls, and *Gayane*, though a suitably melodramatic tale of betrayal, dastardliness and the triumph of true love, is set somewhat limply on a collective farm. Fortunately for music-lovers, Khachaturian clothed these unsparkling tales in music of Armenian glow and dash: his scores are really no more than lively folk-inspired movements loosely strung together, and they work magnificently as concert suites. The first *Gayane Suite* has eight movements, including a 'Lullaby', a high-leaping 'Dance of the Young Kurds' and the all-engulfing 'Sabre Dance', a piece equalled in splendiferous barbarity only by *Falla's *Ritual Fire Dance*.
→ *Spartacus* (the eighth movement, a sensuous love-dance, is the famous Adagio); *Masquerade Suite* (including the famous Waltz and Galop); Kabalevsky suite *The Comedians*.

Piano Concerto (1936) This is a big work in the beefiest virtuoso style: the feeling of the soloist out-muscling the orchestra is a main part of its attraction. But Khachaturian's themes are like folksongs and his orchestration is like film music. The collision between *Liszt and a train of Armenian circus-acrobats is an unlikely one, and produces spectacularly hectic fun.
→ Symphony No. 1; Violin Concerto (also folksy, but less of a firework-show); Gershwin *Rhapsody in Blue*; Grieg Piano Concerto.

KODÁLY, Zoltán (1882-1967). *Hungarian composer and educationist.*
Composition was only one of Kodály's musical activities: he was also a folk-music collector, and he devised a system of music-education which is still in world-wide use. His compositions include hundreds of songs and choruses for singers of every kind from infants' choirs to concert soloists; many are based on folksongs he collected with *Bartók in the Carpathian Mountains before the First World War. His concert-music also uses folk material, but expands it into large-scale works in the manner of a twentieth-century *Dvořák. The 'Hungarian-ness' of his music is marked – in the same way as *Vaughan Williams's 'Englishness' or *Sibelius's

'Finnishness' – and it gives his works a sound-quality very much their own: before you hear a new Kodály piece, you know roughly what to expect, and the pleasure lies in seeing what new delights he will unveil in familiar material.

WORKS Apart from his folksong collections and the huge body of his teaching pieces, Kodály wrote several large-scale choral works (including the *Psalmus Hungaricus*, *Te Deum* and *Missa brevis*); Symphony, Concerto for Orchestra, *Peacock Variations* and a dozen shorter orchestral works; two string quartets, Sonata for cello and piano, Sonata for cello alone, several piano suites and other chamber works, and the folk-operas *Háry János*, *The Spinning Room* and *Czinka Panna*.

Háry János Suite (1930). Kodály's opera has spoken dialogue, which seldom works well in translation; the music lives best in this lively concert suite. The story tells of a boastful, drunken soldier, and the movements depict his love-triumphs, his defeat of Napoleon, his single-handed relief of Vienna and his delight at such capital-city wonders as a mechanical clock. Folksongs, and the use of a cimbalom in the orchestra, give the music a Hungarian tang; its satirical wit is Kodály's own.
→ *Dances of Galánta*; Concerto for Orchestra; Arnold overture *Tam o' Shanter*; Falla suite *The Three-cornered Hat*.

Ⓜ *Psalmus Hungaricus* (1923) Written for the fiftieth anniversary of the uniting of the towns Buda and Pest into one Hungarian capital, this is an exuberant setting of Psalm 55 (*Give Ear unto my Prayer, O Lord*), in Hungarian, for solo tenor, choir and orchestra. The marriage of nationalism and religious fervour is rare, and rarely successful, but here leads to music of blazing intensity, whose effect in the concert-hall is at once overwhelming and exhilarating. (*Handel's *Zadok the Priest*, despite its totally different musical style, is the nearest equivalent for majesty and involvement.)
→ *Missa brevis*; Dvořák *Te Deum*; Bernstein *Chichester Psalms*.

L

LEONCAVALLO. See *One-work Composers*.

LISZT, Ferenc/Franz (1811–86). *Hungarian composer and pianist.*

Liszt's father resigned his job with the Esterházy family (*Haydn's one-time employers) to take his prodigy-pianist son on a European concert-tour. The boy studied with Czerny (the leading piano teacher of the day), was fêted by royalty and made friends with such eminent composers as *Chopin and *Berlioz. When Franz was fifteen, his father died suddenly (of typhoid), and the boy decided to stay in western Europe and continue his career. He soon found recital-bookings, piano-pupils and a rich mistress (the first of many throughout his life); he spent the next sixteen years as one of the most flamboyant touring showmen of the age, depicted by cartoonists as a lion-tamer making the piano beg, as a blacksmith chopping it to bits, and – in a different mood – as a pampered poet swooning under the blossoms heaped on him by doting fans.

Liszt was to the piano what Paganini had been to the violin. Nothing was too hard for him: he could sight-read music others took months to learn, and his own pieces were so difficult that he was reputed to stretch his hands with a secret gadget (perhaps electrical), to play under hypnosis or to be in league with the devil. (Like the good businessman he was, he encouraged all such publicity.) More important, he carried European piano-playing to heights unequalled even by Chopin – all later pianists and piano-composers own him debts – and he used his popularity to reveal to audiences music they would otherwise never have heard: *Schubert's songs, *Bach's organ works, *Berlioz's and *Beethoven's symphonies all appeared (in piano arrangements) in Liszt's concerts, and their reputation spread with his.

For all his success, Liszt was a restless, unsatisfied man. He retired from the virtuoso-circuit in 1848, and became music-director to the court at Weimar. He stayed there for thirteen years, concentrated on conducting and composing, and developed the possibilities of the orchestra as he had those of the piano. He invented new styles of harmony and orchestration, and a Romantic new musical form (the symphonic poem); he played orchestral works by *Schumann, *Wagner and Berlioz, and introduced Italian opera (*Bellini, *Donizetti, *Verdi) to German audiences.

Liszt left Weimar in 1861, ostensibly to become a Roman Catholic priest. In fact he went only far enough along that road to be able to call himself 'Abbé' Liszt; he soon returned to concert-giving, teaching and ever-more-scandalous love-affairs. His musical experiments now led him in directions not even his admirers understood, towards harmonies and methods of construction not heard again in Europe until *Debussy and the early twentieth-century atonalists. He made his last concert tour at the age of seventy-five, and at the end of it he died. At his funeral, people showered the cortège with flowers, threw themselves sobbing in front of it, and some even attempted suicide. Liszt the showman would have loved every minute of it; Liszt the musician might have taken quieter pleasure in the thought that he had advanced his art further than any other nineteenth-century composer but Beethoven.

WORKS Sonata, twenty *Hungarian Rhapsodies*, *Transcendental Studies*, four books of *Years of Pilgrimage, Consolations, Mephisto Waltzes*, many other original works and transcriptions for piano of music by Bach, *Mozart, Schubert, Berlioz, *Rossini, Beethoven, Wagner and others; many organ works (including *Fantasia and Fugue on BACH*); *Faust Symphony, Dante Symphony*, twelve symphonic poems, two piano concertos and a dozen other orchestral works; choral music (including two Masses, several psalm-settings and the oratorio *Christ*) and fifty-five songs.

La campanella ('The Bell'; *Transcendental Study* No. 3, 1851) When people think of Liszt's virtuoso piano works, they often imagine fast, thunderous bombardments of notes. But this piece – originally a reworking of a Paganini violin study – is far more typical. It is quiet and concentrates its virtuosity in a glittering shower of semiquavers and in skipping leaps whose delicacy demonstrates and tests a player's dexterity in a way no firecrackers can. *La campanella* is an encore-piece, a soufflé designed to delight rather than to nourish; the replacement of clatter by gracefulness, in such circumstances, tells much about Liszt's character.
→*La leggierezza* (*Concert Study* No. 2); Mendelssohn/Rachmaninov *Scherzo from 'A Midsummer Night's Dream'*; Saint-Saëns *Concert Study* No. 6.

Ⓜ *Fountains of the Villa d'Este* (*Years of Pilgrimage*, Book 3 No.4, published 1890) Liszt's books *Years of Pilgrimage* collect twenty-six pieces, sound-pictures of places visited on his travels. (Book 1 has Swiss scenes, Books 2 and 3 are chiefly Italian.) This one is a shimmering water-picture, concerned with the dazzle of sunlight in spray and with the endless minute changes in an apparently unchanging texture. The piece and its companions are Liszt's recital-music at its most impressionistic and elaborate, poetic self-communing turned into public art.
→*Legend* No. 2 (*St Francis of Paule Walking on the Waters*); Schumann Fantasia Op. 17; Ravel *Jeux d'eau*.

Ⓜ **Piano Sonata** (1853) Though hard enough to play, this is less a showpiece than a one-movement symphony for solo piano, giving depth of musical thought equal place to technical display. Liszt built it in a favourite way, transforming and endlessly redeploying a handful of basic themes. (He learned the method, perhaps, from studying Bach's fugues and fantasies, but although his themes, like Bach's, are made from mere handfuls of notes, their brooding poeticism and the dark Romantic harmony they imply result in entirely unBachian works.) At first hearing, the sonata sounds like a collage of crashing virtuoso passages and wistful meditation; on repeated hearings, the incessant theme-transformation reveals connections and relationships which give the music emotional tension and intellectual weight.

→*Dante Sonata* (*Years of Pilgrimage*, Book 2 No. 7); Alkan Concerto for solo piano; Rachmaninov Sonata No. 2.

Piano Concerto No. 1 (1849, revised 1853) A gaudy showpiece, intended to bring the audience cheering to its feet. There are pounding cadenzas, soulful tunes with rippling accompaniments, tinkly marches and skittering display of every kind - and, like the Piano Sonata but more smilingly, the whole piece is bound together by the endless transformation of two innocent-seeming themes. Liszt wrote subtler works, but few more shrewdly planned: he set out to slay 'em in the aisles, and that's what he does.

→Ⓜ Piano Concerto No. 2 (less prancing; more poetic); Rachmaninov Piano Concerto No. 1; Saint-Saëns Piano Concerto No. 2

Les préludes (1856) Based on a poem (by Lamartine) about how mortal life is a series of preludes to some unknown future existence, this symphonic poem sets out to depict the formless, ambitious striving of the human race. Love, honour, passion and pageantry determine the music's moods, and riding through it all is a sumptuous tune which gives the whole work (and, by implication, the human race?) a feeling of bravura optimism.

→Symphonic poem *Mazeppa* (depicting military heroism); Janáček *Taras Bulba*; Elgar overture *Cockaigne*; Strauss *Don Juan*.

Ⓜ *Faust Symphony* (1854-7) This large work, for soloist, chorus and orchestra, sets passages from Goethe's *Faust* not as a drama but as a symphony, with all the solemnity and seriousness that implies. Its subject was close to Liszt's heart: the story suits his brand of Romantic endeavour, and Faust's character was remarkably like his own. The outer movements, *Faust* and *Mephistopheles*, represent respectively the striving and the darkly assured sides of human nature, and the middle movement, *Gretchen*, is a lovely depiction of simplicity and beauty, often separately performed.

→*Dante Symphony* (similar treatment of Dante's *Inferno* and *Paradisum*); symphonic poem *Hamlet*; Tchaikovsky symphonic fantasy *Francesca da Rimini*.

LITOLFF. See *One-work Composers.*

LUTOSŁAWSKI, Witold (born 1913). *Polish composer.*

Lutosławski suffered from the same blanket Nazi censorship of the arts as *Henze, and found his style late in life: not his early works, but the scores of his fifties and sixties pulsate with a young man's experimental energy. (Of twentieth-century composers, only *Janáček and *Tippett have been such outstanding late developers.) The breakthrough came when he began using aleatory methods (that is, telling the players what notes to play, but leaving the precise timing and placing up to them). Lutosławski frames these improvised sections with precisely-controlled brass fanfares, arrowy woodwind runs and packed string chords. For ordinary concert-goers (as opposed to modern-music specialists) he has been a recent discovery, but his music is now firmly in the repertoire and (like Tippett's, to which its sound is similar) suggests that, in some respects at least, late joys are best.

WORKS Three symphonies, Concerto for Orchestra, *Venetian Games*, *Livre* ('Book'), *Mi parti* and other orchestral works; Cello Concerto; *Paroles tissées* (for tenor and chamber orchestra, a *Britten-like song-cycle composed for Peter Pears), *The Spaces of Sleep*, *Silesian Triptych* and several smaller vocal works; String Quartet, *Paganini Variations* for two pianos and a handful of shorter chamber-music works.

Variations on a Theme of Paganini (1941) During the Nazi occupation of Warsaw, Lutosławski earned his living as a café pianist, barred from musical experiment. Defiantly, he met to play piano duets with a colleague after hours – and hence this piece. It uses the same theme as *Brahms's *Paganini Variations* and *Rachmaninov's *Rhapsody on a Theme of Paganini*, but shows sides of it neither they nor Paganini could have dreamed of: jazz, pigeon-toed spoof-*Stravinsky, *Bartókian folk-dance. It's a slight work, but no less delightful for that. (A sparky orchestral version also exists.)
→*Dance Preludes* (clarinet and piano); Stravinsky *Three Easy Pieces* and *Five Easy Pieces* for piano duet (also known as *Two Suites* for small orchestra); Poulenc *L'embarquement pour Cythère*.

Ⓜ **Concerto for Orchestra** (1954) As its title suggests, this work is kin to Bartók's, and like it tempers orchestral virtuosity with folk-music verve and tunefulness. Lutosławski's harmony, however, is more self-consciously 'delectable' than Bartók's (like *Ravel, he set out consciously to seduce the ear), and his orchestration is both spikier and silkier.
→*Venetian Games*; Milhaud *Suite Provençale*; Piston Symphony No. 6.

Ⓜ **Cello Concerto** (1970) A stunner: written for Rostropovich (and taxing even his virtuoso muscles), and crammed with enticing orchestral sounds. (Trumpets and horns keep breaking out in pattering shrieks, like guests at a kindergarten party; strings provide a slithering, mysterious background to the soloist's rapturous line.)
→Symphony No. 1; Schuller Double Bass Concerto; Tippett Concerto for Orchestra.

M

MAHLER, Gustav (1860–1911). *Austrian conductor and composer.*

Mahler's first ambition was to be a composer. But the works he wanted to write were large-scale, autobiographical and intellectual (musical equivalents of Nietzsche's philosophical writings), and there was no market for them. So he turned to conducting, and by the time he was twenty-five was one of the leading opera-conductors of the day. For the rest of his life he spent nine months each year in the opera-house or concert-hall, and composed during his summer holidays. Like *Wagner, he thought that an opera-production should be a single, unified experience, as much under one person's control as possible: as well as rehearsing the music, therefore, he organized scene-painting, lighting and stage-movement, and even extended his interest to artists' contracts, ticket-sales, poster-design and the efficiency of cleaners and backstage staff. (His ten years as director of the Vienna Court Opera are still remembered, eighty years on: he was peppery with self-important singers or players, and mercilessly sacked any who fell short of his standards.)

Mahler never wrote an opera of his own. As a composer, he had two main musical outlets. One was the all-embracing, Nietzschean work he had planned from boyhood, and for this he chose not stage-music but symphonies. (He said that a symphony 'should contain the world'.) The second was German folk-poetry, with its simple rhythms and direct, heartbreaking images of love and death. When he wrote songs, he often set folk-words, to tunes as naive and plaintive as folksongs. When he wrote symphonies, he used huge orchestras (and sometimes choirs as well), and composed in 'advanced' forms and harmonies derived from *Berlioz and *Liszt as well as Wagner. Often these orchestral works include wistful, folksong-like themes, giant's tears; otherwise they are forceful, dramatic and passionate, designed to express all the heroic enterprise and nostalgic brooding of humanity. Of other composers, only *Tchaikovsky so nakedly, so magnificently, turned private obsessions and emotions into such public art.

WORKS Ten symphonies (No. 10 completed by Deryck Cooke); *Das Klagende Lied* and *Das Lied von der Erde*; song-cycles with orchestra *Lieder eines fahrenden Gesellen* and *Kindertotenlieder*; several dozen songs with piano, many setting folk-poems; chamber works (early; unripe) including Piano Quintet.

Lieder eines fahrenden Gesellen ('Songs of a Wayfarer') (1885, revised 1890s) These four songs, to Mahler's own poems inspired by an unhappy love-affair, evoke the leafy forests, apple-cheeked maidens and broken-hearted peasant boys of the Grimm fairytales – and the music is suitably pastoral and gentle, matching the words' vision of happiness snatched beyond recall. (The original versions had piano accompaniment; the revised versions, with orchestra, are better.)

→'Ich atmet' einen linden Duft' ('I breathed a delicate fragrance') (from *Five Rückert Songs:* orchestral accompaniment again preferable to piano original); Symphony No. 4 (especially finale); Humperdinck *Hansel and Gretel Suite* (especially 'Dream-pantomime': this Grimm-fairytale opera is in no way merely a children's work).

Symphony No. 1 (1888) Because of its folksong melodies, this is the most approachable of Mahler's large-scale works: its slow-movement Funeral March (based on a gloomy, minor-key version of 'Frère Jacques') and its bitter-sweet Viennese-waltz Scherzo are Mahler at his most unexpected and most inspired. Nearest to it in charm and simplicity is the Ⓜ Symphony No. 4 (1901): this begins with sleighbells and ends with a child's song about the delights of paradise, a place where St Peter goes fishing and the blessed sing and dance while angels bake bread for a party. The Symphony No. 3 (1896) uses similarly wide-eyed folk-poems, set for boys' choir and orchestra; but it is also tinged with Mahler's other main preoccupation, death. Funeral marches and witches' sabbaths are the main forces in the Ⓜ Fifth, Ⓜ Sixth and Ⓜ Seventh symphonies (1902; 1904; 1905), a trilogy of vast works for orchestra alone, each intended to fill most of an evening and to dominate any concert they appear in. For many Mahler-lovers, the Symphony No. 6 is the best of them, one of his finest works; a good first approach to them is the *adagietto* slow movement of the Fifth Symphony, separately famous thanks to its use on the sound-track of Visconti's film *Death in Venice*. Symphonies 2 and 8 (1894; 1906) are really choral cantatas on the largest scale: the theme of No. 2 is the Resurrection, and No. 8, using so many performers that it earns the nickname 'Symphony of a Thousand', glowingly sets parts of Goethe's *Faust*. Death haunts the Ⓜ Ninth and Ⓜ Tenth Symphonies (1908–11; 1910), for orchestra alone: they are prolonged, elegiac meditations with an autumnal feeling close (except that they are audibly Austrian, not English) to *Elgar's end-of-Empire musings.

→Good follow-ups to the lighter symphonies are Mahler's own songs, Reger *Folksongs* for choir and Orff *Carmina Burana*; good follow-ups to the serious works are Strauss *Ein Heldenleben* (heroic), Pfitzner *Palestrina Preludes* and Symphony (mystical) and Mahler's own elegiac song-cycle for two voices and orchestra, Ⓜ *Das Lied von der Erde*.

MARTINŮ, Bohuslav (1890-1959). *Czech composer.*

Martinů began his career as a violinist in the Czech Philharmonic Orchestra, but moved abroad in 1923 and lived thereafter from composing and teaching. At first, in 1920s Paris, he followed the prevailing musical fashions: ragtime rhythm, smart discords spiking otherwise simple harmony, slick orchestration and clockwork-toy tunes, with not a hair out of place and all emotion out of sight. But as his (self-imposed) exile continued, he began filling his works with reminiscences of the folk music and peasant dance rhythms of his native land, and this completely changed his style. The 'Czech' feeling in his music, added to soaring tunes, straightforward harmony and seductive orchestration, makes some critics call him a twentieth-century *Smetana – and so he is: his works are equally enjoyable, equally unflustered and often equally inspired.

WORKS Six symphonies, Double Concerto, *Concerto grosso, Frescoes, Parables* and a dozen other orchestral works; sixteen concertos (including five for piano and two for violin); nine operas (including *Julietta*, serious, and *Comedy on the Bridge*, farcical); six ballets (including *The Kitchen Revue*); *Field Mass, The Epic of Gilgamesh* and several other choral works (many based on Czech folk poetry); seven string quartets, two violin sonatas, two cello sonatas, two piano trios, Wind Quintet and dozens of other chamber works; sets of piano pieces (e.g. *Czech Dances; Études and Polkas*) and a handful of songs.

La revue de cuisine ('The Kitchen Revue') (1927) This spoof-jazz ballet (about kitchen implements that come to life) is typical early Martinů: cheeky red-nosed fun, a romp.
→Ballet suite *Spaliček*; Ibert *Divertissement*; Milhaud *Le boeuf sur le toit.*

Ⓜ *Frescoes of Piero della Francesca* (1955) Relaxed recollection of three Renaissance paintings, the delicacy of Piero's inspiration uncannily matched in sound.
→Ⓜ *Sinfonietta giocosa*; Respighi *Botticelli Triptych* (similarly limpid, but with older-fashioned harmony); Schuller *Seven Studies on Themes of Paul Klee.*

Ⓜ **Double Concerto** (1938) This fine *concerto grosso* (for two string orchestras, piano and timpani) was written at the time of the German invasion of Czechoslovakia, and the tragedy turned Martinů's mind from the simple entertainment-piece he'd planned (like so many he'd produced throughout the 1930s) to grief-stricken lament. The grave, chordal slow movement is often used to accompany films of war-devastated landscapes or of concentration camps, and fits them perfectly. But the outer movements are fast and sinewy, with a kind of serious joviality which is one of Martinů's most characteristic moods.
→ Ⓜ *Memorial to Lidiče*; Lutosławski *Funeral Music*; Honegger Symphony No. 2.

MASCAGNI. See under 'Leoncavallo', *One-work Composers*.

MAXWELL DAVIES. See *Davies, Peter Maxwell*.

MENDELSSOHN, Felix (1809-47). *German composer.*
The name Felix means 'lucky', and fits Mendelssohn perfectly. His family was large and loving, his parents were wealthy and his home was always filled with interesting, amusing visitors: politicians, poets, businessmen, artists and musicians. He was outstandingly gifted: he had a photographic memory (he only needed to read a piece of writing once to remember it forever), he could speak half a dozen languages, he wrote poetry and sketched, he was interested in philosophy (which he studied at university). He could have followed any of a dozen careers. But from childhood his supreme gifts were musical. He played piano (to virtuoso standard), organ and violin, conducted, and above all composed: by fifteen he had written an opera, a dozen symphonies and more than 100 chamber works and songs; at seventeen, thanks to his Octet and *Midsummer Night's Dream* overture, he was one of the most admired composers in Europe.

After university, Mendelssohn decided to make music his career. His graduation-present from his parents was a three-year Grand Tour of Europe, and he used it to make friends and contacts everywhere (he became an especial favourite of the British royal family) and to gather impressions for musical works (the *Fingal's Cave* overture, the 'Scottish' and 'Italian' symphonies). At twenty-four he became conductor of the Lower Rhine Music Festival and at twenty-six he was appointed conductor of the Leipzig Gewandhaus Orchestra, a post he kept for the rest of his life. He was the first conductor to do away with the old variety-bandbox kind of concert (in which a *Beethoven symphony, say, might have its movements interrupted by songs, instrumental solos and even novelty interludes such as yodelling): he insisted that works be played complete, and brought music by *Bach, *Handel, *Haydn, *Mozart and others from obscurity to public fame. He spent weeks and months of each year touring (he visited Britain, for example, ten times in twelve years), and in order to fit composing into his schedule he got up at five every morning and worked until breakfast. No one could keep up such a life forever. In 1847, already suffering from overstrain and in the middle of an exhausting British tour, he was shattered to hear of the death of a beloved sister, hurried home, and shortly afterwards suffered two strokes and died.

The music Mendelssohn wrote in his teens and early twenties is inspired: it has the same zestfulness as *Schubert's, and the same knack of sounding absolutely inevitable, as if it had been discovered fully-formed,

needing nothing more than to be set down on paper. He favoured disciplined, eighteenth-century forms rather than Romantic mood-explorations:
his music's elegant good taste is among its greatest charms. In his later,
busy years he wrote in the same clear-headed style, but lost some of his
early freshness; even so, whenever he returns to top form (as in the Violin
Concerto), few composers' music has such power to lift the heart.

WORKS Five symphonies (including the 'Scottish' and the 'Italian'); six
overtures (including *Midsummer Night's Dream*, *Fingal's Cave* and *Calm
Sea and Prosperous Voyage*); twelve short symphonies for strings; six concertos (three for piano, two for violin, one for two pianos) and several
shorter works for soloist and orchestra; one opera and several sets of
incidental music (including *A Midsummer Night's Dream*); six large
choral-and-orchestral works (including *Elijah*, *St Paul* and *Hymn of
Praise*); six string quartets, three piano quartets, two string quintets, Sextet, Octet, two violin sonatas, two trios for piano, violin and cello and
several shorter chamber-music works; three piano sonatas, six organ sonatas, *Songs without Words* for piano and a couple of dozen other solo-
keyboard works (including *Variations sérieuses* for piano and *Three Preludes
and Fugues* for organ); fifty-five part-songs for choir and sixty-eight solo
songs.

Ⓜ *Fingal's Cave* (or *The Hebrides*), Op. 26 (1830) Inspired by Mendelssohn's
visit to Scotland in 1829, this sea-picture begins with gentle ripples, builds up to
a spectacular storm and then subsides again to sunny calm. The idea is highly
Romantic – nineteenth-century creative artists drew inspiration from nature as
easily as the rest of us draw breath – but Mendelssohn's use of eighteenth-century
sonata form (the calm ripples are exposition, the storm development) gives the
music intellectual drive as well as poetic charm.
→Ⓜ Overture *A Midsummer Night's Dream* (depicting Shakespeare's fairies, mortals and galumphing peasants; tuneful, marvellously scored – and followed seventeen years later by a suite of incidental music including the thistledown, Puckish
Ⓜ Scherzo); overture *Ruy Blas* (heroic and chivalric); Schubert overture *Rosamunde*; Smetana overture *The Bartered Bride*.

Ⓜ **Symphony No. 4** (the 'Italian'), Op. 90 (1833) Like the *Fingal's Cave* overture, this sets Romantic sound-pictures (of sunny olive-groves, pilgrims to Rome,
shepherds in the Tuscan hills, carnival dancers) in the frame of eighteenth-century
style: it is tone-poem and symphony all in one. Few other works, even of Mendelssohn's, equal the first movement's fizz and the Scherzo's lilt and flow; the
whole symphony is happiness turned into notes.
→Symphony No. 3 (the 'Scottish'); Smetana 'Vltava' from *Má vlast*; Schumann
Symphony No. 1 ('Spring').

Songs without Words There are forty-eight *Songs without Words*, in eight books. They are short piano pieces, sometimes with descriptive titles (e.g. 'Venetian Gondola Song', Op. 19 No. 6), but generally exploring mood rather than theme: each book contains one gently-flowing piece, one agitated, one sprightly and so on. The fame of two of them ('Spring Song', Op. 62 No. 6, and 'The Bee's Wedding', Op. 67 No. 4) has far outstripped the rest; the others (especially such *Schumannesque meditations as Op. 19 No. 1, Op. 53 No. 4 and Op. 85 No. 4) are well worth rediscovery.

→*Andante and Rondo capriccioso*; Grieg *Lyric Pieces*; Bizet *Children's Games* (piano-duet version).

Ⓜ **Violin Concerto No. 2, Op. 64 (1844)** Mendelssohn's First Violin Concerto was an apprentice work, and is now hardly ever played; his Second is one of the best-loved concertos in the repertoire. There are few big-concerto heroics: its slow movement is delicately sentimental and its outer movements revel where those of other concertos strut. Grown-up Mendelssohn rarely recaptured the elfin elegance of such teenage works as the *Midsummer Night's Dream* overture; in this concerto, he throws off the solemn cloak of age and dances.

→Piano Concerto No. 1; Mozart Violin Concerto No. 3; Paganini Violin Concerto No. 1.

Ⓜ **Octet, Op. 20 (1825)** Mendelssohn was sixteen when he wrote this work, and he took care to make it his grandest piece so far: its scoring is unusual (two string quartets), its layout is spacious (four extended movements, 40 minutes long), its predecessors are such weighty chamber-music works as *Mozart's string quintets and Beethoven's 'Razumovsky' Quartets. Mendelssohn easily matches his models in originality and composing skill, and adds a fresh-faced charm very much his own: it's as if he's just discovered how marvellous each turn of phrase, each harmony, each tune can be and is bubbling with eagerness to share his excitement.

→Ⓜ String Quintet No. 1; Mozart String Quintet K 174; Dvořák String Sextet.

Elijah, Op. 70 (1846) In its day, this was Mendelssohn's most popular work (especially in Britain, where it set a choral-music trend for 100 years). It is a dramatic oratorio in the footsteps of *Handel's, telling the life of Elijah the prophet (from the Old Testament of the Bible) in recitatives, arias and powerful, monumental choruses. Its effect is distinctly reduced in the living-room: it was composed to take up a full evening in the concert-hall, and the solemn pleasure of watching soloists in evening dress, massed chairs and a full symphony orchestra is an important part of its appeal. Pomp is out of fashion nowadays; but it was something people of Mendelssohn's time thoroughly enjoyed, and few nineteenth-century oratorios are more gloriously full of it.

→Oratorio *St Paul*; Handel *Samson*; Elgar *The Kingdom*.

MESSIAEN, Olivier (born 1908). *French composer and teacher.*

Like *Franck before him, Messiaen combined composing with a brilliant career as organist and composition-teacher. In 1931 he was appointed organist-in-chief at the Church of the Trinity, Paris, and has played there regularly ever since. His composition-pupils have covered three generations of European composers (including such major avant-garde figures as *Stockhausen and *Boulez), and his essays on harmony and rhythm have influenced countless musicians who never knew him personally. Outside his busy professional life, he has had a phenomenal variety of interests: he has catalogued the songs of every known French bird, as others catalogue folksongs, and also those of tropical birds in Africa, India and South America; he has written poetry, and become expert in ancient Greek and Indian verse; he is a religious philosopher, well-read both in Christian Catholic thought and in the beliefs and ideals of all the other major world religions.

All Messiaen's interests colour his music. Roman Catholic Christianity is the inspiration for much of it: a celebration of God's love for human beings and the yearnings for God in the human soul. (Messiaen often gives his movements titles like 'Praise to the Eternity of Jesus' or 'Serene Hallelujahs of a Soul that Yearns for Heaven'.) Even when the works are not Christian, they often concern love or religion: the subject of *Turangalîla*, for example, is sexual love; *Des canyons aux étoiles* ('From the canyons to the stars') pictures the whole world joining with stars and galaxies to praise the loving power which created them. Many of Messiaen's works use birdsong, transformed into patterns of his own and rescored for instruments; others use the un-Western rhythms of Greek poetry and Indian music; still others employ the *ondes martenot*, an electronic instrument whose sound is a swooping, other-worldly wail which the player can manipulate up and down the scale.

Messiaen's music is as complicated, and as fascinating, as all this suggests. Each piece is like a barrel stuffed with sweets, and unwrapping and savouring them all takes time. But he is also one of the easiest of all modern composers simply to sit back and enjoy: the pure sound of his music is luxuriant, sumptuous and endlessly varied, meant to carry its listeners away as much as to stretch their minds.

WORKS Opera *St Francis of Assisi*; *The Transfiguration of our Lord*, cantata for choir and orchestra; *Turangalîla, Et exspecto resurrectionem mortuorum, Chronochromie, Des canyons aux étoiles* and several shorter orchestral works; *Réveil des oiseaux* and *Oiseaux exotiques* for piano and orchestra; *Regards sur l'Enfant Jésus, Catalogue d'oiseaux* and several smaller piano-solo works; *Visions de l'Amen* for two pianos; *Quartet for the End of Time* for chamber group; *The Ascension, The Nativity, Meditations sur le mystère de la Sainte*

Trinité and many other organ works; *Poèmes pour Mi, Harawi, Cinq rechants* and other vocal works.

Ⓜ *Réveil des oiseaux* ('Dawn Chorus') for piano and orchestra (1953) This short (15-minute) work gives an ideal first glimpse of Messiaen's sound-world. It begins with the singing of a nightingale, continues with the stillness of night (interrupted only by owls, nightjars and woodlarks), then suddenly, as dawn approaches and the birds wake up, opens out in sound until every orchestral instrument seems to be independently whistling, cheeping, chirruping, rustling and hooting. The sun rises, and the sound fades to a single cuckoo's call. How such a concoction of (authentic) birdsongs, advanced harmony and Greek and Indian rhythm manages to be a coherent piece of music (even a 'proper' piano concerto), let alone a masterpiece, is a mystery. It is unlike anyone else's music, and it is splendidly approachable and unforgettable.
→*Oiseaux exotiques* (companion-piece, also for piano and orchestra, depicting exotic birds in a jungle setting); Ⓜ *Catalogue d'oiseaux* ('Bird Catalogue', for solo piano: twenty-one individual birds, each given a single piece and surrounded by forest-sounds and the cries of the birds associated with its habitat); Tippett Concerto for Orchestra.

Ⓜ *Quatuor pour la fin du temps* ('Quartet for the End of Time') (1940) This quartet for piano, violin, cello and clarinet is a sound-picture of the Day of Judgement (when, Christians believe, God will call all human beings to answer for their deeds on earth). Its eight movements have titles like 'Song of the Angel Announcing the Day of Judgement', 'Dance of Fury for the Seven Trumpets' and 'Prayer to the Immortality of Jesus'. It is partly a depiction of the awesomeness and panic of the end of mortals' time on earth, and partly a meditation on the life to come, the rapture of Christian souls united at last with God. As always with Messiaen, the music is moving and exciting in its own right, quite apart from its inspiration: the movements named above are particularly fine.
→Ⓜ *L'Ascension* ('The Ascension', for organ solo: visionary, powerful and spectacularly discordant; at once typical of Messiaen's organ works and one of the best); *Et exspecto resurrectionem mortuorum* ('And I Await the Resurrection of the Dead', a parallel work to the *Quartet for the End of Time*, but for full orchestra); Hindemith Quartet for clarinet, violin, cello and piano.

Ⓜ *Turangalîla-symphonie* (1948) A ten-movement symphony for solo piano, solo *ondes martenot* and enormous orchestra. Its musical inspiration is Indian rhythm, and the idea behind it is a series of linked love-songs, using in particular the *ondes martenot*'s ability to suggest soaring ecstasy. (Movement 6, 'Garden of the Sleep of Love', the heart of the whole work, is especially sensuous.) The piano, with the orchestral strings and brass, turns irregular Indian rhythms into something syncopated and snappy, like giant's jazz. The complete symphony, like *Mahler's Symphony No. 8, is designed to fill a whole concert and 'to contain the world': engrossing enough on records, it becomes a superbly all-engulfing experience in the concert-hall.

→Ⓜ *Chronochromie* ('Time-colour', for soloists and orchestra); Szymanowski Symphony No. 2; Scriabin *Poem of Ecstasy*.

MILHAUD, Darius (1892-1974). *French composer.*

Apart from a year in Brazil as secretary to the French ambassador (his friend, the poet Claudel), Milhaud earned his living exclusively from music. In the 1920s he was one of the avant-garde Paris group *Les Six*, 'The Six', and composed lively nonsense-works with the best of them. (Good examples are the ballets *Le boeuf sur le toit*, 'The Ox on the Roof', and *Les mariés de la Tour Eiffel*, 'The Eiffel Tower Newlyweds', on which he collaborated with other members of *Les Six*: like Keystone film comedies set to music.) In 1940 he emigrated to the USA, where he taught composition, played and conducted his own music, and poured out works of every kind from sonatas to film-scores.

Although he wrote dozens of large-scale works, operas, concertos and symphonies, Milhaud's best music is short and sweet: he was a showman rather than a thinker. His mind was an Aladdin's cave stuffed with other people's discoveries: jazz, Brazilian folk-dances, Jewish religious chant, *Debussyish harmony and *Stravinskian rhythm, and his music is reminiscent of the cubist collages of Picasso or Braque, bland backgrounds decorated all over with exotic snippets stuck on for no other reason than the pretty shapes they make. Prettiness is the point: the less seriously Milhaud took himself, and the less seriously we take his work, the more sure it is to please.

WORKS Twelve ballets (including *The Creation of the World*, *Le boeuf sur le toit*); ten operas (including *The Oresteia*, *Columbus* and *David*); twelve symphonies, sixteen concertos (including five for piano and three for violin), several suites (including *Souvenirs of Brazil*) and other orchestral works; Septet, eighteen string quartets, Trio, a dozen sonatas, suites and other chamber works; Sonata, *Scaramouche* (for two pianos) and many other piano pieces; over 200 songs and choral works.

Ⓜ *Scaramouche* (1939) This two-piano suite, adapted from incidental music to Molière's farce *The Flying Doctor*, frames a pastoral slow movement (like tender lovers' murmurings) with a skittering, jazzy first movement and a *samba*-finale which is often played separately (a pity, as the other movements are just as much fun). If French farce had notes instead of words, it would sound like this.

→ *Le bal Martiniquais* (lively two-piano suite based on Caribbean tunes); Ⓜ *Le Carnaval d'Aix* (piano-and-orchestra suite based on jazzily-arranged French folksongs); Benjamin *Jamaican Rumba*.

(M) *La cheminée du roi René* (1939) Typical of Milhaud's quieter style, this gentle suite (for wind quintet) is an evocation of the countryside round Aix-en-Provence where he was born, and of the restrained pageantry of the medieval 'King René' who ruled there. Unlike (say) *Scaramouche*, the piece avoids red-nosed horseplay: its harmonies are cool, its melodies calm and its scoring notably serene.

→ *Suite d'après Corrette* (for wind quintet; based on Renaissance dance-tunes); (M) *La muse ménagère* (for solo piano: a charming suite depicting the ordinary activities of everyday housework, ironing, dusting, washing-up etc.); Ibert *Trois pièces brèves*.

(M) *La création du monde* (1923) This ballet tells the Bible creation story in terms of 1920s jazz, with a black Adam and Eve and the creatures of Eden transformed into hip-wiggling night-club dancers. The music ranges from a slow blues (on saxophone) to a snappy jazz fugue (exploiting drum-kit, doublebass and slithering trombone). There are very few 'serious' works making effective use of jazz; this is one of the very best.

→ *Le boeuf sur le toit* (jolly ballet, musically unsubtle but enormous fun, especially in the concert-hall); Percussion Concerto; Gershwin *An American in Paris*.

MONTEVERDI, Claudio (1567-1643). *Italian composer.*

It was a dazzling stroke of luck for Monteverdi when, in his early twenties, he was appointed one of the court musicians of the Duke of Mantua. Monteverdi (a village chemist's son) was famous (as a string-player and madrigal-composer) but penniless; the Duke was one of the richest and most cultured princes in Italy. Their association lasted for over twenty years. The Duke took his musicians everywhere: they went to Flanders when he took a water-cure for gout; they even followed him to battle in Hungary, playing for his relaxation when each hard day's fighting was done. He made Monteverdi the head of his musical household, financed the publication of his music, and gave him a free hand to write what works he liked (e.g. operas - a new, untried musical fashion - for the Mantua court). Monteverdi married an opera-singer in 1599, and lived a prosperous and contented life.

Then, when he was in his late forties, everything went wrong. His beloved wife died; he had a nervous breakdown and took several years to recover; his employer died and the new Duke, for all Monteverdi's fame, unceremoniously sacked him; he was unemployed for a year and had to live with his aged parents; a fire destroyed all the sheet-music for twelve of his operas; when he did find a job, as head of music at St Mark's, Venice, he was attacked by highwaymen on his way there and robbed of all he owned. This chapter of misery changed his character. He turned from stage music and madrigals to church works, and busied himself less with glittering Venetian social life than with the service of God and the quiet, efficient running of St Mark's. In 1630, with the opening of public opera-houses in Venice, he returned briefly to secular music to write four new operas, among them his two masterpieces *Orfeo* and *Odysseus' Home-coming*.

Like his life, Monteverdi's music falls into two distinct halves. In Mantua, he wrote mainly secular works: madrigals, solo songs and above all operas. In Venice he concentrated mainly on religious music. But for all this split in its purpose, his work was always unified in style: all his music, church or secular, sets out to give the singers luscious, technically demanding sounds, and to upholster the drama with rich orchestral or choral harmonies. Until Monteverdi's time, most Italian vocal music had been governed by strict polyphonic rules (see *Sixteenth-century Music*); his sumptuous style – as revolutionary in its day as *Bellini's was in the nineteenth century – played a major part in the development of a new, 'dramatic' musical idiom.

WORKS Three surviving operas (*Orfeo, Il ritorno d'Ulisse*, 'Odysseus' Home-coming'; *L'incoronazione di Poppea*, 'The Coronation of Poppaea') and a dozen shorter stage works (chiefly choral ballets on stories from Greek myth); twelve books of secular vocal works (which he called 'madrigals', 'canzonets' or 'musical humours'), songs and choruses about the battle of the sexes, many with instrumental accompaniment; *Vespers*, Masses, Psalms and a handful of shorter religious works.

'**Hor che'l ciel e la terra**' ('Now that Heaven and Earth are Still') (published 1638) The night is still, but a storm of passion seethes in the lover's heart; his quarrel with his beloved tears him apart as war rends a country. Monteverdi sets this highly dramatic scene (as romantic as anything produced in the nineteenth century, 300 years later) with anguished discords, passionate outbursts like screams made into melody, and pattering fast notes to represent the lover's pounding heart, all contrasted with quietly-flowing harmonies depicting the night's stillness. It is a six-minute opera for chamber choir, typical of his madrigals at their most affecting and most intense.
→ Madrigal 'O Primavera, gioventù del anno' ('O Spring, Youth of the Year'); Lassus 'La nuit froide et sombre'; Weelkes 'O Care, thou wilt despatch me'.

Ⓜ *Vespers of the Holy Virgin* (1610) This group of evening motets sets sacred words for soloists, choir and orchestra in the new, operatic style of the time. Monteverdi's music is bluff, fast-moving and full of dramatic harmonies, very different from the flowing church style of composers like *Palestrina: one of the solo arias ('Nigra sum', 'I am dark but fair') is a straightforward operatic love-song; the duet 'Two Seraphim' shows us two angels having a musical argument, trying to outdo each other in trills, runs and long-held notes. The *Vespers* were very much to Venetian taste (they probably got Monteverdi his job at St Mark's); they are his finest work, and one of the masterpieces of the age. Two sections, the 'Magnificat' and 'Sancta Maria', are often performed separately, and give splendid samples of the whole work.

→ Mass *In illo tempore*; motet *Iste confessor*; Gabrieli *Jubilate Deo*.

Ⓜ *Orfeo* (1607) The story of this opera – Orpheus's quest to the underworld to rescue his beloved wife Eurydice, his conquering of the Shades by the beauty of his singing, and his despair when he looks back and loses Eurydice forever – was clearly close to Monteverdi's heart. He wrote it in the year of his own wife's death, and the key scene, where Orpheus sings in Hades to try to win Eurydice back, is heartrending and poignant in a way unequalled in opera for another 200 years. For modern listeners, one of the great joys of *Orfeo* is its breezy instrumental interludes, nothing to do with ancient Greece but magnificently conjuring up the pomp and swagger of Renaissance Italy.

→ *Il combattimento di Tancredi e Clorinda* ('The Duel between Tancred and Clorinda', 20-minute chamber-opera, ideal introduction to Monteverdi's dramatic style); Ⓜ *l'incoronazione di Poppea* ('The Coronation of Poppaea', opera of intrigue set in ancient Rome, with splendidly funny minor characters); Cavalli *La Calisto* (comic opera on a story from Greek myth).

MOZART, Wolfgang Amadeus (1756–91). *Austrian composer.*

At three years old Mozart could pick out tunes on the harpsichord, and cried when anyone played too loudly or too discordantly. At four he could play the harpsichord and the violin as fluently as ordinary children three times his age; at five he began to compose minuets and other short pieces. These were phenomenal gifts, and they must have filled his father (a stern, unimaginative man) with as much alarm as joy. He had no idea how to 'teach' his son – the boy would spend half an hour working at even the most complex problem, then know it perfectly – and it never occurred to him to give him a normal child's upbringing instead of that of a freak. He took him on tours round the princely and aristocratic houses of Europe, performing musical party-tricks and making a fortune. By the time Mozart was twelve, he had visited a dozen countries, proposed marriage to Queen Marie Antoinette of France (who smilingly said 'Ask again when you're older'), written three operas, half a dozen symphonies and 100 other works, stunned musical Europe with his talent (one admirer wrote 'If I had stayed longer in the presence of his genius I should have gone mad with admiration') – and lived his life not in a secure, happy home but in stage-coaches, unfamiliar lodgings and the glittering drawing-rooms of people who treated him less as a human being than as some kind of amusing toy. He continued touring for another ten years, hoping (in vain) as he grew older that someone would offer him a job as well as admiration.

This incredible childhood made its mark on Mozart's personality. He was sunny and charming, instantly at ease with people he met, but he found it hard to make permanent friendships or deep relationships. He could never settle: even in adult life, married and with a family, he would move house several times a year (the record was nine times). He was utterly unable to manage his money, and although he made large sums (from operas and from giving concerts), he frittered them away as fast as he earned them. Until his father died (in 1787, when Mozart was thirty-one) he depended on him for guidance and approval (their letters still exist, and give fascinating insight into a testy but affectionate relationship); if he had married a wife capable of running the family affairs his whole career might have been different, but Constanze was as feather-headed over money as he was. His last four years, though musically rich, were spent in racking poverty and debt.

None of this personal inadequacy appears in Mozart's music. From about the age of twelve he was a fully fledged, expert composer: though his music increased in maturity and magnificence, its style stayed basically the same throughout his life. His years of travel gave him a composing-habit which staggered everyone he met: he planned works in his head down to the smallest detail (often while doing something else, like teaching, eating or playing billiards), and as soon as he was able to sit down with manuscript-paper wrote them out as fast as most people write a letter. He gave the impression that music flowed unstoppably from him – and the impression was true, for in the seventeen years of his mature working life (aged eighteen to thirty-five) he produced an average of four compositions (including at least one masterpiece) a month.

If Mozart's father had had his way – he nagged about it unceasingly till the day he died – Mozart would have settled with a single employer and tailored his inspiration to fit the job. But he steadfastly refused. He preferred the variety and freedom of freelance life, for all its financial riskiness. It suited him to have new commissions out of the blue, for works of every kind. (If the money was right, or if he was intrigued by the idea, he would happily write for anything, even a clockwork organ or a set of wine-glasses filled with different levels of water and organized to sound a scale.) He wrote dance-music, teaching pieces, show-arias to spice up other people's operas, even a *Requiem Mass* for a nobleman who intended to pass it off as his own composition – and he turned hackwork, every time, to genius. His greatest genius, however, was kept for his own music-making, or for his favourite musical forms. He thought of himself first and foremost as an opera-composer, and his operas (especially *The Marriage of Figaro, Don Giovanni, Così fan tutte* and *The Magic Flute*) are of all his works the ones he himself most admired. He spent much of his adult life giving concerts, and wrote superb piano concertos and symphonies to perform at them. His favourite instrument was the viola, and he often played it in chamber music with friends (such as *Haydn): his string quartets and quintets, and his chamber works with piano, are not only among his own best works but stand, for imaginative genius and musical excellence, head and shoulders above most music of the century. One of his biographers (after deploring his unhappy life, in which he was 'an adult throughout his childhood and a child throughout his adulthood') described him as 'the most consummate musician who has ever lived' – and to this day there are countless music-lovers who would agree.

(Most composers' works are identified by Opus numbers (e.g. Piano Concerto No. 1, Op. 15; opus means 'work') or by putting the publication-date after the title (e.g. Symphony in C (1940)). Mozart's works are given K numbers instead (e.g. Piano Concerto No. 27, K 595). K is short for Ludwig Köchel, a nineteenth-century scholar who catalogued Mozart's works.)

ORCHESTRAL WORKS Forty-one symphonies; twenty-seven piano concertos; five violin concertos; four horn concertos; Flute Concerto; Oboe Concerto; Clarinet Concerto; Bassoon Concerto; *Sinfonia concertante* for violin, viola and orchestra; *Sinfonia concertante* for four wind instruments and orchestra; Concerto for two pianos; Concerto for three pianos; Concerto for flute and harp; *Concertone* for two violins; seventeen divertimentos, thirteen serenades (including *Eine kleine Nacht-musik*), more than 100 minuets, gavottes, marches and other dance-pieces, often grouped in sets of six; *Masonic Funeral Music.*

Lighter orchestral works *Eine kleine Nachtmusik* ('A Little Serenade'), K 525 (1787) Mozart wrote his serenades, divertimentos and dance-sets for aristocratic enjoyment: some (e.g. the 'Haffner' Serenade K 250, written to accompany a wedding-feast) were large works for large occasions; others (e.g. the dances; *Eine kleine Nachtmusik*) were smaller-scale, meant to be danced to or to provide an agreeable background for cards or conversation. He built the works on a standard four-movement pattern (fast opening movement, slow movement, minuet, rondo), adding extra movements (usually variation sets or second minuets) if longer works were required, and sometimes beginning and ending with a march. Most of it was hackwork, and he would have been surprised to find works like *Eine kleine Nacht-musik* still popular today. (Their vigorous life is proof that even 'musak', in a genius's hands, can be magnificent, and the loss is his patrons', who probably never listened hard enough to appreciate what delights they were getting for their money.) Occasionally, in his serenades for wind instruments, Mozart intensified his style with deepest inspiration: Serenade No. 10, K 320 (1781), for thirteen wind instruments, for example, is one of his most sublime compositions of any kind, with a soul-easing slow movement, a superb set of variations and a rollicking finale. (How can people have talked through music of this quality?)

→ After *Eine kleine Nachtmusik*, the most tuneful of the lightweight works are *Serenata notturna*, K 239, and *Six German Dances*, K 600; good follow-ups to the Serenade for thirteen wind instruments are the Serenade No. 12, K 388 (sombre), and Serenade No. 11, K 375 (cheerful). Of other composers' music, the nearest equivalents still heard today are Haydn's divertimentos and German Dances, Beethoven's Septet and (for the wind serenades) Dvořák's Serenade Op. 44 and Gounod's *Petite symphonie*.

Concertos Ⓜ Piano Concerto No. 21, K 467 (1785) Throughout his life Mozart wrote piano concertos for his own concert use: he composed the first when he was eleven and the last in 1791, the year of his death. The last ten are masterpieces. He often gave concerts in the towns where his operas were being performed, and wrote piano concertos for them combining 'serious' thought (the musical argument is as packed as in a symphony) with extrovert, whistleable themes as bubbly as the hit tunes in his operas. (In No. 21 – nicknamed 'Elvira Madigan' not in Mozart's time but after a film which used the slow movement – the first movement is brisk and march-like, the slow movement sets a gentle, soaring melody against a pulsing string accompaniment, and the finale is a chattering rondo with half a dozen themes, each chirpier and cheekier than the last.) Of Mozart's concertos for other instruments, only the Clarinet Concerto and Ⓜ *Sinfonia concertante* K 364 (one of his very finest works) scale the same heights; the others are cheerful and charming, music for relaxation and never pondering. (The most unbuttoned of all are the Horn Concerto No. 3 and the Flute Concerto No. 1; the finest are the Concerto for two pianos and the Violin Concerto No. 3.)
→ Ideal follow-ups to the Piano Concerto No. 21 are Nos. 17, 19 and 23; Nos. 25 and 27 might well come next. Good follow-ups to the lighter-weight concertos are the Violin Concerto No. 5 and Oboe Concerto K 314 (also arranged, by Mozart, as the Flute Concerto No. 2). Of other people's concertos, the best follow-ups to Mozart's lighter works are Haydn's Cello Concerto in C and Trumpet Concerto; the more serious concertos might lead to Beethoven's Piano Concerto No. 1.

Symphonies Ⓜ Symphony No. 29, K 201 (1774) Most of Mozart's symphonies are meant as entertainment-music, a cheerful counterpart to his divertimentos and serenades (though intended for concert-listening rather than to be chatted through). Even in his last ten years, his favourite orchestral form was not the symphony but the piano concerto, and his symphonies tend to be tuneful, fluent and undemanding (though No. 29 opens with a dozen bars of deliciously tortuous counterpoint and ends with extrovert whooping horns). The exceptions are Symphony No. 38 (the 'Prague'), written for a visit to Prague to produce *The Marriage of Figaro*, and sharing all that masterpiece's good-humoured zest, and his three last symphonies, written not for patrons or specific public occasions but to please himself. Ⓜ No. 39 is a mellow counterpart to Haydn's symphonies, in a similarly witty, not-a-note-wasted style; Ⓜ No. 40 is heartfelt and sombre; Ⓜ No. 41 ('the Jupiter') begins ceremoniously and ends with a glorious intellectual frolic, half a dozen themes put through their paces like circus thoroughbreds. The three symphonies together are not only the summit of Mozart's own creative work, but dwarf most other music of the century: they sum up exactly what eighteenth-century orchestral music was trying to do, and what – at least in the hands of genius – it might achieve.

→ After No. 29, the best follow-ups are Nos. 31 ('Paris') and 33; No. 38 might lead to the more statuesque but no less tuneful No. 36 ('Linz'). Of other composers' symphonies, good follow-ups to Mozart's more genial works are Schubert's Symphonies Nos. 2 and 3 and Mendelssohn's 'Italian' Symphony; Bizet's Symphony is a good counterpart to Mozart No. 39, as Haydn's Symphony No. 95 is to Mozart's No. 40; Mozart's No. 41 leads on well to Beethoven's First.

VOCAL MUSIC Nineteen Masses (including *Requiem*), four cantatas, *Vespers*, and a dozen shorter choral-and-orchestral works; twenty-four operas and other stage works (including *Idomeneo*, *The Abduction from the Seraglio*, *The Marriage of Figaro*, *Così fan tutte*, *Don Giovanni* and *The Magic Flute*); twelve concert-arias, cantata *Exsultate, jubilate* and a handful of shorter pieces for solo voice and orchestra; fifty songs for voice and piano.

Masses and other religious works (M) Mass No. 16 ('Coronation'), K 317 (1779). Like Haydn and Schubert, Mozart had little time for solemnity in his religious music. His Masses are cheerful and showy, with lively orchestral accompaniments, operatic-style arias and choruses as down-to-earth and bustling as any in a *Handel oratorio. The 'Coronation' Mass, as its title suggests, was written for a glittering occasion, and is suitably triumphal and ceremonial; others (e.g. Mass No. 6, K 192) are shorter, lighter-weight and intended for ordinary Sunday use; only one, the unfinished *Requiem*, K 626 (1791, completed by Süssmayr), is solemn and devotional in style. His shorter vocal works include a moving setting of the *Vesper* psalms ((M) *Vesperae solemnes de confessore*, K 339); a jolly cantata for solo voice and orchestra, *Exsultate, jubilate* ('Exult, Rejoice'), K 165, like a three-movement vocal concerto; and the tiny but exquisite motet (M) *Ave verum corpus* (K 618) for unaccompanied choir.
→ Mass No. 10, K 220; Haydn Mass No. 3 ('St Cecilia' Mass No. 1); Beethoven Mass in C.

Operas (M) *Le nozze di Figaro* ('The Marriage of Figaro') (1786). Complete opera. For all their delights of melody or harmony, Mozart's dozen early operas are straightforwardly in the styles common at the time: *Mitridate* is serious and heroic, *La finta giardiniera* is bubbly farce, and so on. Even in (M) *Idomeneo*, his most magnificent grand opera, he kept to the conventions: despite the splendour of the music, the libretto is undramatic, the dialogue is wooden and the characters have no more life than people in a comic strip. The exception is *Die Entführung aus dem Serail* ('The Abduction from the Seraglio'), a kind of Arabian Nights comedy set in Turkey: spoken dialogue keeps the characters believable and the arias are Mozart at his wittiest and most affectionate. In 1786 he began working with the librettist Da Ponte, and his style of opera-composing changed. He still used the old conventions (recitatives, arias, formal duets and patter-songs), but extended and transformed them into something entirely new. His late operas are *opera buffa*, i.e. comedies with unlikely stories of seduction, bluff, disguise and magic (or pretend-magic) tricks, but instead of the usual cardboard characters he makes his people, by the sheer power of his music, seem to have real-life emotions, to touch our hearts despite the ridiculous things they do. (The nearest non-musical equivalents are such bitter-sweet Shakespeare comedies as *Twelfth Night* or *As You Like It*.) *The Marriage of Figaro* deals with the outwitting of a self-important Count, but Mozart is less interested in the story than in the characters, the unhappy Countess, the amorous page-boy Cherubino, the baffled and angry Count and above all Figaro, a fast-thinking manservant, and the mischievous Susanna, who manipulate the others like puppet-masters, setting up tangled situations seemingly just for the pleasure of wriggling out of them. Ⓜ *Don Giovanni* is a darker, more serious tragi-comedy about the seducer Don Giovanni, who snaps his fingers at the world, does just as he pleases and even goes to his doom (he is dragged into Hell as the last act ends) with a cry of proud defiance. Ⓜ *Così fan tutte* ('Women are all Alike') is musically the most beautiful of Mozart's last operas. Its plot is even less like real life than any of the others, but few operatic characters are more touchingly portrayed or given lovelier tunes to sing than the four lovers at the heart of it. Ⓜ *The Magic Flute* is a mixture of comedy (the adventures of the bird-catcher Papageno) and unearthly, fairy-tale events involving a magic battle between the powers of light and darkness.

→ No one wrote operas like Mozart's four great masterworks: *The Marriage of Figaro, Don Giovanni, Così fan tutte* and *The Magic Flute* are each other's most satisfying follow-ups. Rossini's *The Barber of Seville* has many of the same characters as *The Marriage of Figaro*, and its plot is (if anything) faster and funnier, but the music lacks Mozart's depth. In the twentieth century, Strauss (in *Der Rosenkavalier*) and Stravinsky (in *The Rake's Progress*) wrote comedies of manners modelled on *Così fan tutte* and *Don Giovanni*, and Tippett's *The Midsummer Marriage* is a 'magic' opera modelled on *The Magic Flute*, but in each case, though the mood is similar, the sound of the music is utterly unMozartian. Perhaps the best eighteenth-century follow-ups are Haydn's comic operas *The World on the Moon* and *The Desert Island*, and Mozart's own concert arias (composed as individual showpieces for singers he admired, or as replacements for arias in his own or other people's operas): among the best are Ⓜ *Ch'io mi scordi di te*, K 505, and *Bella mia fiamma*, K 528.

PIANO AND CHAMBER WORKS Seventeen sonatas, thirteen sets of variations, four fantasias and a score of shorter works for solo piano; five sonatas, variations and other short works for piano duet; Sonata and Adagio and Fugue for two pianos; six string quintets; twenty-three string quartets; Clarinet Quintet; Horn Quintet; Quintet for piano and wind; Oboe Quartet; six flute quartets; two piano quartets; six piano trios; Trio for clarinet, viola and piano; String Trio; Divertimento for violin, viola and cello; Sonata for bassoon and cello; two duos for violin and viola; thirty-five violin sonatas; a dozen minuets, adagios and other short movements for various chamber groups.

Piano music Ⓜ Piano Sonata No. 11, K 331 (1778). Mozart's piano compositions range from teaching-pieces (pretty but trivial) to large, inspired works for his own personal use. In this sonata, one of the finest, a set of variations is followed by a minuet and a dashing Rondo 'in Turkish Style', often played separately. Of the other solo sonata works, the best are the Ⓜ Fantasia K 396 and Sonata No. 14 (K 457), written at different times but usually played as one group, and the gentle sonatas Ⓜ No. 10, K 330, and Ⓜ No. 16, K 570, notable both in their own right and because they influenced Beethoven's early piano sonatas. Mozart's piano-duet and two-piano works were almost all written to play with his sister Nannerl; they are extrovert and domestic all at once, full of sly echoes between the partners, the players picking up and repeating the same music in delightfully different ways. Most of the works are small-scale, but two, the Ⓜ Sonata No. 5 for piano duet, K 521, and the Ⓜ Sonata for two pianos, K 448, are magnificent, keyboard symphonies.

→ Piano Sonata No. 8, K 310 (grand); Piano Sonata No. 12, K 332 (relaxed); *Variations on 'Unser dummer Pöbel meint'*, K 455 (extrovert; also known in an orchestral arrangement, as the last movement of *Tchaikovsky's Suite No. 4). Of other composers' piano music, the best follow-ups to the solo sonatas are Beethoven's sonatas 4 and 6, and to the duet-sonatas Schubert's Sonata in B flat.

Chamber music Ⓜ Quintet No. 3, K 515 (1787). Mozart composed over 200 chamber works; 100 are substantial compositions (quintets, quartets etc.); over forty of those are of the highest quality. In such circumstances, picking the plums is more than usually a matter of personal taste. By and large, the first dozen string quartets, the first twenty violin sonatas, all the flute quartets and the piano trios are light-weight, pieces for teaching or for relaxation. The finest string quartets are the six inspired by and dedicated to Haydn (Nos. 14-19; Ⓜ No. 19, the 'Dissonance', K 465, is magnificent) and the three 'King of Prussia' Quartets (Nos. 21-23), whose texture is enriched because of the prominent cello part (written for the King himself to play) and by the extra weight given to the other parts to balance it. Exploration of the rest of the repertoire might begin with the delectably spiky Ⓜ Oboe Quartet and the silky Ⓜ Clarinet Quintet, and move on to the Ⓜ Quintet for piano and wind, K 452. Mozart's greatest chamber music, indeed for many people the most sublime of all his compositions, are the Ⓜ Divertimento for violin, viola and cello, K 563, and the string quintets 3-6. They are true chamber music, written for the players' private pleasure as much as for an audience; their richness comes chiefly from the fact that Mozart himself played the viola in them, and, by giving himself interesting music, both enriched the inner parts and spurred himself to heights of inspiration not always reached in his music meant for others. (The same is true of other works he wrote for himself, e.g. the piano concertos.) The Quintet No. 3 is the most extrovert of all these works; Ⓜ No. 4 is a dark cousin of the Symphony No. 40, which shares its key; Ⓜ Quintets 5 and 6 are packed with contrapuntal ingenuity in the manner of his Serenade for thirteen wind instruments.

→ Piano Quartets 1 and 2; Violin Sonata No. 35, K 547; Horn Quintet. Of other composers' chamber music, Haydn's is the nearest match: his piano trios are, if anything, better than Mozart's, and his last string quartets equal Mozart's quintets for inventive genius and chirpy tunefulness. (The most Mozartian of all are Nos. 81-2, Op. 77.)

MUSORGSKY, Modest (1839–81). *Russian composer.*

The son of a nobleman, Musorgsky planned an army career, and became a junior officer at seventeen. Unfortunately for him, his regiment was as famous for hard drinking as for fighting. By the age of nineteen he was an alcoholic; the whole of the rest of his life was punctuated by drinking-bouts; he died at last of alcoholic poisoning. (Things were made even worse for him by poverty: when he was twenty-five his parents went bankrupt, and he had to support himself by working as a clerk in the Forestry Department of the Russian Civil Service.)

Throughout this miserable life, Musorgsky struggled to put his music on paper and to get his works performed. He was unquestionably a genius, but lack of training and lack of concentration (thanks to drink) sapped his powers, and critics and audiences of the time found his works magnificent but uncouth. After his death, *Rimsky-Korsakov and others completed and revised many of his scores, and he came at last to be considered one of the most original and most talented composers of his generation.

WORKS Five operas (including *Boris Godunov*, the only one he finished); *Night on the Bare Mountain* for orchestra; *Pictures at an Exhibition*, three other suites and several shorter piano works; three song-cycles (including *Songs and Dances of Death*) and several dozen single songs (including *Song of the Flea*).

Ⓜ *Pictures at an Exhibition* (1874) This work has a brilliantly simple basic idea. A set of pieces, each a musical representation of a picture, is linked by a 'promenade', a short tune suggesting someone walking round an art-exhibition, changing moods as each new picture comes in sight. Many of the pictures are grotesque (witches, gnomes, devils), and Musorgsky's music is suitably fantastical (rather in the way of *Stravinsky's *Firebird Suite*); the work comes to a triumphant, bell-pealing conclusion with 'The Great Gate of Kiev'. As well as Musorgsky's piano-solo original, *Pictures at an Exhibition* is known in a spectacular orchestral arrangement by *Ravel. (Both versions are equally recommended).
→ *Night on the Bare Mountain* (orchestral picture of a witches' sabbath); Balakirev *Islamey*; Debussy *Children's Corner Suite*. Good follow-ups to the orchestral version: Holst *The Planets*; Rimsky-Korsakov *Spanish Caprice*; Arnold overture *Tam o' Shanter*.

Ⓜ *Boris Godunov* (1869; revised 1872) Musorgsky originally designed this as a historical pageant (based on real events) rather than as an opera, and filled it not with arias but with bustling crowd-scenes, plots and counter-plots expressed in fast-moving recitative (see Glossary), and colourful characters such as secret policemen and crooked monks. But the personality of Tsar Boris (a tyrant tormented by his conscience) came to interest him more and more, and he revised the work to highlight Boris's self-hatred, adding arias and even a love-scene (for Boris's chief enemy and the Polish princess who helps him). This revised version (re-orchestrated later by Rimsky-Korsakov) is well known and close in style to 'ordinary' opera; the original version is much more sombre and brooding (like one of Eisenstein's films set to music). *Boris Godunov* is a rewarding work to discover (because Boris's character is so fascinating, and his music expresses it so movingly), but it is highly complicated (because of all the intrigues), and an English libretto is an essential aid to understanding it.

→ Ⓜ *Khovanschina* (complete opera, finished by Rimsky-Korsakov); Glinka *A Life for the Tsar*; Verdi *The Force of Destiny*.

N

NIELSEN, Carl (1865-1931). *Danish composer*.

Like *Donizetti, Nielsen owed his musical education to the army: soon after his fourteenth birthday he enlisted as a trumpeter, and five years later he was a good enough all-round musician to study violin and composition at the Royal Danish Conservatoire. After he graduated he played the violin in the orchestra of the Opera House, and later became famous as a conductor, both of operas and of the choir and symphony orchestra of the Copenhagen Music Society. The Danes considered him the finest musician Denmark had ever produced, and he was honoured throughout Scandinavia as a genius in the class of *Sibelius or even *Brahms.

Outside Scandinavia, however, comparisons with Sibelius did Nielsen more harm than good. For most audiences in Europe and the USA, there was room only for one great Scandinavian composer, and that was Sibelius: Nielsen's music was rarely played, and even now, over fifty years after his death, it is far less well-known than it deserves. The loss is ours, for although it is very little like Brahms's (and even less like Sibelius's) it is warm-hearted, easy-going and unfailingly tuneful – comparisons with *Dvořák would be closer to the mark.

WORKS Two operas (*Saul and David*; *Maskarade*); six symphonies, three concertos, four symphonic poems, *Helios* overture and half a dozen shorter orchestral works; *Hymnus amoris*, *Sleep*, *Springtime on Fyn* and other choral-and-orchestral works; chamber music including four string quartets, String Quintet, Wind Quintet, two violin sonatas; Suite, Theme and Variations, Chaconne and a dozen shorter piano-solo works; *Twenty-nine Short Preludes* and *Commotio* for organ; original songs and arrangements of Danish folksongs for voice and piano.

Maskarade (overture) (1906) Nielsen's opera is a frothy farce of mistaken identity, cheeky servants, pompous town officials and dewy-eyed young lovers outwitting censorious relatives, all set in the eighteenth century and as high-spirited as a pantomime. The overture sets the party atmosphere, a bubble of tunes made even livelier by unexpected twists of melody and harmony.
→ 'Dance of the Cocks' (also from *Maskarade*); Nicolai overture *The Merry Wives of Windsor*; Rezniček overture *Donna Diana*.

Ⓜ **Symphony No. 3** (*'Sinfonia espansiva'*) (1911) Nielsen's six symphonies are his finest works. Nos. 1 and 2 are grand and ceremonious, No. 4 ('The Inextinguishable') and Ⓜ No. 5 are heroic, striving and in his beefiest, most serious style; No. 6, after a swaggering first movement, takes on a secretive, ironic mood unlike anything else he wrote. The best symphony to hear first is No. 3. Its first movement is a gigantic waltz, its second is an evocation of the countryside (one of the most sheerly beautiful pieces of music of the century), its third is a folk-dance interrupted by furious outbursts from the strings, and its finale is a rondo on a gloriously-scored, stirringly-harmonized 'big tune'.

→ Violin Concerto; Brahms Symphony No. 2; Dvořák Symphony No. 5.

Ⓜ **Wind Quintet** (1922) This piece was composed for five friends, and Nielsen gave each of them music to match his character: the flute music is gentle, the clarinet music impetuous, the bassoon music abrupt and joky, and so on. The work has folk-like tunes and open-air harmonies, and ends with a set of delectable variations on a poker-faced mock-chorale.

→ Flute Concerto; *Serenata in Vano*; Janáček wind sextet *Mládi*.

NINETEENTH-CENTURY MUSIC

THE GROWTH OF MUSIC Music was probably more popular in the nineteenth century than at any other time in history. The coming of the industrial age brought prosperity to towns and cities everywhere, and created vast centres of populations eager for entertainment. For many of the actual workers, the people who tended the machines, leisure time was scarce, and they filled it with pub-songs, church-going (some of the most popular hymns ever written date from this time), visits to the theatre, pub or music-hall and, on special occasions, dancing. Many industrial firms had concert-rooms, and created bands and light orchestras to play in them. For anyone who could afford a holiday, there was a flourishing leisure industry (which still survives in seaside piers and fairgrounds) offering musical entertainment of every kind.

For people who had more leisure - factory-managers, shopkeepers, teachers, ministers, lawyers and others - music meant something very different. Enjoying music was a sign that they were cultured, that they cared about the finer things in life and had time and money to spend on them. People took the musical activities of the old aristocrats, opera, dancing, orchestral concerts and chamber-music recitals, and made them their own. They built opera-houses and concert-halls, and flocked to hear the musicians who played in them. Home music-making (especially singing and piano-playing) became as regular a pastime in ordinary houses as it had once been in noble palaces, and hundreds of music publishers sprang up, printing everything from opera-fantasies for piano to marches and sentimental songs.

In such an atmosphere, those who made music ruled supreme. Great performers were idolized as pop-stars are today. Adoring crowds showered Paganini with kisses wherever he played, and threw roses at his feet; people shrieked and swooned for love of *Liszt, and fought for the silk handker-chiefs he used to wipe his brow; the singer Melba travelled in a private train, and even had a pudding (Peach Melba) and a kind of toast (Melba Toast) named after her. With the coming of steam-trains and steam-ships, performers could quickly and easily travel the world. Melba (an Australian) triumphed not only at home but also in Europe and the USA; another singer (Caruso) had a suite of cabins permanently booked for the trans-atlantic crossing; *Albéniz toured South America as calmly as if it had been his native Spain.

'SERIOUS' AND 'LIGHT' MUSIC For composers, all this activity had two effects. First, they now wrote for the general public and not for a narrow circle of aristocratic patrons. Performers and publishers clamoured for new works, and success could bring fortune and enormous fame. (*Rossini began his life in poverty, but retired a rich man at thirty-eight; *Mendelssohn and *Wagner treated royalty as equals; *Brahms was an international celebrity whose every deed made news.) The art of music split in two. At the grand end of the scale were writers of operas, symphonies, concertos and chamber works: they were 'serious' artists, and their works were a musical equivalent of the masterpieces of painters, architects or poets. At the other end were ordinary composers, producing parlour-pieces, dances, hymns, music-hall songs and other pieces of the same workaday kind. Some 'serious' com-posers turned their hands to popular music (*Schubert wrote dances, for example); some 'light' composers also wrote large-scale works (*Sullivan, for example, composed oratorios and a symphony); but by and large the two kinds of music stayed apart, and have continued to do so ever since.

The second effect of music's popularity, at least for 'serious' composers, was that it completely changed the way they thought of themselves. In the eighteenth century the idea had begun that composers were not merely craftsmen working to order, but individuals expressing their own person-alities in the notes they wrote. Now, in the nineteenth century, this idea became all-important. What mattered above everything else was a work's content: what it had to say, the way it expressed its composer's emotions and the way it aroused emotions in its listeners. This kind of music, full of personal feeling, is called 'Romantic'; the 'Romantic movement' covered poetry, painting, fiction and drama too.

When content matters most of all in music, form and harmony are secondary, and can be changed to suit it. Some composers (e.g. Mendelssohn) still found eighteenth-century forms ideal, and used them more or less unchanged. Others (e.g. *Beethoven) used eighteenth-century forms (sonata, symphony, concerto) as starting-points, but expanded or adapted them as the music went its own individual way. Still others (e.g. *Berlioz and Liszt) abandoned earlier ideas, inventing a form, style and musical language to suit the emotional needs of each new piece. (They sometimes drew ideas from art or literature. Berlioz's *Romeo and Juliet*, for example, is a 'dramatic symphony' based on Shakespeare's play; Liszt's *The Slaughter of the Huns* is a musical account of an enormous battle-painting. Other composers, often called 'Nationalists', tried to express the character of their native land in music: *Smetana's works, for example, are deliberately 'Czech', *Borodin's 'Russian', *Grieg's 'Norwegian' and so on.)

Once each work a composer writes is thought of as something entirely new, without reference to earlier styles and ideas, the feeling of unity typical of eighteenth-century music is replaced by one of extreme diversity. Each Romantic symphony or opera demands to be considered entirely on its own, as a work creating and satisfying its own standards. Some composers found that this emphasis on uniqueness made it difficult to write large, long works, and preferred to express themselves in shorter forms. Songs (sometimes grouped into sets or 'cycles'; see *Vocal Music*) became a major part of many composers' output, far more so than in the eighteenth century. Instrumental pieces often had titles like 'Nocturne' (literally 'night-piece', but applied more generally to music expressing a mood of quiet calm) or 'Fantasy' (a piece like a country walk, long or short, seeming to wander in whatever direction the composer decides as he or she goes along). The huge number of such pieces shows, more than anything else, how marked the change had been from outside discipline to the discipline of the composer's own imagination, whether this was refined and delicate (like *Chopin's), passionate (like *Tchaikovsky's) or tormented (like *Mahler's). The sheer variety of mood in nineteenth-century Romantic music is a major part of its appeal.

Listening There is no room in this book to do justice to the enormous range of nineteenth-century popular music; fortunately, many of the hymns (e.g. 'Rock of Ages'), ballads (e.g. 'The Old Folks at Home'), parlour-pieces (e.g. 'Home Sweet Home') and music-hall songs (e.g. 'Daisy, Daisy') are still well-known today and hardly need introduction. For some of the best 'light' music of the century, see the articles on Delibes, Offenbach, *One-work Composers* (Adam, Hérold), Strauss family and Sullivan. Of 'serious' composers, the best to hear first are Bizet, Borodin, Chopin, Grieg, Mendelssohn and Saint-Saëns; exploration could move on to Dvořák, Rimsky-Korsakov and Schumann, and from them to such giants as Beethoven, Brahms, Schubert, Tchaikovsky, Verdi and Wagner. See also Albéniz, Balakirev, Bellini, Berlioz, Bruckner, *Chamber Music, Choral Music, Concerto*,

Fauré, Franck, Granados, *Keyboard Music*, Liszt, Mahler, Musorgsky, *One-work Composers* (Bruch, Chabrier, Leoncavallo, Litolff, Mascagni), *Opera*, *Orchestral Music*, Rossini, Scriabin, Smetana, *Sonata*, *Song*, *String Music*, *Symphony*, *United States Composers*, *Vocal Music*, Weber, Wolf and *Woodwind Music*.

O

OFFENBACH, Jacques (1819–80). *German/French composer.*

After ten years as a virtuoso cello soloist, Offenbach turned at twenty-nine to his real musical love, stage comedy. For six years he conducted the orchestra of the Comédie Française, but in 1855, angry because the theatre authorities (used to Molière, Corneille and other great French dramatists) refused to stage his works, he formed a small theatre-company of his own, the Bouffes-Parisiens. *Bouffes* is a word he invented, a mixture of the grand Italian name for comic opera, *opera buffa*, and the French exclamation *ouf!*, the sound people make when the breath is knocked out of them. The company's name suits the works Offenbach wrote for it: they are mercilessly witty comedies, making fun of everything from Greek myth to the opera-style of the Comédie Française and the huffing and puffing of pompous Parisian officials – and above all, they are crammed with songs. Because the plays were topical and the language was fast and slangy, they have had a bumpier reception outside France, and most are now hardly known; but the music (songs, galops, waltzes, cancans) is international and imperishable – nineteenth-century Paris at its most elegantly frivolous.

WORKS Operas *The Rhine-spirits, The Tales of Hoffmann*; ballet *The Butterfly*; ninety operettas ('bouffes') including *La belle Hélène, Orpheus in the Underworld, The Grand Duchess of Gérolstein, Robinson Crusoe* and *La vie Parisienne*; six suites for two cellos; several short pieces for cello and orchestra; a dozen songs.

Barcarolle (from *The Tales of Hoffmann*) Hypnotically swaying, gentle piece depicting the lapping of water on the Grand Canal in Venice (where Act 3 of *The Tales of Hoffmann*, a love story, is set). This is one of those pieces of music so often parodied by comedians that everyone knows it and mocks it; the original (especially with the words) is seldom heard, and is simple, sincere and beautiful. (There is one similar song in every Offenbach work, and they are as sentimental and charming as his other songs are knockabout.)
→ 'Il était une fois' ('Once upon a Time', from the same opera); Ⓜ 'When I was King of the Boeotians' (from *Orpheus in the Underworld*); Sullivan 'Take a Pair of Sparkling Eyes' (from *The Gondoliers*).

Gaîté Parisienne ('Parisian Gaiety', arranged Rosenthal, 1938) Nine of Offenbach's most sparkling pieces arranged as a lively ballet suite. Few musical stage-
works offer more stylish fun. The music's good-humoured gusto sweeps everything before it.
→ Overture *La Périchole*; Britten *Soirées musicales*; Strauss (arranged Dorati) ballet
Graduation Ball.

Ⓜ *Orpheus in the Underworld* (1858) Complete operetta. The Greek myth of
Orpheus and Eurydice is turned on its head: Orpheus is a boring violin teacher,
Eurydice a flirt in love with their next-door neighbour, a bee-keeper (who is, little
does she know, really the King of the Underworld in disguise); the Paris police
keep bursting in to make sure that the story is decent and respectable; the whole
second half is a glorious party down in the Underworld, with the Shades (drunk
on Lethe-water) singing and watching a cabaret of dancing-girls (whose act ends
with, of all things, the famous Cancan). Like a twentieth-century musical, *Orpheus
in the Underworld* needs to be seen, in English, for full enjoyment (the feeling of
ouf! Offenbach hoped for); records, highlighting the music, are like snapshots,
giving no more than a glimpse of the total fun.
→ Ⓜ *La belle Hélène* ('Pretty Helen', an even more uproarious send-up of the myth
of Helen of Troy); *Barbebleu* ('Bluebeard': fewer hit numbers, but his funniest
farce); Rodgers musical *The Boys from Syracuse*.

ONE-WORK COMPOSERS

Some composers are internationally famous for one work above all others.
In some cases, the 'one-work' tag is justified, and the well-known piece is
the only one which deserves to be known at all; but sometimes it puts a
composer's whole output unfairly in the shade, and exploration of his other
music will lead to equal (or even greater) delights.

ADAM, Adolphe (1803–56): Ⓜ *Giselle* (1841). Adam was at one time or
another a critic, an organist, a conductor, a theatre-owner and a professor
of counterpoint. He wrote thirty-nine operas and operettas and a dozen
ballets, and the best of them, *Giselle*, is not only his masterpiece but one
of the most popular of all Romantic ballets (outstripping even *Swan Lake*).
It is best heard complete, as an accompaniment to dancing in the theatre;
but a suite of extracts is often heard on record, and has carried Adam's
reputation round the world.
→ Overture *If I were King*; Delibes *Coppélia*; Hérold (arranged Lanchbery) *La fille
mal gardée*.

ALBINONI, Tomaso (1671–1751): *Adagio*. Although he wrote fifty-five operas
and over 100 concertos and chamber works, Albinoni's name lives today
because of this haunting piece, to which he actually contributed only a

handful of notes. (He wrote a bass line, repeating the same notes over and over again; his twentieth-century editor, Giazotto, added elegiac harmonies and an expressive, elusive tune.)
→ Oboe Concerto, Op. 7 No. 3; Pachelbel *Canon*; Barber *Adagio for Strings*.

BENJAMIN, Arthur (1893-1960): *Jamaican Rumba* (1938). This rumba-rhythm, jazz-harmony folksong arrangement is the second of *Two Jamaican Pieces*, and has completely (and unjustly) eclipsed the first. Written for piano duet, it is liveliest in that form, though it has been rearranged for orchestras, chamber groups and dance-bands of every shape and size.
→ Harmonica Concerto; Milhaud 'Braziliera' (from *Scaramouche*); Albéniz *Tango*; Falla *Ritual Fire Dance*.

BRUCH, Max (1838-1920): Violin Concerto No. 1, Op. 26 (1868). In a long and prolific composing career, Bruch was struck by true creative lightning just once, in the touching Ⓜ slow movement of this concerto. It ranks with the most beautiful works ever composed for violin, puts Bruch briefly in the league of *Mendelssohn or *Tchaikovsky, and dwarfs its companion movements (which are competent, enjoyable and second-rate).
→ *Kol Nidrei* for cello and orchestra; Svendsen *Romance*; Saint-Saëns Violin Concerto No. 3.

CANTELOUBE, Joseph (1879-1957): 'Baïlero' (from *Songs of the Auvergne*). This music (a heart-breaking lament) started life as a folksong; Canteloube gave it and two dozen others sumptuous harmonies and a gorgeous orchestral accompaniment; it is regularly used as background music for TV wild-life films showing lonely mountain pastures, but is far more robust and fine than that suggests.
→ 'Lou coucut' ('The Cuckoo', also from *Songs of the Auvergne*); Villa-Lobos *Bachianas Brasilieras* No. 5; Fauré 'Pie Jésu' (from *Requiem*).

CHABRIER, Emmanuel (1841-94): Ⓜ *España* (1883). Bouncy, breezily tuneful evocation of picture-postcard Spain. (The main tune was a hit song in the 1950s, with the unlikely words 'Hot Diggety'.) Chabrier (like *Borodin, an amateur of genius) produced only a handful of works; the best of them share this piece's glittering high spirits, like brash musical equivalents of the posters of Toulouse-Lautrec.
→ *Joyeuse marche*; Bizet *Carmen Suite*; Tchaikovsky *Spanish Caprice*.

DUKAS, Paul (1865-1935): Ⓜ *The Sorcerer's Apprentice* (1897). Hyper-critical Dukas tore up all but twelve compositions; this orchestral scherzo (based on Goethe's engaging story of the young sorcerer who tries his master's spells to make brooms fill buckets, with disastrous, hilarious results) is the best of them all. Walt Disney filmed it (in *Fantasia*, with Mickey Mouse battling against the brooms); it is a virtuoso orchestral showpiece, a sparkling example of musical wit.

→ *La Péri*; Rimsky-Korsakov suite *The Golden Cockerel*; Ravel *Boléro*.

GLINKA, Mikhail (1804–57): overture *Ruslan and Lyudmila* (1842). Regarded in his day as 'the father of Russian music' (see Balakirev), Glinka is now chiefly remembered for this lively operatic overture, a combination of forthright tunes, hammering drums and frenzied scales for wind and strings. He was a wealthy amateur, and composed few works; all have the same straightforward charm.

→ *Kamarinskaya*; Rezniček overture *Donna Diana*; Rossini overture *The Thieving Magpie*; Hérold overture *Zampa*.

GOUNOD, Charles (1818–93): ballet music from opera *Faust* (1859). Gounod wrote church music, symphonies and oratorios, but is chiefly remembered for his 'Ave Maria' (a rapt melody fitted to *Bach's Prelude No. 1 from the *Well-tempered Keyboard*), and for this hugely popular suite from one of his eleven operas. The story of *Faust* suggests weight and seriousness; Gounod's music is bright and light, akin to *Offenbach's or *Sullivan's.

→ 'Juliet's Sleep' (orchestral interlude from opera *Romeo and Juliet*); Ponchielli 'Dance of the Hours' (from opera *La Gioconda*); Rossini-Respighi *La boutique fantasque*; Tchaikovsky *Nutcracker Suite*.

LEONCAVALLO, Ruggero (1857–1919): 'Vesta la giubba' ('On with the Motley'). This sobbing tenor aria (sung by a broken-hearted clown) comes from Leoncavallo's one-act opera Ⓜ *I pagliacci* ('The Strolling Players'), usually performed in a double-bill with Ⓜ *Cavalleria rusticana* ('Rustic Chivalry') by Pietro MASCAGNI (1863–1945). Both operas are passionate tear-jerkers; their music is as melodramatic as a film-score, and their chief glory is the scope they give for full-throated, barrel-chested singing, Italian *bel canto* at its red-blooded best. ('Vesta la giubba' gives a splendid sample of the whole experience; just as swaggering, though more optimistic, is the drinking-song 'Viva il vino' from *Cavalleria rusticana*.)

→ Leoncavallo 'Testa adorata' ('Adored One', from his version of *La bohème*, on the same libretto as *Puccini's opera); Mascagni 'Ed anche Beppo' ('And Beppo Too', from opera *L'amico Fritz*); Puccini 'Nessun dorma' ('None shall Sleep', from opera *Turandot*); Puccini 'O My Beloved Father' (from opera *Gianni Schicchi*).

LITOLFF, Henry (1818–91): Scherzo (from *Concerto symphonique* No. 4). Litolff was a conductor and piano soloist as well as a composer, and wrote this (and other piano-and-orchestral works) for himself to play. In this gossamer music, a pattering dance leads to a mock-solemn chorale, and the two ideas are then combined as deftly and enjoyably as in a conjuring trick. Litolff's other works are *Mendelssohn-and-water; this one is champagne.

→ Finale (also from *Concerto symphonique* No. 4); Liszt *La campanella* (piano solo); Saint-Saëns *Wedding-cake Caprice*.

RODRIGO, Joaquin (born 1902): *Concierto de Aranjuez* (1939). The huge popularity of the guitar in the last forty years has made this concerto one of the most beloved of all classical works, and placed its second movement (a solemn melody like an Andalusian folksong, with throbbing accompaniment) high in the hit parade. Rodrigo's huge catalogue of works includes a dozen other concertos, for various instruments – all of them as delightfully bitter-sweet as this.

→ *Fantasia para un gentilhombre* (guitar and orchestra); Castelnuovo-Tedesco Guitar Concerto No. 1; Villa-Lobos Guitar Concerto.

SINDING, Christian (1856-1941): 'Rustle of Spring' (from *Six Piano Pieces*, Op. 32). This is the kind of piano piece everyone plays in their dreams: a glorious left-hand tune accompanied by rippling waterfalls of right-hand notes. It's hardly great music (in the way that a chocolate-box photograph is hardly great art), but (again like a chocolate-box photograph) it does perfectly and entertainingly exactly what it sets out to do.

→ Serenade, Op. 33 No. 4; Liszt *La campanella* and *Liebestraum* No. 3; Debussy 'Clair de lune' (from *Suite Bergamasque*).

VILLA-LOBOS, Heitor (1887-1959): Ⓜ *Bachianas Brasileiras* No. 5 (1938). Two pieces for voice and eight cellos: a lovely, wordless song and a fast-moving finale. The first piece, the voice floating seductively above a plucked-string accompaniment, is one of those works everyone instantly recognizes but finds it hard to name: a melody as simple and haunting as a childhood song.

→ *Bachianas Brasileiras* No. 2 ('The Little Train of the Caipeira', a bustling orchestral portrait of a self-important village steam-train); Guitar Study No. 1; Falla 'Jota' (from *Seven Popular Spanish Songs*: voice-and-piano version).

OPERA

Opera (the word is Italian for 'work', and was adopted for the dramatic genre in seventeenth-century England) was invented in Florence in the late sixteenth century. Artists, writers and architects of the time were eagerly reviving the culture of ancient Greece and Rome (hence the name Renaissance, 'rebirth', given to this period of history); opera was an attempt to re-create the effect of ancient Greek drama, in which the words were chanted or sung as well as spoken. Music was essential: just as much as words or stage actions, it revealed character, fixed the pace of the story, expressed emotion and created or heightened tension.

SEVENTEENTH-CENTURY OPERA The earliest operas were hardly more than chanted plays, giving everyone much the same kind of music regardless of situation or character. But by the beginning of the seventeenth century, little more than a generation after opera's birth, two composers of genius, first *Monteverdi and then Cavalli, developed the idea of marking high spots in the plot by giving the characters **arias** (florid songs), which stopped the action in order to explore feelings and sentiments. (This was – and is – quite unlike what happened in a spoken play, where continuous, uninterrupted action was the norm.) Monteverdi's *Orfeo* (1607) and *The Coronation of Poppaea* (1642) and Cavalli's *L'Egisto* (1643) and *La Calisto* (1651) still offer a musical experience as gorgeous as the peacock-clothes, full-bottomed wigs and high-society manners of the age for which they were composed. (See *Seventeenth-century Music*.)

EIGHTEENTH-CENTURY OPERA In the seventeenth and early eighteenth centuries opera flourished as an entertainment for the rich. Gradually the conversational parts of the action (called **recitative**, or 'recitation') took second place to the arias, and all attention focussed on the singers. Then (as now) what the audience liked best in an opera-singer was a combination of acting-skill and vocal dexterity, and performers who could provide both trod an international circuit of honours, fame and wealth. The orchestra's role was chiefly to give the singers discreet accompaniment; the chorus parts were skimpy (they usually played cheering or panic-stricken crowds); the plots gave opportunities for spectacular stage effects (e.g. burning towns) and for intrigue (screens and doors, suitable for hiding behind, were standard scenery); the operas moved from one show-aria to the next, so that the effect was rather like a stunning vocal concert loosely held together by a story from classical mythology or ancient history. Many writers of this kind of opera were hacks; but in the first half of the eighteenth century the style was used by one composer of consummate genius: *Handel.

In the mid-1700s fashions in opera changed, and the undramatic, singer-centred style fell out of use. Composers in northern Europe, led by *Gluck, favoured an entertainment nearer to modern music-drama than to seventeenth-century Italian opera. The action was continuous, and the arias, instead of being there for their own showy sakes, fitted into the plot and were justified by it. Operas such as Gluck's *Orfeo* (1762) and *Iphigenia in Aulis* (1774) revived the art of moving their audience as well as impressing them, and the music-drama style has been the main form of opera ever since, favoured in the nineteenth century by Romantic composers like *Weber or *Berlioz, and carried by *Wagner to heights unequalled by any previous stage composer.

Meanwhile, in the eighteenth century, the new ideas of dramatic unity, and of making the music an intellectually satisfying whole in its own right, affected the style even of composers who otherwise retained the old Italian recitative-and-aria method of construction. The greatest of them all was *Mozart, and his *Marriage of Figaro* (1786), *Così fan tutte* (1790), *Don Giovanni* (1787) and *The Magic Flute* (1791) have musical unity (as powerful as any symphony's or sonata's) without losing the dash appropriate to stage entertainment.

NINETEENTH- AND TWENTIETH-CENTURY OPERA In early nineteenth-century Italy there was a brief and glorious revival of the singer-centred style: few operas offer singers more challenges and audiences more thrills than *Bellini's *La sonnambula* (1831), *Donizetti's *Lucia di Lammermoor* (1835) or *Rossini's *Cinderella* (1817). But for most other composers, from *Beethoven to *Verdi, the changes pioneered by Gluck were the making of the art. The combination of intellectual unity in the music and barnstorming swagger in the stories was enhanced by a switch to passionate, Romantic and often highly melodramatic plots. Gone were the decorous (if bloodthirsty) eighteenth-century scheming and measured discussion of classical history and legend; nineteenth-century composers turned instead to writers like Shakespeare, Walter Scott, Byron and Goethe, and found in their treatment of the steamier episodes in Medieval and Renaissance history exactly what they wanted: doomed lovers, poisoned chalices, political plotting and mad scenes on the one hand, and on the other nobility of soul, resignation, selfless heroism and pure-hearted love. *Wagner went a step further back in time, turning to epic history and myth for his subject-matter. Many of the finest and most popular operas in today's repertoire use these elements, and in the hands of genius – Verdi's *Force of Destiny* (1862), *Don Carlos* (1867) or *Otello* (1887) come to mind – the music turns preposterous plots into affecting, passionate statements about human life at large. Other composers took their stories not from history or Romantic literature, but from everyday life, newspaper accounts and the 'realistic' plays and novels of writers like Dumas, Dickens or Victor Hugo. *Bizet's *Carmen* (1875) is about a gipsy, murdered by the man she rejects for a handsome bullfighter. *Puccini's *La bohème* (1896) is set among poverty-stricken artists in the attics of Paris; the heroine of Verdi's *La traviata* (1853) is a courtesan dying of consumption.

From Mozart's time to the present day, opera has been the most lavish, the grandest and for many people most satisfying of all musical forms. It combines spectacle, technical dazzle and emotional pulling-power to a degree unequalled in any other performing art. Those unmoved by it may complain that there have been no advances since the 1890s, that the great opera-composers of this century – *Berg, *Britten, Menotti, *Henze – use methods and styles very little different from Verdi or Puccini. Opera-devotees might answer that the reason the form has stayed unchanged for so long is that it works so well: if a machine does to perfection the job for which it was devised, why change it?

Listening Good, short samples of early operatic style are *Monteverdi's *Il combattimento di Tancredi e Clorinda* (heroic), Alessandro Scarlatti's cantata *Non, non ti voglio Cupido* (dramatic) and *Pergolesi's *La serva padrona* (comic). For further recommendations, see Handel, Monteverdi and Purcell. Good samples of eighteenth-century operatic style are Mozart's concert-arias (e.g. *Per pietà, non ricercate*, K 420); Cimarosa's *Il maestro di cappella* amusingly sends up the backstage problems of singers, conductor and producer. For further recommendations, see Gluck, Haydn and Mozart. Good, brief samples of nineteenth-century opera are Donizetti's *The Night Bell* (comic) and Leoncavallo's *I pagliacci* (tragic). For further recommendations from this, the great age of opera, see Bellini, Bizet, Donizetti, Dvořák, Musorgsky, Offenbach, Puccini, Rossini, Smetana, Sullivan, Tchaikovsky, Verdi, Wagner and Weber. Good samples of twentieth-century opera are Poulenc's one-act, one-singer tragedy *La voix humaine* (sent up in Menotti's jolly *The Telephone*) and Britten's chamber opera *Curlew River* (based on a Japanese *Noh* play). For further recommendations see Berg, Britten, Gershwin, Henze, Janáček, Ravel, Richard Strauss, Stravinsky and Tippett.

ORCHESTRAL MUSIC

The word 'orchestra' originally meant not people but a place: the part in front of the stage where the chorus sang and danced in ancient Greek theatre. In the Renaissance, musicians occupied the same area, their jobs being to accompany the singers and to frame the stage action with preludes, interludes and postludes. It was not until the seventeenth century that 'orchestra' took on the meaning it has today.

EARLY ORCHESTRAS The growing fashionableness of opera in the seventeenth century made orchestras popular too. Composers like *Purcell and Lully took music from their theatre works and arranged it as orchestral suites, to be played at parties and other aristocratic gatherings. Other composers developed the idea of works with orchestral accompaniment in two different ways: some wrote church music in operatic style (with soloists, choruses and orchestras); others used instrumental soloists instead of singers (and so created the *concerto).

EIGHTEENTH-CENTURY ORCHESTRAS By the beginning of the eighteenth century, orchestral music was popular everywhere, and there was plenty available, in the forms of suites (usually, by then, written specially, not assembled from theatre-works), concertos and *concerti grossi*. The standard orchestra of the time was a group of strings with harpsichord or organ, strengthened if required by woodwind (oboes and bassoons in fast movements, flutes or recorders in slow movements) and in the grandest works of all by horns, trumpets and drums. The leading orchestral composers of the time were *Corelli (*concerti grossi*), *Telemann (suites and concertos), *Bach and *Vivaldi (concertos) and *Handel (concertos and *concerti grossi*).

As the century wore on, more and more people came to prefer orchestral music above most other kinds, and players, instead of dividing their time between opera-house, church and orchestra, began to specialize. All over Europe, large and well-drilled orchestras were formed; the standard of playing improved (especially on once-Cinderella instruments like the viola, bassoon and double bass), and composers began writing virtuoso orchestral works, showing off the skills of a whole band as concertos showed off soloists. One orchestra in particular, at Mannheim in Germany, staggered everyone who heard it. It was large (over forty players, twice the usual size for the time); it regularly used woodwind and brass instruments as well as strings (and welcomed newly-respectable instruments such as clarinets); its musicians played so skilfully that, as one awed visitor remarked, they were 'like an army of generals'. Composers for this orchestra developed a new musical form, the *symphony, designed especially to show it off. Orchestras were formed elsewhere to equal it (*Mozart thoroughly approved of the orchestras in Paris and Prague; *Haydn thought one London orchestra finer even than his own at Esterháza), and by the end of the century public orchestral concerts were common everywhere.

NINETEENTH-CENTURY ORCHESTRAS In the time of Mozart, Haydn and the young *Beethoven, an orchestra might consist of two dozen strings (eight first violins, eight second violins, four violas, three cellos and one double bass), one flute, two oboes, two horns, two trumpets and timpani (drums). This group provided an immense variety of sound and tone-colour; it was not too big for the concert-rooms of the time, and it was the right size to accompany such (fairly quiet) solo instruments as wooden-frame pianos and gut-string violins. But as bigger concert-halls were built and pianos and violins grew stronger and louder, orchestras too began to grow. Beethoven regularly used two flutes and two clarinets, and often added a third horn and two trombones to the basic band; *Berlioz standardized woodwind and brass, added harp(s) and percussion, and doubled or trebled string-numbers to balance the sound. (He also firmly fixed the type and number of instruments in the orchestra by writing a book on how to orchestrate.) By the 1830s the orchestra was the basic group we know today: woodwind (two or three each of flutes, oboes, clarinets and bassoons), brass (four horns, two or three trumpets and three trombones), harp, timpani, percussion and strings – about sixty to eighty players altogether.

These large, highly-skilled orchestras encouraged composers to write ever more lavish and spectacular sounds. Several composers (e.g. *Liszt, writing for the orchestra at Weimar) devised new musical forms (concert overture; symphonic poem) specifically to show off the orchestra's expressive power; *Wagner and *Verdi used the orchestra in their stage-works not as an accompanist but as a main participant, setting the emotional mood and guiding the reaction of the audience. Other composers (e.g. *Mendelssohn, writing for the Leipzig Gewandhaus) used the standard forms of symphony and concerto, but built into their music the colourful new sounds available from the modern orchestra. In the hands of some composers (*Bruckner, *Mahler, Richard *Strauss) orchestras grew enormous, using as many as 200 players and incorporating previously-rare instruments like the cor anglais, bass clarinet, bass tuba and Chinese gong. The art of orchestration became a major composing skill: some of the most magnificent orchestral showpieces (by such composers as Richard Strauss, *Tchaikovsky, *Rimsky-Korsakov and *Debussy) date from this time.

TWENTIETH-CENTURY ORCHESTRA There have been two separate orchestral developments in this century: large and small. When the century began, most towns and cities in Europe and America had concert-halls, and many had professional orchestras to play in them. When broadcasting became common, most networks established new orchestras of their own; radio and records have made orchestral music more widely popular in this century than ever before. Most of these orchestras were large (80–120 players), and specialized in the great orchestral masterpieces of the eighteenth and nineteenth centuries. Twentieth-century composers also took advantage of their expertise, and continued writing 'big' works, complex to play and full of glittering sound. (*Stravinsky's *Firebird Suite*, *Walton's Symphony No. 1 and *Messiaen's *Turangalîla* are sumptuous examples.) At the same time, the rediscovery of 'early music' led to an interest in the small orchestral groups of the seventeenth and eighteenth centuries, and to the writing of many twentieth-century works for similar forces. This century has been the great age of the chamber orchestra (nine to twenty-five players), and composers nowadays can specify exactly the orchestral size they want, and be sure of finding professional groups to cope with it. (*Webern's Symphony requires nine instruments, compared to his *Six Pieces for Orchestra*, which need 120; Stravinsky's *Rite of Spring* uses 150 players, and his *Dumbarton Oaks* sixteen.)

As the century moves to its end, there is no sign of orchestras decreasing in popularity: orchestral works are for many people the most enjoyable of all classical music, and the symphonies, concertos, overtures and other orchestral works of the eighteenth, nineteenth and twentieth centuries provide the bulk of their listening enjoyment. Present-day composers, even of the *avant-garde, continue to find new sounds and new ways of using old ones (e.g., in *Boulez's and *Stockhausen's works, modifying them by computers). It took the orchestra a century to leave the opera-house and come of age; but ever since then it has inspired some of the world's finest composers to their finest work; orchestral concerts are, with opera, the art of music at its most spectacular.

Listening In the last twenty-five years, research into early dance music has turned up some delightful 'pre-orchestral' suites: records of Susato and Praetorius are particularly enjoyable. Good introductions to seventeenth-century orchestral music are Purcell's overtures (e.g. *The Married Beau*) and theatre-music suites (e.g. *Distressed Innocence*). They might be followed by Telemann's suites (e.g. *Hamburg Ebb and Flow*), Bach's *Brandenburg Concerto* No. 1 and Handel's *Arrival of the Queen of Sheba* and '*Alexander's Feast*' concerto grosso. Good introductions to later eighteenth-century music are J. C. Bach's Symphony Op. 9 No. 1 and Clementi's Symphony No. 3; typical of eighteenth-century orchestral music at its grandest are Haydn's Symphony No. 97 and Mozart's 'Jupiter' symphony and *Sinfonia concertante*, K 297*b* (for four wind instruments and orchestra). (For other eighteenth-century recommendations, see C. P. E. Bach, J. S. Bach, Boccherini, *British and Irish Composers*, *Concerto*, Corelli, Handel, Haydn, Mozart, *Eighteenth-century Music*, *Symphony*, Telemann and Vivaldi.) Good introductions to nineteenth-century orchestral music are *Glinka's overture *Ruslan and Lyudmila* and Schubert's 'Unfinished' symphony (early) and Debussy's *Prélude à l'après-midi d'un faune* and Rimsky-Korsakov's *Spanish Caprice* (late); works in grandest style are Beethoven's overture *Egmont* and Symphony No. 7, Berlioz's *Symphonie fantastique*, Dvořak's 'New World' symphony and Strauss's *Don Juan*. (For other nineteenth-century recommendations, see Balakirev, *Ballet Music*, Beethoven, Berlioz, Bizet, Borodin, Brahms, Bruckner, *Concerto*, Delibes, Delius, Dvořák, Fauré, Franck, Grieg, Liszt, Mahler, Mendelssohn, Musorgsky, *Nineteenth-century Music*, *One-work Composers* (Adam, Bruch, Chabrier, Dukas, Glinka), Rimsky-Korsakov, Saint-Saëns, Schubert, Schumann, Scriabin, Smetana, R. Strauss, *Symphony*, Tchaikovsky and Weber.) Good introductions to twentieth-century music for large orchestra are Ravel's *Boléro*, Holst's *The Planets*, Britten's *Four Sea Interludes* and Copland's *Billy the Kid*; good introductions to chamber-orchestral music are Delius's *On Hearing the First Cuckoo in Spring* and Milhaud's *La création du monde*; twentieth-century orchestral music at its grandest can be heard in Nielsen's Symphony No. 5 and Stravinsky's *Symphony in Three Movements*. (For other twentieth-century recommendations, see *Avant-garde Music*, *Ballet Music*, Barber, Bartók, Berg, Bernstein, Bloch, Boulez, *British and Irish Composers*, Britten, *Concerto*, Copland, Debussy, Elgar, Falla, Gershwin, Henze, Hindemith, Holst,

Ives, Janáček, Khachaturian, Kodály, Lutosławski, Martinů, Davies, Messiaen, Milhaud, Nielsen, Poulenc, Prokofiev, Rachmaninov, Ravel, Respighi, Schoenberg, Shostakovich, Sibelius, Stockhausen, Stravinsky, *Symphony*, Tippett, *Twentieth-century Music*, *United States Composers*, Vaughan Williams, Villa-Lobos, Walton and Webern.)

ORFF, Carl (1895–1982). *German composer.*

Orff founded a music-school, and invented a system of music-education (based on singing and percussion-playing) which is still used in kindergartens and primary schools throughout the world. His compositions were all for voices, and most were for the stage. Their musical style is unique, allying nursery melodies and harmony to pounding, pulsating rhythms and orchestration as garish as a film-score. Some pop composers (Lloyd Webber, Sondheim, Hamlisch) have reached similar goals from a different direction; Orff's subjects are more 'serious' (and the words he set were as often in Latin, ancient Greek or medieval French as in his own language German), but his music's tunefulness and dramatic power are just as immediate.

WORKS A dozen stage-works including *Trionfi* (trilogy consisting of *Carmina Burana*, *Catulli carmina* and *Trionfo di Afrodite*); six operas (including *Antigone*, *King Oedipus* and *The Clever Girl*) and three oratorios (one each for Christmas and Easter and one depicting the Day of Judgement); three sets of songs for chorus and orchestra; *Schoolwork*: several hundred pieces for children to sing and play.

Ⓜ *Carmina Burana* ('Songs of Beuron') (1936) Twenty-one medieval poems (mostly in Latin) for soloists, choir and huge orchestra. It sounds dry, but Orff's subjects (spring, wine and sex), his wonderful tunes and his all-engulfing rhythms make it one of the most foot-tapping of all twentieth-century concert works, a deserved hit wherever it's performed. Its companion-works in *Trionfi* are less compelling, but *Carmina Burana*'s seductive brilliance is equalled in the fairy-tale operas Ⓜ *The Moon* and Ⓜ *The Clever Girl*. (Orff's serious works, especially Ⓜ *Antigone*, Ⓜ *King Oedipus* and Ⓜ *Comedy for the End of Time*, are magnificent but are best explored after his other music – and, as with all his works, knowing what the words mean is vital.)

→ *Die Kluge* ('The Clever Girl'); Britten *Spring Symphony*; Lloyd Webber *Cats*.

P

PALESTRINA, Giovanni Pierluigi da (*c.* 1525-1594). *Italian composer.*

Palestrina spent his life in the service of the Church. In Rome, he sang in the choir of the Sistine Chapel, directed the choir of the Cappella Giulia and was choirmaster of the churches of St John Lateran and St Maria Maggiore. In 1567 he joined the household musicians of Cardinal Ippolito II d'Este at Tivoli, but five years later he returned to the Cappella Giulia as choirmaster, remaining there for the rest of his life. Soon after the death of his first wife, in 1581, he married a rich widow and took over her late husband's fur-trading business, making an excellent job of it.

Palestrina is the finest of all composers in the polyphonic choral style of the Roman Catholic Church (see *Sixteenth-century Music*). His long, sinuous vocal lines seem to intertwine and coil through the church, drawing in the entire congregation to an atmosphere of prayer. The beauty of the music guarantees pleasure even for non-believers; those who can enter into and share its devotional meaning (of whatever denomination) find it crowded with emotion, intense and spiritual in a way few other church works begin to match.

WORKS Ninety-four Masses, 273 motets and many shorter pieces for church use; two books of madrigals to non-religious words.

Missa Papae Marcelli ('Pope Marcellus Mass') (published 1567) The story is that Pope Marcellus ordered his composers to reform their style, to abandon musical frills and self-indulgent showing-off and concentrate on expressing the meaning of the words – and that this Mass was Palestrina's response. Whether the tale is true or false, few Palestrina works better express the longing and love for God which lies at the heart of the Roman Mass. It is familiar music (regularly used on television and film soundtracks to accompany pictures of Renaissance churches); when heard without distraction in the concert-hall, or better still, in church, it both satisfies the mind and touches the heart.

→ Ⓜ *Stabat mater*; *Missa brevis*; Victoria Mass *O quam gloriosum est regnum* (based on his motet of the same name, which is also recommended).

PERGOLESI, Giovanni Battista (1710–36). *Italian composer.*

From Pergolesi's childhood it was clear both that he was a musical genius and that (because of tuberculosis) he had not long to live. He took a good musical job as soon as possible (as musician-in-chief to the Viceroy of Naples), and composed with hectic speed, writing several operas, trio-sonatas, concertos and large-scale church works every year. By 1735 his health was so poor that he retired into a monastery hospital, where he died soon afterwards.

WORKS One work, *La serva padrona* (see below), made Pergolesi's name not long after his death. It was so popular, and his manuscripts were so numerous and so chaotic, that theatre managers and publishers began announcing 'new Pergolesi discoveries' every season, whether they were actually his work or not. This makes it hard to say what music he actually *did* compose: perhaps half a dozen operas, twenty or so church pieces, a few solo songs and not much else. But it hardly matters, now, who penned the music: all of it is delightful. (Stravinsky's *Pulcinella* uses 'Pergolesi' trio-sonata movements and songs, full of vigour and tunefulness, and they are as entertaining in the original eighteenth-century versions as in Stravinsky's luscious score.)

La serva padrona ('The Maid Mistress') (1733) Complete opera. This cheerful comic opera, only 45 minutes long, tells of a flirtatious maidservant who pretends to be her mistress in order to fool a lover. Its tunes are catchy, its story is funny, and its characters are memorable: if Pergolesi had lived to develop this style, he might have rivalled even *Mozart (whose *Così fan tutte* is a disguise-opera in very similar vein).
→ *La contadina astuta* ('The Clever Country Girl'); Telemann *Pimpinone*; Mozart *The Impresario.*

Ⓜ *Stabat mater* (1736) Pergolesi set out to write a serious church work, for two soloists, choir and orchestra – and for all his solemn intentions, comic-opera tunefulness and split-second stage timing (he knows exactly when to stop; his movements are never a note too long) kept breaking through. If ever a 40-minute church work could be called 'delightful', this is it.
→ *Magnificat*; Vivaldi *Gloria*; Rossini *Petite Messe solennelle.*

POULENC, Francis (1899–1963). *French composer and pianist.*

When he was twenty-four, Poulenc composed a lively, Stravinskian and highly successful ballet (*Les biches*) for Diaghilev's Ballets Russes. Its success made him the toast of fashionable Paris, and he spent the 1920s and 1930s as a kind of serious-music Noël Coward, writing bright, lightweight pieces which exactly suited the frivolous high-society mood of the time.

In his mid-thirties, Poulenc's approach to music changed. He became a devout Roman Catholic, and composed a dozen serious and solemn works on Catholic subjects. He began a partnership with the singer Pierre Bernac, and for the next twenty-five years toured the world as his accompanist; for Bernac, he composed songs as moving and serious as any written since *Fauré's time. Occasionally in his later years, the red-nosed jollity of his early style resurfaced (e.g. in the high-spirited Piano Concerto of 1949); but his finest late music is tuneful and Romantic instead of jazzy, and he is one of the most enjoyable second-rank composers of the age.

WORKS Three operas (including *Dialogues of the Carmelites*); two ballets (including *Les biches*); Sinfonietta, two suites, four concertos (for harpsichord, piano, organ and two pianos) and several shorter orchestral works; Sextet, String Quartet, Trio, eight sonatas for assorted instruments and many shorter chamber works; fifteen volumes of piano music (including *Mouvements perpétuels*, Sonata for four hands and *L'embarquement pour Cythère*); *Babar the Little Elephant* for speaker and piano; 125 songs (including the song-cycles *Cocardes* and *Fiançailles pour rire*, both frivolous, and the deeply-felt *Tel jour, telle nuit* and *Banalités*).

Mouvements perpétuels ('Perpetual Movements') (1918) Three tiny, witty piano pieces with popular-song tunes and up-to-the-minute, jazzy harmonies. Poulenc admired *Stravinsky and *Satie, and these piano pieces are like those composers' music at its gayest.
→ *Suite Française* (spiky arrangements of seventeenth-century French dances, also available in a toothsome orchestral version); *L'embarquement pour Cythère* (two pianos); Ibert 'Le petit âne blanc' (from *Histoires naturelles*).

Ⓜ **Flute Sonata** (1947) Unsolemn, brilliantly written for both flute and piano and full of the sorts of tune that haunt the memory for days. The first movement is urbane and unhurried, the second touching, the third boisterous. (The piece is also known in a concerto-version with orchestra; the piano accompaniment, however, has a clangy glint which suits the music better.)
→ Sextet for piano and wind; Ⓜ Organ Concerto; Ibert Flute Concerto.

Ⓜ *Four Motets for a Time of Penitence* (1939) These deeply-felt religious pieces (for unaccompanied choir) date from Poulenc's conversion, and are passionately spiritual in a way quite unlike his earlier music. Fauré's *Requiem* is their musical ancestor, and Poulenc's inspiration is worthy of that pedigree.
→ Ⓜ *La figure humaine*; Mass in G; Britten *Rejoice in the Lamb*.

PROKOFIEV, Sergey (1891-1953). *Russian composer.*

There was a custom at the Moscow Conservatoire that piano students, on the day they graduated, should play a concerto by *Beethoven, *Grieg or *Tchaikovsky. Prokofiev caused a sensation by playing his own Concerto No. 1: its music struck the professors as outlandishly ugly, but he played so brilliantly that they swallowed their annoyance and awarded him a special prize. For the next twenty years he regularly appeared as pianist in his own works, and gave the first performances of most of his concertos and sonatas. Just after the 1917 Russian Revolution he toured the USA, and then settled in Paris for ten years (not for political reasons, but chiefly to work for Diaghilev's Ballets Russes). He returned to the USSR in 1933, and for the rest of his life, despite occasional wrangles with the authorities (who said his music was too intellectual and too discordant), was considered one of his country's leading composers.

Prokofiev's music *was* sometimes discordant and intellectual: especially in his twenties, he experimented with jagged discords, keys piled up together whether their notes fitted or not, barbaric piano-thumping and screeching orchestral sounds. But this was only in a handful of works (e.g. the intentionally horrendous *Scythian Suite*). Most of his music is tuneful, easy on the ear and in a Romantic style spiced with unexpected harmonies and lively twentieth-century rhythms. His *Peter and the Wolf*, a tale with orchestra for children, designed to show off every instrument in the orchestra, is typical of his music at its best: easy-going, flowing and irresistibly melodious.

WORKS Eight operas (including *Love for Three Oranges* and *War and Peace*); seven ballets (including *Romeo and Juliet* and *Cinderella*); seven symphonies, Sinfonietta and half a dozen shorter orchestral works (including *Scythian Suite*); five piano concertos, two violin concertos, two cello concertos; ten sonatas, two sonatinas, four studies and many shorter piano works; two string quartets, two violin sonatas, Cello Sonata and other chamber works; choral works (including the cantata *Alexander Nevsky*, based on the music for Eisenstein's epic film) and a score of solo songs.

Lieutenant Kijé, Op. 60 (1934) This orchestral suite began life as music for a comedy film (about bumbling officials forced to invent a whole life for a non-existent army officer in whom the Tsar takes an interest). The film is forgettable, but the suite is gorgeous, five short scenes from Kijé's life including his birth, wedding and heroic death on the battlefield; 'Troika' ('Sleighride') is, next to *Peter and the Wolf*, Prokofiev's best-loved piece.
→ Suite *Love for Three Oranges*; Shostakovich *The Gadfly*; Kodály *Háry János*.

Ⓜ **Symphony No. 1** ('Classical'), Op. 25 (1917) Prokofiev set out to write the sort of symphony *Haydn might have composed if he'd lived in the twentieth century: it uses a small orchestra, the same sequence and style of movements as Haydn's symphonies, and has the same good-mannered proportions. (It was meant as an antidote to the long, emotionally extrovert symphonies of composers like *Tchaikovsky.) Prokofiev's tongue-in-cheek melodies, witty harmony and sparkling orchestral writing make it a symphony Haydn would certainly have enjoyed; instead of fettering his inspiration, eighteenth-century formulas gave it wings.

→ Violin Concerto No. 2; Bizet Symphony; Poulenc Sinfonietta.

Ⓜ *Romeo and Juliet*, Op. 64 (1936) Prokofiev set Shakespeare's story in a series of dazzling self-contained movements, mazurkas, polkas, galops, *pas de deux* and so on, very much in the manner of Tchaikovsky's great ballets. (Its slow love-music, and the leaping, energetic fight-music, are magnificent.) It is a marvellous ballet to see performed (and has been superbly filmed); it is recorded complete, and there are also two popular suites, recommended in their own right.

→ *Cinderella* (complete ballet; also suites 1 and 2); Tchaikovsky *The Sleeping Beauty*; Ravel *Daphnis et Chloé* (suites 1 and 2 before complete ballet).

Ⓜ **Piano Concerto No. 3**, Op. 26 (1921) A splendidly light-hearted piece, beginning with a march (full of delicious 'wrong-note' harmony), continuing with a delicate theme and variations and ending with a pompous waltz which whips itself up to a frenzied, glittering conclusion. Twentieth-century concertos are usually either hefty showpieces or unhurried conversation; this one is a romp.

→ Piano Concerto No. 1; Shostakovich Piano Concerto No. 2; Britten Piano Concerto.

PUCCINI, Giacomo (1858-1924). *Italian composer.*

The descendant of five generations of musicians, Puccini knew from boyhood that he wanted to make music his career, and that he wanted to concentrate on opera. His first three operas were only moderately successful, but the three that followed, *La bohème*, *Tosca* and *Madama Butterfly*, went straight into the international repertoire and have remained ever since among the most popular operas ever composed. Their success was financial as well as artistic: they made Puccini a millionaire, and he bought a lakeside villa near Lucca, his native town, spent his life in semi-retirement (he was a keen wild-fowler), and in the next twenty-five years produced only four more works.

WORKS Apart from a Mass and a handful of short instrumental pieces (e.g. *Chrysanthemums* for string quartet), all written when he was a student, Puccini composed nothing but operas: *Le Villi*, *Edgar*, *Manon Lescaut*, *La bohème*, *Tosca*, *Madama Butterfly*, *The Girl of the Golden West*, *The Swallow*, *The Triptych* (*The Cloak*, *Sister Angelica*, *Gianni Schicchi*) and *Turandot*.

Ⓜ *La bohème* ('The Bohemian Girl') (1896) Complete opera. The stories of Puccini's operas are like popular films or novels: it is always clear who the villains and victims are, what the story is about and how it will end, and our interest is chiefly in the characters and in the unusual locations where the events take place. *La bohème* is about artists in 1890s Paris, a dying girl and the young men who love her; *Tosca* is set in Rome during the 1800 revolution, and its characters include a sadistic police chief, a suspected terrorist and the girl who loves him; Ⓜ *Madama Butterfly* shows us the pathetic love of a Japanese girl for a heartless American sailor; *The Girl of the Golden West* is a cowboy opera; Ⓜ *Turandot* is about a fairy-tale Chinese princess. On their own, the stories are overheated rubbish. What makes the operas masterworks is the way Puccini's music constantly reminds the audience of the characters' feelings and destinies, telling us things of which his people are often unaware. (For example, when Rodolfo in *La bohème* sings to Mimi 'Your Tiny Hand is Frozen', the music makes it quite clear that she is dying and that their love is doomed, and this tragic knowledge makes us care about the characters in a way their plain words never could.) Emotion in the music, added to full-throated, soaring tunes – a good example is the heart-broken 'One Fine Day' from *Madama Butterfly* – gives Puccini's operas their power: even though the people on the stage are clearly singers, accompanied by a perfectly-visible orchestra and a conductor in evening dress, we forget that they are characters in a drama, and believe in them as real people – and this emotional sympathy wrings the heart.

→ *La bohème*, *Madama Butterfly* and *Tosca* are the best Puccini operas to hear first, together with his marvellous one-act comedy Ⓜ *Gianni Schicchi* (about a man who pretends to be dying in order to see which of his family and neighbours love him most); good individual moments, ideal samples of his style, are the two arias mentioned above ('Your Tiny Hand'; 'One Fine Day'), 'O My Beloved Father' (from *Gianni Schicchi*) and 'None shall sleep' (from *Turandot*). Good follow-up operas by others are Giordano *Andrea Chénier*, Leoncavallo *I pagliacci* (see *One-work Composers*) and Verdi *La traviata*.

PURCELL, Henry (1659–95). *English composer.*
Purcell's father was one of Charles II's household musicians, and both his sons (Henry and his younger brother Daniel) entered royal service as soon as they were old enough. Henry's rise was meteoric: at fifteen he was merely an 'organ-tuner' (i.e. employed to pump the bellows), at eighteen he was 'composer to the King's violins' (i.e. writing for a string orchestra modelled on that of Louis XIV), and at twenty he was appointed organist of Westminster Abbey.

Purcell composed music of the specialist kinds required by all his appointments: orchestral suites and dances, chamber music for royal enjoyment, odes and other ceremonial pieces for state occasions, anthems and other works for church. But his main love was the theatre. Under Cromwell, the London theatres had all been closed; when Charles II came to the throne there was an explosion of theatre-life, and dozens of new plays, operas and masques were performed each year. In the last fifteen years of his life, in addition to all his other musical activities, Purcell wrote a dozen large-scale music-theatre works, incidental music for over forty plays, and hundreds of individual songs and dances. After his death he was remembered chiefly for his ceremonial works; it is mainly for his theatre music (and especially his songs) that he is esteemed today.

WORKS Apart from incidental music (often later published in suites named after the plays, e.g. *Distressed Innocence*, *Abdelazer*, *The Married Beau*), Purcell wrote one opera (*Dido and Aeneas*: see below) and several 'stage-spectacles' involving spoken dialogue, songs, ballet and orchestral interludes: the best-known are *Dioclesian*, *King Arthur*, *The Fairy Queen* (based on Shakespeare's *A Midsummer Night's Dream*), *The Indian Queen* and *The Tempest*. His over four dozen choral works include two *Birthday Odes for Queen Mary*, *Ode on St Cecilia's Day* and many anthems (e.g. *My Heart is Inditing*), and he wrote more than 100 separate songs (including *Music for a While*, *Nymphs and Shepherds* and *Evening Hymn*). His non-vocal music includes eight suites, two dozen marches and other short pieces for harpsichord, *Chacony* and fifteen fantasias for strings, twelve violin sonatas, eleven trio-sonatas and a dozen shorter chamber works.

Music for a While (?1692) Purcell's songs, like *Schubert's, fit music to words so expertly that they seem always to have gone together; also like Schubert, he could make rubbishy words (like these) seem sublime poetry simply through his music's emotional strength and tunefulness.
→ This song, slow and tender, could well be followed up by 'Lord, What is Man?' and Ⓜ *Evening Hymn*; 'Nymphs and Shepherds', 'Man is for the Woman Made' and Ⓜ 'Sweeter than Roses' show him in more sprightly mood. The nearest equivalents by others are Arne's Shakespeare-settings (e.g. 'Under the Greenwood Tree'; 'Where the Bee Sucks') and Haydn's *English Canzonets*.

Ⓜ *Dido and Aeneas* (1689) Complete opera. This short work is utterly unlike the ponderous recitative-and-aria Italian operas of the time (see *Opera*): in emotional directness and depth of character-drawing it is closer to the 'reform' operas of *Gluck a century later. Particular delights are its breezy choruses (e.g. 'Sailors' Farewell'), the spectacular 'Sorceress Scene' (using almost nineteenth-century 'magic' harmonies), and Dido's grief-stricken song 'When I am Laid in Earth', as she prepares to commit suicide after Aeneas deserts her.
→ *The Fairy Queen* (jolly with the spoken dialogue; but the music works perfectly well without it); Handel *Acis and Galatea*; Vivaldi solo cantata *Amor, hai vinto*.

Ⓜ *Ode on Saint Cecilia's Day* (1692) Triumphant celebration of music, dedicated to its patron saint, and to fine words by the poet Dryden. The choir sings of trumpets, drums, sighing flutes and cheerful dancing – and Purcell's music matches every idea in joyous sounds.

→ (M) 'Come, Ye Sons of Art' (*Queen Mary's Birthday Ode* No. 1); Blow 'God Spake Sometime in Visions' (*Coronation Anthem*, 1685); Handel 'Let God Arise' (Chandos Anthem No. 11).

R

RACHMANINOV, Sergey (1873-1943). *Russian composer and pianist.*

Until the 1917 Russian Revolution, Rachmaninov divided his time between Russia, Eastern Europe and the USA, and was well-known as a composer, solo pianist and conductor (notably of opera). After the Revolution he settled in the USA and never returned to Russia. He was one of the leading virtuoso pianists of the first half of this century, famous for his interpretations of *Chopin, *Liszt and above all his own music. He had little time to devote to composing, and wrote slowly; but his major compositions, and especially his piano works, are of lasting quality.

WORKS Two sonatas, twenty-four preludes, fifteen *Études-tableaux*, two variation-sets (on a theme of Chopin; on a theme of *Corelli) and a dozen shorter solo-piano works; two suites and *Russian Rhapsody* for two pianos; three operas; three symphonies, *Isle of the Dead*, *Symphonic Dances* and four shorter orchestral works; four concertos and *Rhapsody on a Theme of Paganini* for piano and orchestra; choral music (including a choral symphony, *The Bells*, and a setting of the *Easter Vigil* of the Russian Orthodox Church); two trios, Cello Sonata and other chamber works; fifty-six songs.

Ⓜ **Prelude in C sharp minor**, Op. 3 No. 2 (1892) Rachmaninov wrote this swaggering, Romantic piece when he was nineteen, and it haunted him for the rest of his life: it was beloved all over the world, recorded, rearranged and regularly requested at his concerts (even of large-scale pieces; even of other people's music). The other preludes (there are twenty-four altogether, in every major and minor key) are equally attractive (together, they are a showcase of every kind of piano style) and several (e.g. Op. 23 No. 5 in G minor; Op. 32 No. 5 in G) are almost equally well-known. Of Rachmaninov's larger piano works, composed for his own recitals, the best are the Ⓜ *Études-tableaux* ('Study-pictures'), mood-pieces combining technical spectacle with poetic impressions of Romantic scenes, rather in the manner of Liszt's *Années de pélerinage*. His *Chopin Variations* and Ⓜ *Corelli Variations* are alternatively heroic and dexterous, companion-works to *Brahms's *Paganini Variations*; his sonatas are big and energetic. Less well-known than his solo music, but perfectly delightful, are the two suites for two pianos: No. 2 has a march, waltz, nocturne and tarantella as winsome as anything he ever wrote. The best follow-ups are the works by others mentioned in this paragraph; also recommended are Godowsky's rearrangements of Chopin's studies, gorgeously, preposterously extending their difficulty (e.g. by running two together, or giving them to the left hand alone); they used to be known only to virtuoso pianists, but now, thanks to records, everyone can share the fun.

Ⓜ **Piano Concerto No. 2, Op. 18 (1901)** Already well-known, this work became an international hit when it was used as sound-track music for the 1940s film *Brief Encounter*. It is still, with Tchaikovsky's Concerto No. 1, the best-loved piano concerto in the repertoire – and one of the finest: Rachmaninov's ability to blend finger-dexterity with luscious harmony and sumptuous tunes (each one, it seems, more memorable than the last) was never more stunningly displayed. The work has had a thousand imitations, ten thousand parodies: it dwarfs them all.
→ Ⓜ Piano Concerto No. 3 (if anything, finer music: harder-edged, but just as tuneful); Grieg Piano Concerto; Liszt *Hungarian Rhapsody* No. 2 (version for piano and orchestra).

Ⓜ *Rhapsody on a Theme of Paganini*, Op. 43 (1934) Paganini's famous theme (also varied, by, among others, *Schumann, Liszt, Brahms, Blacher, Lutosławski, Lloyd Webber and Paganini himself) is here given twenty-four sparkling variations, organized to make a scintillating, continuous concerto for piano and orchestra. Variation 18 (which turns the theme upside-down and quarters its speed) was detached and made into a soupy pop-song; heard in context, it is the climax of a dazzling work.
→ Piano Concerto No. 1; Dohnányi *Variations on a Nursery Song* (giving the same glittering treatment to 'Baa Baa Black Sheep'); Franck *Symphonic Variations*.

Ⓜ **Symphony No. 2 (1907)** Rachmaninov's symphonies, once overshadowed by his piano music, have recently found their place triumphantly in the repertoire. They are passionately Romantic, in a line from the symphonies of Tchaikovsky; and though they may take time to make their full effect (perhaps because we keep subconsciously waiting for a non-existent piano soloist), they are Rachmaninov's music at its sombre, sober best.
→ Ⓜ Symphony No. 3; Ⓜ *Symphonic Dances*; Nielsen Symphony No. 2.

Songs Rachmaninov's songs are usually hidden away in the middle of recital-programmes or in afternoon broadcasts heard by half a dozen listeners and a cat. They are worth seeking out, especially on record: his gift for melody and his passionate melancholy give them a wistful, haunting power. The best-known include *Vocalise*, Op. 34 No. 14 (also arranged for violin and piano), 'In the Silent Night', Op. 4 No. 3, and 'To the Children', Op. 26 No. 7; the best collection is *Six Songs*, Op. 38.
→ Good follow-ups by others are songs by Tchaikovsky (e.g. 'Over the Golden Cornfields', Op. 57 No. 2) and by Duparc (e.g. *Chanson triste* or *L'invitation au voyage*).

RAVEL, Maurice (1875-1937). *French composer.*

Although he published his first compositions in his twenties (including *Pavane for a Dead Infanta*, which made his name), Ravel went on studying at the Paris Conservatoire until he was thirty, polishing an already dazzling technique. He was a first-class pianist and conductor, and took an active part in French music-making before the First World War, giving concerts, writing criticism, and composing for Diaghilev's Ballets Russes. After the war his health broke down, and he spent the last ten years of his life in semi-retirement, composing only another half-dozen works.

Ravel found a style early in life and kept to it: all his works have the same polish, the same harmonic pepperiness and the same dazzling exploitation of the instruments they use. He was particularly interested in developing piano-style, and his piano works (the major part of his output) explore the instrument's possibilities in a way as revolutionary for their time as *Chopin's music was for its. He was also one of the most skilful orchestrators in the business: few composers ever invented more dazzling or original orchestral sounds.

WORKS Two operas (*L'heure Espagnole*; *L'enfant et les sortilèges*); two ballets (*Daphnis et Chloé*; *Boléro*); *Pavane*, *Jeux d'eau*, *Sonatine*, *Miroirs*, *Ma mère l'oye*, *Gaspard de la nuit*, *Valses nobles et sentimentales*, *Le tombeau de Couperin* and several shorter piano works, many also arranged for orchestra; two piano concertos; *Rapsodie Espagnole* and *La valse* for orchestra; String Quartet, Piano Trio, Sonata for violin and cello, Violin Sonata, *Tzigane*, *Introduction and Allegro* and a few shorter chamber works; fifty songs (including *Sheherazade* for voice and orchestra and *Histoires naturelles* for voice and chamber group).

Boléro (1928) Ballet score, often heard in the concert-hall. This piece consists of a single thirty-two-bar tune, repeated over and over again (with ever more subtle harmony and orchestration) for seventeen minutes. (A hypnotic, insistent side-drum beat keeps the rhythm taut.) It says a lot for the quality of Ravel's tune, and for his wizardry at devising orchestral sound effects, that instead of being boring, *Boléro* is one of the most stunning pieces in the whole orchestral repertoire.
→ *Rapsodie Espagnole*; *La valse*; Stravinsky *Firebird Suite*.

Ⓜ *Introduction and Allegro* (1906) Written to show off a newly-invented pedal harp, this septet (for flute, clarinet, harp and string quartet) is delectably cool and poised, as fresh-sounding as its scoring might suggest. None of Ravel's works better show off his fastidious ear for sound, or his gift for weaving tiny scraps of melody into a musical texture as delicate and strong as lace.
→ String Quartet; Debussy Sonata for flute, viola and harp; Damase *Sonate en concert*.

Ma mère l'oye ('Mother Goose') (1908) Suite of gentle nursery-story pieces for piano duet, later extended and adapted for a ballet (and seductively orchestrated). In the same placid, filigree piano style are *Jeux d'eau* ('Fountains'), *Sonatine* and ⓜ *Le tombeau de Couperin* (also for orchestra); more substantial, and among Ravel's finest works, are ⓜ *Gaspard de la nuit*, *Miroirs* and *Valses nobles et sentimentales* (also for orchestra).

→ Good follow-ups to the smaller works are Debussy *Petite suite*, *La cathédrale engloutie* and suite *Pour le piano*, and Poulenc *Mouvements perpétuels*; good follow-ups to the larger works are Rachmaninov *Études-tableaux*, Op. 39, and Prokofiev *Toccata*, Op. 11.

ⓜ *L'heure Espagnole* ('Spanish Time') (1911) The setting of this one-act farce (a clockmaker's workshop) allows Ravel to indulge in whirring, jingling, ticking and chiming orchestral sounds of every kind. (His hobby was collecting clocks and musical toys.) Against the fanciful, fairy-tale background these sounds provide, he tells a tongue-in-cheek story of a foolish clockmaker, his flirtatious wife and her lusty but brainless lover.

→ ⓜ *L'enfant et les sortilèges* ('The Child and the Apparitions', fantasy-opera about a naughty little boy whose nursery tea-set, maths book, stuffed toys and pet animals rise against him); Puccini *Gianni Schicchi*; Menotti *Amelia Goes to the Ball*.

ⓜ **Piano Concerto for the Left Hand Alone** (1931) Ravel's Piano Concerto in G is a light, jazzy piece influenced by *Gershwin; his left-hand Concerto is darker, much more profound and (though no one listening to a record would ever guess) scored for one hand only. The mysterious opening, like huge creatures stirring from sleep in a nightmare wood, leads to brighter and livelier sounds, culminating in a clattery, no-nonsense march: the piece is over and gone as quickly as a dream. Only in *Gaspard de la nuit* (herewith recommended) did Ravel create such a ghostly, suspenseful atmosphere, and its fearful imaginings inspired him to a masterpiece.

→ Piano Concerto in G; Piano Trio; Martinů Concerto for two pianos.

RESPIGHI, Ottorino (1879–1936). *Italian composer.*

In Italy, Respighi is remembered as a composition-teacher and as the composer of several successful operas. In the rest of the world, his reputation comes from a series of orchestral suites in a no-holds-barred, technicolor style learned from *Rimsky-Korsakov and passed on to Hollywood film-composers of the brashest and most flamboyant kind. His work is like an iceberg – and the submerged nine-tenths (especially his concertos, chamber music and songs) are placid, restrained and entirely untouched by the swagger of his more familiar scores. He is a composer tailor-made for gramophone enjoyment.

WORKS Seven operas (including *Belfagor* and *The Sunken Bell*); twelve suites (including *The Birds*, *The Pines of Rome*, *Botticelli Triptych* and *Church Windows*) and half a dozen other orchestral works (including *Dramatic Symphony*); three concertos and other works for soloists and orchestra; choral and vocal works including *Spring* (soloists, choir and orchestra), *Praise for Our Lord's Nativity* (soloists, choir and orchestra), *Forest Gods* (voice and chamber group) and several dozen songs; two string quartets; Quintet; Violin Sonata; numerous arrangements (including the ballet *La boutique fantasque*, after Rossini).

The Birds (1927) Charming suite for small orchestra, weaving dexterous patterns round half a dozen eighteenth-century bird-pieces (e.g. Daquin's *The Cuckoo*). Unpretentious and charming, as cheerful as the birds whose name it bears.
→ *Ancient Airs and Dances* (three suites, giving other sixteenth- to eighteenth-century works the same delightful treatment); Fauré suite *Masques et bergamasques*; Warlock *Capriol Suite*.

Pines of Rome (1924) The first of three Roman suites (the others are *Fountains of Rome* and *Roman Festivals*), this uses every ounce of orchestral mastery to conjure up children playing, the catacombs, moonlight on the Janiculum Hill (complete with nightingale) and legions marching in triumph up the Appian Way.
→ *Church Windows*; Debussy *Nocturnes*; Elgar overture *Cockaigne*; Ibert *Escales*.

Ⓜ *Concerto gregoriano* (1922) Respighi's homage to the great Italian polyphonic music of the such sixteenth-century composers as *Palestrina is a concerto for violin and orchestra, in modern concerto form and with Respighi's own styles of rhythm and harmony, but based on plainsong melodies and filled with the un-hurried, gravely devotional atmosphere of the Renaissance music it celebrates. There are few 'concertos' like it, but it is utterly characteristic of Respighi's quieter work at its most inspired.
→ Piano Concerto; cantata *La primavera* ('Spring'); Malipiero Violin Concerto No. 1.

RIMSKY-KORSAKOV, Nikolay (1844-1908). *Russian composer.*
In the nineteenth century it was commonly believed that nothing was impossible, that people could achieve anything if only they were prepared to make sufficient effort - and Rimsky-Korsakov's early career seems to prove the point. His family wanted him to be a naval officer, and sent him at twelve to a naval academy, where music was a minor item in a busy timetable. He was unable to study it properly until he was twenty-one, by which time he had spent six years at sea. Then he went to *Balakirev for advice, and Balakirev told him, 'Write a symphony. Four movements. E flat major'. He did, even though he knew nothing of harmony, counterpoint

or orchestration. After that, his musical self-education progressed so quickly and so remarkably that at twenty-seven, without a single academic qualification to his name, he was appointed head of the St Petersburg Conservatoire.

This amazing success was due partly to Rimsky-Korsakov's choice of friends – he lodged with *Musorgsky and regularly met *Borodin and others to discuss music and try over new works – and partly to his incredible musical ability. He soaked up skills like blotting-paper: by the time he was thirty he was the most learned professor in Russia, a teacher sought out by all young composers worth their salt and a composer famous for the brilliance and technical mastery of his music. Unlike some other professor-composers, however, he avoided dryness: he was fascinated by folk music, and filled his music with its colourful rhythms and fresh, cheerful tunes.

WORKS Fifteen operas (including *The Snow Maiden*, *The Tale of the Invisible City of Kitezh* and *The Golden Cockerel*); three symphonies, *Russian Easter Festival Overture*, *Sheherazade*, *Spanish Caprice*, four fantasies and half a dozen other orchestral works; Piano Concerto; Clarinet Concerto; Trombone Concerto; String Sextet, String Quintet, Quintet for piano and wind and other shorter chamber works; four cantatas for choir and orchestra; many folksong arrangements and solo-piano works.

Spanish Caprice (1887) A dozen Spanish folktunes are the basis of this glowing orchestral fantasy, with prominent solo parts for violin, harp and clarinet. A very few pieces of music seem to overflow with the zest of life: this *Caprice*, with *Berlioz's overture *Roman Carnival*, Litolff's Scherzo and *Mozart's *Marriage of Figaro* overture, leads the dance.
→ *Russian Easter Festival Overture*; Brahms *Academic Festival Overture*; Dvořák overture *Carnival*.

Ⓜ *Sheherazade* (1888) This lilting score began life as an orchestral suite, and was later turned by Diaghilev into an opulent ballet which made the name of the star dancer Nijinsky. It is based on the *Arabian Nights*, and depicts in music Sheherazade's stories of pirates, genies, fabulous treasure-caves and harems bursting with dusky maidens. It is as colourful as the stories – irresistible.
→ Overture *May Night*; Glinka *Kamarinskaya*; Tchaikovsky *Italian Caprice*; Strauss *Till Eulenspiegel*.

The Tale of Tsar Sultan (suite from the opera, 1900) Because of the problems of translation, Rimsky-Korsakov's fairy-tale operas are rarely heard outside Russia, and are chiefly known through the gorgeous orchestral suites he assembled from their music. The best-known number in this one is 'Flight of the Bumble Bee'; the suite also contains such other intriguingly-titled movements as 'The Three Miracles' and 'The Tsarina at Sea in a Barrel'. One effect of this lively music, for record-listeners at least, is to whet the appetite for an English-language libretto and a recording of the complete opera – and anyone who tries them will reap rich rewards.

→ Ⓜ *The Golden Cockerel* (suite and complete opera); 'Dance of the Tumblers' (from opera *The Snow Maiden*); Khachaturian *Gayane* Suite No. 1.

RODRIGO. See *One-work Composers*.

ROSSINI, Gioachino (1792–1868). *Italian composer*.

The son of a town trumpeter, Rossini was destined from childhood for a musical career (despite a brief apprenticeship, in his early teens, to a blacksmith). He wrote his first opera at eighteen, and by twenty-five was in demand in all the great Italian opera-houses. For thirteen more years he composed three or four operas a year, and travelled all over Europe supervising their production. The strain of this work ruined his health, and in 1830 he retired from composing. He suffered from a nervous disease whose main symptom was lassitude: he found it physically exhausting even to lift a pen, and his enemies eagerly and unfairly caricatured him as a lazybones, fonder of a nap than of tussling with sharps and flats. In his seventies, after twenty-five years of silence (broken only by one religious work, the *Stabat mater*), he recovered sufficiently to compose again, and the Mass, songs and piano pieces of his last years show that his creative powers remained undimmed.

In his lifetime, Rossini was renowned not only for the comic operas still heard today, but for serious works on subjects from history (*William Tell*; *Moses*; *The Siege of Corinth*) or from great literature (*Otello*; *Tancredi*). When operatic fashion changed in Italy, his style (with its ornate and immensely difficult arias for the singers) was thought old-fashioned, and his serious operas fell out of the repertoire. Nothing, however, dislodged the comedies: their overtures give many an orchestral concert a sparkling start, and a handful of them (especially *Cinderella* and *The Barber of Seville*) still draw crowds wherever they are performed.

WORKS Thirty-eight operas (including *The Italian Girl in Algiers*, *The Barber of Seville*, *Cinderella*, *Semiramide* and *William Tell*); six cantatas, two Masses (including *Petite Messe solennelle*) and *Stabat mater*; six sonatas for strings; six wind quartets; numerous solo songs (including *La danza*), chamber works and piano pieces (many also known in arrangements, e.g. *Respighi's ballet *La boutique fantasque* and *Britten's suites *Soirées musicales* and *Matinées musicales*).

Ⓜ *La gazza ladra* ('The Thieving Magpie') (overture; 1817) Because of the speed at which he worked (he liked to compose a complete opera in less than a fortnight), Rossini built his overtures to a formula: a slow introduction (based on one of the opera's more seductive tunes), a fast section (based on two of its cheekier tunes), a whipped-up frenzy (nicknamed 'the Rossini crescendo') created by repeating the same few bars of music half a dozen times, louder and louder, and a riotous conclusion. Like all successful formulas, it was fool-proof: with tunes as effortless and orchestration (especially for the wind) as bubbling as Rossini's, overture after overture is a delight – and they are toothsomely consistent: like one, and you'll like them all.

→ Ⓜ Overture *William Tell*; Smetana overture *The Bartered Bride*; Rezniček overture *Donna Diana*; Schubert *Overtures in the Italian Style*, Nos. 1 and 2.

Ⓜ *The Barber of Seville* (1816) Complete opera. In the 1770s, the French playwright Beaumarchais wrote three farces, with the standard ingredients of sighing young lovers, wily servants and pompous, doddering elders. The second, *The Marriage of Figaro*, full of satire at the aristocracy of the time, was turned into a superb opera by *Mozart; the first, *The Barber of Seville*, a more straightforward farce, became Rossini's operatic masterpiece. It is full of individual delights – the Overture, the arias 'Una voce poco fa', 'La calunnia' and above all 'Largo al factotum' ('Figaro, Figaro, Figaro') – but its chief pleasure is the way the action speeds along, as smooth and hilarious a sequence of comic disaster as in any spoken farce, all enlivened by Rossini's marvellous tunes and musical wit. For newcomers to opera, *The Barber of Seville* is unbeatable; for old hands, it remains a lasting joy.

→ *Cinderella*; *The Italian Girl in Algiers*; Donizetti *Don Pasquale*.

S

SAINT-SAËNS, Camille (1835-1921). *French composer.*

Except that he rarely conducted orchestras, Saint-Saëns was rather like a French *Mendelssohn: it seemed that he could do anything in music, and whatever he turned his hand to he did with a grace and skill which charmed even jealous rivals. His piano- and organ-playing were legendary (as was his habit of practising scales with the morning newspaper propped on the music-desk); his composition-classes were always crowded with pupils; his operas were hits all over Europe; his symphonic works (especially his 'Organ' Symphony and five piano concertos, if he himself was playing in them) drew throngs of fans. His music is not, perhaps, the greatest ever composed – he never rivalled Mendelssohn at his best – but it is beautifully constructed, a fountain of delight from first to last.

WORKS Twelve operas (including *Samson and Delilah*); three symphonies, four symphonic poems (including *Danse macabre*), two suites, marches, overtures and other orchestral works; five piano concertos, three violin concertos, two cello concertos and a dozen shorter works for soloists and orchestra (including *Carnival of the Animals*); *Requiem, Christmas Oratorio* and a dozen less grand choral works; chamber music including two string quartets, Piano Quintet, Piano Quartet, Septet, two piano trios, two violin sonatas, two cello sonatas and sonatas for bassoon, oboe and clarinet; twelve studies, six bagatelles, three fantasias and six fugues for solo piano; *Variations on a Theme of Beethoven* and other shorter two-piano works; three preludes and fugues, three fantasias and three shorter organ works.

Carnival of the Animals (1886) Delightful suite of animal portraits (darting fish, braying asses, bone-clattering fossils, roaring lions) for two pianos and small orchestra. Witty, graceful and hilarious. One movement, 'The Swan', was used for Pavlova's once-famous solo ballet *The Dying Swan*, and is still a favourite concert piece: a limpid cello melody over rippling piano chords.
→*Danse macabre* (rollicking orchestral tone poem about skeletons dancing in a graveyard; wonderfully sinister rattling from the xylophone); Britten *The Young Person's Guide to the Orchestra*; Tchaikovsky *Nutcracker Suite*.

ⓜ **Piano Concerto No. 2** (1868) With the Third Symphony, this is Saint-Saëns's most substantial concert work. Its first movement is mock-ponderous (like a *Bach organ toccata with tongue in cheek); its second is a scherzo with a gorgeously galumphing middle section; its finale is a quicksilver tarantella (cousin to the last movement of Mendelssohn's 'Italian' Symphony).
→ ⓜ *Introduction and Rondo capriccioso* (violin and orchestra); Piano Concerto No. 3; Chopin Piano Concerto No. 2.

ⓜ **Symphony No. 3** ('Organ' Symphony) (1886) Though it was written in memory of *Liszt, this is more a celebration of life than a long-faced funeral piece. Saint-Saëns uses Liszt's construction method, basing the whole work on constant variations of the same few ideas – but though his material is solemn (a chorale), his variants are increasingly cheerful and frolicking, until the work climaxes with solemn organ chords given a halo of energetic ripples and arpeggios on two pianos. Saint-Saëns cheekily called the piece a symphony, but it's about as close to *Beethoven or *Brahms in symphonic mood as P. G. Wodehouse is close to *War and Peace*.
→ Cello Concerto No. 1; Mendelssohn 'Italian' Symphony; Harty *Irish Symphony*.

ⓜ *Variations on a Theme of Beethoven* (1874) Unusually for a virtuoso keyboard-player, Saint-Saëns left no large-scale piano or organ music: even this piece is for two players, not one. It takes the minuet from Beethoven's Piano Sonata No. 18 and at first treats it seriously, in Beethovenian mood, but soon gets carried away by its own virtuosity, the pianists shaking double octaves and arpeggios out of their sleeves like raindrops, and bringing the whole work to an end with a so-called 'double fugue' which is more like a comic-opera chase. 'Serious music', meant exclusively to delight: just what Saint-Saëns did best.
→ Fantasia No. 2, Op. 101 (solo piano); Schubert Fantasia in F minor (piano duet); Brahms *Variations on the St Anthony Chorale* (two-piano version).

SATIE, Erik (1866–1925). *French composer.*
Satie was an eccentric: his ways of thought were quite unlike anyone else's and his life was held together by small rituals of behaviour which seemed quite crazy even to his friends. He lived alone in a room whose threshold no one else was ever allowed to cross; he collected umbrellas by the hundred; summer and winter, wherever he was, he wore striped trousers and a morning-coat; he gave his pieces ridiculous titles (like *In Horse Costume* or *Pesterings and Posturings of a Big Wooden Dummy*), and told the performers 'open your head' or 'play like a nightingale with toothache'.
Despite this foolery, musicians in Satie's own lifetime (and since) always took him very seriously. The reason is that he was just as eccentric in the harmonies and melodies he used, avoiding tradition and breaking new ground – and once he had pioneered a style of writing, many other com-

posers imitated him. Rather against his will, he was a kind of musical guru, and *Debussy, *Ravel, *Stravinsky, *Poulenc and many others all learned from him. Nowadays, when others have used his methods to produce far greater works than he ever could, it is sometimes hard to see just what the fuss was all about. But for all their triviality and weirdness, his pieces are always charming, and some (e.g. *Gymnopédies*) have a grave beauty which raises them far above eccentricity.

WORKS Over 150 solo piano pieces, usually grouped into sets or suites (with titles like those mentioned above); fourteen songs; six stage works (including the ballets *Parade* and *Relâche*); Mass for voices and organ; *Socrate*, cantata for four voices and orchestra.

Piano pieces *Trois gymnopédies* (1888). Inspired by pictures on a Greek vase, these pieces set out to capture the peaceful dignity of the classical world. No. 1, a sweetly-flowing tune over plain, unemotional chords, has become an international hit; Nos. 2 and 3 are just as evocative. (They are also known in arrangements for orchestra.) In similar quiet mood are *Trois gnossiennes*. Other Satie works use his experience of cabaret and music-hall – he earned his living as a night-club pianist in Montmartre. The best are *Trois morceaux en forme de poire* ('Three Pear-shaped Pieces' – actually six) for piano duet and its sequel *En habit de cheval* ('In Horse Costume'). In another mood, Satie wrote perfectly straightforward pieces, and then filled the score with strange comments (e.g. 'The Captain loves this!') and descriptions (e.g. 'He packs for his holiday'): the best such work (musically as well as humorously) is *Sports et divertissements* ('Sports and Pastimes'), twenty-one pictures of different activities from golf and riding a seesaw to flirting.

→ Good follow-ups by Satie himself are *Avant-dernières pensées* ('Next to Last Thoughts'), *Trois préludes flasques* ('Three Limp Preludes') and *Embryons desséchés* ('Desiccated Embryos'). Good follow-ups by others are Poulenc *Mouvements perpétuels* (frivolous), Gershwin *Three Preludes* (bluesy and frivolous) and Debussy *La cathédrale engloutie* and *Six épigraphes antiques* (serious and beautiful).

Other works Apart from his piano music, Satie is best-known for a lunatic ballet, *Parade*, and the cantata *Socrate*. Ⓜ *Parade* (1917) depicts the passing of a circus parade, and is full of raucous red-nosed musical slapstick. It was famous in its day because its orchestra included typewriters, pistols, factory-sirens and aeroplane engines; it survives today because the music is splendidly funny, like a Keystone-Cops custard-pie comedy transferred to sound. Ⓜ *Socrate* (1919) is utterly different. It is a setting of passages from Plato's dialogues concerning the teaching and death of the Greek philosopher Socrates. Satie gives the voices plain, unmelodic lines to sing, deliberately avoiding the rise and fall of notes which would create emotion, and he accompanies them with equally plain, unconnected chords. The result is not, as it might seem, monotonous, but restrained and moving, like overhearing a quiet conversation – exactly the effect Plato himself was aiming for.

→ Good follow-ups to *Parade* are Satie's own *The Adventures of Mercury* and *Relâche* ('Theatre Closed'), Chabrier *España*, Milhaud *Le boeuf sur le toit* and Ibert *Divertissement*; good follow-ups to *Socrate* are Satie *Three Songs*, Vaughan Williams *On Wenlock Edge* and Barber *Dover Beach*.

SCARLATTI, Domenico (1685-1757). *Italian composer.*

Scarlatti was the son of a famous opera-composer (Alessandro Scarlatti, 1660-1725), and soon entered his father's profession. For the first thirty-five years of his life he led a busy but undistinguished musical existence, playing the harpsichord (e.g. for *Handel's Italian opera company in London), composing Masses for St Peter's, Rome, operas for Venice and Naples and concertos and chamber works for anyone who asked. He was famous as the finest harpsichordist of the day, but as a composer he was competent and not inspired.

In about 1720 Scarlatti went to Lisbon as harpsichord-teacher to Princess Maria Barbara, and when she became Queen of Spain eight years later he followed her to Madrid and stayed there for the rest of his life. For Maria Barbara, he composed over 500 harpsichord pieces, works of dazzling brilliance which place him abruptly in the front rank of composers: the change is like a butterfly emerging from a chrysalis.

(Scarlatti's sonatas have been catalogued and numbered three times, by the Italian scholars Longo and Pestelli, and by the American scholar Kirkpatrick. L numbers were once common (and are still sometimes seen); but Kk numbers are based on more up-to-date research and are now most commonly used.)

WORKS Masses, *Stabat mater*, *Salve regina* and many other religious works; fifteen solo cantatas (similar to those of his father Alessandro, in all but quality); twelve *concerti grossi*; fugues and other solo-organ works; 500 harpsichord 'sonatas'.

Sonatas All Scarlatti's sonatas are one-movement works, three to six minutes long and divided into two equal (and repeated) halves. He grouped them in pairs, usually contrasting slow and fast, grave and gay; even so, many are separately performed today. (Good examples are the bouncy Kk 132, the clattery jig Kk 119, the 'hunting-call' Kk 96 and the pastoral Kk 175.) Recommending specific works is pointless: each player groups the sonatas to suit himself or herself, and all sonatas offer the same blend of exuberant finger-dexterity, scrunchy harmony and open, simple melody. The sonatas sound best on their own instrument, the harpsichord; but they are often played on the piano (in some cases, e.g. Horowitz's recording of Kk 232, 455 and 531, dazzlingly); arrangements for guitar, brass group, recorder group, strings and even mandolins exist. (Two splendid 'spin-off' works are Avison's (eighteenth-century) twelve *concerti grossi* for strings, each movement of which is a Scarlatti sonata, and Tommasini's (twentieth-century) ballet *The Good-humoured Ladies*, a reworking of Scarlatti as cheerfully irreverent as *Stravinsky's *Pulcinella* is of *Pergolesi.)

→ Bach Fantasia in C minor; Soler (a Scarlatti pupil) Sonatas; Handel Chaconne in G.

SCHOENBERG, Arnold (1874–1951). *Austrian composer and teacher.*

Schoenberg was one of the finest composition-teachers of the century. At first in Vienna, then (after he fled from Europe because of Nazi persecution) in the USA, he trained and encouraged many of the leading figures of 'contemporary' music, insisting not only on unfettered self-expression but also on a firm grounding in the harmonic, contrapuntal and orchestral techniques of the sixteenth to nineteenth centuries. (His university textbook *Harmony Method* is still one of the best.)

In his own music, Schoenberg was restless, unsatisfied, always pushing at the boundaries of experiment: he never wrote two works alike. From the start of his career, his ambition was to express 'pure emotion' in sound; along with such other creators as the playwrights Strindberg and Kaiser and the painters Munch and Kandinsky, he believed that one way to achieve 'truth' in art was to let the unconscious mind freely express itself. (Freud, at the same time, was encouraging his patients to remember and retell their dreams; 'expressionist' painting, drama and music of the time often seem to have the logic of dreams, not of waking life.) In the 1900s the search for ever-more-expressive harmonies led Schoenberg to replace ordinary keys and scales in his music with a continuously-changing musical texture where every individual sound had equal importance. (His admirers called it 'atonality'; shocked audiences found it an aural nightmare.) In the 1920s he refined the idea still further, and perfected the 'twelve-note system' (see Glossary): this discovery affected the music of almost every serious composer since.

Schoenberg's quest for new sounds, for the ultimate musical expressiveness, makes his work either very seductive (if you follow his obsessions) or very hard on the ear (if you don't). He is something of a composer's composer, more admired by professional musicians than enjoyed by ordinary music-lovers. But although at first hearing the music does sound as chaotic and disorderly as dreams, it is logically and honestly constructed, and with each repeated hearing its logic becomes more apparent, adds to its emotional impact and makes it powerful and moving where once it seemed cacophonous.

WORKS Four operas (including *Moses and Aaron*); oratorio *Jacob's Ladder*; *Verklärte Nacht*, *Pelléas and Mélisande*, *Variations*, *Five Pieces*, two chamber symphonies, *Accompaniment for a Film Scene* and several other orchestral works; Piano Concerto; Violin Concerto; *Gurrelieder*, *Pierrot lunaire*, *Ode to Napoleon*, *A Survivor from Warsaw* and a dozen other vocal and choral works; four string quartets, Serenade, Suite and other chamber works; Suite and several sets of pieces for piano; three dozen songs (including the song-cycle *Book of the Hanging Gardens*); many arrangements and recompositions of other composers' works (e.g. *Handel's *Concerto grosso* Op. 6 No. 7 reworked for string quartet and orchestra; *Brahms' Piano Quartet No. 1 rescored as a symphony).

Ⓜ *Verklärte Nacht* ('Transfigured Night'), Op. 4 (1899) Originally for six solo strings, this sumptuous piece was rescored for large string orchestra (and much improved). It is a sound-picture of two lovers walking in a moonlit wood, she tearfully confessing adultery, he forgiving her and assuring her of eternal love. The music's style is close to *Wagner's *Tristan and Isolde*, and Schoenberg's score contains some of the most ravishing sounds ever drawn from a string orchestra. → String Quartet No. 1 (just as sumptuous sounds, but less rhapsodic and more intellectually compact); Strauss *Metamorphosen*; Tippett *Fantasia concertante on a Theme of Corelli*.

Ⓜ *Pierrot lunaire*, Op. 21 (1912) Twenty-one expressionist poems, about a love-sick, moon-struck clown (Pierrot), set for voice and five instrumentalists. The voice-part is half-spoken, half-sung, and the instruments provide a shimmering, eerie background: of all Schoenberg's works, this is one of the most dreamlike, but the shortness of the poems and the constant variety of mood make it easier to grasp than most, an excellent introduction to his style. (An English libretto is crucial.) → *Five Orchestral Pieces* (shifting, blurring sounds of much the same kind, but no voice); Boulez *Le marteau sans maître*; Maxwell Davies *Eight Songs for a Mad King*.

Ⓜ **String Quartet No. 3**, Op. 30 (1927) If *Bach had written twelve-note music, it might have sounded like this: brisk, lithe, disciplined and sounding not random but absolutely inevitable. No twelve-note music is easy on the ear at first hearing, but this quartet (though you'd be hard put to it to go away whistling its tunes) is one of the most sparkling twelve-note works ever composed. → Ⓜ String Trio; Bartók String Quartet No. 4; Carter String Quartet No. 1.

SCHUBERT, Franz (1797-1828). *Austrian composer.*
Like many an impoverished genius before and since, Schubert owed his artistic education to a scholarship. At the age of eleven he became a boy

soprano at the Imperial Chapel in Vienna, and in his five years there he not only confirmed his life-long love of the human voice (and of the German poetry he was to set for it), but also learned composition, piano and violin (on which he became expert enough to lead the college orchestra). At sixteen he joined his father's school as an apprentice teacher; but thanks to his classroom manner (a mixture of over-strictness and wool-gathering) he had no success at teaching, and four years later gave it up to devote his time to music.

From then on, the problem was money. There was no support from the family – his father and brother barely earned enough to support themselves – and very little from wealthy patrons (e.g. the Esterházy family, who employed Schubert in the summer holidays to teach their daughters the piano, but had no permanent post to offer him). From the start, influenced by *Rossini (who was currently all the rage in Vienna), he determined to make his fortune by writing successful operas – and failed. (His operas were lovely music but hopeless drama: the least popular ran for two nights, the most popular for twelve.) In the end, he found an outlet: composing piano pieces, songs and chamber works to satisfy the growing amateur demand for home music (see *Nineteenth-century Music*). He did this expertly and brilliantly, adding genius to what in other hands was merely a chore, and throughout his life publishers provided him with a steady if meagre income.

Schubert spent every morning, every day, at his desk. His concentration on work was total: as a friend once remarked, 'He has now long been at work on an Octet, with the greatest zeal. If you visit him during the day, he says, "Hello. How are you? Good." and goes on writing, whereupon you leave'. It was thanks to such singlemindedness that he managed to write so much: as many works, for example, in twenty years as *Brahms composed in fifty. (He composed with almost unbelievable fluency: he once wrote 150 songs in a single year, and his friends claimed that he could invent music for a song in the time it took most other people to read the words.) In the afternoons he liked to visit friends, walking or picnicking in the countryside or visiting one of Vienna's coffee-houses to read the paper, drink hot chocolate and discuss the world and its problems. In the evenings, four or five times a week, Schubert and his friends met at one another's houses for talk, party-games, food and drink, and above all music: so many of Schubert's works were first heard on these occasions, and he was so much the life and soul of the party, that the evenings were nicknamed 'Schubertiads'.

Next to composing, friendship was the hub of Schubert's life. He knew everyone: clerks, poets, customs officers, actors, rich young idlers, postmen and opera singers (e.g. Johann Vogl, for whom he wrote many of his songs and with whom he went on concert-tours and summer walking-holidays).

To the outsider, his life sounds placid but monotonous: a great deal of eating, drinking, horseplay and music-making interrupted only by occasional shortages of cash or, in his last five years, by days and weeks in hospital. But it must have been a happy life to live, and it provided exactly the easy-going, good-humoured background he needed to compose, a good-humouredness which is reflected in virtually every work he wrote.

(The D numbers sometimes used to identify Schubert's works refer to a catalogue made of them by the twentieth-century scholar Deutsch.)

VOCAL WORKS Over 600 songs (including the cycles *The Maid of the Mill* and *Winter Journey*, and the group *Swan Song*); three dozen choral works (including *Song of the Spirits over the Water*); ten operas and operettas; seven Masses, *Salve regina*, oratorio *Lazarus* and half a dozen smaller church works.

Songs Ⓜ *An die Musik* ('To Music'), D 547 (1817). The 1500 pages of Schubert songs are a mine of treasures, equal in diversity and magnificence to Shakespeare's plays or *Haydn's symphonies, and recommendable *en masse* in much the same way: whatever your first enjoyment, scores of equal and greater pleasures await further exploration. *To Music* is typical of Schubert's own favourite kind of song, a simple, ecstatic melody with plain accompaniment, repeated for several verses, a musical outpouring as clear and instantaneous-seeming as the poetry he set. (Other well-known songs of this kind include Ⓜ *Die Forelle* ('The Trout') and Ⓜ *Der Tod und das Mädchen* ('Death and the Maiden'), used as the basis for sublime variation-movements in the 'Trout' Quintet and 'Death and the Maiden' Quartet, respectively; *Nähe des Geliebten* ('Praise of the Beloved'), Ⓜ *Du bist die Ruh'* ('You are Peace') and *Gretchen am Spinnrade* ('Gretchen at the Spinning-wheel'). In other songs he extended and elaborated the piano accompaniments, with results less like simple poems than lyrical, one-movement cantatas for voice and piano: these include many of his greatest songs, e.g. Ⓜ *Erlkönig* ('The Erlking'), Ⓜ *Ganymed* ('Ganymede'), *Der Musensohn* ('Son of the Muses') and *Die junge Nonne* ('The Young Nun'). Fourteen *Lieder* of this type were published together after Schubert's death as Ⓜ *Schwanengesang* ('Swan-song'): they are usually performed as a group, and make a fine introduction to his songs. In his two song-cycles, Ⓜ *Die schöne Müllerin* ('The Beautiful Maid of the Mill') and Ⓜ *Winterreise* ('Winter Journey'), he extended the drama of the *Lied* to cover a set of songs lasting forty minutes or more, telling a developing story and exploring depths of character or feeling not possible in the span of a single song. (Both cycles concern hopeless love. *The Maid of the Mill* is lighter-hearted, with bubbly piano accompaniments symbolizing both the mill-stream and the hope in the heart of the young man who confides in it his hopeless love. *Winter Journey* is more sombre and more tragic in tone, though its melodies are some of the most heart-easing Schubert ever wrote.)

→ Other well-known Schubert songs include *Hark, Hark the Lark, Lachen und Weinen* ('Laughing and Weeping'), *Seligkeit* ('Purity'), *Ständchen* ('Serenade') and *Der Hirt auf dem Felsen* ('The Shepherd on the Rock', cantata for voice, clarinet and piano). Good follow-ups by others are Schumann *Die Lotosblume*, Op. 27 No.

7, and *Der Sandmann*, Op. 79 No. 13; Brahms *Ständchen*, Op. 106 No. 1, and (to *Swan-song*) Wolf *Italian Songbook*.

Other vocal works Ⓜ *Gesang der Geister über den Wassern* ('Song of the Spirits over the Water'), D 714, is a wistful, peaceful song for choir and orchestra, somewhat in the ecstatic mood of *To Music* or *Ganymede*. Schubert's operas and Masses, by and large, are less well known (and less good): the best of the operas is the Rossini-inspired comedy *Die Zwillingsbrüder* ('The Twins', with a bravura central role for one singer playing both twins); the best of the church works are the Mass in G (D 167: short and cheerful) and Mass in A flat (D 678: large-scale and ceremonial). Of other people's music, a good follow-up to the operas is Weber's *Abu Hassan* (whose overture is especially Schubertian), and good follow-ups to the Masses are Haydn's Mass No. 6 ('St Cecilia' Mass No. 2) and Mozart's Mass No. 10, K 220.

CHAMBER AND PIANO WORKS Octet, String Quintet, 'Trout' Quintet (for piano and strings), string quartets, Violin Sonata, Arpeggione Sonata, three sonatinas for violin and piano, two piano trios and a few shorter chamber works; twenty-one sonatas, *Wanderer Fantasy*, six *Moments musicaux*, eleven impromptus, forty-eight waltzes, several variation-sets and other assorted solo-piano works; *Hungarian Divertissement*, Grand Duo, Sonata, Fantasia, three *Marches militaires*, variation-sets, rondos and other four-hand piano works.

Chamber music Ⓜ Octet, D 803 (1824). Few other works better show Schubert's ability to respond to a humdrum commission with work of overwhelming, lyrical genius. He was asked for a companion-piece to Beethoven's Septet, and produced a work with the expected minuets, variations, bouncy finale and songlike slow movement – but instead of tossing it lightly off, and without sacrificing an ounce of jollity or tunefulness, built in all the expansive seriousness of his symphonies (the 'Great C major' was in his mind at about this time). The 'beefing-up' process was repeated in his last three string quartets (Ⓜ No. 14, 'Death and the Maiden', is particularly fine), in the two sunny piano trios, and above all in the Ⓜ String Quintet, as majestic and compelling as the late string quartets of his admired *Beethoven, but with a directness and simple-heartedness not even Beethoven achieves. His other chamber works are slighter, accessible to amateur players as well as professionals, and crammed with tunes. The Ⓜ 'Trout' Quintet is the jolliest, the leaping accompaniment and sparkling tune of the song (used here for variations) setting the mood of the whole piece; the early string quartets are close in style to Symphonies 1-6 (see below), and the violin sonatas and Arpeggione Sonata (for an instrument midway between cello and guitar) are Schubert at his most smiling and serene.

→ Good follow-ups by Schubert are the symphonies mentioned above and the piano works discussed below; good follow-ups by others are, to the lighter works, Beethoven's 'Spring' Sonata (Violin Sonata Op. 24), Dvořák's 'Dumky' Trio and Berwald's Septet, and to the more serious works Mozart's String Quintet K 614, Beethoven's String Quartet No. 9, Op. 59 No. 3, Mendelssohn's Octet and Brahms's Clarinet Quintet.

Piano music Sonata No. 6, D 568 (1817). Like Beethoven, Schubert used his piano sonatas throughout his life as a kind of musical notebook, a place to experiment with forms, styles and ideas – and none the less, as if he could hardly staunch the flow of inspiration, made several of them masterworks as well. They range from unpretentious, merry works (e.g. No. 6, recommended above, or No. 13, D 664), ideal for himself to play at a Schubertiad, to 'big' sonatas on the grandest heights of inspiration (Nos. Ⓜ 18, D 894, and Ⓜ 21, D 960, are among his most satisfying pieces of any kind: No. 21, in particular, ranks in magnificence with the String Quintet). Two non-sonata works are of parallel stature: the Ⓜ *Wanderer Fantasy* for solo piano and Ⓜ Fantasia for piano duet, D 940. The rest of Schubert's piano music is delectable: its purpose is to please, and it fulfils it perfectly. The best works to hear first are the *Four Impromptus*, D 899: No. 4, a cascade of right-hand arpeggios over a sumptuous left-hand tune, is one of his best-loved pieces.

→ Good follow-ups to the lighter works are the *Three Marches militaires* ('Military Marches': No. 1 is also well-known for orchestra, and is affectionately sent up in *Stravinsky's *Circus Polka*, accompanying a march-past of elephants) and the Rondo in A for piano duet, and *Six Moments musicaux* ('Musical Moments'), D 780 (No. 3, variations on a plaintive melody, is particularly loved); good follow-ups to the more serious works are Sonata No. 19, D 894, and the relaxed, flowing Ⓜ Grand Duo, D 813 (another companion-piece to the 'Great C major' symphony). Good follow-ups by others are Beethoven's piano sonatas Nos. 21, 24 and 26 and (for the lighter works) Chopin's nocturnes, Op. 32, and waltzes, Op. 64.

ORCHESTRAL WORKS Nine symphonies (No. 7 unorchestrated; No. 8 unfinished); five overtures (including two 'in the Italian style'); *Rosamunde* incidental music (overture, entractes, ballet music and songs); rondo for violin and orchestra; assorted dances and other slight works.

Ⓜ **Symphony No. 5** (1816) Schubert's first six symphonies were written for amateur or semi-professional orchestras, and the emphasis is less on grandeur than on pleasure, both for players and audience. The Fifth is the finest, an orchestral jewel of which Mozart himself might have been proud. (Its slow movement, strutting minuet and bouncy finale are especially Mozartian.) Of the other early symphonies, Nos. 1–3 most nearly match its elegance (though not its profundity), and their tongue-in-cheek wit is also a feature of the *Rosamunde* overture (and its attendant pieces, of which the ballet music in G is the best-loved) and of the two glittering overtures 'in the Italian style'. In the mid-1820s Schubert's views on orchestral music changed. He was impressed by Beethoven's symphonies (especially Nos. 4 and 7), and set out to emulate their relaxed expansiveness. His Seventh Symphony (not played nowadays) was a large-scale, forty-minute piece and his Ⓜ Eighth (the 'Unfinished'), although only two movements exist, notably combines a symphonic energy worthy of Beethoven with the soaring tunes Schubert composed so effortlessly. (It is a companion-piece, in style and beauty, to the Piano Sonata No. 18, D 894.) The Ⓜ Symphony No. 9 (nicknamed the 'Great C major' to distinguish it from the Sixth, also in C major) is Schubert's finest orchestral work, as noble a companion to Beethoven's symphonies as Schubert's

Fifth is to Mozart's. For all its length and grandeur, the main impression it gives is of good humour: *Schumann once compared hearing Schubert's music to strolling through beautiful countryside, and this is the kind of work he meant.

→ Good follow-ups to the lighter-weight symphonies are the *Four Impromptus*, D 899, for piano and the Arpeggione Sonata; good follow-ups by others are Mozart's Symphony No. 33, Beethoven's Symphony No. 2 and Mendelssohn's 'Italian' Symphony. Good follow-ups to the *Rosamunde* music are the Rondo for violin and orchestra, the Octet and Mendelssohn's *Midsummer Night's Dream* overture and incidental music. Good follow-ups to the more expansive works are the String Quartet No. 15, D 887, and the *Wanderer Fantasy* and Grand Duo for piano (*Wanderer Fantasy* also arranged by Liszt for piano and orchestra; Grand Duo also orchestrated by Weingartner; both arrangements recommended); good follow-ups by others are the Beethoven symphonies mentioned above (not to mention No. 6) and such sunny late-nineteenth-century pieces as Strauss's *Aus Italien*, Brahms' *Academic Festival Overture* and Mahler's Symphony No. 4.

SCHUMANN, Robert (1810–56). *German composer.*

A bookseller's son, Schumann spent much of his boyhood exploring his father's stock, and the works of such Romantic writers as Byron, Goethe and Jean Paul were almost as real to him as reality itself. He studied law at university, but wanted to make his career either in music or in literature. His first idea was to become a concert pianist, and at nineteen he went to live and study with the great teacher Friedrich Wieck; later, however, he crippled his right hand (with a gadget invented to strengthen his fourth finger), and abandoned playing for composition and the writing of music criticism. He became one of the finest and most influential critics of the age, particularly helpful to young composers like *Chopin and *Brahms, and a mine of enthusiasm for *Bach, *Mozart and other great composers of the past.

Almost as soon as Schumann went to study with Wieck, he fell in love with Wieck's daughter Clara, then a teenager. Her father was scandalized, and did everything he could to break up the affair. There were years of rows, bitter letters and lawsuits, ending only when the lovers finally married on the day before Clara's twenty-first birthday. Clara had her own career as a concert-pianist (she was one of the greatest performers of the nineteenth century), and spent many months each year on tour; but when she was at home she guided and encouraged Robert's composing career, and many of his best works were written either for her or under her inspiration.

Despite this domestic security, there was from the start a dark cloud over Schumann's life. His family had always shown traces of mental illness (his brother, for example, committed suicide at sixteen), and he himself showed early signs of a split personality (half 'Eusebius', an impractical, head-in-the-clouds dreamer, half 'Florestan', an impetuous, fiery and equally impractical man of action). The strain of his rows with Wieck further damaged his mental balance; and finally, after their marriage, Clara put him through a composition-régime which was exciting (and which produced marvellous results) but which mentally exhausted him. (1840 was a year dedicated to writing songs, 1841 a year of symphonies, 1842 a year of chamber music, and so on.) In the mid-1840s Schumann began suffering severe depression; in the early 1850s (the time of his friendship with the young *Brahms) he began hearing voices and talking with angels; in 1854 he threw himself into the Rhine, was rescued and committed to a mental hospital, where he died after two more years of suffering.

The only sign of this personal distress in Schumann's music is that some of his piano works are in two carefully-separated styles, 'Eusebius' pieces and 'Florestan' pieces. Otherwise, his work is as serene and organized as *Mendelssohn's, as tuneful as *Schubert's. He found concentration on large forms difficult, and his symphonies and chamber works, though they are full of inspired moments, tend to rather frigid academic rambling; but his short pieces, especially his songs and piano suites, are among the most inventive and poetic compositions of the age.

WORKS Three sonatas, twenty-five suites and other large collections (including *Papillons, Carnaval, Symphonic Studies, Abegg Variations, Scenes from Childhood* and *Davidsbündlertänze*), Fantasia and several other individual piano pieces (including *Arabeske*); four symphonies (plus an unfinished fifth, published as *Overture, Scherzo and Finale*) and two overtures for orchestra; Piano Concerto; Cello Concerto; Violin Concerto; Concert Piece for four horns and orchestra; *Introduction and Allegro* for piano and orchestra; opera *Genoveva*; chamber music including two string quartets, Piano Quintet, Piano Quartet, three piano trios, two violin sonatas and a dozen works with romantic titles (e.g. 'Fairy-Tale Pictures' for viola and piano); *Scenes from Faust*, *Requiem* and half a dozen other choral works; sixty partsongs (including four volumes of *Romances and Ballads*); over 250 solo songs (including the cycles *Dichterliebe* and *Frauenliebe und -Leben*, and two other groups called simply *Liederkreis* ('Songcycle')).

Piano music Ⓜ *Carnaval*, Op. 9 (1835). Most of Schumann's piano music was written during the years he was courting Clara, and is full of ardour and rich fantasy: it can be as heady as lovers' conversation, like two besotted people eagerly sharing views, dreams and private jokes. *Carnaval* is typical: it is a musical picture of a costume-ball, whose guests include the *commedia dell'arte* lovers Harlequin and Columbine, the dreamer Eusebius and the darkly handsome Florestan, as well as such notables as Paganini and Chopin: at the end, the ball is invaded by a band of humourless killjoys, and all the fantastical characters unite and rout them in a triumphant march. (The work also exists as a ballet, to much the same story; the music is best on piano.) Other works in similar fantastical vein are *Papillons* ('Butterflies'), Ⓜ *Kreisleriana* and *Faschingsschwank aus Wien* ('Carnival Procession from Vienna'); the Ⓜ *Kinderscenen* ('Scenes from Childhood') are gentler and quieter (and have splendid counterparts, designed for Schumann's own children and easy to play, two *Albums for the Young*). Of his other piano music, the three sonatas are fiery, virtuoso works; the Ⓜ Fantasia and *Arabeske* are warmly Romantic (like Schubert or Chopin at their gentlest); the Ⓜ *Études symphoniques* ('Symphonic Studies') are variations as trippingly tuneful and varied in mood as any of his character-pieces, lacking only explanatory titles to guide our imagination.

→ A good follow-up to the dreamier music is the Ⓜ *Andante and Variations*, Op. 46 (best in its piano-duet form, though it also exists for piano with cellos and four horns); good follow-ups to the heroic music (especially the sonatas) are the *Overture, Scherzo and Finale* for orchestra and the Piano Quartet; good follow-ups by others are Schubert's impromptus, Chopin's Ballades and *Variations brillantes*, Op. 12, and Brahms's Scherzo Op. 4, *Variations on a Theme of Schumann,* Op. 23 (four-hands) and *Piano Pieces* Op. 118.

Songs Ⓜ *Widmung* ('Devotion'), Op. 25 No. 1 (1840). If all Schumann's music but his songs disappeared overnight, his reputation would still stand unimpaired. They are like gems, single moments of emotion or description frozen in sound, polished, poetic and precise. Like Schubert, Schumann had a genius for clothing the thought of a poem in simple, inevitable-sounding notes, and then letting the piano accompaniment flesh out the emotional meaning implicit in the words. The tune of *Widmung*, for example, is as plain as a folksong; with guitar-chords the piece would be as straightforward as *The Ash Grove* or *My Love is like a Red, Red Rose*. But the hectic piano accompaniment gives it a blurted, breathless fervency, making it a declaration of passion too insistent to be held in check. In *Der Nussbaum* ('The Nut-tree'), Op. 25 No. 3, an equally straightforward description of a nut-tree is given yearning intensity by rippling left-hand arpeggios and discordant, suspenseful right-hand notes: this is not the idyll the words might make us think. The technique is carried to its apogee, and produces Schumann's greatest work in any form, in the song-cycle Ⓜ *Dichterliebe* ('Poet's Love'), Op. 48, where the hope forever springing in the poet's voice (that his beloved will respond to him) is constantly undercut by elegiac turns of harmony and mocking distortions of the melodic phrases he sings, until at the end, as he accepts his beloved's loss, the piano suddenly flowers into a most moving epilogue, a beautiful recollection of happiness snatched beyond recovery. Writing *Lieder* of this quality is a subtle art, and at his best Schumann is its subtlest master, outclassing even Schubert.

→ *Frauenliebe und -Leben* ('Woman's Life and Love', a cycle taking its protagonist through every stage of her adult life from first love to marriage, childbirth and betrayal; darkly coloured, but some of Schumann's most beautiful tunes); *Six Songs*, Op. 89; Schubert *Frühlingsglaube, Ganymed*; Brahms *Feldeinsamkeit, Magelone Romances*.

(M) **Piano Concerto, Op. 54 (1841; 1845)** The first movement of this concerto began life as a present for Clara in 1841 (the second year of their marriage), and is full of the same springing happiness as his most passionate songs; like them, too, it is like a single inspiration, a single polished jewel. Miraculously, four years later he was able to pick up the inspiration where he'd left off, and added a wistful slow movement and an energetic finale full of witty cross-rhythms and energetic, upward-leaping themes, to complete one of the sunniest concertos in the repertoire.

→ *Introduction and Allegro appassionato* (piano and orchestra); *Davidsbündlertänze* (solo piano); MacDowell Piano Concerto No. 1.

Symphony No. 1 (the 'Spring'), Op. 38 (1841) Schumann's symphonies are like *Mendelssohn's, concerned as much with happy-go-lucky entertainment as with the solemn working-out of themes. Energy bursts from the very first half-dozen bars, and the pace seldom flags (save for a song-like slow movement) from first bar to last.

→ Symphony No. 3 (the 'Rhenish'); Weber Symphony No. 1; Gounod Symphony No. 2.

SCRIABIN, Alexander (1872-1915). *Russian pianist and composer.*

Virtuoso pianists in the second half of the nineteenth century tended to follow in *Liszt's footsteps: that is, they favoured what they called a 'masculine' playing-style (full of assertive technical display, so that even quiet music had a kind of steely strength) instead of the 'feminine' style of such men as *Chopin or *Schumann (where technical brilliance was built into the sound-texture of the music). Scriabin was an exception: he played in the Chopin style, and composed the kind of piano music Chopin might have written if he'd lived another half-century: poetic, ornate, dependent on a cloud of subtly-changing harmony (helped by the sustaining pedal) and dreamy right-hand decoration.

For the first ten years of his professional life, Scriabin taught the piano in Moscow, toured Europe and the USA as a composer-pianist, and wrote a Chopin-like Concerto, four sonatas, preludes, studies and other pieces for his recitals. But in the 1900s he became interested in theosophy (a form of religious mysticism), and changed both his life and his composing style. He began to think of himself as a divinely-appointed superman who would bring humanity to its senses and rescue the world from destruction, and thought that the means of salvation, the revelation, would come through a union of all the arts. His concerts were more like religious meetings than musical events; the audiences were assailed with incense, coloured lights, poems and prayers as well as with choirs, orchestras and Scriabin himself as pianist and conductor. He invented (or discovered) a 'magic' chord which he claimed underlay all music, and his last six sonatas and two orchestral works (*Poem of Ecstasy*; *Prometheus*) are built on it. For all its eccentric, even crazy inspiration, this music is often very fine: he may not have succeeded in saving the world, but by shaking off Chopin's influence Scriabin certainly found himself.

works Two symphonies (early; not good), *Divine Poem, Poem of Ecstasy, Prometheus* (*Poem of Fire*) for orchestra; Piano Concerto; ten sonatas, twenty-four studies, eighty-five preludes and many shorter piano pieces.

Ⓜ **Piano Sonata No. 5, Op. 53** (1908) Lovers of Chopin may find Scriabin's early piano music disappointing: it tends to sound exactly like Chopin's with the tunes removed. (*Preludes*, Op. 11, is the best selection.) With the Sonata No. 5, however, the change in his style begins. Without losing its poetic dreaminess, the music is tougher, more directed, as if written out of need rather than merely to fill a concert programme. The sonata is a sound-picture of the 'mysterious, submerged forces' in human life, and of the performer-magician summoning them from the depths. It is also a spectacular display of piano sounds, ranging in one packed movement from the tender to the hectic. (It is a great favourite with virtuoso soloists.)

→ Sonata No. 7 (a headlong toccata); Prokofiev Sonata No. 4; Medtner Sonata, Op. 25 No. 2.

Ⓜ *Poem of Ecstasy*, Op. 54 (1908) This symphonic poem sets out to show how if the spirit is allowed to 'float free', it will gather, unite and harmonize all human fear, protest, longing, ambition and will in a single, all-satisfying experience. Musically, this programme involves five themes (symbolizing each of the five emotions above) at first presented separately, then united by a sixth theme (Spirit). For all its complex inspiration, the music is sensuous, Romantic and deliciously heady. The best thing to do with the *Poem of Ecstasy* (as with most of Scriabin's later works) is not to puzzle out what it means but simply to wallow in its gorgeous sounds.

→ *Divine Poem*; Schoenberg *Verklärte Nacht* (string-orchestra version); Strauss *Also sprach Zarathustra*.

SEVENTEENTH-CENTURY MUSIC

In the seventeenth century, Western music changed direction. Until then the emphasis of serious composers had been on elaborate sacred works, dignified offerings for the house of God, with music for entertainment playing a very secondary role. Now the balance shifted. Apart from a few individuals of genius (Gibbons, Schütz, Buxtehude), church musicians were obscure, and leading composers preferred the newly-perfected secular forms of *opera, *concerto and *sonata. The eclipse of Catholic church music meant the decline of the sumptuous polyphonic style created for it (see *Sixteenth-century Music*), and harmonic music, using instruments, took its place. To modern ears, whereas sixteenth-century music can sound magnificent but remote, the art of an alien age, seventeenth-century music is close to the art as we know it today.

CHURCH MUSIC The decline of polyphony had two causes. The first was the religious reformation begun by Martin Luther (1483-1546). Among other changes, Luther proposed that church services should be in native languages, understandable by everyone, and should involve the congrega-tion as much as professional priests and choirs. At a stroke, this did away with Latin services and the intricate music written for them. Instead, Lutherans based their worship on sermons and Bible readings, and on chorales: hymns in rhyming verse and with simple, slow tunes which everyone could sing. It was not until the end of the seventeenth century, with Buxtehude, that any Lutheran church music was written to equal what it had replaced – and even so, Buxtehude is still remembered chiefly because he prepared the way for J. S. *Bach.

The second cause of polyphony's decline was a single building, the church of St Mark's in Venice. Like all great churches and cathedrals, it employed some of the leading composers of the age, and two of them, Giovanni Gabrieli (who worked there from 1585) and *Monteverdi (who worked there from 1613), changed the style of Roman Catholic church music in such a radical way, and wrote works of such imaginative power, that they influenced every composer who followed them. St Mark's is not cross-shaped like most cathedrals, but circular, and its musicians' seats are not all at one end but are set round the walls, some at floor-level, others in raised galleries. This suggests a style of church music which surrounds the congregation with sound, the choirs from each gallery echoing and answering each other across the church. Unlike most Catholic churchgoers (e.g. those at the Papal Chapel in Rome where *Palestrina worked), the Venetians liked instruments as well as voices, and so the 'choirs' in St Mark's galleries included as many players as singers. By experiment, com-posers found that polyphonic counterpoint suited neither the instruments nor the need for overlapping blocks of sound; accordingly, they replaced long lines of melody with short groups of chords and harmonies, self-contained nuggets of sound which could be contrasted and repeated intact instead of the endlessly-winding traceries of the polyphonic style.

Not everyone liked Venetian church music. Spanish-speaking Catholics, in particular, preferred the old polyphonic ways, and have gone on using them ever since. But in royal and noble chapels throughout France and Italy, Venetian music set the fashion, and composers everywhere imitated its way of blending instruments and voices, and the harmonic composing-style that went with it. (The trend was particularly welcomed by noblemen interested in new secular-music styles like opera, as it allowed them to employ the same musicians, and to enjoy the same kind of music, both in and out of church.)

STAGE MUSIC Until the seventeenth century, stage music had been a matter of short songs or dances (e.g. jigs for clowns) stuck into plays. But in the 1580s a group of Italian composers and writers, working in Florence, set out to re-create the splendour of ancient Greek drama, with its mixture of words, dance and song – and invented *opera. The fashion spread like fire: by 1630 there were regular opera performances in a dozen Italian cities, scores of composers were writing operas, and several lasting masterpieces (e.g. Monteverdi's operas) had already been composed. Opera offered the dandyish, fashion-loving aristocrats of the time ideal entertainment: it was varied and colourful, adding singing and dancing to the well-known stories from Roman history or Greek myth taught in every schoolroom, or sending them up in a deliciously witty way. Opera became the century's main entertainment medium, and though few works of the time are nowadays ever heard complete, more operas were composed between 1600 and 1700 than at any other period before or since.

Italian opera spread to many places outside Italy. But in northern Europe (especially France and Britain) people favoured other musical stage entertainments too. One was the masque, a mixture of song and dance more like modern pantomime or musical than opera (but with more serious music than that suggests): it was especially liked in England, where authors as distinguished as Milton and Dryden wrote librettos and composers like *Purcell provided music. The other form was ballet, stories told in dance and music alone, without words. This was a favourite form with the courtiers of Louis XIV of France, who also enjoyed what we might call 'mixed media' events: opera-ballets (such as those with words by Molière and music by Lully), ballet-pantomimes and plays with elaborate operatic interludes.

MUSIC FOR INSTRUMENTS Once instruments began to be used in church, and to accompany operas and other stage-shows, the standard of players quickly improved. There had always been a few virtuosos, famous for their skill on lute, viol or harpsichord, but by and large the playing of instruments had in the past tended to be a small-scale and unimportant activity, an accompaniment for dancing or a pastime for amateurs. Now, as more skilled professionals appeared, and as instruments improved in reliability and sound-quality, people began to think that listening to instrumental music, as well as playing it, might be worthwhile. Patrons began asking their church- or stage-instrumentalists to give concerts, and composers devised new forms of music to show off their skills.

Instrumental music was of three main kinds. First were fantasias, variation-sets and short pieces of much the same sort as in previous centuries. (Good examples are Couperin's solo-harpsichord pieces, and Purcell's *Fantasias of three, four, five and six parts*.) Second were suites. Often these were groups of dances, unconnected except that they were in similar keys: good examples are the dance-suites Lully composed for Louis XIV's court orchestra, or the brass-group suites of Locke in Britain and Petzold in Germany (still regular items in brass-ensemble concerts). Gradually, however, composers began linking the movements of the suite by basing them on the same melody throughout, by echoing and repeating phrases or by deliberately setting out to create a single mood. (Purcell's solo-harpsichord suites are of this kind; the form reached its peak at the beginning of the next century, in the orchestral suites of *Telemann and the solo suites and partitas of J. S. Bach.) Third were *sonatas. These were more highly-organized even than suites, with the movements (usually four or five) following a standard order and a standard style. In the last quarter of the century composers like *Corelli developed the sonata to a point where it (and its large-scale equivalents, concertos and *concerti grossi*) rivalled opera as the most popular musical-entertainment form of all.

Listening Typical Venetian pieces by Giovanni Gabrieli (*c.* 1555-1612) are his canzonas and one-movement sonatas for multiple instrumental groups (e.g. *Sonata pian' e forte* for brass), and his motets for groups of mingled voices and instruments (e.g. *In ecclesiis*; *Jubilate Deo*). The finest seventeenth-century Lutheran composer was Buxtehude (*c.* 1637-1707): his organ works (e.g. Prelude and Fugue in G minor) foreshadow J.S. Bach's, and his cantatas (e.g. the solo-voice Christmas cantata *In dulce jubilo*) have a brisk, fresh charm even Bach seldom equalled. More austere devotional music is by Schütz (1585-1672): his *Requiem* (*Musikalische Exequien*) and *St Matthew Passion*, for unaccompanied voices, combine the grandeur of Palestrina's polyphonic style with German words and Lutheran sentiments in a unique and moving way. The Italian operatic style is heard at its liveliest in the work of Alessandro Scarlatti (1660-1725), uncle of the harpsichord-virtuoso *Scarlatti. Good examples of his work are single arias like 'Gia il sole del Gange', from the opera *Pompey*, and the religious works of the end of his life, e.g. the *Stabat Mater*, in a cheerful operatic style like *Pergolesi's. The greatest composer of the English masque was Henry Lawes (1596-1662): his individual songs (e.g. *Gather Your Rosebuds*) are as light and charming as any by Purcell, who greatly admired him. Lawes's 'setts' and the suites of Schmelzer (*c.* 1623-1680) are splendid examples of the lighter kind of instrumental music. For music by the century's greatest composers, see the articles on Corelli, Couperin, Monteverdi and Purcell; see also *Ballet Music, British and Irish Composers, Chamber Music, Opera, Sonata, String Instruments* and *Woodwind Instruments*.

SHOSTAKOVICH, Dmitry (1906-75). *Russian composer*.

When he finished studying, at nineteen, Shostakovich was undecided whether to be a composer or a concert pianist. (He was equally talented at both; his preference, if any, was for the piano.) In the end, events made his mind up for him: his Symphony No. 1, written as a graduation exercise, unexpectedly became a world success, and before he was twenty-one he found himself hailed as the leading young composer of the new Soviet state.

This was a difficult position to keep up. The Soviet rulers were suspicious of the arts, and regarded experimentalism, modernism, as 'hostile to the interests of the working class'. They wanted patriotic music, and that meant folk-tunes, harmonies everyone could understand and wherever possible a glorification of the Revolution and what it had achieved. For his part, Shostakovich admired the spiky, joky modernism of such men as *Milhaud and *Prokofiev. In the 1920s he worked hard to adapt their kind of Parisian, jazzy music to Soviet subjects (e.g. in the ballet *The Golden Age*: see below), and by the time he was thirty he seemed to have built a style which was both acceptable to the authorities and satisfying to him personally, suitable for 'great' music as well as hack-work.

Then, in 1936, disaster struck. Stalin objected to his opera *The Lady Macbeth of the Mtsensk District* (because he found the music discordant and the staging decadent), and Shostakovich was officially disgraced. He climbed laboriously back into favour (e.g. by writing his Symphony No. 5, subtitled 'a Soviet artist's practical creative reply to just criticism') and consolidated his new reputation with music for patriotic cantatas (on such subjects as forestry schemes) and for heroic films. None the less, his reputation remained precarious throughout his life: in 1946, 1948 and 1962 he was in disgrace; in 1966, by contrast, he was given the title Hero of Socialist Labour, the highest honour in the USSR.

Shostakovich's music veers between the inspired and the trivial. He wrote more hack-work than any other great composer of the century, and much of it (e.g. the patriotic cantatas, the Symphony No. 12, on the Revolution, the film scores) is rubbish. At the same time he poured out symphonies, concertos and string quartets of the highest quality, in a musical style which is by no means 'modern'. With Prokofiev and *Copland, he is one of the most accessible of all twentieth-century composers; like *Britten, he uses a straightforward style to say things which are complex, deep and dark.

WORKS Fifteen symphonies, eleven suites (mainly from film music), *Festival Overture* and a dozen shorter orchestral works; six concertos (two each for piano, violin and cello); three operas, four ballets and incidental music for a dozen plays and thirty films; eight cantatas, a dozen song-cycles with orchestra and three dozen solo songs (including the cycle *Suite on Verses of Michelangelo Buonarroti*); fifteen string quartets, Piano Quintet, two piano trios and other chamber works; two sonatas, thirty-seven preludes, twenty-four preludes and fugues, three *Fantastic Dances* and other piano works; Suite, Prelude and Fugue and Concertino for two pianos.

The Golden Age (1932) For this 'social-realist' ballet (a satire on Fascism and capitalism) Shostakovich provided a jazzy, witty score in the manner of Prokofiev. When the ballet flopped (mainly because people found its story ludicrous) he took five of its sections (Introduction, Waltz, Adagio, Polka and Russian Dance) and made them into a rollicking orchestral suite, one of the most exuberant of all his works.

→ Suite *The Bolt*; Piano Concerto No. 1; Gershwin *An American in Paris*; Piston *The Incredible Flutist*.

Ⓜ **Symphony No. 10** (1953) Shostakovich's finest work, and a magnificent example of his 'private' music: its most heartfelt moments even use a note-pattern based on letters from his name (DSCH, representing the notes D, E flat, C, B natural). The grave first and third movements are balanced by a scherzo (second movement) and finale whose glittering orchestral show recalls the march-movement in *Tchaikovsky's Symphony No. 6; the contrast between this spotlit ebullience and the melancholy of the rest of the symphony is unforgettable.

→ Ⓜ Symphony No. 1; Ⓜ Cello Concerto No. 1; Roussel Symphony No. 3.

Ⓜ **Piano Quintet** (1940) This begins solemnly enough (with a prelude and fugue), but then throws seriousness away in one of Shostakovich's scampering, Russian-dance scherzos and a finale intended to depict a circus parade. The two sides of Shostakovich's personality are brilliantly juxtaposed, and the whole work, as unlike the solemn procession of themes and developments suggested by the name Piano Quintet as a fawn is unlike an elephant, is skittish, appealing and unique.

→ Piano Trio No. 2; Ravel Piano Trio; Harris Piano Quintet.

SIBELIUS, Jean (1865-1957). *Finnish composer.*

Until his late twenties, Sibelius was a violin teacher and a talented but second-rank composer following in the footsteps of *Tchaikovsky or *Brahms. Then, in the 1890s, he began studying the *Kalevala* (a huge Finnish epic poem dealing with the creation of the universe, the coming of the gods and above all the birth of Finland itself from the cold northern sea). He used this epic as the basis for cantatas and symphonic poems; their first performances coincided with an enormous upsurge of Finnish nationalism, the climax of years of struggle to free Finland from Russian rule, and because Sibelius's epic works caught the patriotic mood, he found himself a national hero.

From then on, Sibelius was honoured as Finland's greatest composer: he was showered with medals and honorary degrees and was given a state salary for life. He composed music of every conceivable kind: piano pieces, songs, incidental scores for plays, choral works, and above all the kind of large-scale orchestral pieces that had made his name. His shorter works – three-quarters of his output – are cheerful and tuneful, quite deliberately un-grand; his symphonies and symphonic poems, by contrast, are massive and heroic, a counterpart to the fjords and forests of Finland or the *Kalevala*'s sombre magnificence.

WORKS Seven symphonies; twelve symphonic poems (including *En Saga*, *Finlandia*, *Pohjola's Daughter* and *Tapiola*); ten suites (based on incidental music for the theatre, including *Karelia*, *King Christian II* and *The Tempest*); several dozen shorter orchestral works; Violin Concerto; fifty part-songs and other choral works (many to words from the *Kalevala*); String Quartet, Violin Sonatina and six volumes of pieces for violin and piano; Sonata, three sonatinas and twenty-one volumes of solo piano pieces (similar to *Grieg's *Lyric Pieces*); two pieces for organ (thought to be the 'lost' movements of his never-published Symphony No. 8); seventy-nine songs.

Symphonic poems and symphonies Ⓜ *En Saga* ('A Saga'), Op. 9 (1892, revised 1902). Sibelius's unique style, a combination of bare harmony, luscious nineteenth-century orchestration and instantly-striking snippets of melody worked up into substantial and powerful movements, is heard at its most stirring in his symphonic poems. *En Saga* has no story, and instead evokes the stark, heroic world of Scandinavian sagas (in the same way as *Finlandia* evokes the Finnish landscape, or Ⓜ *The Oceanides* the sea); other symphonic poems, notably Ⓜ *Pohjola's Daughter* and Ⓜ *Tapiola*, his grandest orchestral works, have *Kalevala* inspiration. Of his symphonies, the first two are lush, tuneful and Tchaikovskian (Ⓜ No. 2's irresistible finale has made it one of the best-loved of all Sibelius's works); from the Third Symphony onwards, the epic mood of the symphonic poems takes over, and the Fourth, Ⓜ Fifth and Ⓜ Seventh are compact, emotionally powerful and bleakly grand. But in No. 5, after a sombre opening movement, Sibelius warms the music with a placid intermezzo and a striding finale built on a 'big tune' accompanied by bell-like chanting on the horns: this hypnotic tunefulness also lightens the Third and Sixth symphonies, and makes them the most accessible of his later works.

→ Good follow-ups by others are, to the symphonic poems, Liadov *The Enchanted Lake*, Rachmaninov *Symphonic Dances* and Copland *Quiet City*; to the Romantic early symphonies, Nielsen Symphony No. 1, Ives Symphony No. 2 and Martinů Symphony No. 4, and to the late, great symphonies Harris Symphony No. 3 and Vaughan Williams Symphonies Nos. 3 and 5.

Karelia Suite, Op. 11 (1893) Originally written for the theatre, this music has a lilt to its harmony and a bustle to its scoring which surprise people expecting the cool grandeur of Sibelius's symphonies, but which is typical of his sparkling light-music style. Often performed after the *Karelia Overture*, Op. 10, the suite consists of an Intermezzo, a Ballade and a whistleable, foot-tapping March.

→ Suite *King Christian II*; *Scènes historiques*, Set 1; Elgar *The Wand of Youth Suite* No. 1.

Violin Concerto, Op. 47 (1903, revised 1905) This is a concerto in swaggering nineteenth-century show-style, with a heavyweight, 'symphonic' first movement, a songlike slow movement and a scampering, folk-dance finale. (The patterns of Grieg's Piano Concerto and Tchaikovsky's Violin Concerto were much in Sibelius's mind.) Some of the bareness of his symphonic style is also there (e.g. at the very start), and gives a personal flavour to what is otherwise delightfully high-spirited musical showing-off.

→ *The Swan of Tuonela* (a slow piece for cor anglais and orchestra, very much in the mood of this concerto's slow movement); Saint-Saëns *Introduction and Rondo capriccioso*; Lalo *Symphonie Espagnole*.

SINDING. See *One-work Composers*.

SIXTEENTH-CENTURY MUSIC

In most parts of Europe, the old fifteenth-century division between sacred and secular music still applied. Sacred music was large-scale and serious. It used voices, largely unaccompanied – instruments were considered too frivolous for church – and was the highest art to which a composer might aspire. Secular music was shorter, simpler and jollier. It used instruments and voices (haphazardly: pieces were described as 'apt for instruments or voices'), was often in dance-forms of the time (pavan, galliard, coranto), and incorporated folk-songs and popular tunes (e.g. *Greensleeves*, a 'hit' in Britain for most of the century). It was not until the late 1580s that composers began to treat music as a single, undivided art (see Monteverdi), and it was not until the next century that these experiments produced real fruit (see *Seventeenth-century Music*).

POLYPHONIC CHURCH MUSIC Once or twice in the history of Western music, composers have evolved near-perfect musical forms, ideal for their purpose and seemingly beyond improvement. Examples are the string quartets and symphonies of the eighteenth century, Italian grand opera in the nineteenth, and polyphonic Roman Catholic church music in the sixteenth.

Polyphonic means 'many-voiced': polyphonic music is like a tapestry of interweaving vocal lines. It is as if each group of voices in the choir (sopranos, altos, tenors, basses) has a separate melody throughout the music, and the melodies blend and harmonize to make the effect. Usually one vocal line begins alone, and the others follow, at first imitating the notes of the first group but soon branching out in new melodies of their own. The whole experience is like led prayer, the voices picking up, repeating and varying ideas proposed by the leader; it also suggests to some listeners the branching pillars and arching ceiling-ribs of the cathedrals for which it was composed.

Polyphonic music developed slowly, through the works of such as Machaut, Dufay and *Josquin, to reach an emotional and devotional peak in the sixteenth century. Its heyday was short (the lifetime of *Palestrina or Lassus) and in the seventeenth century it had a glorious but decadent aftermath as composers (e.g. Gibbons or Schütz: see *Seventeenth-century Music*) adapted it to new ideas both in music and in religion, so corrupting it even as they practised it. Like such later forms as symphony or opera, it was an international style with well-established rules, and this means that at first hearing the music of second-rate composers can seem little different from that of the greatest masters. But the Masses of Palestrina, Lassus and *Byrd touch the listener's mind and soul in ways lesser works never do. The music is relaxed and restless, challenging and fulfilling all at once, an exact parallel to the religious experience it glorifies. The Mass (with its five sections, Kyrie, Gloria, Credo, Sanctus and Agnus Dei, as unified and tightly-organized as the movements of a symphony) shows the polyphonic style at its finest, but it is also ideal for shorter works: psalm-settings, prayers (e.g. *Ave Maria*), canticles (e.g. *Magnificat*), anthems and motets.

SECULAR MUSIC In their secular vocal music, many sixteenth-century composers tried to find equivalents for polyphonic religious structures. They wrote madrigals, for example, with a tapestry of imitation in true polyphonic style. But most of it, lacking the inspiration of sacred words, sounds pretentious and empty. Palestrina's madrigals, for example, are just as skilful as his church music, but are all head and no heart: they go through the motions of describing love or loss without ever convincing the listener that Palestrina cared tuppence about the meaning of what he wrote.

More successful secular vocal music was usually in a four-square style based less on interweaving melodies than on the chords and strummed harmonies used by lutes, guitars and keyboard instruments. The *chansons* of Claude le Jeune, the *chansons* and madrigals of Lassus or *Monteverdi and the madrigals of the 'English school' (Byrd, Morley and others) are among the glories of the age – and their glory comes from restraint, from an emotional match between words and music and above all from brevity: they are as precise as poems.

Composers of instrumental music, unfettered by words, had more success with polyphony, writing fantasias and toccatas in a 'learned' style as
rich as that of *Bach's fugues 150 years later. For non-polyphonic music,
they favoured sets of variations, often on folk-tunes or popular songs (a
lovely example is Sweelinck's *Mein junges Leben hat ein End'*), and
'mood-pieces' (e.g. Byrd's *The Battel* for harpsichord solo, complete with
imitations of trumpet-calls, galloping hooves, clashing weapons and
victory-cheers).

Listening As with the fifteenth century, record-anthologies give a good sound-
sample of sixteenth-century music: madrigals, instrumental pieces and short
church works are particularly well served. The work of three composers in particular demonstrates the range and scope of sixteenth-century styles, and offers
listening-delights of rare quality. Orlando de Lassus (*c.* 1532-1594) was the *Telemann of his age: he was enormously prolific (there are over 2,000 surviving works),
and was fluent in all styles from Palestrina-like Masses (e.g. the fine *Missa pro
defunctis* of 1580), through madrigals and dialect-songs (e.g. the drunken soldier's
serenade *Matona mia cara*) to instrumental dances and teaching-fantasias in the
most learned style. Tomás Victoria (1548-1611) wrote church music of a sonority
and passion second only to Palestrina's: his motets (e.g. *Vexilla regis* or *O quam
gloriosum est regnum*) are polyphonic counterpoint at its most moving and ornate.
Jan Pieterszoon Sweelinck (1562-1621) specialized in instrumental works, and his
fantasies (e.g. *Echo fantasia 12*) and variation-sets (e.g. *Mein junges Leben hat ein
End'*, on a folk-tune, or *Puer nobis natus est*, on a Christmas hymn) are perfect
miniatures. For many listeners, sixteenth-century British music is some of the
finest in our history; for recommendations see the article on *British and Irish
Composers*. For music by the finest sixteenth-century composers of all, see the
articles on Byrd, Monteverdi and Palestrina.

SMETANA, Bedřich (1824-84). *Czech composer.*
When Smetana was born the Czech nation, as we know it today, did not
officially exist. 'Bohemia' (as it was called) was a province of the huge
Austrian empire, and Smetana grew up speaking German and regarding
'Czech' culture as something localized, small-scale and out of the mainstream of life. But in the 1840s there were Czech nationalist uprisings in
Prague and elsewhere, and Smetana became a fervent partisan, even at one
point an urban terrorist fighting the Austrians. The revolt was fiercely
crushed, and in 1856 Smetana went to live in Sweden, where he earned a
living as director of the Göteborg Philharmonic Society.

In the 1860s the political atmosphere in Prague lightened, and it was
possible for Smetana not only to return, but to act as a spokesman for
Czech culture and the Czech language (which he had studied while in

Sweden). He composed and conducted choral works and operas on nationalist subjects, and was given the important job of music-director to the Prague Provisional Theatre (a centre of Czech culture). In 1866, after the success of his folk-opera *The Bartered Bride*, he was regarded everywhere as the creator of a truly Czech musical style, one admired and imitated by many later composers (among them *Dvořák, *Janáček and *Martinů). His Czech inspiration lives on today in the verve and dash of his music: it is as sunnily tuneful and as happy as the country-dances of his beloved native land.

works Eight operas (including *Dalibor*, *The Bartered Bride* and *The Kiss*); cantatas and partsongs for choir, many with patriotic words; *Triumph Symphony*, nine symphonic poems (including the cycle of six together called *My Country*), *Festival Overture* and *Carnival in Prague* for orchestra; two string quartets, Piano Trio and other chamber works; polkas, Czech dances and other piano works in folk-dance style.

Ⓜ 'Vltava' (from *Má vlast*, 'My Country') (1879) The six symphonic poems of *My Country* depict landscapes from Bohemia (modern Czechoslovakia) and episodes from Bohemian history. The best-known are 'From Bohemia's Woods and Fields' and this one, 'Vltava', a picture of the river (also called 'Moldau') from its beginnings in the hills to its majestic, wide-flowing passage through Prague to the sea. In Smetana's day, 'Vltava''s patriotic theme made it popular; nowadays it lives because of its colourful, folksong harmonies, its bright orchestration and above all the heart-stirring, all-enfolding tune which grows from the woodwind ripples at the start as unstoppably as the river grows from its trickling tributaries. *My Country* is now usually played complete (and fills most of a concert); 'Vltava' is a good sample of its tuneful style, and is gloriously worth hearing on its own. → *Carnival in Prague* (chirpy folk-dance merriment); Mendelssohn overture *Fingal's Cave*; Alfvén *Swedish Rhapsody* No. 1 ('Midsummer Watch').

Ⓜ *The Bartered Bride* (1866) Complete opera. Several of Smetana's operas (e.g. *Dalibor*, *The Brandenburgers in Bohemia*) are serious historical epics, but *The Bartered Bride* uses patriotic inspiration in a refreshing and different way. It is a comedy about two village lovers, and the misunderstandings and masquerades which finally result in their wedding. Smetana took the chance to depict the old customs and manners of Czech rural life, and filled his score with folk-dance rhythms and folksong-like tunes instead of arias. Several items (Ⓜ Overture, Polka, Furiant and the ecstatic song 'Our Dream of Love') are separately known, but there are few musical pleasures to equal sitting down to enjoy the complete opera. (English libretto essential.)
→ *The Two Widows* (complete opera, in the same lighthearted, folksy style); Martinů *Comedy on the Bridge*; Sullivan *The Gondoliers*.

SONATA

A sonata is a piece of music for one instrument alone (usually keyboard), or for one or two solo instruments with keyboard accompaniment. (A few exist for solo instrument without accompaniment, e.g. *Bach's or *Bartók's for solo violin; but they are very rare.) Most sonatas have three or four movements; a few composers (e.g. *Scarlatti) specialized in one-movement sonatas.

EARLY SONATAS AND TRIO-SONATAS Until the 1650s, the word 'sonata' had no special meaning: it was short for *musica sonata* ('music to be sounded', i.e. played on instruments), and contrasted with *musica cantata* ('sung music'). Then, in the work of composers like *Corelli, the sonata became a distinct musical form: a work in several movements for soloist(s) and accompaniment.

The accompanying part usually consisted of a bass line of music (for bass viol, cello or bassoon), sometimes with figures written underneath to signify what chords the composer wanted. The keyboard player (usually on harpsichord or organ) played the written-out bass line with the left hand, and made up a right-hand part to fit the 'figured' chords. (This kind of two-performer accompaniment, bass-player and keyboard-player, is called 'continuo'. A sonata for one instrument and continuo, therefore, involves three players; a trio-sonata, for two instruments and continuo, involves four.)

In the seventeenth century, two kinds of sonata were popular. 'Church sonatas' (so-called because of their sober style) generally had four movements (slow, fast, slow, fast); 'chamber sonatas' had five or more movements (often in dance-rhythms, e.g. minuet, gavotte, jig). Gradually, however, dance-movement works came to be called suites, and all sonatas and trio-sonatas followed the four-movement pattern.

EIGHTEENTH-CENTURY SONATAS The heyday of the four-movement sonata and trio-sonata was the first fifty years of the eighteenth century. Chamber-music of this kind was a favourite recreation, and hundreds of composers provided it. The sonatas and trio-sonatas of Bach, *Handel, *Vivaldi and *Telemann are nowadays among the best-known of all music of that time, and (though they never aimed at profundity, being written simply for entertainment) they are some of their composers' most attractive and characterful works.

As the century went on, and particularly as the piano began to replace the harpsichord (see *Keyboard Instruments*), the style of sonatas completely changed. The continuo dropped out of use, and the piano became the standard accompanying instrument, with the music for both hands fully written-out. Solo sonatas (for keyboard alone) became common, and the old, four-movement pattern changed to three: a substantial, fast opening movement (in a new musical form, developed for sonatas and named after them; see Glossary: *Sonata form*), with two shorter movements (slow and fast) to balance it. This kind of sonata was perfected at the same time as string quartets (see *Chamber Music*) and the *symphony, and, with them, became the grandest kind of music an instrumental composer could write. The later sonatas of *Haydn and *Mozart, and *Beethoven's sonatas, are like chamber-music symphonies, full of their composers' most elaborate and adventurous thoughts.

LATER SONATAS Sonatas have kept this high status ever since. Because they are written for soloists, they are often challenging to play and full of virtuoso show. But their 'symphonic' cast of thought gives them a seriousness and grandness other virtuoso music lacks. Since *Chopin's time, few composers have written more than a handful of large-scale sonatas (compared, say, with Handel's sixty or Telemann's hundreds), and sonatas have been regarded, with concertos, as the peak of the solo repertoire.

SONATINAS For teaching purposes, or for non-virtuoso players, 'Sonatinas' ('little sonatas') were devised in the nineteenth century: easy-going, short and melodious, they offer similar listening pleasure to the entertainment sonatas and trio-sonatas of the early eighteenth century. Clementi's Sonatina Op. 36 No. 1 for piano and *Dvořák's Sonatina Op. 100 for violin and piano are delightful examples.

Listening For those new to sonatas, recommended early eighteenth-century works are Handel's Violin Sonata Op. 1 No. 10, Bach's Flute Sonata No. 6, BWV 1035, and Telemann's Trio-sonata in F for recorder, viola da gamba and continuo (from *Essercizii musici*: it may be complicated to locate the exact sonata in a record shop, but the search is worth it); good follow-ups are more sonatas by these composers (especially Bach's *Six Violin Sonatas* BWV 1020-5 and the rest of Telemann's *Essercizii musici*), and the sonatas and trio-sonatas of Corelli, Quantz and Vivaldi. Good introductions to later sonatas are Mozart's Piano Sonata No. 12, K 332, Beethoven's Sonata No. 5 ('Spring') for violin and piano and Brahms's Sonata No. 1 for clarinet and piano; good follow-ups are Beethoven's Piano Sonata No. 8 ('Pathétique'), Schubert's Arpeggione Sonata and Brahms's Sonata No. 1 for violin and piano. For further recommendations (including some of the grandest and most delightful sonatas in the repertoire), see C. P. E. Bach, J. S. Bach, Bartók, Beethoven, Brahms, Carter, *Chamber Music*, Chopin, Corelli, Franck, Handel, Haydn, Ives, *Keyboard Music*, Liszt, Mozart, Poulenc, Prokofiev, Schubert, Scriabin, *String Music*, Telemann, Vivaldi and *Woodwind Music*.

STOCKHAUSEN, Karlheinz (born 1928). *German composer.*

In the turmoil of German reconstruction after the Second World War, Stockhausen worked as a farm-labourer and a conjurer's piano-accompanist in order to finance his studies. At first he floundered, musically speaking, in a morass of *avant-garde styles, but in the 1950s he found his feet, first as a disciple of *Messiaen and then, crucially, as assistant director of the electronic-music studio of Radio Cologne. He has worked with electronics ever since, and (with *Boulez) is the greatest 'serious' composer ever to use them.

Since the 1970s, Stockhausen has directed and led a chamber group, which has toured the world performing his music. He gives the players not precise notes, but rough instructions to the mood and style of the sounds he wants; they improvise on these instructions, and he filters the results through a computer. His music is gentle and meditative, and its other-worldly effect is increased by Stockhausen's use of Far Eastern rhythms, note-patterns and instruments. He is still something of a specialist's composer (with a following as fanatical as, say, Mike Oldfield's or the Modern Jazz Quartet's); but his best work has pleasures to offer ordinary music-lovers as well as fans.

WORKS Of Stockhausen's 100 or so compositions, the best-known include *Groups* (three chamber orchestras), *National Anthems* (tape), *Procession* (percussion and tape), *Sirius* (voices and tape), *From the Seven Days* (chamber group), *Song of the Young Man* (boy's voice and tape) and *Light* (dancers, solo trumpet, orchestra, chamber group and electronics).

Stimmung ('Tuning') (1968) In this (very typical) piece, six solo singers listen to electronic sounds (which the audience can also hear), then 'tune' into them, echoing them, developing them and adding new music of their own. The effect is hypnotic (and the piece needs all of its seventy-five minutes to make its full effect), similar to Buddhist chanting: appreciating it is less like listening to ordinary music in a concert than taking part in a religious service – and because of this, listening to records in one's own at home is less satisfactory than experiencing a live performance.

→ 'Michaels Reise um die Erde' (*Licht*, 'Light', Part 2); *Inori* ('Adorations'); Boulez *Domaines*.

STRAUSS, Johann (II) (1825-99). *Austrian composer and conductor.*

The Strauss family of Vienna was a musical phenomenon. There were half a dozen of them, Johann I (1804-49) and his sons and nephews, and throughout the nineteenth century they ran a successful dance-orchestra, touring the world to provide waltzes, galops, polkas and other fashionable pieces. (As well as playing for dancing, the orchestra performed on its own: Strauss waltzes are fully worked-out compositions, substantial and satisfying on their own account.) As well as conducting, the Strausses composed (over 1200 waltzes between them), ran a music publishing business and made a fortune from sheet-music sales alone.

Johann Strauss II was incomparably the family's best composer, and one of the finest light-music composers of the century, imitated by *Offenbach, admired by *Wagner and envied by *Brahms. Until 1871 he specialized in waltzes and other orchestral works; then, at Offenbach's suggestion, he began writing operettas, and for the next fifteen years no season at the Viennese Theater an der Wien was complete without a new work from him. (His popularity came at the same time as Gilbert and Sullivan's in London, and his operettas are as highly regarded in German-speaking countries as theirs are in Britain and the USA.)

WORKS 400 waltzes (including *The Blue Danube, Tales from the Vienna Woods, Artist's Life, Morning Papers, Emperor, Roses from the South* and *Wine, Women and Song*); 300 polkas, galops, marches and other orchestral pieces (including *Thunder and Lightning Polka, Champagne Galop* and *Perpetuum mobile*); sixteen operettas (including *Die Fledermaus, The Gipsy Baron* and *A Night in Venice*).

Ⓜ *The Blue Danube*, Op. 314 (1867) Like all Strauss's finest waltzes, this is not so much a single dance-movement as a continuous suite of waltzes, linked by a swaying tune, warm orchestration and the lilting 'three-quarter time' of the rhythm. The waltz so instantly conjures up pictures of couples in evening dress, swirling round the dance-halls of Imperial Vienna, that it is easy to give in to nostalgic reverie, and in the process miss just how good the music is. (Even *The Blue Danube*'s use on the sound-track of the film *2001*, accompanying shots of lazily-tumbling space-craft, hardly altered its image.)
→ Ⓜ *Roses from the South; Emperor Waltz*; Josef Strauss waltz *Delirien*.

Tritsch Tratsch Polka, Op. 214 (1858) Shorter, lighter and more straightforward than his waltzes, Strauss's polkas are now treated less as dance-music than as novelty orchestral items (e.g. at the Vienna New Year Concert). They use lively sound-effects (popping corks, rifle-shots, thunder-rolls), but their chief delights are witty tunes and high-spirited orchestral showing-off.
→ *Pizzicato Polka; Perpetuum mobile*; Chabrier *Joyeuse marche*; Edouard Strauss polka *Bahn frei* ('Full Speed Ahead').

Ⓜ *Die Fledermaus* ('The Bat') (1874) Complete operetta. Like Offenbach's operettas, Strauss's are a blend of catchy tunes and frantic, spoken farce (full of misunderstanding, disguises, tricks and intrigue). They need stage performance (and singers able to act comedy) to make their effect: records, and extracts (e.g. the Overture), for all their fizzy fun, offer only a fraction of the full delight. (More satisfying on record is the gorgeous score arranged from Strauss pieces by Dorati for the ballet *Graduation Ball*: without words, the music swirls easily to the mind's centre-stage.)

→ *The Gypsy Baron*; Lehár *The Merry Widow*; Oscar Straus (no relation) *The Chocolate Soldier*.

STRAUSS, Richard (1864–1949). *German composer and conductor.*

When Strauss was eighteen, one of his teenage works (Wind Serenade, Op. 7) was so successful that Hans von Bülow, director of the Meiningen Court Orchestra, asked him for a sequel and invited him to conduct it himself. This led to more conducting, and by the age of twenty-two Strauss was one of Germany's busiest conductors. He divided his time between operas (he was music-director of the Munich Opera and assistant conductor at *Wagner's theatre in Bayreuth) and orchestral work, where he specialized in *Mozart, *Liszt and his own music. He began composing symphonic poems in Lisztian style, and by the time he was thirty-five several of them (e.g. *Don Juan, Till Eulenspiegel*) had made him world-famous.

In the 1900s Strauss turned from symphonic poems to operas. His *Salome* and *Elektra* were sensations: their librettos were condemned as indecent, their music was said to be the most discordant ever composed – and the public flocked to see them. In 1911, however, with his comic opera *Der Rosenkavalier*, Strauss abandoned discord, and began composing in a serene, mellifluous style closer to Wagner than to any twentieth-century sounds. He went on using it for the rest of his long life, composing mainly songs (he was one of the supreme masters at this) and operas until he was in his eighties, when he unexpectedly returned to instrumental music and produced half a dozen masterworks (e.g. the Oboe Concerto; *Metamorphosen*), lyrical and gently-moving, like opera-ensembles re-imagined for instruments.

WORKS Two symphonies, ten symphonic poems (including *Don Juan, Don Quixote, A Hero's Life, Till Eulenspiegel* and *Death and Transfiguration*), suites, serenades and other orchestral works; four concertos (two for horn, one each for oboe and violin) and other works for soloists and orchestra; fifteen operas (including *Salome, Elektra, Der Rosenkavalier, Ariadne, Arabella* and *Capriccio*); two ballets; a dozen choral works and over 200 songs (including the *Four Last Songs*); piano and chamber works (mainly early).

Symphonic Poems Ⓜ *Till Eulenspiegel*, Op. 28 (1895) Strauss's symphonic poems are orchestral equivalents of swashbuckling technicolor films: their subjects are larger-than-life heroes; every emotion is plain and clear; every event (scattering a flock of sheep, climbing a mountain, bathing the baby) is lovingly depicted (in brilliant orchestral sound); no ounce of gusto or sentiment is omitted. Of other orchestral composers, only *Berlioz can equal Strauss's pictorial gifts, and Strauss's tunes and harmonies are more gorgeous even than Berlioz's. The most full-blooded of all the symphonic poems are *Till Eulenspiegel* (about a practical joker), Ⓜ *Don Juan* (about a legendary lover) and Ⓜ *Ein Heldenleben* (a general picture of a 'Hero's Life', except that the hero in question is the composer); no less pictorial, but on soberer subjects, are *Don Quixote* (scenes from the life of Cervantes' doleful knight), *Also sprach Zarathustra* ('So Spake Zarathustra', a picture of the striving and ecstatic fulfilment of the whole human race) and the elegiac, Wagnerian *Tod und Verklärung* ('Death and Transfiguration'). Of the other symphonic poems, the best is *Aus Italien* ('From Italy', a lovely sound-travelogue of Italian scenes).

→ A good Strauss follow-up to the wilder works is the *Alpine Symphony* (partly a picture of a strenuous climbing expedition, but full of the majesty and grandeur of the Alps); follow-ups to the gentler works could include the Horn Concerto No. 2 and the lovely Ⓜ Oboe Concerto. Good follow-ups by others, in swaggering Straussian style, are Tchaikovsky's *Romeo and Juliet* and *Italian Caprice*, Elgar's overture *Cockaigne* and Arnold's *Tam O'Shanter*, and (to *Don Quixote*) Berlioz's *Harold in Italy*, Smetana's *Vltava* and Rimsky-Korsakov's *Sheherazade*.

Ⓜ *Four Last Songs* (1948) Calm reflections on sunset, autumn and death, set with heart-stoppingly beautiful harmony and meltingly scored for orchestra: a lifetime's instrumental and vocal mastery distilled.

→ Songs with orchestra *Zueignung* ('Dedication'), Op. 10 No. 1, *Ruhe, meine Seele* ('Rest, my Soul'), Op. 27 No. 1, and *Morgen* ('Morning'), Op. 27 No. 4; Ⓜ *Metamorphosen* ('Metamorphoses', for twenty-three solo strings); Sibelius *Luonnotar* (symphonic poem for soprano and orchestra).

Ⓜ *Der Rosenkavalier* ('The Knight of the Rose') (1911) Complete opera. This comedy was composed in homage to Mozart, and is set in the same period and among the same elegant aristocrats as *Così fan tutte*. Its vocal writing (e.g. in the scene of the Presentation of the Rose) is some of the most ravishing in all Strauss's music, and libretto and words match perfectly in a way achieved only by a handful of the greatest operas. (English libretto useful.) It is best seen, and seen complete; there are separate orchestral items (Ⓜ *Rosenkavalier Waltzes*; *Rosenkavalier Suite*) to whet the appetite.

→ *Capriccio*; *Ariadne auf Naxos*; Wagner *Die Meistersinger*.

STRAVINSKY, Igor (1882-1971). *Russian composer.*

Stravinsky's father was an opera-singer, and was determined that his children would have less chancy professional lives. Stravinsky read law at university, and it was not until his father's death in 1902 that he was able to study musical composition properly (with *Rimsky-Korsakov). In 1909 one of his early works, a spectacular orchestral piece called *Fireworks*, caught the attention of Diaghilev (founder of the Ballets Russes), and Stravinsky was commissioned to write music for a fantastical ballet based on a Russian folk-tale, *The Firebird*.

The Firebird was the sensation of Diaghilev's 1910 Paris season, and was followed by two even greater successes, *Petrushka* and *The Rite of Spring*. By 1914 Stravinsky was established as one of the world's leading composers. During the First World War he stayed in Switzerland, and when the Russian Revolution of 1917 stripped him of his Russian estates and property, he became a permanent exile. (He took French nationality in the 1930s and US citizenship in the 1940s, and only went back once to the USSR, for an eightieth-birthday tour in 1962.)

Stravinsky's early works were inspired by Russian folklore, and were in a sumptuous Romantic style influenced by Rimsky-Korsakov. In Switzerland, however, he began discovering and experimenting with jazz, and its 'clean' sound, sparse scoring and spiky rhythms soon made their mark on his music. In 1920, for Diaghilev, he wrote *Pulcinella*, a ballet with a Harlequin-and-Columbine story and music based on pieces by the eighteenth-century composer *Pergolesi. Stravinsky used Pergolesi's tunes and some of his harmonies, but spruced up the rhythm, added witty discords and scored the result sparklingly for a modern orchestra. He called this kind of music, eighteenth-century ideas viewed through twentieth-century eyes, 'neo-classical', and it was his main musical style for the next thirty years, inspiring a couple of dozen of his finest works.

In the 1920s and 1930s, as well as composing, Stravinsky spent some time as solo pianist and conductor, usually of his own works. (In old age he calculated that he had conducted his *Firebird Suite* over a thousand times in fifty years – i.e. on average twenty times a year or once every two to three weeks.) In 1939, after his mother, wife and daughter had died of tuberculosis, he emigrated to the USA and settled in Hollywood with his second wife, strenuously refusing all offers to compose film music (e.g. one million dollars to write music for *The Bible*, or two million if he agreed to let someone else write the music and use his name). In the 1950s, in his own seventies – and just as everyone thought his inspiration was drying up – he began to study *Webern, and the music of his last fifteen years (chiefly religious) is serial (see Glossary: 'Twelve-note system') and intellectually compact without losing any of the familiar 'Stravinsky sound'. His enormous fame in old age – he was the modern composer everyone had heard of, the Picasso of music – led to two other fascinating projects: a complete recording of his works, under his own supervision, and a series of 'Conversations', books of memoirs in the form of witty and entertaining answers to questions by his friend Robert Craft.

Stravinsky's early music (e.g. the three great ballets for Diaghilev) is sensationally glittering and barbaric, and the taste for dazzle was one he never lost: apart from *Ravel, no one has ever created more striking instrumental sounds. Even when he stripped down his style towards neo-classicism, this inventive exuberance remained – he truly does what people say, 'makes you hear each sound as if he'd just invented it'. His music is tuneful, perkily harmonized, freshly-scored, and above all filled with a sense of timing as sure as Charlie Chaplin's: its rhythms are crisp, constantly varied and have the quality of sounding utterly inevitable, of tickling and satisfying the senses all at once.

STAGE WORKS Ten ballets (including *The Firebird, Petrushka, The Rite of Spring, Apollo, Orpheus* and *Agon*); four operas (including *Oedipus Rex* and *The Rake's Progress*); three music-theatre works (*Renard, The Soldier's Tale, The Flood*).

Ballets Ⓜ *Petrushka* (1911), about a puppet who comes to life only to fall agonizingly in love, is the best introduction to Stravinsky's 'Russian' ballets, and (perhaps because he began the score intending to write a piano concerto) works just as well in the concert-hall as on stage. (There is also a spectacular solo-piano arrangement.) Its predecessor, *The Firebird*, is simpler music, but less 'modern' (his nearest piece in sound to Rimsky-Korsakov, and, in the form of the *Firebird Suite*, a twentieth-century classical 'pop'). Ⓜ *The Rite of Spring* is relentlessly discordant, driving music, a picture of a stone-age human sacrifice whose compulsive energy makes it an overwhelming experience (if anything, more so in the concert-hall than in the theatre). The neo-classical ballets begin with *Pulcinella*, and include three gravely beautiful masterworks on ancient Greek myths and inspired by Greek ideas of symmetry and poise: Ⓜ *Apollo*, Ⓜ *Orpheus*, Ⓜ *Agon*. → Good follow-ups to the 'Russian' ballets are Ⓜ *Les noces*, a picture of a Russian peasant-wedding for chorus and percussion, and the glittering symphonic poem *The Song of the Nightingale*, based on his opera (see below); good follow-ups by others are Rimsky-Korsakov *Sheherazade*, Falla *The Three-Cornered Hat* and Ginastera *Panambi* (a sound-clone of *The Rite of Spring*). Good follow-ups to the 'Greek' ballets are *Jeu de cartes* (brisk and breezy, about a poker game) and *Duo concertant* (for violin and piano, reflective and pastoral); good follow-ups by others are Debussy *Jeux*, Roussel *The Spider's Banquet* and above all Britten *Four Sea Interludes* and Copland *Appalachian Spring*.

Operas *The Nightingale* (1908, completed 1914) is a gorgeously exotic version of Andersen's fairy-tale about a Chinese emperor who falls in love with a nightingale. The score is full of mock-Chinese effects and pantomime-like transformations, and centres on one of Stravinsky's most heartfelt, touching tunes for the fisherman who finds the nightingale. *Mavra* is a twenty-five-minute farce, a homage to *Rossini with catchy tunes and a bubbly accompaniment. Ⓜ *Oedipus Rex* sets Sophocles' tragic play in Latin: it is monumental, crystal-clear in purpose and style, and for all its deliberate dryness of tone, overwhelming and moving, like a ritual enacted before our eyes. *The Rake's Progress*, a musical homage to *Mozart, uses the orchestra, harpsichord-continuo and aria-style of Mozart's *Don Giovanni* and *Così fan tutte* to tell an eighteenth-century story of a young man who falls into the devil's hands and is redeemed, after great suffering, by the pure devotion of the girl who loves him.

→ Good follow-ups by Stravinsky are (to *The Nightingale*) *The Firebird*, (to *Mavra*) *Renard*, (to *Oedipus Rex*) *Persephone* and (to *The Rake's Progress*) *Orpheus*. Good follow-ups by others are (to the more sumptuous operas) Ravel *L'enfant et les sortilèges* (opera) and *Daphnis et Chloé* (ballet), and to the others Henze *The English Cats*. Poulenc *Stabat Mater* is closely modelled in style and sound on *Oedipus Rex*.

ORCHESTRAL AND CHORAL WORKS Three symphonies, *Symphonies of Wind Instruments, Dumbarton Oaks, Danses concertantes, Four Norwegian Moods, Huxley Variations,* Concerto and Capriccio for piano and orchestra, Violin Concerto, *Ebony Concerto* for clarinet and jazz band and many shorter orchestral works; *Symphony of Psalms,* Mass, *Perséphone, Canticum sacrum, Threni, Requiem Canticles* and several shorter works for soloist(s), choir(s) and orchestra.

Orchestral works Ⓜ *Dumbarton Oaks* (1938). Most of Stravinsky's orchestral works are like this cheerful piece (a twentieth-century cousin of *Bach's *Brandenburg Concertos*): alert, full of perky rhythms, bubbling with happiness. His concertos (Concerto and Capriccio for piano, Concerto for violin) are very similar, among the gayest in the repertoire, and there is a profusion of smaller works in the same unbuttoned style (good samples are the two suites for small orchestra, *Four Norwegian Moods* and the jazz-band *Ebony Concerto*). His symphonies are more substantial and more serious: No. 1 (1907) is a solemn 'Russian' piece in the manner of *Balakirev or *Borodin; the Ⓜ Symphony in C and Ⓜ *Symphony in Three Movements* are masterpieces from the pinnacle of his career.

→ Good follow-ups to the lighter works are the *Danses concertantes* and Ⓜ Concerto in D for strings; good follow-ups to the last two symphonies are the Ⓜ *Symphonies of Wind Instruments* and *Symphony of Psalms*. Of other composers' music, Prokofiev's Piano Concerto No. 3 and Martinů's *Sinfonietta giocosa* breathe the same cheerful air as Stravinsky's jolliest pieces, and his serious works are paralleled by Tippett's Symphony No. 2 and Bartók's *The Miraculous Mandarin*.

Choral works Ⓜ *Symphony of Psalms* (1930). Stravinsky was a devout Christian, and his religious works are among his most deeply-felt and personal scores. The *Symphony of Psalms* sets three psalms (38, 39 and 150) in a serene, timeless way, suggesting to some listeners the stillness and devotion of Russian religious paintings; the Ⓜ Mass and Ⓜ *Requiem Canticles* apply the same monumental clarity to Roman Catholic words. (*Canticum sacrum, Threni* and the other late religious works are even more serious: a good, brief sample of their austere sound-world is *Introitus: T. S. Eliot in memoriam*.) Another work, Ⓜ *Perséphone*, tells the Greek myth of Persephone in the same mystical, reflective way, to miraculous effect: it is unaccountably little-known, a masterpiece.

→ Because of their 'private' inspiration, these works are best followed up by one another, though the *Symphonies of Wind Instruments* comes close to matching their solemnity and ecstasy. Good follow-ups by others are Bernstein's *Chichester Psalms* and Britten's *Missa brevis* (matching Stravinsky's more glittering religious inspiration note for note), Rachmaninov's *Vesper Mass* (matching the intensity of the *Symphony of Psalms*) and (to the late, serial works) Webern's *Second Cantata*.

CHAMBER AND PIANO WORKS Octet, Septet, *Duo concertant,* Concertino for string quartet and many other chamber works; Concerto for two solo pianos, Sonata for piano duet, two sonatas and Serenade for solo piano and several shorter piano works; works for voices and chamber group including *Cantata, In memoriam Dylan Thomas* and *Pribaoutki.*

Ⓜ Octet (1923, revised 1952) Although there are a few serious, large works in this category of Stravinsky's music (e.g. the Ⓜ Concerto for two solo pianos), most of his chamber and piano works are chips from his workshop, light, unpretentious and just for fun. The Octet is typical: it came to him in a dream, and he scribbled it down in the next few days, a *Pulcinella*-like procession of tunes and rhythms as unfussy as a circus band. His piano music inhabits the same brightly-coloured world: good samples are the Serenade for solo piano, the Sonata for piano duet and the galumphing, tongue-in-cheek *Tango.*

→ A good follow-up to the Octet (though pastoral rather than posturing) is the *Duo concertant* for violin and piano; the Violin Concerto, by contrast, is a superbly prancing counterpart. Stravinsky's songs (e.g. *Pribaoutki, In memoriam Dylan Thomas*) give attractive brief glimpses of his style, and their mood is extended (despite a boring middle movement) in the sprightly *Cantata on Old English Songs.* Good follow-ups by others are (to the songs) Falla's *Psyché* and Ravel's *Chansons Madécasses,* and (to the chamber and piano music) Poulenc's Sextet for piano and wind and Milhaud's *La cheminée du Roi René.*

STRING INSTRUMENTS

There are two kinds of string instrument: bowed and plucked. The bowed instruments used until the late seventeenth century were the **viol** family (treble, tenor and bass viols) and after the seventeenth century the **violin** family (violin, viola, cello and double bass). The plucked instruments most commonly used are **lute** and **guitar**.

VIOL FAMILY The viol was perfected in the early sixteenth century, and was the main bowed instrument of European music for some 200 years. It comes in three different sizes, treble, tenor and bass, and is held not under the chin but on the player's knees or, in the case of the bass viol, between the legs like a cello – hence the Italian name, *viola da gamba,* 'leg viol'.

In the sixteenth century people thought that the sound of a 'chest' of viols (a group consisting of two of each different size) was a close instrumental equivalent to a choir of voices. They wrote music accordingly: ornate, intertwined and polyphonic (see *Sixteenth-century Music*). British composers were particularly fond of this kind of music, and their viol fantasias are among the only instrumental music of the time to rival Masses or madrigals in quality. (*Byrd and Morley were leading Elizabethan viol-composers; in the seventeenth century Gibbons, Jenkins and *Purcell carried the tradition on.)

There were few solo works for the upper viols: although their sound blended well in a consort, it was too quiet for solo work, much less satisfactory than a violin's. But the bass viol was a favourite solo instrument, especially in seventeenth-century France. Many composers wrote for it (e.g. Marin Marais), and their pieces – similar, except for the scoring, to *Couperin's fanciful harpsichord pieces – are still often heard. The finest bass solos of all are *Bach's three sonatas BWV 1027-9. These are, however, the end of a line: except in chamber music (where it played as part of the continuo: see *Sonata*), the bass viol was seldom used after about 1725.

VIOLIN FAMILY The reason for the decline of viols in the late seventeenth century was the growing popularity of the violin family. This was the time of leading makers like Guarneri and Stradivari, who took the medieval 'fiddle', or *viella*, and improved and strengthened it to produce the powerful, beautifully-toned instruments we know today. Violins were the most popular, with cellos next, violas third and the double bass last.

Perfecting the violin family changed the face of music. String orchestras became common (a large string group is still the core of the orchestra today), and their power and playing-skill led many composers to turn from writing vocal to orchestral music. New forms (*sonata and trio-sonata, *concerto) were developed, and for about fifty years (from the 1670s onwards) they were the core of the instrumental repertoire: the string sonatas and concertos of *Corelli, *Telemann, *Vivaldi and Bach are among the finest music of this time.

The growing popularity of the piano in the eighteenth century (see *Keyboard Instruments*) meant that the members of the violin family, in their turn, went into eclipse as solo instruments. Composers writing 'show' sonatas or concertos composed for keyboard; violin and cello solo works (there were few for viola, fewer still for double bass) were smaller-scale, written mainly for amateur music-making or teaching. (*Mozart's violin concertos and *Haydn's cello concertos are typical: light and insubstantial, on nothing like the scale of Mozart's piano concertos or Haydn's symphonies composed at the same time.) Paradoxically, this move away from solo-string music led to the development of two of the most magnificent of all musical forms, both centred on violin-family sound: the string quartet

(see *Chamber Music*) and the *symphony. If solo music was at a compara-
tively low ebb – and there were a few exceptions, e.g. Mozart's sublime
Sinfonia concertante K 364 – ensemble string-music now took the dominant
place in the repertoire it still holds today.

In the nineteenth century, the idea of a virtuoso string soloist resurfaced,
and – particularly after Paganini, the most stunning concert violinist of the
century – violinists came to rival pianists and opera-singers as the most
flamboyant performers of the age. Their popularity and staggering dexterity inspired composers, and from the time of *Beethoven onwards string
concertos and sonatas again became grand, fully-fledged concert works. In
the nineteenth century the violin led the field, with magnificent concertos
(e.g. those by Beethoven, *Mendelssohn, *Brahms and *Tchaikovsky) and
sonatas (e.g. those by Beethoven and Brahms); there were a few solo works
for other string instruments (e.g. Beethoven's and Brahms's cello sonatas,
Dvořák's Cello Concerto and Brahms's Double Concerto for violin and
cello), but by and large players of the lower strings had to content themselves with orchestral work or playing in string quartets. Twentieth-
century composers, however, have made up for this. While they have not
neglected the violin (few great composers are without a violin concerto or
sonata to their name), they have poured out solo works for viola, cello and
even (in the last ten years) for double bass. The cello concertos of *Elgar,
*Shostakovich and *Lutosławski and the viola concertos of *Bartók and
*Walton are masterworks, as fine as any composed for piano or violin.

PLUCKED STRING INSTRUMENTS In the sixteenth century, the favoured
plucked string instrument was the lute. For the most part it had eleven
pairs (or 'courses') of strings, and it was able to play not only chords
(strummed, like a modern guitar), but also polyphonic music of considerable complexity. Its main use was in chamber music (as one of a 'consort'
of instruments), but in Britain especially it was used for accompanying
songs (the 'lute songs' of Dowland, Campion and Rosseter are magnificent)
and for solo dance-movements or fantasias in polyphonic style (e.g. Dowland's *Lachrimae*). Later composers occasionally used the lute, but in the
heyday of string sonatas and concertos it fell out of fashion, and such
works as Bach's five lute suites and Vivaldi's handful of lute concertos,
though delightful music, would have been regarded as curiosities, for a
museum-instrument, even in their own day.

Until the late eighteenth century, the guitar was practically unknown in
classical music. It was a folk-instrument, for strumming with songs. Even
in the nineteenth century, musicians who played it (among them *Schubert, *Berlioz, Paganini and *Wagner) regarded it more as a toy than as a
serious musical instrument, and specialist guitar-composers (e.g. Fernando
Sor, 1778–1839) were few and seldom first-rate. The great age of the guitar

began with the concert début of Segovia (born 1893), a virtuoso genius to rival *Chopin on the piano or Paganini on the violin. Inspired by his playing, makers improved and strengthened the instrument (until it was loud enough to hold its own in a concert-hall), concert-promoters began booking guitar-recitalists, the lute-music of the past was rediscovered and published, and hundreds of new guitar-works were composed. By now, seventy years on, the guitar is a favourite concert-instrument, there are a dozen world-ranking soloists, and there is a huge repertoire of music of every kind, from the tuneful sonatas, studies and concertos of Ponce, Arnold, Villa-Lobos and Rodrigo (see *One-work Composers*) to large-scale compositions by such avant-garde masters as *Henze, *Tippett and Berio.

Listening *Viol family*: Byrd *In nomine a 5* No. 2, Gibbons *Pavan* and Purcell *Fantasia on One Note* (all for viol consort); Marais *Sonate à la Marésienne* and Bach Sonata No. 1, BWV 1027 (both for bass viol and harpsichord). See also *Chamber Music*. *Violin family*: Handel Sonata Op. 1 No. 15, Schubert Sonatina No. 1, D 384, Ravel *Tzigane* (all for violin and keyboard); Bach Violin Concerto No. 2, BWV 1042, Vivaldi *The Four Seasons*, Mozart Violin Concerto No. 5, Mendelssohn Violin Concerto and Dvořák Cello Concerto. For further recommendations, see the articles on J. S. Bach, Bartók, Beethoven, Berg, Bloch, Boccherini, Brahms, *Chamber Music*, *Concerto*, Corelli, Delius, Dvořák, *Eighteenth-century Music*, Elgar, Franck, Handel, Haydn, Mendelssohn, Mozart, Nielsen, *Nineteenth-century Music*, Schubert, *Seventeenth-century Music*, *Sonata*, Stravinsky, Telemann, *Twentieth-century Music*, Vivaldi and Walton. *Lute and guitar*: Dowland *Semper Dowland semper dolens* and Bach Suite No. 3, BWV 1006 (both for solo lute); Sor *Variations on a Theme of Mozart* and Villa-Lobos Prelude No. 1 (both for solo guitar); Rodrigo *Concierto de Aranjuez* (guitar and orchestra).

SULLIVAN, Arthur (1842–1900). *English composer.*
If Sullivan's career had gone the way he planned it, he would have climbed the ladder of the English musical establishment from choirboy to cathedral organist to oratorio-composer to Master of the Queen's Music. (Throughout his life he composed 'serious' works as if yearning for establishment respectability: they range from the hymn *Onward, Christian Soldiers* to three *Mendelssohnian oratorios on biblical subjects.) But for all these strait-laced ambitions, his real flair was for writing popular melodies (e.g. the famous ballad *The Lost Chord*), and for the stage. In 1871 he began collaborating with the comic playwright W. S. Gilbert, and their operettas were so popular that they swept Sullivan's other music out of the public mind. Rather to his irritation, he became known as the purveyor of frothy, satirical musical comedies, among the most high-spirited and entertaining in the business. For all his expressed distaste (and his quarrels

with Gilbert, who found him stuffy and whom he regarded as an unserious prankster), he went on turning out operettas, one a year, for twenty years – and in the process revealed the genius and originality his other music lacks.

WORKS Twenty-two operettas (the 'Savoy operas', i.e. the operettas he wrote with Gilbert, which were performed at the Savoy Theatre, are *Trial by Jury*, *The Sorcerer*, *HMS Pinafore*, *The Pirates of Penzance*, *Patience*, *Iolanthe*, *Princess Ida*, *The Mikado*, *Ruddigore*, *The Yeomen of the Guard*, *The Gondoliers*, *Utopia Limited* and *The Grand Duke*); grand opera *Ivanhoe*; three oratorios and three cantatas for chorus and orchestra; Symphony; Violin Concerto; two overtures and a few shorter orchestral works; songs, hymns, anthems, organ voluntaries and other minor works.

Operettas Ⓜ *The Mikado* (1885). Gilbert learned his trade writing satirical articles for *Punch*, and greatly admired the stage farces of such masters as Labiche (who wrote *An Italian Straw Hat*). When he began a libretto for Sullivan, he liked to take some aspect of officialdom (the police, the law, the forces, the House of Lords) and poke fun at it, stirring in mockery of fashions of the time (e.g., in *The Mikado*, the 1880s craze for everything Japanese). This topical side is balanced by simple plots: boy meets, loses and regains girl; pompous asses get their come-uppance; virtue is rewarded in unlikely but charming ways. Gilbert's librettos are fresh and witty, and Sullivan's music matches every twist and turn of mood. *The Mikado*, a young-lovers-separated-by-circumstances story set in a splendidly ridiculous ancient Japan, is the best operetta to see first, and its individual numbers (e.g. 'Three Little Maids from School are We' or 'Tit Willow') are some of Sullivan's best tunes; of the other operettas, *Trial by Jury*, *HMS Pinafore*, and Ⓜ *The Pirates of Penzance* are spectacularly farcical (full of comic policemen, rollicking pirates who are really terribly nice at heart, and stuffy officials who revel in their own pomposity); Ⓜ *The Gondoliers*, set in Italy, is a bandits-and-peasants tale similar in style to such European light operas as *The Bohemian Girl* or *Fra Diavolo* (both of which are recommended); Ⓜ *The Yeomen of the Guard*, Sullivan's masterpiece, by making its characters seem real human beings instead of farcical puppets, is moving as well as frivolous, and pushes the operetta form as near as Sullivan ever went towards true opera. (His only serious opera, *Ivanhoe*, is awful.)

→ The Gilbert and Sullivan operettas are each other's best follow-ups; other Sullivan pieces in similar bouncy style are the overture *Di Ballo* and the ballet *Pineapple Poll* (arranged Mackerras). Good follow-ups by others, in true 'Savoy opera' style, are German *Merrie England* and Ellis *Bless the Bride*; good follow-ups from other countries are Lehár *Land of Smiles* and Romberg *The Student Prince* and *The Desert Song*.

SYMPHONY

A symphony (from the Greek for 'sounding together') is an orchestral work in one or more movements (usually four). Unlike a suite (which is a fairly haphazard assembly of movements: extracts from a ballet or opera, dances or mood-pictures), a symphony is a rounded-out, fully-organized work: each of its movements dovetails with the others, and it would sound mutilated if any of them were omitted or replaced.

EARLY SYMPHONIES In the seventeenth and early eighteenth centuries, symphonies were short orchestral pieces played before, during or after vocal works. (The 'Pastoral Symphony' in *Handel's *Messiah* is typical: a single, brief movement depicting the shepherds in the fields before the angel appears to them to announce Christ's birth.) Many such 'symphonies' appeared at the start of operas (taking the place of what we might call today 'overture' or 'selection'): they used tunes from the opera, and were often in three short movements, fast, slow, fast. (The overture to *Mozart's opera *Die Entführung aus dem Serail*, 'The Seraglio', works in just this way.)

EIGHTEENTH-CENTURY SYMPHONIES At some time in the early eighteenth century, the custom began of writing and playing 'operatic'-style symphonies separately, as orchestral entertainments in their own right. The three-movement pattern remained, and the music was as cheerful and simple as its operatic ancestors. (Typical works of this kind are *Haydn's first few dozen symphonies, written for and named after Count Morzin. They have three tiny movements, each three or four minutes long, and usually follow the pattern bustle-relaxation-dance.)

The new form proved popular, especially in places where there was a large, skilful orchestra (e.g. Mannheim, Esterháza or Paris). Composers began to extend the range of symphonies: they expanded the first movements (by using the newly-developed sonata form: see Glossary), added balancing fourth movements (usually rondos: see Glossary), and formalized the pattern of the lightweight middle movements into a gently-flowing slow movement and a prancing minuet. (Mozart's Symphony No. 19 is a splendid example of this kind of work, halfway between the simple, 'operatic' symphonies of a generation before and the large-scale symphonies he went on to write.)

STORM AND STRESS In the late 1760s a new musical fashion swept Europe. Instead of the well-mannered 'galant' style (see *Eighteenth-century Music*), many composers began to write instrumental works full of what they called *Sturm und Drang* ('storm and stress'). Their idea was to fill symphonies, sonatas and concertos as full of emotion as operas, to let the music express feelings other than good-natured charm. The symphony was a particularly suitable form for this kind of music. It could make use of the full resources of an orchestra, with all its variety of sound, and its four movements already had contrast built into them, from the heroic thoughtfulness of the opening and the reflectiveness of the slow movement to the lighthearted wit of minuet and finale.

The 'storm-and-stress' fashion itself lasted only a dozen years or so. But it completely changed people's ideas about symphonies. Feelings of grandness and emotional power remained, and composers began approaching symphonies as large, intellectually weighty and profound musical works, the most powerful pieces they could write for orchestra. Haydn's first storm-and-stress symphonies are No. 44 ('Mourning') and No. 45 ('Farewell'); the symphonies he wrote after them have a masterful dignity quite unlike those he wrote before. Mozart's first storm-and-stress symphony was No. 25; although he wrote a few 'entertainment-only' symphonies after that (e.g. No. 32), his progress generally was swift and true to the symphonic masterpieces we know today. And as well as geniuses, many lesser composers (Stamitz, Cannabich, Mysliveček) polished and improved symphonic style, until by the end of the century only the *sonata rivalled it as a leading instrumental form.

NINETEENTH-CENTURY SYMPHONIES The composer who did more than any other to give the symphony its modern reputation was *Beethoven. Haydn and Mozart had written great symphonies before him – among the finest in the history of the form – but they were little known; his symphonies, by contrast, were played, reviewed and discussed everywhere, and influenced every subsequent orchestral composer. His first two symphonies (and Nos. 4 and 8) are amiable and straightforward, not too different from eighteenth-century symphonies in size. But No. 3 (the 'Eroica'), No. 5 and No. 7 are huge pieces: their movements are often as long as some other people's whole symphonies, their thought is complex, and their emotional impact is enormous. (Nos. 6 and 9 go still further: No. 6 (the 'Pastoral') expresses emotions roused by country scenes; No. 9 (the 'Choral') is a titanic celebration of the unity and dignity of humankind.) Above all, Beethoven made the symphony a single, multi-movement experience: each movement follows on from or adds to the feelings and ideas expressed in all the others – and must be heard, in correct sequence, for the symphony to make its full effect.

Beethoven's symphonies were so grand and so magnificent that they frightened some nineteenth-century composers away from symphonies entirely. (*Liszt, for example, devised the symphonic poem instead, as a way of showing emotion in sound; even the two works he called 'symphonies' are really long symphonic poems.) Some others (among them *Mendelssohn, *Dvořák and *Bizet) avoided grandeur, and deliberately wrote light-hearted entertainment symphonies in a graceful, simple style. But many other composers took up what they thought of as Beethoven's 'challenge': the symphonies, for example, of *Bruckner, *Mahler, *Brahms and *Tchaikovsky are works of enormous power, both intellectual and emotional; *Wagner and *Verdi thought of their stage-works as 'symphonic dramas'.

TWENTIETH-CENTURY SYMPHONIES In the twentieth century, symphony-writing has continued unabated. Several composers (e.g. *Sibelius, *Nielsen, *Shostakovich, *Tippett) have set out their finest thoughts in symphonic form. Others (e.g. *Prokofiev, *Copland and *Martinů) have treated the symphony as something jollier, a twentieth-century counterpart to *Schubert's early symphonies, or to the symphonies of Mendelssohn and *Saint-Saëns. Other composers again, while avoiding the title 'symphony', have written works of a seriousness and grandeur to rival anything composed in symphonic form. (Good examples are Debussy's *La mer*, *Bartók's *Music for Strings, Percussion and Celesta* and *Stravinsky's *The Rite of Spring*.)

Listening For those new to symphonies, recommended works are Mozart's Symphony No. 33, Schubert's No. 5 and Prokofiev's No. 1 ('Classical'), and they might be followed by Mendelssohn's 'Italian' Symphony, *Schumann's No. 1 ('Spring'), Dvořák's No. 9 ('From the New World') and Beethoven's No. 4. For further recommendations, the works mentioned in this article will give guidance to the different kinds (and 'weights') of symphony available; see also the articles on Beethoven, Borodin, Brahms, Bruckner, Dvořák, Haydn, Mahler, Martinů, Mendelssohn, Mozart, Nielsen, *Orchestral Music*, Prokofiev, Saint-Saëns, Schubert, Schumann, Shostakovich, Sibelius, Stravinsky, Tchaikovsky, Tippett, Vaughan Williams and Walton.

T

TCHAIKOVSKY, Pyotr (1840–93). *Russian composer*.

In the whole history of nineteenth-century arts, there was only one other creative genius whose character matched Tchaikovsky's: the painter van Gogh. Both men were seemingly at odds with themselves, unable to understand or cope with their own personalities; both produced works which, although clamorous with personal pain, nevertheless speak directly and disarmingly to millions who share none of the Romantic agonies of soul which gave birth to them.

From the age of ten (when he was sent away to boarding school), Tchaikovsky lived in a state of permanent mental anguish, haunted by self-induced terrors which no one else could understand or alleviate. He was terrified of human contact, whether it was intellectual or physical. He had few friends (and made their lives a misery by the sharpness of his tongue) and no lovers. (He thought he was homosexual, like his brother, and hated himself for it. But there is no evidence for or against homosexuality: the truth may rather have been that he was, at one and the same time, physically frigid and emotionally boiling; he certainly behaved to women exactly as he behaved to men.) His musical judgements were acidly cruel, and he stood aloof from *Balakirev, *Borodin and the rest of the 'Russian' school. He hated conducting, but forced himself to do it (hunching up his shoulders, it seems, so like a roosting bird that the orchestra could hardly make out his beat); he loathed travelling, but went on constant tours both in Russia and abroad; he despised establishment honours (such as honorary degrees) and yet was sick with disappointment when no offers came. He was obsessed with the idea that Fate was stalking him, fist poised to hammer on his door; a week after the première of his Symphony No. 6 (the 'Pathetic', full of presentiments of death), he drank a glass either of polluted water or of poison (the evidence is unclear) and died.

In this nightmare life only two things seem to have given Tchaikovsky happiness. One was his extraordinary friendship with a rich widow, Nadezhda von Meck. For fourteen years, 1876–90, she paid him an annual salary (of 6,000 roubles, enough to live on in comfort) on condition that they never met – a condition which suited Tchaikovsky perfectly. They sent each other reams of letters (sometimes as many as four a day), and discussed music, the other arts, politics, religion, the beauty of nature and their own feelings as avidly as two lovers. It was passion without contact, intellectual rapture without emotional involvement – and when it ended, as abruptly as it had begun (Mme von Meck, thinking that she was going bankrupt, ceased both payments and letters without explanation), Tchaikovsky was devastated: this 'separation' began the obsession with Fate and the mental decline of his last three years.

The second source of serenity in Tchaikovsky's life was the simple act of putting notes down on paper. He found the mechanics of writing music a soothing discipline, and established a set routine on which his mental equilibrium depended. At nine-thirty every morning he sat down at his desk (for, as he put it, 'the Muse keeps unfailing hours'); he began every afternoon with a walk and ended it by revising and orchestrating his morning's work, correcting printers' proofs and writing letters; every evening he played cards (whist if friends were there, patience if not); every night he drank a tumbler of whisky to relax his mind for sleep. If this routine was upset (e.g. on tour, in foreign hotels), his gnawing self-torture quickly returned: it was as if routine were a drug that kept him sane.

If Tchaikovsky's music were as contorted and anguished as his character, it would be unbearable. But while his life was evasive, hesitant and withdrawn, his music is gloriously direct. His own favourite composer was *Mozart, and he strove to equal Mozart's blend of emotional openhandedness and formal discipline. (Tchaikovsky's forms were Romantic and nineteenth-century rather than 'classical', but the effect on the music was the same.) He loved Russian folk-tunes, and used or imitated them in many works, so giving an uncomplicated, sunny lilt to his music even at its most emotional. He was a brilliant orchestrator, with a flair for technicolor sound outmatching even *Rimsky-Korsakov's. His music's personality comes from its frankness: he is like a stranger plucking your sleeve and blurting out fascinating, incredible stories before you can speak a word. But unlike, say, film music (which has a similar instant attractiveness), his works twist and turn in unexpected directions, saying expected things but never in the expected way – and this quality of surprise, of endless self-discovery, makes them sound new-minted, not hackneyed, each time they are played.

WORKS Six symphonies, four suites, two symphonic fantasies, two fantasy overtures (*Hamlet, Romeo and Juliet*), two overtures (including the *1812*), *Serenade for Strings, Italian Caprice* and several shorter orchestral works; four concertos (three for piano; one for violin), *Variations on a Rococo Theme* and half a dozen shorter pieces for soloist and orchestra; ten operas (including *Eugene Onegin* and *The Queen of Spades*); *Liturgy* and *Vespers* for choir; three ballets (*Swan Lake, The Nutcracker, The Sleeping Beauty*);

three string quartets, Piano Trio, String Sextet (*Souvenirs of Florence*); two sonatas; suite *The Seasons* and ten books of pieces for solo piano; ninety-five songs.

Orchestral music (other than symphonies and concertos) Ⓜ *Romeo and Juliet* (1869, revised 1870 and 1880). Tchaikovsky was attracted by the idea of the symphonic poem (see Liszt), a work providing a musical impression of a famous play, novel, painting or other work of art. He began by assembling in his mind the ideas or emotions he thought paramount (e.g. in *Romeo and Juliet*, ecstatic love, fast-moving fighting and religious serenity), and giving each a musical theme. Then he used those themes as if they were the straightforward basis for a sonata form (see Glossary) or other symphonic movement, thus building the underlying ideas into a homogeneous texture by musical rather than extra-musical means. (The result seldom follows the pattern of the original artworks: Tchaikovsky's Ⓜ *Hamlet, Francesca da Rimini, The Tempest* and *Romeo and Juliet* are meditations on the originals rather than transpositions of them to another medium; the *1812 Overture* reworks history – a famous battle between Napoleon and the Russians – in the same personal way.) The use of 'emotional' pegs, each clearly distinguishable by tune, orchestration and level of orchestral 'busyness', makes the works easily understandable; their dazzling orchestration and soaring tunes imprint them on the mind. For other orchestral works, Tchaikovsky went emotionally downmarket (*Marche Slave* is a brassily assertive march, no more; *Capriccio Italien* is a glossily gaudy evocation of Carnival), or into more abstract regions where the basic ideas had no emotional or dramatic associations outside the music: in the first three suites, for example, or the marvellously tuneful Ⓜ *Serenade for Strings*. (The fourth suite is an orchestration of piano works by Mozart.)

→ Good Tchaikovsky follow-ups to the more extrovert works are the Fifth and Sixth Symphonies and the *Sleeping Beauty Suite*; good follow-ups by others are Strauss's *Don Juan*, Dukas' *The Sorcerer's Apprentice*, Berlioz' overture *Carnaval romain*, Liszt's *Les préludes* and Musorgsky's *Night on the Bare Mountain*. Good Tchaikovsky follow-ups to the gentler works (especially the *Serenade for Strings*) are the String Quartet No. 1, the *Rococo Variations* and *The Seasons*; good follow-ups by others are Liadov's *The Enchanted Lake*, Wagner's *Siegfried Idyll*, Elgar's *Introduction and Allegro for Strings* and Arensky's *Variations on a Theme of Tchaikovsky*.

Symphonies and concertos Ⓜ *Symphony No. 4* (1878). Tchaikovsky considered the Fourth Symphony his most perfect work, achieving his intentions exactly. Until then, his symphonies had been lightweight: No. 1 and No. 3 are like ballet music, No. 2 (the best) is a Russian 'folksong' symphony in the manner of Balakirev or Borodin. With No. 4, he began treating the symphony as a major form for expressing personal emotion and feeling: it begins in an uncertain, questing way (like many of Liszt's orchestral works), and gradually grows in power and authority until the last movement explodes in a Russian dance of frenzied gaiety. The Symphony No. 5 is concerned with Fate (in mood it is not unlike *Berlioz's Fantastic Symphony*, alternating a kind of doomed brightness with solemn, portentous reminders that all human joys end in tears); Ⓜ No. 6 (the 'Pathetic') frames a fractured waltz (in five-time instead of three-time) and a quicksilver march (one of Tchaikovsky's most stunning pieces of orchestral writing) with heartrending, funeral-march slow movements. Of the concertos, the Ⓜ Piano Concerto No. 1 and Ⓜ Violin Concerto are glittering display-works, rightly at the heart of the Romantic concerto repertoire; the Second Piano Concerto is more ruminative, a companion-piece to the orchestral suites; *Variations on a Rococo theme*, for cello and orchestra, is eighteenth-century in inspiration and nineteenth-century in emotion, like a *Haydn cello concerto with its heart worn firmly on its sleeve.

→ Good Tchaikovsky follow-ups to the later symphonies are *Romeo and Juliet*, *Hamlet* and the *Swan Lake Suite*; good follow-ups by others are Dvořák's Symphony No. 9, Franck's Symphony and Rachmaninov's Symphony No. 1. Good Tchaikovsky follow-ups to the big concertos are the *Capriccio Italien* (dazzling) and Piano Trio (extrovert/sad); good follow-ups by others are Rachmaninov's Piano Concerto No. 2, Beethoven's 'Emperor' Piano Concerto, Brahms's Violin Concerto and Lalo's *Symphonie Espagnole*; good follow-ups to the *Rococo Variations* are Haydn's Cello Concerto No. 1 and Rodrigo's *Concierto como un divertimento* (cello and orchestra).

Ballets Until *Delibes, it never seems to have occurred to anyone that ballet music, instead of being a sequence of pretty but unconnected tunes, could be organized like a symphony or opera, outlining the story's emotional development as well as accompanying the dancers' steps. In *Coppélia* and *Sylvia* Delibes went some way towards achieving this, but he was still seduced away from symphonic unity by a love of (rather short-winded) tunes. Tchaikovsky admired his work, took up where he left off, and wrote what are still three of the finest ballet-scores in the repertoire. The form ideally suited his flair for giving emotional feeling a precise, immediate sound, and his ability to give free-seeming, rhapsodic music a loose but satisfying overall structure. *The Nutcracker* is the most Delibes-like of the ballets, a fairy-tale companion-piece to *Coppélia*; Ⓜ *Swan Lake* inhabits that characteristically nineteenth-century Romantic world of moonlight, grottoes, misty forests and dark secrets of the heart; Ⓜ *The Sleeping Beauty* uses the most symphonic structure of all the ballets to tell a story of magic, pageantry and passion as inconsequential as a dream. The ballets work best in the theatre – Tchaikovsky planned them in detail, bar by bar, with the choreographer, and music and dance are inextricably linked – but they are often heard, to good effect, in the concert-hall. There is an orchestral suite from each of them, the *Swan Lake Suite* and *Sleeping Beauty Suite* darkly passionate, the *Nutcracker Suite* a collection of some of the most immaculate light music Tchaikovsky ever wrote.

→ Good Tchaikovsky follow-ups to the complete ballets are the Symphony No. 6, the Suite No. 3 and the Piano Concerto No. 2; good follow-ups by others are Delibes's *Coppélia* and *Sylvia*, Adam's *Giselle* and Stravinsky's *The Fairy's Kiss* (complete ballet; suite). Good follow-ups to the suites are Tchaikovsky's *The Seasons* (piano), Mendelssohn's *Midsummer Night's Dream* music, Rossini-Respighi *La boutique fantasque* and the orchestral suites of Fauré and Sibelius.

Other works Of Tchaikovsky's shorter works, the best are his songs, which (perhaps because singers are chary of Russian) are less well known than, say, *Schumann's or *Brahms's, but are every bit as good. The best known is *None but the Lonely Heart*, Op. 6 No. 6; other recommendations are *Simple Words*, Op. 60 No. 5, *Legend*, Op. 54 No. 5 (sometimes heard as a carol, and in a cello-and-orchestra arrangement; the source of Arensky's *Variations* mentioned in 'orchestral works' above); and above all *Why did I Dream of You?*, Op. 28 No. 3. Good follow-ups are the songs of *Sibelius (especially *Six Songs*, Op. 50) and *Vaughan Williams (especially *Silent Noon*). The only Tchaikovsky opera well known outside Russia is *Eugene Onegin*, a tale of doomed love and destroyed innocence lifted from sentimentality by the robustness of its tunes: Ⓜ Tatiana's Letter Scene and Lensky's aria are well-known concert extracts, excellent samples of the whole work. Good follow-ups are Tchaikovsky's *The Queen of Spades*, Verdi's *La traviata* and Puccini's *Madama Butterfly*. From Tchaikovsky's piano and chamber music, only three works have flourished in the repertoire: a suite of twelve slight but picturesque piano pieces, *The Seasons*, the elegiac, heroic Piano Trio, and the tuneful String Quartet No. 1, whose slow movement, under the title 'Andante cantabile', is a separately-known string-orchestra 'pop'. Good follow-ups are (to *The Seasons*) Grieg's *Lyric Pieces*, (to the Piano Trio) Mendelssohn's Piano Trio No. 1, and (to the Quartet) Borodin's Quartet No. 2 and Dvořák's Quartet No. 12 (the 'American').

TELEMANN, Georg Philipp (1681–1767). *German composer.*

Telemann had the enviable ability to soak up knowledge as bread soaks up gravy: whatever caught his interest, he taught it to himself, completely and thoroughly. As a boy he favoured science (especially medicine and astronomy), and this was his chosen university study. But while he was at university he also learned all the European languages, became a competent performer on all the wind and string instruments of the day, and taught himself to compose in the musical styles fashionable in France, Germany and Italy. Above all, he learned the harpsichord and organ, well enough to be appointed (in 1704) organist and choirmaster to one of the lesser churches in Leipzig. In 1721 he was offered the job of music-director at St Thomas's Church, Leipzig (the equivalent of a modern cathedral organship), but turned it down, whereupon it went to the second person on the list, J. S. *Bach. Telemann took instead the post of music-director of the town of Hamburg, and stayed there for the rest of his life.

Telemann's restless mind and phenomenal technique led him to compose more prolifically than almost anyone else before or since: every musical form of the time, from church cantatas to trio-sonatas, was graced with not one example from his pen, but dozens or even hundreds. In the nineteenth and early twentieth centuries his work was scorned as empty and mechanical. But recent study and proper performance have proved this judgement ludicrously wrong. His music is utterly un-Romantic, to be sure, and (in true eighteenth-century style) prefers sentiment to emotion and easy flow to rant. But the same is true of *Handel, and Telemann's instrumental music, at least – his vocal music is scarcely ever performed, and is therefore difficult to assess – is every bit as good as his.

WORKS Telemann's thousands of works are still being catalogued, but those so far known include over 500 church cantatas, forty-four Passions, forty operas (of which the best known is the comedy *Pimpinone*), 600 orchestral overtures (i.e. suites), and more than 1000 concertos, sonatas and trio-sonatas, using almost every instrument then available.

Table Music (third collection) (date unknown) The sheer number of Telemann's works makes identification difficult: he badly needs a Köchel or a Deutsch to make a definitive list. The best introduction to his music is one of the sets of pieces he published in his lifetime (thinking them his finest achievement): There are three main sets, the *Essercizii musici* (sonatas and trio-sonatas), *Der getreue Musikmeister* ('The Reliable Music Tutor'; solos, suites and sonatas) and *Table Music* (three collections). Each collection of *Table Music* includes an orchestral suite, at least one concerto, a trio-sonata and one or two solo sonatas. The third contains six such works, all for wind instruments (flutes, oboes, horns) and strings or harpsichord continuo. The opening Suite and the Concerto for two horns and strings are the jewels of the set, but the whole is typical of Telemann's effortless, amiable and personable style.
→ *Overture des nations ancients et modernes* (orchestral suite); Trio-sonata in F (from *Essercizii musici*); Vivaldi Trio-sonata R63 (*La folia*).

Ⓜ **Suite in A minor** (date unknown) This charming suite for recorder (or flute) and strings is as shapely and satisfying as Bach's better-known Suite No. 2 (for flute and strings). Particularly delightful are the dances in national styles (e.g. Polonaise) which follow the bustling, contrapuntal opening movement.
→ Ⓜ Concerto in E minor (recorder, flute and strings); Concerto in G (viola and strings); Vivaldi *The Four Seasons* (violin and strings); Bach *Brandenburg Concerto* No. 1.

TIPPETT, Michael (born 1905). *English composer.*
A small private income (eked out with money earned by teaching and conducting) allowed Tippett to go on studying composition until he was in his thirties. His first international success came with his Concerto for double string orchestra in 1939; even then, it was not until the 1970s (when he himself was over sixty) that he became a cult figure, one of the best-loved and most influential composers of the century.

This late flowering was of enormous importance to the acceptance of 'modern' music in the concert-world at large. Tippett's music sidesteps all the crabbed, music-for-computers complexity of the 1950s avant-garde, replacing it with wiry exuberance (in fast movements) and lyrical mysticism (in slow movements): younger composers (some young enough to be his grandchildren) learned from this style and began opening out their own compositions from clever but ugly sounds towards a kind of controlled rhapsody which is far more seductive to the ear.

At first, the mixture of athleticism and mysticism in Tippett's music makes it hard for some listeners to comprehend. (*Messiaen's music is just the same.) In particular, the words of his later vocal works – which he writes himself – are philosophical, visionary, elliptical and not a little difficult. (His opera librettos for *The Knot Garden* and *The Ice Break*, for example, though they lead to fascinating music, are dramatically ludicrous.) But his earlier vocal works (e.g. *A Child of Our Time*; *The Midsummer Marriage*) and virtually all his instrumental works are ravishing: he understands fully that one of music's main purposes is to give sensual as well as intellectual pleasure, and his work fulfils it perfectly.

WORKS Four symphonies; Triple Concerto (violin, viola, cello); Piano Concerto; Concerto for orchestra; Concerto for double string orchestra; *Fantasia concertante on a Theme of Corelli*; suites, Divertimento and other short orchestral works; four operas (including *The Midsummer Marriage* and *King Priam*); *A Child of Our Time*, *The Vision of St Augustine*, *The Mask of Time* and other shorter choral works; four string quartets, four piano sonatas, Sonata for four horns and other chamber works; song-cycles *Boyhood's End*, *The Heart's Assurance*, *Songs for Achilles*, *Songs for Ariel*, *Songs for Dov*.

Ⓜ *Ritual Dances* (1953) Few even of Tippett's works are more ecstatic than these orchestral dances, adapted from his opera *The Midsummer Marriage*. The scoring (gutsy strings, chattering trumpets, whistling flutes) is zestful and original, the harmony is lush and the tunes and rhythms are exuberant. The whole opera (Tippett's masterpiece) is a fascinating allegory in the manner of *Mozart's *The Magic Flute*; anyone who enjoys opera and is drawn by the sound of these dances will find *The Midsummer Marriage* an absorbing experience.

→ Ⓜ Concerto for double string orchestra; Ravel *Daphnis et Chloé Suite* No. 1; Martinů *Frescoes of Piero della Francesca*.

Ⓜ **Symphony No. 2** (1957) Inspired by *Vivaldi and *Stravinsky, this symphony is full of their lithe rhythms and bright, open harmonies, and adds Tippett's own brand of mystical murmuring (especially in the beautiful slow movement) and his soaring, ecstatic tunes (the last five minutes of the symphony are a long-drawn-out, swooping tune accompanied by trickles of notes on the woodwind as endlessly varied as water swirling over pebbles). Audiences (and orchestras) used

to think twentieth-century symphonies a pain in the ear: this one, like Martinů's or Stravinsky's, enthusiastically proves them wrong.
→ Concerto for orchestra; Piano Concerto; Copland Symphony No. 3.

Ⓜ *A Child of Our Time* (1941) This oratorio for soloists, choir and orchestra tells a story not from the Bible but from our own tormented century: an act of heroism against the Nazis and its brutal punishment. The choruses (as with *Handel's oratorios) are the work's great glory, either fluting and fluttering in panic or gloriously, heart-easingly, offering comfort in the form of Negro spirituals. (The spirituals are sometimes sung separately; but in context they bring tears to the eye.) Tippett's other choral works are veiled and mysterious in meaning; the ghastly (real-life) event which provoked this one, and his response (which was to find hope even in the deepest despair then known to humanity), make *A Child of Our Time* direct, unequivocal and radiant.
→ Song-cycle *Boyhood's End* (voice and piano); Britten *War Requiem*; Stravinsky *Oedipus Rex*.

Symphony No. 4 (1977) In the mid-seventies (his own seventies), Tippett developed his style in a new direction. Without abandoning the ecstasy or fervour of his earlier music, he added a kind of reflective fascination with the abstract sounds of music, as if turning each of them over to reveal every facet of its making. This symphony, in one long movement, is composed like a mosaic: short sound-blocks (snapping brass chords, string-clusters, flurries of notes on harp and wind, the clonk of a xylophone and the sigh of a wind machine) are endlessly reordered and regrouped, to hypnotic and seductive effect. (The same procedure is used in the Ⓜ Symphony No. 3 – the slow movement is one of the most beautiful of all Tippett's orchestral compositions – and the work then closes with three blues-songs for soprano, flugel-horn and orchestra, a conclusion as startling as the choral ending of Beethoven's Ninth Symphony, which inspired it.)
→ Ⓜ Triple Concerto; Ⓜ String Quartet No. 4; Lutosławski Symphony No. 2.

TWENTIETH-CENTURY MUSIC

RECORDING Experiments with sound-recording began in the 1880s; music-hall stars began recording their hit songs in the 1890s and 1900s; the first ever recording of a complete symphony (*Beethoven's No. 5) was made in 1909. Since then, music and recording have progressed side by side – and no other invention so changed the art. It became possible, without hiring chairs, music-stands and enormous rooms, to invite favourite performers, even whole orchestras and opera companies, into the home, and to hear favourite pieces not once or twice a year but as often as the record-owner chose. For the first time in the history of music anyone could listen to anything they chose, cheaply, easily and anywhere.

The effect on music-lovers (again for the first time in music's history) was to make them shy away from novelty. Once, people had thronged to hear the latest sounds, and music of the past was hardly known. But now past music (the sort most frequently recorded) became all the rage, and new music, 'modern music', turned into a specialist pleasure, ignored or disliked by the majority of music-lovers. In the same way, once people were free to choose, the gulf between 'serious' and 'popular' music spectacularly widened. Most people chose pop, and never listened to a note of 'serious' music in their lives; 'serious' music-lovers were equally ignorant of pop. It was a new brand of snobbery, and it still exists.

No one benefited more from recording than performers. Record-sales brought royalties, and one day's work could turn a lucky performer into a millionaire. Records took a performer's fame to every corner of the world, to hundreds of places he or she might never see. Many pop stars nowadays spend most of their energies in making records (and the videos that go with them); touring and live performances are much rarer events, and their purpose is to promote records as much as to meet the fans. In 'serious' music, records are nearly as important: for many soloists and orchestras, they pay the bills, and they popularize particular works and particular ways of playing above all others. (We talk of 'X's Beethoven' or 'Y's Rachmaninov' as if the performers owned the composers instead of merely playing their works.)

COMPOSERS The availability on records of so much great music of the past, and the popularity, thanks to records, of such 'light' musical styles as ragtime, jazz, swing, pop and rock, have given 'serious' twentieth-century composers immense inspiration. Some (e.g. *Nielsen, *Rachmaninov or *Respighi) have gone on developing past ideas or styles, writing 'neo-Romantic' works (in a nineteenth-century manner) or 'neo-classical' works (based on the styles of the eighteenth century or before). Others (e.g. *Copland or *Milhaud) have borrowed ideas from jazz and swing, giving their works colourful rhythms and harmonies unknown in 'serious' music before this century. Others (e.g. *Falla, *Sibelius, *Vaughan Williams) have found inspiration in the scenery, legend or folk music of their native lands. Others again (including two of the greatest musicians of the century, *Bartók and *Stravinsky) have taken inspiration from all these sources and blended it into new and utterly personal styles.

The work of all these composers, because it has some audible connection with the mainstream of music, has been accepted by most audiences, and is now regularly played alongside music by *Mozart, Beethoven, *Tchaikovsky and other great composers of the past. But there is another, equally flourishing kind of twentieth-century music, and it is one the average music-lover seldom hears. This is experimental music, an attempt to organize sound in completely new ways, unknown to previous generations.

Sometimes the sounds are ordinary notes made by ordinary instruments, and it is the way of organization that is new: *Schoenberg, for example, did away with scales and keys, and treated all twelve semitones of the octave as exactly equal in the makeup of melodies and harmonies. At other times, the sounds themselves are made in new ways by new instruments: *Boulez, *Stockhausen and others, for example, use synthesizers and computers either alongside or instead of conventional instruments.

A fair number of these experiments are bizarre. Some orchestral musicians, trained to play *Bach or *Brahms, find them difficult and ugly; audiences hate hearing them. (For some wild ideas, and some extreme reactions, see *Avant-garde Music*.) It takes a generation, on average, for a composer's true worth to become obvious, for people to get used to his or her work and to welcome the sound it makes. Some of the century's finest composers (Bartók, Stravinsky, Schoenberg, *Webern, *Tippett, *Messiaen, Boulez) were once reviled, and only time has shown them for the giants they really are. Of all twentieth-century composers, this group has benefited most from being recorded: records give us time to familiarize ourselves with what they wrote and, even if we still end up hating it, to stretch our ears and give new sounds a chance.

Listening A good introduction to twentieth-century music is work by composers who blend new ideas (e.g. jazz) with traditional styles and harmonies: the best to begin with are Falla, Milhaud and Walton, and exploration could move on first to Britten, Debussy and Vaughan Williams and then to Sibelius, Stravinsky and Bartók. (See also Bernstein, Bloch, Gershwin, Henze, Hindemith, Ives, Janáček, Kodály, Martinů, *One-work Composers* (Benjamin, Canteloube, Dukas, Rodrigo), Orff, Poulenc, Prokofiev, Ravel, Satie, Shostakovich, Richard Strauss, Tippett and Villa-Lobos.) The best composers of 'new sounds' to hear first are Berg and Lutosławski, followed by Boulez and Messiaen, and then by Webern, Maxwell Davies and Schoenberg. (See also Carter and Stockhausen.) For the most traditionally-styled composers of all, see Barber, Delius, Elgar, Holst, Khachaturian, Nielsen, Rachmaninov and Respighi; for general twentieth-century recommendations, see *Avant-garde Music*, *Ballet Music*, *British and Irish Composers*, *Chamber Music*, *Choral Music*, *Concerto*, *Opera*, *Orchestral Music*, *Sonata*, *String Instruments*, *Symphony*, *United States Composers*, *Vocal Music* and *Woodwind Instruments*.

U

UNITED STATES COMPOSERS

The United States have an extraordinarily varied musical experience. On to the traditions of the original native inhabitants have been grafted importations of every kind: Spanish-Catholic plainsong, Puritan hymns, African work-songs, European music-hall ditties and the complex composition-methods of nineteenth-century German symphonists. For a long time, the effect of these influences, together or separately, was that American art music seemed to have no voice of its own (as, say, Italian music did, or French). It was not until the twentieth century that recognizably 'American' styles began to appear, tempering European influences with hymns, slave-songs and the popular music (ballads; ragtime; jazz) derived from them. Two things special to the USA, from the nineteenth century onwards, have been the power of light music (Foster's songs; Sousa's marches; the show-tunes of Berlin or Kern) and the way 'serious' composers have tapped that power in works as different as sonatas and Broadway musicals.

NINETEENTH-CENTURY COMPOSERS The first US composers whose works linger in the international concert repertoire were pianists: Louis M. Gottschalk (1829-69) and Edward MacDowell (1860-1908). Both travelled in Europe and were hailed there as geniuses, Gottschalk by *Chopin and MacDowell by *Liszt. Both used local ideas in their works, Gottschalk (born in New Orleans) employing Creole folksongs and negro slave-melodies, MacDowell writing sound-pictures of the woods and placid landscapes of New England. There, however, the resemblance between them ends. Gottschalk was mainly a showman, and his pieces (e.g. *Creole Ballad*; *Bananaboat*; *Fantasy on Old Folks at Home*) alternately woo the audience with sentimental tunes and stun with virtuosity: musical substance - even in his 'symphony' *A Night in the Tropics* - is consistently replaced by dazzle. MacDowell is a heavyweight by contrast, an American *Grieg. He is best-remembered today by the slight drawing-room piece 'To a Wild Rose' (No. 1 of *Ten Woodland Sketches*), but as well as several dozen such effusions (typical collections are *Forest Idylls* or *Ten New England Sketches*) he wrote four substantial piano sonatas, several large symphonic works (e.g.

Hamlet and Ophelia) and two piano concertos which are deservedly still played. For all his toying with music's lighter side, he is a far more inspired figure than any of his contemporaries, even than such high-minded, academically-correct composers as the so-called 'New England Classicists' (one of whom, Horatio Parker, taught *Ives), whose (unsuccessful) life's mission was to build American music in the image of Bach or *Brahms.

EARLY TWENTIETH-CENTURY COMPOSERS The shadow of Europe lay particularly darkly over the turn-of-the-century generation. Many of America's great orchestras were established at this time, and their founders and committees imported European conductors and European masterworks, relegating local composers to the dance-hall, parade-ground or vaudeville (where, somewhat ungratefully, they flourished). In the welter of third-rate pomposity which followed, only two composers stood out from the crowd. One was Ives, and he generally kept his work to himself, so that its originality was recognized and influential only thirty or so years after it was written. (Cowell and Ruggles are his finest followers; Ruggles's orchestral *Sun-treader* is the most Ivesian work not actually by Ives.) The other was Howard Hanson (born 1896). He based his style on *Sibelius (he is best-known for a series of massive symphonies), and the orchestra he conducted (The Eastman-Rochester in New York) introduced more than 1500 new works by young composers over forty years, a record equalled by few other orchestras, and an activity which regularly rejuvenated Hanson's own rather heavy-featured Muse.

FROM THE 1920S TO THE PRESENT DAY After the First World War, everything changed. The twin causes were jazz and *Stravinsky. Young composers (notably *Copland, Harris and Thomson) were drawn to Paris by the reputation of Diaghilev's Ballets Russes (and particularly by word of its scandalous successes, *Debussy's *L'après-midi d'un faune* and Stravinsky's *The Rite of Spring*). They took French and Russian ideas back to the USA, and looked for some recognizably American ingredient to add to the exoticism of their models. The choice – in the 1920s, how could it be otherwise? – was jazz, and its rhythm, harmony and free-ranging solo expression, coupled with the scalpel-clean scoring and formal directness learned from Stravinsky, banished Teutonic heaviness from American scores for good. (Not even the discovery of *Schoenberg's twelve-note method affected this: American twelve-note composers like Riegger and Sessions are among the liveliest in the field.)

As the century progressed it became clear that several apparently vital compositions of the 1930s–1950s were in fact destined for the attic. Roy Harris (1898–1979) once seemed the greatest American composer; but of his many works (several on local themes like the life of Lincoln or High

School marching songs) only the Symphony No. 3 is likely to survive. Virgil Thomson (born 1896) took Gertrude Stein as his librettist (e.g. in the nonsense-opera *Four Saints in Three Acts*) and *Satie's dadaist simplicity as his musical inspiration: this guaranteed him a reputation in the 1930s, but his music now seems as faded as his models. Henry Cowell (1897-1965), with his sixteen league-of-nations symphonies (incorporating every musical style under the sun) and his 1000 chord-cluster piano pieces, and George Antheil (1900-1959), who added aeroplane-engines, rifles and popping balloons to his orchestras, were considered deliciously outrageous geniuses - once. The music which has lasted blends directness of expression with a kind of open-air busyness or quietness which now (thanks, for better or worse, to a million imitations in Hollywood film-scores) seem uniquely American characteristics. The finest composer in the style - one of the dozen or so leading composers of the century - is Aaron Copland, but others of distinction include Samuel *Barber, Leonard *Bernstein, Elliott *Carter, Gunther Schuller (born 1925), and the expert symphonists Walter Piston (1894-1976) and William Schuman (born 1910), whose pieces are less well known outside the USA than their quality deserves. There are flourishing experimentalists, from the dadaist John *Cage and Morton Feldman (born 1926) to the electronic Milton Babbitt (born 1916) and 'guided-improvisation' Lukas Foss (born 1922); and, most 'American' of all, there is a large group of composers who have turned the usual way of inspiration inside-out, using 'serious' styles and ideas to strengthen popular music: the greatest was *Gershwin, but the list also includes jazz composers like 'Duke' Ellington (1899-1974) and musical showmen as diverse as Richard Rodgers (1902-79; *Oklahoma!*), Frank Loesser (1910-69; *Guys and Dolls*) and Stephen Sondheim (born 1930; *Chorus Line*).

Listening The most inspired introduction to nineteenth-century American music is MacDowell's Piano Concerto No. 2, which is on a level with anything by (say) *Saint-Saëns; the Germanic school can be sampled at its most serious in Arthur Foote's *Night Piece*, and at its most smiling in the drawing-room ballads and piano mood-pieces of Mrs Amy Cheney Beach. From the twentieth century, ideal works of substance to begin with are Hanson's Symphony No. 2 (the 'Romantic') and Harris's Symphony No. 3, both reminiscent of Sibelius's symphonies, in sound and quality, and also the more characteristically American *Symphony of Chorales* by Lukas Foss. The finest or most typical twentieth-century American composers (Ives, Gershwin, Copland, Carter, Barber, Bernstein) are discussed elsewhere in this book; introductions to some of the others are Piston's bouncy circus-ballet *The Incredible Flutist* and his Stravinskian Symphony No. 2, Schuman's *American Festival Overture* and Violin Concerto, and Schuller's *Seven Studies on Themes of Paul Klee*, one of the most beguiling of all avant-garde orchestral scores.

V

VAUGHAN WILLIAMS, Ralph (1872–1958). *English composer.*

Financed by a private income, Vaughan Williams was able, like *Tippett, to continue studying well into his thirties: he took composition lessons with Parry and Stanford at the Royal College of Music, read history and music at Cambridge, and even spent three months in Paris with *Ravel, giving his orchestration what he called a 'touch of French polish'. This long apprenticeship makes his early works (e.g. *The Wasps* or *A Sea Symphony*) sound accomplished but anonymous: they could have been composed by any of a dozen turn-of-the-century British musicians, from *Delius to Parry.

Vaughan Williams's surge into genius came in the mid-1900s, when he began collecting and studying English folksongs. (At this time he was editing a new hymn-book, *The English Hymnal*, and supplied several fine tunes of his own, some, e.g. *Sine nomine* ('For All the Saints'), in the forthright style of the late nineteenth century, others, e.g. *Down Ampney* and *Monk's Gate*, in flowing folk-music idiom.) His folk-music work irradiated his own music (much as *Bartók's did his): his style began to reflect its melodic turns of phrase and harmonic ease and his music often seems a natural counterpart to the quiet fields and woods of the English countryside.

But there is more to Vaughan Williams than calendar-picture prettiness. Like his friend *Holst, he was interested in mysticism, and particularly in such robust religious visionaries as Bunyan and Blake. He wrote dozens of vocal works to mystical texts, a Bunyan opera and a Blake ballet – and his best non-vocal music (e.g. the Third and Fifth Symphonies) is filled with an ecstatic, soaring beauty which carries it far above folksong simplicities. Works like the *Tallis Fantasia*, *Job* or the Fifth Symphony place him with the finest British composers of his generation, and fix his music securely in concert programmes throughout the world.

WORKS Six operas (including *The Pilgrim's Progress*); five ballets (including *Job*); nine symphonies, *Tallis Fantasia*, *Partita*, *English Folksongs Suite* and a couple of dozen lesser orchestral works; four concertos (for violin, two pianos, oboe and tuba) and several other pieces for soloist and orchestra;

twenty-five large choral works (including *Sancta civitas*, *Five Tudor Portraits*, Mass, *Dona nobis pacem* and *Serenade to Music*) and many shorter works for choir (including dozens of folksong settings); sixty-five songs (including *Linden Lea*, *Silent Noon* and the cycles *Songs of Travel* and *Ten Blake Songs*); chamber music (including a violin sonata and two string quartets), piano pieces, organ pieces and music for a dozen films (including *Scott of the Antarctic* and *The England of Elizabeth*).

Ⓜ *Fantasia on a Theme of Thomas Tallis* (1910) While he was working on *The English Hymnal*, Vaughan Williams rediscovered the hymns and other church music of the sixteenth-century composer Thomas Tallis (see *British and Irish Composers*), and restored several of his fine tunes to the repertoire. This rapt work, for solo string quartet and two string orchestras, is a meditation on one of them: not so much variations as an unbroken series of developments and commentaries, exploring every implication of Tallis's tune in music of radiant inspiration and ecstatic, heart-easing sounds.
→ Ⓜ *The Lark Ascending* (violin and orchestra); *Serenade to Music* (sixteen solo voices, or choir, and orchestra); Tippett *Fantasia concertante on a Theme of Corelli*.

English Folksongs Suite (1923) This chirpy four-movement suite, based on some of the jolliest of all English folk-tunes and sea-shanties, was originally written for brass band, but works even better in Gordon Jacob's sparkling orchestral arrangement. Vaughan Williams was a master of unbuttoned, rumbustious gaiety, and this short suite is one of the most cheerful works he wrote.
→ Overture *The Wasps*; Holst *St Paul's Suite*; Milhaud *Suite Française*.

Ⓜ 'Silent Noon' (from song-cycle *The House of Life*, 1903) Vaughan Williams was at his happiest writing slow, dreamy melodies for the human voice, and this song is one of the best-loved of all. It is a picture of languor, the drowsiness of midday paralleled by lassitude in the singer's soul. The feeling of stillness, of receptivity, is beautifully caught and both tune and harmony are of ravishing simplicity.
→ *Linden Lea* (fresh as a folksong); Purcell *Music for a While*; Brahms *Gestille Sehnsucht* Op. 91 No. 1.

Ⓜ **Symphony No. 5** (1943) Vaughan Williams worked for thirty years on an opera based on *The Pilgrim's Progress*, but the problems of matching Bunyan's language in music and of finding a company willing to mount a mystical, meditative opera made him lay it aside, time and time again, to work on other projects. In the end he used some of its music as the basis for this masterly symphony: the quiet opening movement and the overlapping, arching climax of the slow movement are exactly the Bunyan equivalents he was looking for, and also match the intensity of his own inspiration in (say) the *Tallis Fantasia*. He never wrote a finer work – and writing the symphony spurred him to finish the opera, which many of his admirers now prize among all his finest vocal works. (Of his other symphonies, the best are No. 2, the 'London', Ⓜ No. 3, the 'Pastoral', and the uncompromisingly dissonant Ⓜ No. 4 and No. 6.)

→ Ⓜ Ballet *Job*; Ives Symphony No. 2; Rubbra Symphony No. 6.

VERDI, Giuseppe (1813-1901). *Italian composer.*

When Verdi was ten a local shopkeeper, struck by his musical talent, agreed to finance his education; ten years later Verdi was appointed conductor of the local choir and orchestra, and married his patron's daughter. He had no particular ambition to become an opera-composer, and it was only with the unexpected popular success of his third opera, *Nabucco*, that he took up opera-writing seriously, at the age of twenty-nine. For the next eleven years, determined to make his fortune, he wrote an opera every nine months or so, and by 1853 he was Italy's leading composer. The stories of many of his operas dealt with nations throwing off the tyrant's yoke, and since Italy at this time was freeing itself from Austrian overlordship, he gained a reputation as a political composer, and was regularly in trouble with the censors.

After these years of hard work – he called them his 'years in the galleys' – Verdi settled back on his farm, composing much less intensively (an opera every three to four years). He worked on prestigious commissions – e.g. on a new opera, *Aida*, to celebrate the opening of the Suez Canal – and spent five years as a member of parliament after Italy won self-government from Austria. His operas, particularly *La traviata*, *Il trovatore* and *Rigoletto*, travelled the world (they were particularly popular in the USA), and each Verdi première was a glittering social and musical event. After his sixtieth birthday, it seemed that he had retired from composing operas; but in 1879 (when Verdi was seventy-six) his publisher suggested a new project based on Shakespeare's *Othello*, and a new collaborator, the up-and-coming composer and poet Arrigo Boito. Verdi was reluctant at first, but was so impressed by Boito's libretto that he not only composed *Otello* but also collaborated on another Shakespeare opera, *Falstaff*, whose first performance was given when he was eighty-one. After this he really did retire: he wrote nothing more except a handful of short church pieces, and devoted his energy to setting up a home for impoverished elderly musicians, which still exists today and is handsomely financed from his performance royalties.

WORKS Twenty-six operas (including *Luisa Miller*, *Rigoletto*, *Il trovatore*, *La traviata*, *Sicilian Vespers*, *Simone Boccanegra*, *A Masked Ball*, *The Force of Destiny*, *Don Carlos*, *Aida*, *Otello* and *Falstaff*); *Requiem*, *Four Sacred Pieces* and half a dozen shorter choral works; String Quartet; two dozen early songs.

Operas During his 'years in the galleys' Verdi was reasonably happy to accept whatever librettos were offered him, and to tailor his style to fit each commission and each occasion. He composed comedy (e.g. *Un giorno di regno*, 'King for a Day'), biblical romance (e.g. *Nabucco*, 'Nebuchadnezzar'), stories of high adventure in the manner of *Bellini or *Donizetti (e.g. *Il corsaro*, 'The Pirate'; *Giovanna d'Arco*, 'Joan of Arc'), and above all the historical pageant-operas which made his political reputation (e.g. *I Lombardi alla prima crociata*, 'The Lombards on the First Crusade'; *Attila*; *Ernani*). All these works are dramatically effective and full of opportunities for glorious singing, but none rivals the masterpieces of his later years. In the 1850s he began looking for stories which dealt with personal passions, individual joy and suffering, as much as with battles, political plotting and state affairs. *Rigoletto* is about a deformed jester tormented by a cruel Duke, whose planned revenge backfires and destroys him too; Ⓜ *La traviata* ('The Women who Strayed') is about a 'woman with a past', dying of consumption, who bravely renounces the love of a younger man; *Il trovatore* ('The Troubadour') is a hot-blooded romantic tale involving long-separated brothers (who end up loving the same woman), a gypsy's curse and the inexorable closing of the jaws of Fate. The stories are highly unlikely, but the operas are wonderfully effective, and their individual numbers (e.g. the Anvil Chorus from *Il trovatore*, the Drinking Chorus from *La traviata*, 'Caro nome' and 'La donna è mobile' from *Rigoletto*) contain some of Verdi's best-loved and most stirring tunes. After these operas, he began to compose in a more compact, 'symphonic' style (an Italian equivalent of *Wagner's music-dramas), using the orchestra to draw out the emotional meaning of each scene, and developing it over the whole length of an act or opera: this makes extracts from his later operas less self-contained and less effective than from his middle-period works. Some of the late operas (*Simone Boccanegra*, *The Force of Destiny*, *Aida*) are melodramas about love and betrayal in the old, red-blooded style, but orchestral depth, and the way Verdi makes his characters seem like real people instead of singing puppets, gives them a power few other operas can match. Other of his operas – for many listeners, the most satisfying of all – concern political intrigue, and his music catches every twist and turn of the dark emotions underlying the events: *The Masked Ball* centres on an assassination-plot, and Ⓜ *Don Carlos* is about a tyrant father and his freedom-loving son, at odds both politically and because they love the same woman. Verdi's last two operas are his greatest, some say finer works even than the Shakespeare plays they are based on. In Ⓜ *Otello*, Verdi's music points up Desdemona's innocence, Othello's passionate jealousy and Iago's cold-hearted scheming in a way only the finest actors bring off in Shakespeare, and Boito's libretto for Ⓜ *Falstaff* marvellously tidies up some of Shakespeare's most tangled comedy, a feat which Verdi spectacularly undercuts by the complexity of his music: this comic opera has sonata-form acts and double fugues, which (miraculously) only serve to make it funnier.

→ The best first approach to Verdi is through extracts (e.g. those from *Rigoletto* or *La traviata* mentioned above), followed by a complete opera (perhaps *Il trovatore* or *Aida*). After that might come *Otello*, followed by the political operas (e.g. *Don Carlos*: it helps beforehand to read a clear outline of the story) and *Falstaff*. Of other composers' operas, good counterparts to Verdi's early works are

Bellini's *Norma* and Donizetti's *Lucrezia Borgia*; good follow-ups to *La traviata* and the other middle-period works are Puccini's *La bohème* and Leoncavallo's *I pagliacci*; good follow-ups to *Aida* and *The Force of Destiny* respectively are Puccini's *Madama Butterfly* and *Tosca*; a good follow-up to *Don Carlos* is Musorgsky's *Boris Godunov*; a good follow-up to *Otello* is Tchaikovsky's *Eugene Onegin*, and good follow-ups to *Falstaff* are Wagner's *Die Meistersinger* and Britten's *A Midsummer Night's Dream*.

Other works Ⓜ *Requiem* (1874). Verdi's *Requiem* is opera for the concert-hall. It sets the words of the *Requiem Mass* for soloists, chorus and orchestra in a vibrantly emotional style; the central confrontation, on the Day of Judgement, between angelic avengers and fervently-praying penitents is as dramatic and at-mospheric as any of his operatic scenes, and the orchestra underlines the 'meaning' of the action in true stage style. In the concert-hall, the impact is extraordinary: the work engulfs its listeners, believers and non-believers alike, and turns funereal pomp and show into a transcendental experience. Of Verdi's other choral works, the Ⓜ *Te Deum* (from *Four Sacred Pieces*, a mixed bag assembled in the late 1880s) most nearly matches it for magnificence; the *Stabat Mater* and the unac-companied *Ava Maria* and *Lauds of the Virgin Mary* seem, by comparison, reticent and delicate. His songs and one non-vocal piece, the String Quartet, are luscious but lightweight, musical meringues.

→ The nearest Verdi opera to the *Requiem* in style is *Aida*: its 'Grand March' and the beautiful aria 'Celeste Aida' are especially close kin. Good follow-ups by others are Puccini's *Messa di Gloria*, Mahler's Symphony No. 8 and (in a more secular vein) Orff's *Carmina Burana*; good follow-ups to Verdi's songs are those of Donizetti and Respighi, and a splendid follow-up to the String Quartet is Wolf's *Italian Serenade*.

VILLA-LOBOS. See *One-work Composers*.

VIVALDI, Antonio (1678–1741). *Italian composer*.

Vivaldi studied for the priesthood, and took holy orders in 1703. But from the start he was far less interested in the church than in music and pretty women. He had a job (as music-master to a girls' orphanage in Venice), but spent months each year away from it, touring Italy as violin-virtuoso and opera-composer. He was a fantastically fluent composer, able to write a new concerto in a day and an opera in a week; he was also an extrovert, a showman and something of a rogue, and the swagger of his life is matched by the irrepressible charm of his music, expertly and infallibly made to please.

(The most reliable catalogue of Vivaldi's surviving music is by the Danish scholar Peter Ryom. The R numbers (or RV numbers, standing for Ryom *Verzeichnis*, 'Ryom's Catalogue') attached to his works refer to this.)

WORKS Vivaldi claimed to have written several thousand works, and more than 700 have survived. His operas are his least-known compositions: twenty-one survive, most of them comedies to witty librettos in Venetian dialect by the playwright Goldoni. He also wrote church music (including a well-known *Gloria*) and oratorios, but he is best-known today for his instrumental works: *concerti grossi*, sonatas, trio-sonatas and over 450 concertos for one, two, three or four soloists and string orchestra.

The Four Seasons, Op. 8 Nos. 1–4 (*c.* 1725) Op. 8 is a set of twelve solo-violin concertos, subtitled (in typical Vivaldi style) 'Contest between Harmony and Invention', and these four concertos are the best of them. Each represents one of the seasons, and the music is bright with sound-pictures of icicles, skating, larks, harvesting, hunting and so on. The shape of each, however, is a standard (for their time) four-movement concerto-form, and this balance between fantasy and discipline, combined with Vivaldi's bouncy rhythms and fizzy solo-violin writing, makes the whole set irresistible.

→ The best follow-up to any Vivaldi concerto is more of the same, and there are anthology-recordings to suit every taste, involving every conceivable solo instrument from piccolo to mandolin. The concertos published in his lifetime are the best-known, and the finest of those are the twelve of Op. 3 (subtitled *L'estro harmonico*, 'Harmonious Inspiration'), for violin, and the six of Op. 10, for flute. Of other composers' music, the best follow-ups are the concertos (and sonatas and trio-sonatas) of *Telemann, beginning with the Viola Concerto in G, and the violin concertos Nos. 1 and 2 by J. S. *Bach, one of Vivaldi's most constant admirers.

VOCAL MUSIC

Singing is a human activity as old as speech: Stone Age cave paintings show solo singers accompanied by handclaps and sticks banged on the ground, and the history of vocal music is really no more than an account of the different ways human beings have found of disciplining their singing voices, from straightforward nursery songs or religious chants to such sophisticated art forms as *opera and oratorio (see *Choral Music*).

SONG The simplest vocal music of all is folksong – and yet it has fascinated 'serious' musicians throughout the centuries. In the fifteenth and sixteenth centuries composers based Masses on folksong tunes; in the eighteenth and nineteenth centuries composers as distinguished as *Haydn, *Beethoven and *Brahms responded to the public's taste for folk music with folksong arrangements; and in the twentieth century collecting folksongs has been a major musical activity, and its results have influenced the styles of composers as far apart in sound as *Bartók, *Copland and *Vaughan Williams.

'Art' song has similarly attracted many of the great composers, but it was not until the nineteenth century that it acquired the capacity to rival the vocal music of the opera-house and the church. In the seventeenth and eighteenth centuries the popularity of opera pushed aside the private plaints of the madrigal and the lute-song. People thought of song as a popular form, rarely as 'art' music, and the nearest approaches to 'serious' vocal music were the theatre songs of composers like *Purcell. Vocal music for opera and the church tended to be ornate and showy: works like Alessandro Scarlatti's or Handel's solo-voice cantatas, for example, were far too grand to be classed as 'songs'.

The composer above all others who made songs 'respectable' again was *Schubert. Many of his *Lieder* (the German word for 'songs') are on a large scale (see below), but he also wrote hundreds of straightforward, unaffected songs, as simple as popular songs, as direct as folksongs, and above all of unchallengeable inspiration and quality. After him, many other composers regarded song composition as respectable; singers began to move happily between opera-house and recital-room, and a large repertoire of songs was created for them to sing. Some (e.g. Rossini's 'La danza', Musorgsky's 'Song of the Flea' or Brahms's 'The Vain Serenade') are spectacular encore-pieces, designed to bring the house down; others (e.g. Dvořák's *Songs My Mother Taught Me*, Tchaikovsky's 'None but the Lonely Heart' or Vaughan Williams's 'Silent Noon'), without sacrificing simplicity, are deeply felt, moving and emotionally strong.

LARGE-SCALE SONGS AND SONG-CYCLES In the nineteenth century the popularity of the cantata waned (Beethoven's *Ah! Perfido!* is one of the last), and they were replaced by a particularly rich and elaborate kind of song with piano accompaniment. Once again, Schubert was to the fore in providing *Lieder* of a substance and power to satisfy public and performer alike, developing the piano accompaniments until they played as important a part as the voice in describing the atmosphere evoked by the words. He was followed by *Schumann, Brahms, *Wolf, *Mahler and Richard *Strauss, and only towards the end of the century did composers from other countries than Germany and Austria write songs of equal weight (notably *Fauré, *Debussy and *Poulenc in France, and *Musorgsky, *Tchaikovsky and *Rachmaninov in Russia).

At its most elaborate – e.g. in Schubert's *Ganymed* or Strauss's *Mutter-tanderlei* – the *Lied* is musically as complex as a sonata or symphony movement (and forms borrowed from instrumental genres were often used in its construction), and the listener's enjoyment comes as much from appreciating its musical structure as from the treatment of the words. Even so, for many nineteenth-century vocal composers, this musical density was not enough. They began grouping their songs into sets (called 'song-cycles') that told a developing story or treated a theme (defeated love, enjoyment of country life) in a variety of ways, spreading the emotional impact over several songs. (Beethoven's *An die ferne Geliebte*, 'To the Distant Beloved', was the first important song-cycle, followed by Schubert's *The Maid of the Mill* and *Winter Journey*; Schumann and Fauré were their greatest followers.) Song-cycles are often long (twenty to forty minutes), and depend as much as sonatas and symphonies on being heard complete. They carry the art of vocal music into regions of emotional power and complexity unthought of in previous centuries, until finally, towards the end of the century, the *Lied* took itself out of its original domestic setting, whether private parlour or small recital-room, and moved into the concert-hall, with orchestral accompaniment taking over from the piano (e.g. in Mahler's *Kindertotenlieder*, 'Songs of the Death of Children', and *Lieder eines fahrenden Gesellen*, 'Songs of a Wayfarer').

PART-SONGS The part-song is a pleasant variant on the idea of a simple solo song: a melody accompanied not by instruments but by other voices in harmony. At their grandest, part-songs are indistinguishable from madrigals or other such choral works; at their simplest, they are musical kin to hymns or student songs (e.g. 'Gaudeamus igitur', used by *Brahms as the climax of his *Academic Festival Overture*). Part-singing, with one voice to a part or in small choirs, has been a popular British pastime for four centuries, and there are splendid part-songs by British composers otherwise as different as *Purcell, *Elgar, *Vaughan Williams and *Britten. In the nineteenth century, part-songs were also popular in Europe (usually in a more complex form, with piano accompaniment): Schubert, *Mendelssohn and Brahms composed many sets, and Debussy's *Chansons de Charles d'Orléans* and Ravel's *Trois chansons* are among the gems of the repertoire.

Listening Good introductions to solo vocal music are the songs and *Lieder* mentioned in this article; after that, the best approach to an enormous repertoire is perhaps to find a composer whose style of songs appeals, and explore his or her output. The leading song-composers discussed in this book are Brahms, Britten, Dvořák, Falla, Fauré, Grieg, Mendelssohn, Musorgsky, Schubert, Schumann, R. Strauss, Tchaikovsky, Vaughan Williams and Wolf; see also *One-work Composers* (Canteloube; Villa-Lobos). Good song-cycles to begin with (with an English translation to hand if necessary) are Schubert's *The Maid of the Mill*, Debussy's *Trois ballades de François Villon* (both for voice and piano) and Britten's *Serenade* (for voice, horn and strings); good follow-ups are Schumann's *Dichterliebe*, Britten's *Winter Words* and Mahler's *Lieder eines fahrenden Gesellen* (with orchestra). For further recommendations, see Brahms, Britten, Debussy, Fauré, Grieg, Mahler, Poulenc, Schubert, Schumann, Tippett, Wagner and Wolf. Good introductions to the part-song repertoire are Vaughan Williams's folksong arrangements (e.g. *Just* as the Tide was Flowing), Elgar's O Happy Eyes, Op. 18 No. 1, and *Tippett's Five Spirituals (from A Child of Our Time); good follow-ups are Stanford's The Blue Bird, *Delius's To be Sung of a Summer Night on the Water, Brahms's Love-song Waltzes (in English, if possible), and the Debussy and Ravel part-songs mentioned above.

W

WAGNER, Richard (1813–83). *German composer.*

Wagner may have been the illegitimate son of an actor, Ludwig Geyer, and he was attracted to the stage from childhood. At first his interest was in writing plays, but in his teens he saw a production of *Beethoven's *Fidelio*, and this decided him on a career as an opera composer. He was a gifted poet, and wrote all his own librettos in a highly personal blend of nineteenth-century Romantic melodrama and the archaic turns of phrase and heroic sentiments of the Norse sagas and German legend-cycles whose stories he adapted.

At first Wagner found it hard to establish himself: young opera-composers were ten a penny, and his favoured style (which leaned towards *Berlioz rather than to the fashionable *Bellini or *Rossini) made managers reluctant to accept his works. Then, in 1839, he met Meyerbeer, composer of grand operas for the Paris Opéra, and in him found both a model and a patron. On Meyerbeer's recommendation, Wagner's *Rienzi* and *The Flying Dutchman* were accepted for production, and were sufficiently successful to win him a conducting job (at the Dresden Court Opera). More important, Meyerbeer's own operas – large, melodramatic and spectacular – showed Wagner how to turn the unlikely stories and cardboard characters of legend into powerful stage drama. *Lohengrin*, *The Flying Dutchman* and *Tannhäuser* were all composed in Meyerbeer's shadow, and are among the finest Romantic pageant-operas in the repertoire.

At this point, just as Wagner's professional life seemed more assured, his private life went to pieces. He was an intolerant, opinionated man, convinced that he was a sublime genius, an artist-superman, and that other people existed largely for his convenience. He had a string of mistresses; he lived far beyond his means, borrowing money and skipping from town to town to avoid paying his debts; he made public assertions about politics so violent that he was branded a revolutionary and banished from Germany. He took shelter first with *Liszt in Weimar, then in Switzerland with a rich merchant called Wesendonk, whose hospitality he repaid by seducing his wife.

Apart from Meyerbeer, Liszt and Mathilde Wesendonk were the most crucial influences in Wagner's life. He had long been planning a stage-work based on the heroic legends of Germany (the Nibelung Saga), and had felt that Meyerbeer's operatic style, with its hefty choruses, showy arias and four-square harmony, was unsuitable. He needed a texture more like the sagas themselves, continuous, constantly varied in mood, and with the story-teller's voice as important as those of the characters. Liszt's symphonic poems suggested that instead of aria-and-chorus opera he could write 'music-drama', a kind of symphony with singers, and that he could replace the story-teller by the orchestra, using it to remind the audience of underlying themes and ideas, to shape the events and to give each turn of the plot a context which was musical as well as dramatic. Not only that, but Liszt's adventurous harmonies, not straightforward like Meyerbeer's but sinuous, blurring endlessly into one another, full of 'new' sounds and chords, were the ideal framework for a continuous, developing musical structure. Fired by all this, Wagner wrote the words of *The Ring of the Nibelung* and began composing the music. Then, halfway through, he fell in love with Mathilde Wesendonk, and was so inspired that he laid *The Ring* aside and wrote *Tristan and Isolde*, a music-drama about ecstatic, passionate love which used the new 'symphonic' style and pushed conventional harmony beyond anything then known. *Tristan and Isolde* was, in its day, the most revolutionary piece of music ever composed: it influenced the whole progress of late-nineteenth-century music, paved the way for the harmonic experiments of such turn-of-the-century composers as *Mahler and *Schoenberg – and made very many people share Wagner's own opinion of himself, that he was the greatest composer in the history of stage music, the Shakespeare of his art.

Fame and influence were, however, no guarantee of income. Wesendonk and his wife left Switzerland for a long Italian holiday, and Wagner too was forced to move. He went to Paris to revise *Tannhäuser* for the Opéra, and while he was there fell in love with Liszt's daughter Cosima (wife of the conductor Hans von Bülow). He spent some time in Vienna, working on a comic music-drama (*Die Meistersinger*), but had to leave for the usual reason – debtors hammering at his door. At this point (1864) he met the eighteen-year-old King Ludwig II of Bavaria, who was dazzled by both his personality and his music. Ludwig invited him back to Germany, guaranteed him a steady income, and pressed him to finish *The Ring*. The settled work this required, added to domestic happiness at last – in 1870 Cosima divorced von Bülow and married Wagner – seem to have calmed his restlessness. He put his energies into building a theatre (at Bayreuth, in Bavaria), purpose-made for productions of the huge *Ring* cycle; he supervised the architects, went on concert-tours to raise money and scoured Europe for singers and players fit to take part in one of the most mammoth musical undertakings of its time. In 1876 the theatre opened, and there have been yearly Wagner festivals at Bayreuth ever since. Wagner wrote one more music-drama, *Parsifal*; after this his strenuous life finally began to take its toll: he suffered a series of heart-attacks, and died in Venice in 1883.

There is more than a little truth in the comparison of Wagner with Shakespeare. Both took ideas current at the time (in Wagner's case, the orchestral styles of Berlioz and Meyerbeer, the symphonic grandeur of Beethoven and the harmonic experiments of Liszt) and turned them into unique art-forms by the stupendous quality of their own genius. Like Shakespeare, Wagner has had a thousand imitators, and no equals; the grandeur of his works is self-evident, and the rewards they offer anyone prepared to come to terms with them are a lifetime's engrossing listening and a uniquely overwhelming musical experience.

WORKS 13 operas and music-dramas (including *The Flying Dutchman*, *Lohengrin*, *Tannhäuser*, *The Ring* cycle, *Tristan and Isolde*, *The Mastersingers* and *Parsifal*); *Wesendonck Songs*; *Siegfried Idyll*; two dozen early works (including a symphony, a piano sonata, six overtures, an oratorio and several songs). Wagner's prose-writings include an autobiography and books on *Opera and Drama*, *Religion and Art*, *The Music of the Future* and *Conducting*.

Early Operas The heroes and heroines of Wagner's operas are 'loners', 'outsiders', often cursed by Fate and – like the sea-captain hero of *The Flying Dutchman* – endlessly searching for self-fulfilment. (Wagner saw them as symbols of the creative artist striving in society, and their restlessness parallels his own.) The stories are as unrealistic as fairy-tales: supernatural forces are at work, and the characters must come to terms with them in order to 'find' or 'save' themselves. (*Mozart's opera *Don Giovanni* contains very similar elements, and was another powerful influence on Wagner at this time.) As always with Wagner, the mishmash of influences is there for anyone to see, but what comes across in performance is less other people's ideas than the blazing power of his own inspiration: his conviction that every note he composed was inevitable shines out and dazzles the spectator; he is one of those rare artists whose work demands to be taken on its own terms, insists that we enter its world, dominates the spectator as well as entertains. The best first approach is through orchestral extracts such as the Prelude to Act 3 from *Lohengrin* or the Overture, Venusberg Music and Grand March from *Tannhäuser*. The best first opera to hear complete (because it has the clearest plot and the finest music) is *The Flying Dutchman* (and a good sample of that is its symphonic-poem-like Overture); good follow-ups (complete operas) by others are Meyerbeer's *The Prophet*, Weber's *Der Freischütz* and Verdi's *The Force of Destiny*.

Ⓜ *The Ring of the Nibelung* (begun 1852; completed after interruptions 1874) This vast musical epic (eighteen hours long, in four sections: *Das Rheingold*, 'Rhinegold'; *Die Walküre*, 'The Valkyrie'; *Siegfried*; *Götterdämmerung*, 'Twilight of the Gods') is set in the legendary time of the Nordic sagas, begins with the forging of a magic ring and ends with the destruction of the gods and the collapse of the whole order of the universe. Its cast-list includes humans, gods, dwarves, giants and a shape-changing dragon; its subject matter involves miraculous swords, helmets of invisibility, rainbow-bridges and a circle of magic fire; its settings include the bed of the river Rhine, the dwarves' caverns under the earth and the sky-citadel of the gods. In short, it sounds like a mixture of science-fiction fantasy and pantomime. What makes it sublime is not only Wagner's music but his psychological insight: his supernatural beings are racked with human fears, rages and jealousies, and his human characters are touched with the nobility and majesty of the gods. (The two beings at the heart of the drama are Siegfried, a human hero aspiring to divine purity, and Brünnhilde, a divine being filled with human love. Their criss-crossing, doomed relationship gives the whole *Ring* cycle a clear psychological centre, around which all the supernatural events revolve; it is as simple, and as moving, as the lovers' relationship in *Tristan and Isolde*, and evokes from Wagner music of similar intensity and ecstasy.) Musically, the cycle is unified by a system of *Leitmotive* ('leading-motives'), tags of harmony and melody, each symbolizing a particular person or idea (e.g. jealousy, power of love, magic potion), and woven in and out of the musical texture to let the audience see each action, hear each statement, in its dramatic and psychological context. (The leading-motives appear most often in the orchestra, making it the commentator, the 'story-teller', and giving it the major role in the action that Wagner wanted. It is this orchestral commentary which makes Wagner's music-dramas unlike stage-works by any other composer.) The size of *The Ring* makes it an enormous undertaking for singers, orchestra and audience alike, and although extracts (dismissed by the critic Tovey as 'bleeding chunks') hardly do it justice – one might as well recite individual speeches and call them Shakespeare – they are the only possible way of making a first approach. (The most 'informative' are *Siegfried's Rhine Journey*, Ⓜ *Siegfried's Funeral March* and the closing scene, or Ⓜ *Immolation Scene*, all from *Götterdämmerung*; other popular, if less typical, extracts are *The Ride of the Valkyries* from *Die Walküre* and *Forest Murmurs* from *Siegfried*.) For those approaching *The Ring* complete, an English libretto and some information on the leading-motives are useful aids. Follow-ups (if follow-ups are possible to such a gigantic enterprise) are Wagner's *Tannhäuser* and Berlioz's *The Trojans* (to the more forthright central sections of *The Ring*), and (to the more mystical sections) Wagner's *Parsifal* and Debussy's *Pelléas and Mélisande*.

Other music-dramas *Tristan and Isolde* (1859). At first glance this might be taken for one of the early pageant-operas: its plot, set in medieval Cornwall, is a farrago of poisoned chalices, chastity-vows, pure-hearted passion and beetle-browed villainy. But from the moment the music starts, this impression evaporates. *Tristan and Isolde* is a compelling, ecstatic tone-poem about love, the vocal lines and orchestral harmonies entwining, embracing and flowing into one another in a way which transfigures the experience even as it shows it. Two extracts, Ⓜ Prelude and *Liebestod* ('Love-death'), give the flavour, but the work needs to be heard complete to make its full effect. Ⓜ *Die Meistersinger von Nürnberg* ('The Mastersingers of Nuremberg') is a comedy, involving two young people whose love triumphs over every obstacle: in particular, the hero has to win a song-contest, in the teeth of peppery judges, to earn his bride. The central role, however, is not the young lover but the wise craftsman Hans Sachs, whose soliloquies on life and the transcendental power of art (modelled on Falstaff's soliloquies in Shakespeare's *Henry IV*) are Wagner's most direct exposition of his own personal views, expressed in some of the most relaxed, even-tempered music in all his output. Well-known extracts include Prelude, *Dance of the Apprentices* and Ⓜ *Prize Song*; Ⓜ Act Two is a dazzling, self-contained masterpiece of stage comedy in music, an excellent sample of the whole work. *Parsifal* is unlike any of Wagner's other stage works, a 'sacred festival drama' on the themes of redemption through suffering, the holy fool (someone whose simplicity enables him or her to surmount all obstacles) and the contrast between profane love (men's and women's physical passion) and sacred love (symbolized by the hero's quest for the Holy Grail, the cup from which Christ drank at the Last Supper). *Parsifal* is sincere and moving, and (like Shakespeare's *The Tempest*) gathers together all the ideas and experiences of a creative lifetime. For many Wagner-lovers, it is his supreme creation; others may find it a little over-serious, and prefer extracts (e.g. Prelude and *Good Friday Music*) to the whole work.

→ Good follow-ups to *Tristan and Isolde* are Wagner's *Wesendonk Songs* (see below), Chausson's *Chanson perpétuelle* and Schoenberg's *Gürrelieder*; good follow-ups to *Die Meistersinger* are Mozart's *The Magic Flute* and Strauss's *Capriccio*; good follow-ups to *Parsifal* are Bruckner's symphonies (especially No. 3, directly inspired by Wagner, and No. 7, written in his memory) and Pfitzner's *Palestrina* (first the three Orchestral Preludes, then the complete opera).

Other works Ⓜ *Siegfried Idyll* (1870). This beautiful piece was written to celebrate Christmas Day, the birth of Wagner's son Siegfried, and above all his rapturous love for Cosima. It takes German folk-tunes and themes from Wagner's music-dramas (especially *Siegfried*, on which he was then working), and works them into a serene orchestral tone-poem, radiant with domestic happiness. Of all his non-stage works, this is the only one to match the music-dramas for inspiration and mastery; it is close in style to *The Ring* and in atmosphere to *The Mastersingers*, and is by no means dwarfed by them. A sister-work to *Tristan and Isolde* is the set of five *Wesendonk Songs* for soprano and orchestra: luscious Romantic settings of love poetry by Wagner's mistress Mathilde Wesendonk, slight poems turned to gold by the power of Wagner's genius, and some of the most ravishing sounds he ever wrote for the human voice. The finest of his other works, all early, is his *Faust Overture*: if it had been by anyone else (*Schumann, say, or Berlioz) it would be far more frequently performed, but Wagner's name suggests more grandeur than this music achieves, and it is unjustly little-known.

→ Good follow-ups to the *Siegfried Idyll* are Wagner's *Siegfried's Rhine Journey* (from *Götterdämmerung*) and *Forest Murmurs* (from *Siegfried*), Dvořák's *Serenade for Strings* and Strauss's Oboe Concerto; good follow-ups to the *Wesendonk Songs* are Wagner's *Liebestod* (from *Tristan and Isolde*) and Strauss's *Der Rosenkavalier* (Closing Scene); good follow-ups to the *Faust Overture* are Wagner's overtures to *Rienzi* and *Tannhäuser*, Bruckner's Overture in G minor and Berlioz's overture *King Lear*.

WALTON, William (1902–83). *English composer.*

When he was seventeen Walton went to live with the eccentric Sitwell family, and was a kind of unofficial relative for the next ten years. Life with the Sitwells was excellent for his reputation. They were at the hub of the fashionable 1920s artistic scene, and knew everyone from cubist painters and dada poets to nightclub pianists. In 1921 Walton composed *Façade*: a witty, jazzy score to accompany nonsense-poems by Edith Sitwell. Its performers were hidden by a curtain; the speaker declaimed Sitwell's verse through a huge megaphone; the whole thing would not have been out of place in a P.G. Wodehouse novel, and it was a scandalous success.

It was not until he was twenty-seven that Walton shook off this kind of frivolous cleverness, and began to write music of substance. He worked slowly, and in the 1930s and early 1940s produced on average one large-scale work every two to three years: concertos for viola and violin, the cantata *Belshazzar's Feast* and the magnificently brooding Symphony No. 1. He spent the years during and after the Second World War writing music for patriotic films (e.g. Olivier's *Hamlet* and *Henry V*), and in the late 1940s settled on Ischia, in the Bay of Naples. By this time he was internationally famous, and travelled all over the world to conduct and record his great 1930s scores. In 1954, after the critics savaged his opera *Troilus and Cressida* (because its hot-blooded Romantic harmony seemed closer to the nineteenth century than to the poker-faced avant-garde techniques then fashionable), his compositions dwindled both in number and quality. (The same thing happened to Samuel *Barber: he seemed out of step with the times and backed out of what had once been a dazzling career.) Walton's output was small, but a high proportion of it is excellent, and now that the critical snobberies against neo-Romantic music have withered away, he can be heard for what he is: the finest English composer of the between-wars generation, *Elgar's heir.

works Two symphonies, three concertos (violin, viola, cello), *Sinfonia concertante* (piano and orchestra), three overtures (including *Portsmouth Point*), Partita, *Variations on a Theme of Hindemith* and a dozen shorter pieces for orchestra (including two Coronation marches, *Fiesta, Capriccio burlesco* and the *Spitfire Prelude and Fugue*); two operas (*Troilus and Cressida; The Bear*); two ballets; four large choral works (including *Belshazzar's Feast*) and a dozen anthems and smaller pieces for choir (including *Missa brevis*); String Quartet, Violin Sonata and half a dozen shorter chamber-music works; songs, piano duets and scores for a dozen films, many (e.g. *Hamlet, Henry V*) subsequently quarried for light-music suites; *Façade*, for reciter and chamber group.

Façade (1921, frequently revised) Edith Sitwell's poems (in nonsense, imitations of the work of Gertrude Stein) use vigorous musical rhythms – waltz, pasodoble, tarantella, etc. – and these are also the basis of Walton's glittering accompaniments, with cheeky tunes (some his own, others, e.g. 'I do like to be beside the seaside', remakings of popular songs), jazzy harmony and bright instrumental dazzle. The entertainment is available complete, and also (without reciter) in two tongue-in-cheek suites for orchestra.

→ Coronation march *Crown Imperial* (more majestic, but with the same cocky exuberance); Arnold *English Dances*, Set 1; Benjamin *Jamaican Rumba*.

Portsmouth Point (1925) For this sound-picture of a bustling port (based on Rowlandson's satirical cartoon), Walton used snappy, syncopated rhythm, jazz harmony and perky tunes; the result is spectacularly cheerful, a joy to watch in the concert-hall. He composed a dozen pieces of this kind, masterly without being masterpieces (they have no such high ambitions), amongst the best 'light classical' music of the century.

→ *Johannesburg Festival Overture*; *Capriccio burlesco*; Ireland *A London Overture*.

Ⓜ *Belshazzar's Feast* (1931) Though Walton composed this Old Testament cantata (on the barbaric feast of King Belshazzar of Babylon, and the destruction of his city that followed it) for a solemn choral festival, he seems to have had in mind a musical equivalent of Cecil B. de Mille's then-popular Old Testament films, full of eye-rolling orgies and fervent, breast-beating piety. Walton turned a stuffy oratorio commission into just such an event: his chorus and orchestra never break out into an orgy, but the music constantly suggests one. The dazzle and barbarism of the Babylonian scenes is balanced by a beautiful setting of the elegiac psalm 'By the Waters of Babylon' (sung by the exiled Jews), and the work culminates in a sumptuous paean of triumph after the God of the Jews weighs Belshazzar in the balance, finds him wanting and destroys Babylon.

→ *Te Deum*; Poulenc *Gloria*; Lambert *The Rio Grande*.

Ⓜ **Symphony No. 1** (1935) This is a work on the largest scale, with substantial musical thought (its inspiration was *Sibelius's Fifth Symphony) and an over-riding Romantic melancholy; at the same time, Walton's stunning orchestration, fiery harmony and marvellous tunes (ending in a jazz fugue) enliven the texture and stir the blood. This symphony is one of those 'perfect' artworks which, even if nothing else by the artist survived, would still trumpet his or her genius from the housetops.

→ Ⓜ Viola Concerto; Bartók Concerto for Orchestra; Stravinsky Symphony in C.

WEBER, Carl Maria von (1786–1826). *German composer.*

The son of an actress and a musician and theatre-manager, Weber was determined from boyhood to make a career composing for the stage. He had a succession of jobs (e.g. music director of the Breslau Municipal

Theatre, the Prague Opera and the Dresden Court Theatre), and travelled widely in Europe to supervise productions of his operas. He was physically frail (he suffered from tuberculosis), but seems to have taken very little care of his health, and bouts of frenzied activity were usually followed by days and weeks in bed. He died after hectic rehearsals of his opera *Oberon*, during a particularly damp London spring.

Weber is one of those composers whose influence in their own time was far greater than the quality of their surviving works suggests. He was a pioneer of German music-drama, adapting Gluck's 'reform' ideas to the German language and to Romantic stories similar to the folk-stories collected by the Brothers Grimm. His music is cheerful and warm, but it is over-shadowed by that of the masters he inspired (e.g. *Wagner). As with Clementi (who influenced *Beethoven) and Field (who paved the way for *Chopin), Weber has enough pieces still in the repertoire to ensure the survival of his name, and although his music never treads the heights of inspiration, it is unfailingly and unpretentiously enjoyable, a pleasure both to discover and to explore.

WORKS Six operas (including *Der Freischütz*, *Euryanthe* and *Oberon*); three Masses and three oratorios; two symphonies, two overtures, five concertos (two for piano, two for clarinet and one for bassoon), two concertinos (clarinet; horn) and other shorter orchestral works; Piano Quartet, Clarinet Quintet, Trio (flute, cello, piano) and half a dozen lesser chamber works; four sonatas, *Invitation to the Dance*, several variation-sets and books of dances for piano; songs, part-songs and incidental music for the stage.

Oberon (overture; 1826) Although of Weber's operas only *Der Freischütz* is heard complete (their librettos, even by operatic standards, are ludicrous), the overtures are regular and delightful concert fare, with a tunefulness reminiscent of *Schubert at his most boisterous, and darkly Romantic interludes suggesting *Berlioz or Wagner – a heady and fascinating potpourri of styles.
→ Overture to *Der Freischütz*; Nicolai overture *The Merry Wives of Windsor*; Schubert overture *Rosamunde*; Berlioz overture *Carnaval romain*.

Clarinet Concerto No. 1 (1811) The slow sections of this charming work swoon and languish with emotion, like operatic arias; the fast sections are in lively dance-rhythms (e.g. polka); Weber consistently prefers sentiment or jollity to depth, and the result is one of the gayest wind-instrument concertos in the repertoire.
→ Bassoon Concerto; Clarinet Quintet; Spohr Clarinet Concerto No. 1.

WEBERN, Anton (von) (1883-1945). *Austrian composer.*

After his first degree at university (in philosophy), Webern went on to work for a doctorate in music. His subject was Heinrich Isaac (*c.* 1450-1517), a church composer noted for the intellectual complexity of his music (pieces, for example, which used the same themes backwards, upside-down and in 'mirror-forms' where the second half was the first half backwards). This complexity, and also Isaac's emotional fervour (which binds together even the most intricate musical constructions), is paralleled in Webern's own musical style.

When he left university, Webern went to study composition with *Schoenberg. He married, and supported his family by teaching, lecturing and conducting. His life was modest and uneventful, utterly belying his growing international reputation as one of the most uncompromising avant-garde composers of the century. In 1938, when the Nazis over-ran Austria, he was declared a 'non-artist', performances of his music were banned, and he had to eke out a living by proof-reading and doing other hackwork provided by his loyal publishers. In 1945, soon after the war ended, he was taking an evening stroll in his son's garden, and lit a cigar; an American soldier, mistaking its glowing tip for light glinting on a rifle, shot him dead.

In the 1900s, when Webern began composing, music in the German-speaking countries was an art of gargantuan extravagance: enormous music-dramas, symphonies or dramatic cantatas, for vast orchestras and using 'advanced' harmony to squeeze the utmost musical meaning out of every phrase. (*Mahler's and Richard *Strauss's works are typical.) Webern followed this path himself until 1905-6; then, perhaps influenced by Isaac's lean, neat works, he stripped his music down to its essential elements (single sounds, tiny rhythms, expressive silences) and refashioned them in a revolutionary new way. His pieces were unprecedentedly short (a movement might last forty seconds, a whole work ten minutes), and instead of melodies and dense chords the players were given ethereal, single sounds whose meaning was in their context, in their relationship with the rest of the piece. There are no discords in a Webern score, and no concords either: the music is a mosaic of 'moments', and the miracle is that despite their brevity they are packed with emotion: they seem to say as much, with a fraction of the effort, as the grandest Romantic opera or symphony.

For most of Webern's life, and indeed for twenty years after his death, performances of his works were few, and were respectful rather than whole-hearted. Orchestras and soloists were trained for expression on the largest scale, and found his tiny pieces baffling and pointless. For a long time his music was mainly a scholarly delight, more popular with other composers than with ordinary listeners. (The generation of *Boulez and *Stockhausen owes him particular debts.) Then, in the 1970s, leading

conductors (notably Boulez and Karajan) and performers (notably Mauri-
zio Pollini) took up his works and at last revealed their true expressiveness.
His use of intellectual procedures, which used to fascinate people who
knew his music only from reading it, now seems irrelevant: as with Isaac,
what matters in his work is its urgent emotion and its ravishing, if spectral,
sound.

WORKS Symphony, *Five Movements, Six Pieces, Five Pieces, Passacaglia,
Variations* and other orchestral works; *Eyesight*, two cantatas and a handful
of other choral works; thirty songs for voice and chamber group and forty
songs for voice and piano; String Quartet, String Trio, Concerto for nine
instruments, Quartet (for violin, cello, saxophone and piano) and several
sets of pieces for various chamber groups; *Variations* and *Piece* for piano;
early works (pre-1905) including Piano Quintet and String Quartet.

Five Movements, Op. 5 (1910, revised 1929) These pieces make a splendid introduction to Webern's ice-crystal style: it is as if single notes, single slivers of
emotion, have been frozen and then re-ordered, and the process has revealed new
beauty not only in the sounds themselves but in their new relationship. (At first
the music sounds random, like scattered letters on a Scrabble-board; but with
repeated hearings the ear makes connections and discovers significance, involving
the listener in the process of 'creating' the musical experience in a way forgotten
since Renaissance Christian times. These five pieces were originally composed for
string quartet; but they work equally well (and sound even more ravishing) in
Webern's 1929 revision for large string orchestra.
→ *Six Bagatelles*, Op. 9; *Five Pieces* for orchestra, Op. 10; Ligeti String Quartet
No. 1.

Ⓜ *Das Augenlicht* ('Eyesight'), Op. 26 (1935) This ten-minute cantata for choir
and orchestra is typical of Webern's vocal music (his best), and its delicate beauty
and fervent emotion can be a revelation to anyone who imagines his music cerebral
or dissonant. Although an English version of the words is a useful aid, it should
be discarded when listening to the actual piece: Webern 'fragmented' the words
much as he did the music, paying great attention to each individual sound, and
this makes performance in German essential to the work's full meaning.
→ Ⓜ Cantata No. 2; Dallapiccola *Canti di prigionia*; Maxwell Davies *Leopardi
Fragments*.

WOLF, Hugo (1860-1903). *Austrian composer*
From his teens onwards, Wolf was able to keep sane, it seemed, only
thanks to regular outbursts of violent, bitter-tongued rudeness: they lost
him job after job, and cost him all but his most patient friends. His mental
instability also made composing difficult. For twenty years he could write

only in a pale imitation of the composers he most admired (*Schumann and *Wagner). In the early 1880s he became a Viennese music critic, and began avidly fanning the flames of the row about whether Wagner or *Brahms was the greater composer; by the fury of his attacks on Brahms (who had a large following among professionals) he soon ensured that very few performers or orchestras would touch his own works.

Then, in 1888, Wolf's creative faculties clicked into place, and for four years he poured out songs (over 200 altogether) of a musical simplicity to equal *Schubert's and a poetic intensity as great as Schumann's. In 1892 the flame of inspiration dimmed; it flickered briefly in 1895-6 (when he wrote more songs, and his opera *Der Corregidor*); but in 1897 he tried to drown himself (as Schumann had before him), and was committed to an insane asylum.

WORKS Apart from his songs, Wolf's only music of quality is his opera *Der Corregidor* ('The Mayor', on the same farcical story as *Falla's *The Three-cornered Hat*) and his *Italian Serenade* (see below). Of his early music, the most interesting is a string quartet and the symphonic poem *Penthesilea*: even so, they are nothing like as good as his mature works, and are more reminiscent of *Franck than of the Wagner or Schumann he idolized.

Songs In Wolf's *Lieder*, voice and piano are equally important, and the song is concerned as much with expressing a specific emotion or mood as with providing a pretty tune or catchy rhythm. (None the less, Wolf's tunes, with Schubert's, are the best in the business, and his piano parts add a friskiness and wit very much his own.) There are five main sets of songs. The fifty-three *Mörike Songs*, twenty *Eichendorff Songs* and fifty-one *Goethe Songs* are predominantly about lost love, and their mood is both lyrical and serious; the *Spanish Songbook* (forty-four songs) and *Italian Songbook* (forty-six songs in two volumes) are lighter-hearted, with folk-dance rhythms and elegant folksong poems. Among Wolf's best-loved songs are Ⓜ'Kennst du das Land?' and the three *Mignon* settings (all from the *Goethe-Lieder*), and 'Der Gartner' and 'Mausfallensprüchlein' (both from the *Mörike-Lieder*); the best first approach to his songs is through an anthology-recording; the *Eichendorff Songs* are his most consistently fine collection. Good follow-ups by others to the lighter songs, especially those in the *Italian Songbook*, are Mahler's *Wunderhorn Songs* (1888) and Chopin's songs Op. 74; good follow-ups to the more serious songs are Schumann's *Liederkreis* ('Song-cycle') Op. 24 and *Liederkreis* Op. 29.

Italian Serenade (1887, revised 1892) This began life as a string quartet, and was later revised for orchestra. It is a scampering dance (something like a very fast waltz), its tunes alternately chirpy and long-breathed, its accompaniment bouncy and its rhythm full of unexpected, delightful hiccoughs. Wolf never captured its light-hearted elegance again in instrumental music, but some of its zest is paralleled by such individual songs as 'Im Frühling' ('In Spring'), 'Jägerlied' ('Huntsman's Song') and ⓜ 'Der Tambour' ('The Drum Major'). Good follow-ups by others are Schubert's *Quartettsatz*, D 703 (serious), and Wirén's *Serenade for Strings* (bubbly).

WOODWIND INSTRUMENTS

The woodwind instruments most commonly found in 'serious' music are flute, oboe, clarinet and bassoon. Each belongs to a family containing other instruments (piccolo, alto and bass flutes; cor anglais; E flat and bass clarinets; double bassoon), and a few other instruments (e.g. recorder and saxophone) occasionally appear, but the bulk of woodwind music is written for the four main instruments.

EARLY WOODWIND INSTRUMENTS Until the end of the seventeenth century, few composers took woodwind instruments seriously. They were peasant instruments, often out of tune, restricted in the notes they could play and better suited to out-of-doors playing (e.g. accompanying dances) than for refined indoor listening. A few composers (e.g. *Monteverdi) used woodwind instruments sparingly in their orchestras, adding their raucous, hard-edged tone to the sound as carefully as a cook adds salt to stew.

At the end of the seventeenth century, things changed. By this time string orchestras were well established as an entertainment medium, and the *concerto was a favourite form. Because their sound contrasted well with strings, wind instruments made ideal concerto soloists, and many composers (e.g. *Telemann and *Vivaldi) eagerly exploited them, writing solo, double, triple and quadruple concertos for every instrument in sight. (Telemann was himself a woodwind player, and his concertos are magnificent.) Some of these experiments (e.g. Vivaldi's concertos for bagpipes) are bizarre, but others (especially recorder and oboe concertos) worked well, and led to woodwind instruments gradually being accepted into the orchestra. As the standard of playing improved (so that woodwind instruments could play in tune with a fixed-tuned instrument like the harpsichord), sonatas and other similar works were added to the repertoire: among the earliest and best are *Bach's flute sonatas and Telemann's and *Handel's sonatas for recorder, flute and oboe.

EIGHTEENTH-CENTURY WOODWIND MUSIC By the mid-eighteenth century, every orchestra of any size included oboes and bassoons, and many had flutes as well. The clarinet, once the most erratic of all woodwind instruments, was standardized and improved in the early eighteenth century, and began to appear more and more in orchestras, until by the 1790s it was a standard orchestral instrument.

The most reliable (and hence most favoured) eighteenth-century wood-wind instruments were flute and oboe. Some composers (e.g. Quantz and C.P.E. *Bach, both of whom worked for the flute-playing King Frederick II of Prussia) concentrated on flute music, providing a lively repertoire of sonatas, concertos and chamber works. Others found the flute tone insipid, and preferred the oboe: *Mozart's Oboe Quartet and Oboe Concerto, for example, are shapely, bright-toned works quite unlike his gentler - and less inspired - quartets and concertos involving flute. (Mozart also wrote a Bassoon Concerto, and three sublime works with solo clarinet, the Trio, Quintet and Concerto, inspired by the playing of a friend, and the first works of genius ever written for the instrument.)

NINETEENTH- AND TWENTIETH-CENTURY WOODWIND MUSIC This haphazard approach to the woodwind continued well into the nineteenth century: *Berlioz, for example, tells entertaining tales of his problems in finding double-bassoonists or cor-anglais players in the European towns whose orchestras he conducted, and of the (often far greater) problem of finding them instruments fit to play. In the 1840s, however, inventors turned their attention to improving woodwind instruments, and Boehm and others devised systems of keys, rods and levers which increased the number of available notes and made them playable without contorting the fingers. These inventions liberated woodwind instruments in the same way as valves and pistons liberated brass (see *Brass Instruments*): from the middle of the century onwards, virtuoso woodwind players were as skilled as pianists or violinists, and dozens of minor composers set about providing them with works to play.

None the less, although excellent players and instruments were now available, and although most nineteenth-century composers regarded them as essential members of the orchestra, very little solo music of quality was composed. *Schumann wrote a handful of woodwind works (e.g. *Fantasy Pieces* for clarinet, *Three Romances* for oboe), *Weber wrote concertos for clarinet and bassoon, and *Brahms (inspired, like Mozart, by the playing of a friend) wrote two clarinet sonatas, a Clarinet Trio and a superb Clarinet Quintet, but among great composers they stand alone. It was not until the twentieth century, when interest in 'unusual' concerto instruments was as great as it had been in the seventeenth century, that the solo-woodwind repertoire began to grow again. Among many other composers, *Nielsen wrote a fine quintet, and concertos for clarinet and flute; *Vaughan Williams, Richard *Strauss and *Henze wrote oboe concertos; *Martinů and *Hindemith wrote concertos for flute, oboe and clarinet; other composers provided sonatas, quartets, quintets and other chamber works by the dozen. (The only woodwind instrument left out in the cold was the bassoon: its solo repertoire is still minute.)

WOODWIND ENSEMBLES Although solo woodwind works have never been numerous, from the eighteenth century onwards works for woodwind ensemble have been extremely popular. The favourite group is a wind quintet (flute, oboe, clarinet, horn, bassoon), but trios, quartets and larger groups are also common. From the eighteenth and nineteenth centuries, composers of this kind of music include Haydn (divertimentos and partitas), Mozart (serenades, among the finest of all woodwind works), *Beethoven (a splendid Quintet for wind and piano), *Dvořák, Gounod and Richard Strauss (serenades and 'symphonies' for large woodwind groups). Among the most sparkling twentieth-century woodwind-ensemble works are Nielsen's Wind Quintet, Poulenc's and Janáček's sextets, Ibert's *Trois pièces brèves* and *Milhaud's *La cheminée du Roi René*; at the other end of the scale of seriousness are chamber works by *Schoenberg, Maxwell *Davies, Henze and *Berg (whose Chamber Concerto, for violin, piano and thirteen wind instruments, is one of his largest and finest works).

Listening Good introductions to eighteenth-century woodwind music are Handel's Recorder Sonata Op. 1 No. 4, Bach's Flute Sonata BWV 1035 and Albinoni's Oboe Concerto Op. 9 No. 2; good follow-ups are Mozart's woodwind works (beginning with the Oboe Quartet K 370 and the Clarinet Concerto, and moving on to the Wind Serenade K 388). Good introductions to nineteenth-century woodwind music are Reicha's Wind Quintet Op. 91 No. 5 and Schumann's *Fantasy-Pieces* Op. 73; good follow-ups are Beethoven's Quintet, Op. 16, Dvořák's *Serenade*, Op. 44, and Brahms's Clarinet Quintet. Good introductions to twentieth-century woodwind music are Ibert's *Trois pièces brèves* and Poulenc's Sextet; good follow-ups are Strauss's Oboe Concerto, Stravinsky's *Symphonies of Wind Instruments* and the clarinet concertos of Nielsen and Copland. For further recommendations see the articles on C.P.E. Bach, J.S. Bach, Brahms, Carter, *Chamber Music*, *Concerto*, *Eighteenth-century Music*, Handel, Milhaud, Mozart, Poulenc, *Sonata*, Telemann and Vivaldi.

GLOSSARY

aria (Italian for 'air'.) A solo song, usually in an opera, oratorio or other long vocal work. Most arias are designed to show off the singer's technique as well as his or her powers of expression.

Baroque (French for 'bizarre'.) First used to describe architecture (the carved traceries and curlicues of seventeenth-century German church interiors), this word is now applied to the clean-lined, extravagantly-decorated music of approximately 1650–1750. *Corelli, *Telemann and *Vivaldi are typical Baroque composers; the greatest Baroque masters, adding individuality to the standard recipe, are J.S. *Bach and *Handel.

canon A piece of music where two or more performers use the same line of notes, starting at different times – and the music fits. Tallis's Canon (sung to the hymn 'Praise God from whom all blessings flow') is a well-known, short example; the placid tune of Pachelbel's Canon has made it a favourite orchestral 'pop'.

cantata (Italian for 'sung'.) Extended vocal work. In the seventeenth and eighteenth centuries, most cantatas were for church use (like *Bach's), or were written for solo voice with instruments or orchestra, and were like one-person, miniature operas, a group of recitatives and arias exploring a single dramatic situation (e.g. the rage and despair of an abandoned lover). In the nineteenth and twentieth centuries, by contrast, most cantatas were large-scale, non-religious choral works with soloists and orchestra (*Brahms's *Song of Destiny*, Stanford's *The Revenge* and *Orff's *Carmina Burana* are typical examples).

Classical Non-musicians (such as many chain-store managers) use this word to mean music which is neither 'easy listening' nor 'pop'. Musicians, by contrast, use it to refer to 'serious' music composed in the second half of the eighteenth century and the first quarter of the nineteenth. Classical music in this sense is poised and formal (see *Eighteenth-century Music*), and concentrates more on perfection of manner than on the unfettered depiction of emotion. Typical 'classical' composers are *Boccherini and *Rossini; *Haydn and *Mozart are the greatest masters of the style.

concord Technical term for a cluster of sounds which 'agree', that is whose combined effect seems to the ear both pleasing and 'complete' (as opposed to a *discord, which seems open-ended and incomplete).

counterpoint Lines of music (or tunes) running horizontally against one another. The contrast is with 'harmonic' music, where a tune or note is set against an accompaniment and subordinates it; in contrapuntal music all the lines are of equal weight, and their weaving together is more important than their individuality. Most composers use counterpoint as one part of their technical vocabulary; its most consistent appearance, and greatest flowering, is in the church music of the fifteenth and sixteenth centuries (see, especially, *Byrd, *Josquin des Prez and *Palestrina), and in the instrumental and choral music of J.S. *Bach.

discord Technical term for a cluster of sounds which 'disagree', that is whose combined effect seems to the ear both pungent and 'incomplete'. (Once, in musical theory, a discord was, exactly, an unfinished chord which needed a *concord to complete its meaning; in the nineteenth and twentieth centuries, reliance on completion was increasingly abandoned, and discords were used for their own colourful or emotional assertive effect.)

divertimento A group of instrumental movements played as an accompaniment to aristocratic meals, parties or entertainments: eighteenth-century muzak. *Mozart's *Eine kleine Nachtmusik* is a sublime example.

fugue A piece of counterpoint whose rules are among the strictest in all music. A fugue begins like a canon, with the same tune chasing itself in part after part; thereafter, the 'subject' (i.e. the tune) can be speeded up, slowed down, played upside-down or backwards, shortened or lengthened – and still fits the musical texture. J.S. *Bach was the supreme master of the form, and his fugues (e.g. the forty-eight of *The Well-Tempered Keyboard*) combine intellectual wizardry with a feeling of effortless musical inevitability.

libretto (Italian for 'little book'.) The 'play', or words, of an opera.

motet Piece of religious music for soloist(s) and/or choir. The words are usually from those parts of the liturgy not forming part of the Mass or other Christian services: the Psalms, for example.

movement Self-contained section of a longer work such as a concerto, sonata, suite or symphony.

recitative Rapid, conversation-like passages in opera, usually half-sung, half-spoken and with a simple accompaniment of chords or long-held notes. In eighteenth-century opera, most recitatives were brisk and inexpressive, accompanied chiefly by the harpsichord; nineteenth-century composers used the orchestra, and added expressive tunes and turns of phrase, until the recitative was to all intents and purposes incorporated into the general musical texture of the opera.

Renaissance (French for 'rebirth'.) This intellectual movement began in Europe in the fourteenth century, and was given impetus when, after the fall of Constantinople in 1453, more and more information about Classical antiquity began to flood the West. The aim was the 'rebirth' of culture after the Middle Ages; the method was to analyse and imitate Greek or Roman styles. In music, since no ancient Greek or Roman music was known, the main influences of the Renaissance were on forms and subject-matter, a move away from such medieval forms as the Mass or courtly love-song towards longer, more dramatic works in the style of ancient tragedy, epic poetry or pastoral. 'Renaissance music', however, has since come to mean little more than the work produced in Europe between about 1450 and 1650. *Palestrina and *Josquin des Prez are two of the most highly regarded of all 'Renaissance' composers – and they have little in common but the name.

Romantic Artistic movement of the second half of the eighteenth century and throughout the nineteenth. For a description of its aims (the unfettered expression of emotion) and methods, see *Nineteenth-century Music*.

rondo (Italian for 'round'.) A piece in which one section keeps coming round again, framing interludes in different moods or styles. It is a favourite last-movement form for concertos, sonatas and symphonies.

serenade Identical to a divertimento, except that it is designed to be played outdoors.

sonata form Commonly used for the first movements of sonatas (hence the name), concertos and symphonies. It has three essential components: exposition (straightforward presentation of the musical theme(s) of the movement), development (in which their shape, harmony, rhythm and other musical implications are explored) and recapitulation (in which they return in more or less their original dress).

suite (French for 'train of followers'.) A group of movements, adding up to a single work but not so tightly unified as the movements of a sonata or symphony. In the seventeenth and eighteenth centuries, most suites were groups of contrasting dances (courante, minuet, jig, etc); in the nineteenth and twentieth centuries they were usually selections from operas, ballets or incidental music, or works (like *Respighi's *Botticelli Triptych* or *Holst's *The Planets*) with pictorial or other non-musical associations.

toccata (Italian for 'touched'.) A showy solo piece, usually for keyboard, designed to demonstrate, equally, the composer's fancy and the player's dexterity. Common in the sixteenth and seventeenth centuries, by the nineteenth century they had been replaced by sonatas, or by genre-pieces (studies, preludes or concert waltzes, etc.), and the word 'toccata' now suggests a show-piece in a slightly archaic style.

twelve-note system Many composers worked towards atonality in the early twentieth century, but *Schoenberg was the first to make the twelve semitones of the octave systematically equal, and his work established it as a major twentieth-century composing method. In the twelve-note system scales and traditional harmony (in which one or more notes or chords dominate the others) are abandoned for a democratic system where all twelve semitones of the octave (twelve consecutive notes on the piano, up or down, black and white) are sorted into a fixed order, which is rigorously repeated throughout the piece, horizontally to make melodies, vertically to make chords and harmonies; no note may be repeated until all other eleven have had their turn. The mathematical possibilities of this 'serial' system have fascinated composers, and are still being explored (nowadays with the help of computers); for listeners, the serial intricacy of the music is often less noticeable than a kind of dreamlike, shifting progression from one sound to the next, quite unlike the determined hierarchies of sound in the music of earlier centuries.

*Works with specific names (e.g.
'Moonlight' Sonata; Don
Pasquale) are indexed under
those names. Other works (e.g.
Sonata no. 7, Suite in G) are
indexed under their composers'
names.
Main entries are in* **bold type.**

Giorno di regno, Un 234
Giovanna d'Arco 234
Gipsy Baron, The 205
'Gipsy Rondo' Trio 53, 99
Gipsy Songs 73
'Girl and the Nightingale,
The' 90
Girl of the Golden West, The
165
'Girl with the Flaxen Hair' see
Fille aux cheveux de lin, La
Giselle 13, 149, 221: Suite 14
Glagolitic Mass 109
Glazounov, Alexander 13
Glinka, Mikhail 11, 30, 142,
151, 158, 173
Gloria (Poulenc) 246
Gloria (Vivaldi) 161
Gluck, Christoph Willibald
von 13, 24, 88-9, 153, 154,
247
'Gnomenreigen' 55
Godowsky, Leopold:
arrangements of Chopin's
Études 169
'God Spake Sometime in
Visions' 167
Goehr, Alexander 45
Goethe Songs 250
Goldberg Variations 10, 14
Golden Age, The 194, 195:
Suite 195
Golden Cockerel, The 174:
Suite 34, 151, 174
Gondoliers, The 200, 214:
'Take a pair of sparkling
eyes' 148
'Good Friday Music'
(Parsifal) 244
Good-humoured Ladies, The
180
Götterdämmerung 242-3, 244
Gottschalk, Louis M. 228
Gounod, Charles 13, 69, 137,
151, 253; Symphony no. 2
189
Goyescas 2, 90
Graduation Ball 149, 205
Granados, Enrique 2, 89-90,
115
Grand Duo 185, 186
Grand macabre, Le 66
Grande messe des morts 29, 56
Grande valse brillante 55
'Grand March' (Aida) 79, 235
Grand Septet 42

'Great C major' Symphony
see Schubert: Symphony
no. 9 in C
Greensleeves 197
Gretchen am Spinnrade: see
'Gretchen at the Spinning-
wheel'
'Gretchen at the Spinning-
wheel 183
Grieg, Edvard 2, 72, 73, 90-1,
128, 146, 197, 222, 228,
238; Piano Concerto 38, 59,
91, 115, 117, 169, 197;
Piano Sonata 91; Songs 91;
Violin Sonata no. 3 86
Griselda 95
Grosse Fuge 23
Gürrelieder 244
Guys and Dolls 230
Gymnopédies 178: no. 1 67, 83,
178

Hába, Alois 3, 4
'Haffner' Serenade 136
Halling 91
Hamburg Ebb and Flow Suite
96, 158
Hamlet (Liszt) 121
Hamlet (Tchaikovsky) 220,
221
Hamlet and Ophelia 229
'Hammerklavier' Sonata 22
Handel, George Frideric 5,
11, 44, 57, 58, 59, 62, 74,
75, 76, 92-6, 116, 118, 128,
153, 156, 158, 166, 167,
179, 201, 215, 223, 254;
cantatas 237; Chaconne in
G 180; chamber music 96;
Concerto a due cori no. 2
93, 96; Concerti Grossi 95-
6: op. 3 no. 4 59: op. 6 no.
12 63; Fifteen Sonatas op. 1
96: op. 1 no. 4 253: op. 1
no. 10 202: op. 1 no. 11 93:
op. 1 no. 15 62, 213;
Harpsichord Suites 96: no.
10 9; operas 94-5; oratorios
57, 92, 93-4, 225; Organ
Concertos 95, 113: no. 4 93:
no. 7 60; Organ or Harp
Concerto op. 4 no. 6 10;
Trio-sonatas op. 2 96;
woodwind sonatas 251
'Handel's Largo' see 'Ombra
mai fù'

Hansel and Gretel 124
Hanson, Howard 58, 229;
Symphonies 229: no. 2 230
Hard By a Crystal Fountain
46
'Hark, Hark, the Lark' 183
Harmoniemesse 100
'Harmonious Blacksmith,
The' 96
Harold in Italy 27, 206
'Harp' Quartet 23
Harris, Roy 58, 229-30; Piano
Quintet 195; Symphonies:
no. 3 196, 230
Harty, Hamilton 15, 95, 177;
Violin Concerto 15
Háry János: Suite 118, 163
Haugtussa 91
Haydn, Josef 5, 6, 19, 32, 44,
52, 53, 57, 75, 76, 77, 78,
84, 94, 96-101, 136, 137,
139, 156, 163, 166, 184,
202, 215, 216, 221, 253,
254; Andante and
Variations 100; baryton
trios 99; Cello Concertos: in
C 137, 211: in D 33, 211,
221; concertos 99;
Divertimento in B flat 99;
folk-song arrangements 236;
horn concertos 42; masses
56, 100-1, 138; organ
concertos 113; Piano Sonata
no. 52 in E flat 23, 99;
piano trios 99, 140; String
Quartets 100, 140; no. 35
op. 20 no. 4 100: op. 33
100: op. 76 100: op. 77 100,
140: no. 81 op. 77 no. 1 23;
Symphonies 98-9: no. 10 in
D 98: no. 18 in G 98: no.
52 in C minor 98: no. 95 in
C minor 98, 131: no. 97 in
C 158: no. 99 in E flat 98,
99: no. 102 in B flat 98, 99;
Trumpet Concerto 42, 59,
99, 137
Haydn, Michael 78, 96, 99;
Concerto for harpsichord
and viola 78
Heartsease 53
'Heavens are Telling, The' 91
'Hebrides, The' see Fingal's
Cave
Heigh Ho Holiday 53
Heldenleben, Ein 124, 206

265